39.95

D1190948

# CARNIVAL, AMERICAN STYLE

1. Street masker, New Orleans, 1987 (photo, Norman Magden)

# CARNIVAL, AMERICAN STYLE

## Mardi Gras at New Orleans and Mobile

### Samuel Kinser

Photographs by

### Norman Magden

THE UNIVERSITY OF CHICAGO PRESS
CHICAGO AND LONDON

**Samuel Kinser** is professor of history at Northern Illinois University, specializing in Renaissance and early modern French history. He is the coauthor of *A L'Amour Comme a la Guerre,* and author of *The Works of Jacques-Auguste de Thou* and *Rabelais' Carnival.*

The University of Chicago Press, Chicago 60637
The University of Chicago Press, Ltd., London

99 98 97 96 95 94 93 92 91 90    5 4 3 2 1

Library of Congress Cataloging-in-Publication Data

Kinser, Sam.
    Carnival, American style : Mardi Gras at New Orleans and Mobile /
Samuel Kinser : photographs by Norman Magden.
        p.   cm.
    Bibliography: p.
    Includes index.
    ISBN 0-226-43729-9 (alk. paper)
    1. Carnival—Louisiana—New Orleans.   2. Carnival—Alabama—
Mobile.   3. New Orleans (La.)—Social life and customs.   4. Mobile
(Ala.)—Social life and customs.   I. Title.
GT4211.N4K56   1990
394.2'5—dc20                                              89-30476
                                                              CIP

# Contents

List of Illustrations     vii
Acknowledgments     ix
Foreword     xi
Introduction     xiii

1   What Is Carnival?     3
2   Colonial Rites     17
3   Meltdown     59
4   Civic Festival     75
5   Sex     119
6   Wildmen     151
7   Africa     195
8   Grotesques     215
9   A Great American Spectacular     250
10   Cultural Codes     275
11   Carnival's American Style     307

Afterword     319
Appendix     321
Notes     325
Bibliography     397
Index     409

# Illustrations

| | | |
|---|---|---|
| 1 | Street masker, New Orleans, 1987 | Frontispiece |
| 2 | Rex on his parade float, New Orleans, 1987 | xvi |
| 3 | Spectators and plastic necklace at nighttime parade, New Orleans, 1987 | xviii |
| 4 | Witch doctor, Zulu parade float, New Orleans, 1940s? | xx |
| 5 | Invitation to Cowbellion Ball, Mobile, 1853 | 87 |
| 6 | Invitation to Comus Ball, New Orleans, 1857 | 95 |
| 7 | Comus Ball, New Orleans, 1873 | 100 |
| 8 | Rex Parade, New Orleans, 1873. "Totila?" | 105 |
| 9 | Advertisement in Mobile Weekly Register, 1874 | 109 |
| 10 | Title Float, Comus Parade, New Orleans, 1906 | 117 |
| 11 | Masked ball, Mobile, 1972 | 123 |
| 12 | Baby Dolls, New Orleans, ca. 1940 | 133 |
| 13 | Street Maskers, New Orleans, 1873 | 139 |
| 14 | "Duke" in nighttime parade, New Orleans, 1987 | 152 |
| 15 | "Boeuf Gras," Rex Parade, New Orleans, 1873 | 154 |
| 16 | "Boeuf Gras," Paris, 1852 | 155 |
| 17 | "Boeuf Gras," Rex Parade, New Orleans, 1899 | 157 |
| 18 | Mardi Gras Indian Chief on Parade, New Orleans, ca. 1978 | 166–67 |
| 19–21 | Costume, Mardi Gras Indian Chief, New Orleans, 1987 | 176–80 |
| 22–29 | Mardi Gras Indian Practice, Tavern, New Orleans, 1987 | 182–91 |
| 30 | Trinidad Fancy Indian Chief on Parade, Port of Spain, about 1970 | 198 |
| 31 | Stick dancers in Carnival, Haiti, ca. 1880 | 203 |
| 32 | "Koo-Koo" or Actor Boy, Variant of "John Canoe," Jamaica, 1830s | 217 |
| 33 | "Kuker" from Padarevo, Bulgaria, mid-20th Century | 220 |
| 34 | Indian Parader in Krewe of Iris, New Orleans, 1987 | 225 |
| 35 | King Zulu and retinue on float, New Orleans, 1923 | 234 |
| 36 | King Zulu and retinue, New Orleans, 1931 | 235 |
| 37 | Witch Doctor, Zulu parade float, New Orleans, 1987 | 237 |

| 38 | King Zulu and page on float, New Orleans, 1987 | 239 |
| 39 | Zulu float-rider, New Orleans, 1987 | 241 |
| 40 | Street masker, "wildman," New Orleans, 1987 | 243 |
| 41–42 | Street masker, "death"(?), French Quarter, New Orleans, 1987 | 244, 246 |
| 43 | Bacchusaurus, float in Bacchus parade, New Orleans, 1987 | 252 |
| 44 | "Lou Babau," carnival float, Nice, 1905 | 253 |
| 45 | Bacchus, float in Bacchus parade, New Orleans, 1987 | 254 |
| 46 | Masker on a balcony, French Quarter, New Orleans, 1987 | 261 |
| 47–50 | Street maskers, French Quarter, New Orleans, 1987 | 264–69 |
| 51 | "Dukes" about to throw, Rex parade, New Orleans, 1987 | 283 |
| 52 | Carnival crowd, nighttime parade, New Orleans, 1987 | 287 |
| 53–54 | Captain emeritus, in the throwing game, Krewe of Iris, New Orleans, 1987 | 288–89 |
| 55 | Boeuf Gras, Rex parade, New Orleans, 1987 | 296 |
| 56 | New Orleans police, nighttime parade control, New Orleans, 1987 | 299 |
| 57 | Wildman troupe, French Quarter, New Orleans, 1987 | 309 |

# Acknowledgments

Special thanks are due to Professor Lawrence Bryant, formerly of Spring Hill College, Mobile; to Professor Steven Reinhardt, formerly associated with the Louisiana State Museum, New Orleans; and to Mr. Caldwell Delany, Mobile City Museum, without whose initial help and local expertise my research would have proceeded much more slowly.

At a later stage of the enterprise Dr. Brune Biebruyck, anthropologist; Professor John Hafner, Spring Hill College, Mobile, Alabama; Collin B. Hamer, Jr., Head of Louisiana Division and City Archives Collection, New Orleans Public Library; Maud Lyon, Curator of Costumes, Louisiana State Museum; Michael Smith, photographer and sensitive friend of many Mardi Gras Indian groups; and Professor Martin Walsh, University of Michigan, offered the clues, contacts, and documents that I needed. My collaboration with Norman Magden has been full of the Carnival spirit, as expected, and that with Cheryl Fuller as enjoyable as it has been indispensable. Finally and most personally I am indebted to my colleagues Sean Shesgreen and Alfred Young for advice of all kinds about the themes and historical perspectives addressed here.

# Foreword

If you are a member of the New Orleans Carnival societies called Rex and Comus, do not read this book!

It is written by a damned Yankee, a northerner from up the river, a "Kaintuck," practically, like those rowdy flatboatmen who used to crowd the docks. Then, too, the book goes on about what is done in Mobile, as if their Alabama festival could contend in interest with the Carnival at New Orleans.

And it takes you, the reveler, seriously. Well, half seriously. Seriously enough, perhaps, to spoil the fun.

Historical, cultural, sociological analysis spoils the fun. If you are a Mardi Gras Indian, if you parade in the Elks Krewe of Orleanians, if you are one of Mobile's Comic Cowboys or Knights of Revelry, do not read this book. . .

Not for your sake, but for ours, the audience, spectators, participants from elsewhere. We need you for our dream of mirthful indolence as much as you need each other for its fabrication.

# Introduction

At the edge of a marsh, in early morning, sunlight lifts the mist from tangled thickets. Birds twitter, and insects flit along the surface of pools. A deer dips its nose toward the water, and then moves off through the underbrush, scattering small animals from its path. In terms of variety of forms the richest place for life is the margin between two ecological areas, two times of day, two moments of activity. Sharp edges draw explorers. Over time the edges produce diversity by encouraging inventive responses. A frontier between water and land juxtaposes forms of life which may be unseen through hundreds of miles of prairie.

Is this why people gather at the springtime margin between old and new seasons in the marshland near the mouth of the Mississippi? Mardi Gras, with its displays of festively feathered human animals, has been celebrated for centuries at New Orleans and nearby Mobile. Founded by the same French colonizers at the beginning of the eighteenth century, these cities have proved to be durable havens for the once French and Catholic festivity. Carnival has changed over time, extraordinarily so. Some say that its colors have never been brighter than they are today.

If this is so, the reasons for it have less to do with Franco-Catholic origins than with social conflict and social tolerance. Boundaries between groups have been drawn and redrawn, as new ethnicities and new circumstances have battered the cities. In most American settings similar large-scale immigrations and eco-political changes have been diluted by the ethos of assimilation and progressive compromise. But in these cities—and more especially at New Orleans—social differences have become enmeshed without resolution. The failure has prompted cultural richness.

In the eighteenth and early nineteenth centuries New Orleans and Mobile were atypical frontier towns, on the verge of multiple kinds of expansion. Depending on the location of the home country's colonies, the two port cities were viewed in political and military terms as situated on the northern, western, or southern edges of colonial conflict between France, England, Spain, and later the United States. Fort Louis de la Louisiane on Mobile Bay, one hundred miles east of the Mississippi Delta, was planned to defend a new French empire in America by the Canadian brothers Bienville and Iberville and their followers in 1699. After exploration of the Delta, the capital of the colony was moved from Mobile Bay and Biloxi, Mississippi, to the site of New Orleans in 1718. Economically the towns were eccentric but essential outposts, especially in the years immediately following the Louisiana Purchase of 1803. They were the southern anchor of the Mississippi drainage of first French and then American fur trading with the Indians. They were on the northern rim of the sugarcane colonies in the Caribbean basin. From the point of view of the cotton economy burgeoning in the South after the American War of Independence, they bade fair to become the main commercial centers for sale and export of this raw material to both Europe and the American east coast.

Like ecological margins, New Orleans and Mobile served as transition-points no less than as barriers between societies, and they facilitated not only commercial but cultural flows. Between and within the lines drawn by white state-builders the old Amerindian cultures, partly hunting-gathering and partly agricultural in character, survived until the mid-nineteenth century and continued afterwards to haunt the imagination with their rebellious exoticism. The Caribbean colonies, faced with black resistance from the era of the French Revolution onward, sent fleeing slavemasters and free and unfree black people to Louisiana. African tribal cultures, however adulterated or suppressed by the old Spanish-French or new Anglo-American slavery, nevertheless found in New Orleans' social miscellany good chances for survival.

What is it about Carnival-time which seems to compel people to place the miscellany on parade? The history of the two port cities' chief annual celebration is fascinating, deriving its uniqueness from the double effects of isolation from European antecedents and immersion in a richly diverse local situation. Yet Gulf Coast Carnival has until now received little attention except from local scholars. This may be because its phenomena have been understood in terms of the wrong model.

The normative model of Carnival today is adapted from the work of anthropologists such as Max Gluckman and Edmund

Leach: in view of its similarities to other seasonal festivals and to rites of passage, Carnival should be analyzed as a set of rituals of "reversal" or "inversion" which turn the everyday world upsidedown.[1] The model certainly applies to some aspects of New Orleans' and Mobile's Mardi Gras. The grandest of Mardi Gras parades are led by a Carnival king enthroned in Elizabethan splendor on a glittering float, served by handsome young "pages" and escorted by the "dukes" and "captain" of a secret society. Atop other floats following the king members of the society throw trinkets to the commoners along the sidewalks below, who raise their hands imploringly. The game is gay, full-throated, gleaming. Social power shines forth and is rewarded with awe and feverish devotion, a power hard to grasp and usually fleeting in this mobile, competitive land. Witnessing this in New Orleans, the Brazilian sociologist Roberto Da Matta has been led to conclude: "The event seems to intend to create a hierarchy. . . . The Carnival of Mardi Gras does not lead to individualization or even to the creation of an egalitarian ambiance. In fact to do this would be not to carnavalizar [to play in a Carnival way] in a society where individualism and equality are precisely the ideas that Mardi Gras inhibits or keeps in the background."

Da Matta sees Carnival in the usual manner as reversing the surface of everyday life in playful fantasy. Carnival, however, plays not only with the surface but with what the surface hides. The game going on between dukes and commoners is governed not by the logic of inversion but by that of ambivalence: surface/depth, past/present, reality/fantasy. Moreover, Carnival's logic is totalizing, a both-and rather than either-or game. Mikhail Bakhtin's work on medieval and Renaissance festive culture, emphasizing the engulfing quality of the carnivalesque no less than its inversive character, offers a more suitable point of departure for study of Gulf Coast Carnival than that of Da Matta, Leach or Gluckman. Inversion theory is not false, but it is falsifying because it neglects the dynamics that connect what Bakhtin calls "debasement"—or, in the case of Rex's parade, exaltation—with incorporation, the dream of ever more inclusive, total ways of feeling, desiring, and acting.[2]

Carnival is a way of dreaming with others, publicly and responsively. Its qualities of inversion, of ambivalence, of conspicuous consumption and excess have to do with removal and escape from social calculations. The floats move through the streets in a mesmerizing atmosphere, isolated from rather than

simply reversing or enhancing the qualities of everyday life. In both cities there is not only one grand Carnival sovereign but also a galaxy of other "rulers," male or female, paraded by their respective societies at different times. During the night parades in particular the monarchs on their floats look like saintly dolls trundled through darkened streets in a time of need, endowed with unnatural power by torchlight and tinsel. In this remotely shining world the blare of trumpets and crash of drums, the hum of motorcycles and hoofbeats of police horses, the sparkle of army-cadet bayonets and of school-band batons blend with sudden bursts of color in the air as glittering plastic-bead necklaces go sailing up, over, down toward leaping, yelping gnomes among whom one will, if one is there, sooner or later be counted.

These are not beads but bits of magic. The men on the floats are guardians and keepers of precious mystic stuff. Their authority comes from their—and our—lack of reflection about the efficacy and the silliness of the magic. Everyone laughs even as they throw and scream and scramble. The king laughs even as he poses and proposes his toasts to the notables of the city who await him along the parade's way.

Carnival deals with the barriers omnipresent in daily life not by tearing them down or turning them topsy-turvy but by stepping over them and back again in an exemplary although impractical enlargement of the everyday. Daily life is enlarged theatrically; it is also enlarged in a particular bodily way. In Carnival, more than in any other festival peculiar to Western industrial mass society, that bodily participation remains which Victor Turner, speaking of "tribal ritual," has eulogized as the employment of "all the sensory codes . . . dance, body languages of many kinds, song, chant . . . incense, burnt offerings, ritualized feasting and drinking, painting, body painting, body marking of many kinds . . ., the application of lotions and the drinking of potions. . . ." It is impossible to list all the guises and disguises which exalt the body in this enchanted time.[3]

Carnival is a specifically Christian festival in its historical origins and it is specifically Western in its psychology. It is obvious that carnivalesque exaltation of the body derives some of its force from its whimsical defiance of the Christian spiritual and Western intellectual faiths which rank mind over body, the immaterial over the material, and the inward *psyche* over out-

2. Rex on his parade float, New Orleans, 1987 (photo, Norman Magden)

ward *physis*. But Carnival behavior, along the Gulf Coast as elsewhere, does not seem so much concerned to undo these hierarchies as to draw attention to their limiting character.

The last few paragraphs veer between several narrative manners, participatory, generalizing, and historical. These differing rhetorics refer to varying methodological as well as theoretical approaches to a protean festivity. They recur throughout the book. The reader is asked to understand Carnival as a psychically involving process, not just as a passing parade of historically articulated images. Given its totalizing, mesmerizing

3. Spectators and plastic necklace at nighttime parade, New Orleans, 1987 (photo, Norman Magden)

thrust, one must participate as well as inquire, meditate as well as compare Gulf Coast features with their relatives and sources. Carnival is gesturally, orally, rhythmically communicated. Its visible, verbal parts, unsupplemented by a feeling for its rhythms and sensual totality, appear absurdly trivial as recorded and photographed in archives. Yet the experience is too striking and too engulfing to be absorbed consciously at the same time as it happens. The participant-observer methods of folklorists, journalists, and anthropologists will seem shallow, however well reported, unless they are given depth by the social scientist's dissections and the historian's search for similar phenomena at other times and places. I have limited myself by and large to two dissecting tools: the sociologist's idea of the connections between economic class, social status, and cultural standards, and the semiologist's idea of cultural activity as an assemblage of signs and codes. If coding of behavior can be observed in Carnival, what is the relation of these repetitive sequences to the shifting of economic and other frontiers among the groups taking part in the festival? Can generalizations be made about the way in which single signs (gestures, words, shouts, song notes) are combined into codes and the codes combined into the characteristic games and rituals of Carnival?

In answering these questions I have drawn on personal participation in Carnivals here and in a number of European locales, no less than on studies of them, in order to measure the distance of the Gulf Coast form from its related modes. Although the history of Carnival and some revision of theories about Carnival have their place in this study, they are subordinate to the purpose just mentioned, the definition of cultural adventures unique to Carnival's American form. Among the many ritually repeated actions whose history, sociology, and semiotics are considered, three are studied in special detail. These three are the most innovative forms, stimulating the most colorful behavior in the rich marshes: the throwing game, like that in the parades to which allusion has been made; the creation of pseudo-kings and, equally important, of pseudo-queens; and the masking and dancing of "wildman" figures.

The character of these rituals substantiates a conclusion which will be drawn from studying historical evolution: playful as it is, richly inventive as it has been, Carnival at New Orleans and Mobile conserves the black-white barriers which can be observed nearly everywhere in American society and which de-

4. Witch doctor, Zulu parade float, New Orleans, 1940s? (photo, Norman Magden, from *Sepia*, 1955, courtesy of New Orleans Public Library)

veloped with force in the slave society of this southern area's first century and a half of existence. The double role of marginality, inviting and forbidding movement across frontiers, has special meaning in these circumstances, for it is etched in black and white. The rituals all make reference, consciously or unconsciously, to race relations.

At New Orleans and Mobile Mardi Gras happens once in the white man's business-land and again in black-town, once in the brightly lit central city and meanwhile also in the neighborhoods. Is this redoubled play, with its implication of hierarchy tinged by racial difference, a kind of spatial enlargement of people's commonplace sense of festivity? Does Carnival everywhere and always happen once in orderly fashion and then also alongside the big parades, in disorderly embroidery upon its official image?

Mardi Gras is mentally as well as physically double in New Orleans and Mobile. It happens once in one's aspirations and again in one's desires, once along Canal Street in front of the Boston Club and again in Bourbon Street or wherever the ideal landscape of one's most lurid lewdness can be given, for that day, a location.

This is the sometimes split, sometimes reiterative duplicity whose sense and sensuousness I want to communicate. The book's subject is a festival which is a fantasy. People's imagination of it is as important as their practice.

# CARNIVAL, AMERICAN STYLE

# What Is Carnival?

Carnival in American speech outside the Gulf Coast has no seasonal or Christian connotation. It refers to a traveling collection of amusements which include games of chance, sideshows, and thrilling rides. The word also carries the more general connotation of gaudy fun; we say that such-and-such an occasion was "a regular carnival" in its extravagance. Department stores and northern college campuses may advertise a "winter carnival"; the city of Saint Paul, Minnesota, sponsors one in late January. How is this modern meaning related to the old Latin ecclesiastical word for Carnival, which refers to pre-Lenten meat-eating, and how is it related to the play with social rules and spiritual traditions exhibited in American Mardi Gras?

The modern meaning of Carnival arose in the fifteenth and sixteenth centuries in Europe. It is a consequence of Catholic and later also Protestant attacks on the celebration of a holiday generally acceptable before 1450. Humanists and churchmen after 1450 began associating Carnival customs with those of the ancient Bacchanalia and Saturnalia. But association of the holiday with ancient Greek and Roman rites was almost certainly a mistake. Five centuries separate the last mention in antiquity of popular festivities that included customs similar to those of Carnival (494 A.D.: the Roman Lupercalia) from the first medieval European mention of the word (965 A.D.: *Carnelevare*, literally, "to lift up" or relieve from "flesh" or "meat").

Between 965 and 1130 Latin and related Italianized words meaning "to leave off meat" appear some dozen times in Italian documents, referring to a regularized time—like Christmas or Easter—for paying off debts and settling feudal contracts.[1] In these cases the word is ambiguous. It may refer to the beginning of Lent rather than to festivities before Lent. But a Roman text written about 1140 reports the public killing of steers and other animals before the Pope and other Roman notables after a parade through the city. This is the earliest document reporting festive customs associated with the approach of meatless Lent.[2]

The Roman Carnival and other European Carnivals, all of which begin to be reported with frequency only in the fourteenth century, have no documentable connection with ancient festivities. Carnival developed its usages first vis-à-vis the church's rules concerning Lent. Along with the prohibition of meat the church prohibited marriage during Lent and also discouraged sexual intercourse. It was easy enough for fifteenth- and sixteenth-century church reformers to associate with pagan materialism and sensuality the boisterous games and bodily self-indulgence that developed in Carnival. From the sixteenth century onwards city and state authorities in both Catholic and Protestant areas sometimes found it useful to support the mistaken notion of pagan origins in their efforts to suppress the festival's disorderliness.

The word "Carnival" gradually broadened its meaning for these polemic reasons until it acquired the commonplace American sense of gaudy and somewhat disreputable pleasure. The modern meaning was especially developed in Protestant England. It passed easily into American semantics from this English form. Perhaps to avoid confusion with the generalized sense of the word, New Orleans and Mobile newspapers tend to use the term Mardi Gras, not Carnival, in referring to the pre-Lenten festival. The French words literally refer only to "Fat Tuesday" preceding Ash Wednesday, but their sense along the Gulf Coast has been extended to cover the entire season of Carnival, a two- or three-week period today. Following local usage, I shall use Mardi Gras interchangeably with Carnival to refer to the Gulf Coast festivities; mardi gras with small letters will indicate Fat Tuesday specifically, while carnival with a small "c" will refer to the generalized meaning of showy amusement.

It is important to disentangle Carnival's origins from its pre-Christian analogues. The Bacchanalia, Saturnalia, Lupercalia, and so on, however frequently they may be invoked in the Gulf Coast parades or in Sunday-supplement explanations of the festivity, have nothing to do with the historical origin of Mardi Gras or with the origins of *its* origin in Europe's Carnivals. A second idea about the origins of Mardi Gras, which may be called the folkloric explanation, has also done more to obscure than to clarify the meaning of the Gulf Coast celebration. Folklore was founded as a discipline in the early nineteenth century by enthusiastic amateurs and some academicians who went to Europe's villages to collect folktales and folk songs and to observe agricultural habits and superstitions which were beginning to disappear with advancing industrialization and with greatly increased migration to towns. These collectors recorded customs associated with springtime plowing and planting which were carried out at Carnival-time. They noticed, too, that the pre-Lenten period was an occasion for giving public, ribald, satiric form to local social scandals, such as the domination of husbands by wives or the adulterous behavior of town notables, male and female. The form of these customs apparently had little to do with Lent or anything else Christian. These collectors therefore conjectured a pre-Christian rural origin for Carnival instead of a pre-Christian urban, Saturnalian one. They asserted that rural pagan rites had been conserved for thousands of years in miraculously pure form in the countryside. It followed that city Carnivals were pale and adulterated versions of rural originals. Such a theory nicely supported the nationalist ideologies of authentic "folk spirit" and anti-aristocratic populism sweeping Europe in the Romantic era when these ideas were elaborated.

One hundred years of careful investigation of these allegedly prehistoric rites and much further collecting of both rural and urban versions of European Carnival have led most scholars to abandon the folkloric explanation.[3] It now seems more likely that Carnival-time, beginning as an urban and courtly reaction to Lenten rules, gradually attracted to itself a variety of agricultural and social practices which were originally celebrated at different points in late winter and early springtime. Many of the agricultural practices were very old, reflecting pre-Christian Celtic, Germanic, Slavic, and Roman sun, wind, and water-worship. But all of them had gone through an unknown number of transformations in the course of one thousand years of Christian and feudal-manorial history, becoming associated with Saints' days, legendary heroes, and local features of landscape such as mountains, ravines, and water sources. Far from being endlessly repeated in the same way, each glimpse of such agricultural, marital, hunting, and politically satiric rites shows a different form. Before one can point to a specific source for a particular usage, one must be able either to point to a specific document—which is almost by definition impossible for customs developed through oral, gestural practice—or to reconstruct through associated documents and comparative materials a plausible line of evolution leading from the supposed source to the form in which it presents itself for explanation.

This second method of plausible comparative reconstruction can be used, for example, to show that the celebration of Mardi Gras in the Cajun country of southern Louisiana has a different origin from the Mardi Gras of New Orleans or of Mobile. The Cajuns are descendants of Acadian emigrants from Canada in the later eighteenth century. Their *courir du mardi gras* ("Fat Tuesday Run") is a transformation of Canadian French customs, not documented for the eighteenth but for the nineteenth and twentieth centuries, and can also be related to nineteenth-century customs in rural Western France, from which area the Acadians migrated to Canada in the seventeenth century.[4]

Carnival celebrations, occurring in early springtime or what is definitely still winter in some places in the Alps and Pyrenees, have always had seasonal as well as Christian meaning. Its Christian moral meaning can be made precise by relating the festivity to Lent. Its seasonal meaning, on the other hand, has varied with climate and way of life (Alpine Carnivals usually include hunting rituals, something of scarce interest either to rural agricultural or to urban mercantile communities), and also with respect to other customary celebrations which occur before and after it. In colonial New Orleans, for example, Twelfth Night was as important a point of articulation for festive customs as Mardi Gras, and in present-day New Orleans Saint Joseph's Day, falling after Mardi Gras, has nearly equal importance in some sectors of the community.

These indications of Carnival's seasonal meaning lead one to question a third explanation of Carnival which sees the festival neither as particularly Roman and pagan nor as rural and agricultural, but more grandly, as something universally human, parallel in both its nature-oriented and socially-oriented customs to rituals practiced in all times and places, such as the celebration of returning sunlight and warmth or the purgative practice of casting out an evil force by drowning, burning, or shooting a puppet-figure. Although bonfires and fireworks and burnt-up or drowned Carnival "kings" are frequently found, they are evidence of Carnival's attractive power over rituals originally celebrated at other times for any number of reasons which are interesting in themselves but not revelatory of Carnival's deepest meanings. If we are to understand Carnival's specifically American style, we must attend to its most proximate sources and geographic connections, and also to its nearest calendrical competitors such as Christmas, Twelfth Night, Mid-Lent, and Saint Joseph's Day. This does not mean, however, that the general history of Carnival is not relevant to understanding a particular festive tradition like that of the Gulf Coast. Knowing the phases of its history not only helps one avoid alluring simplifications but allows one to pick the most likely paths for inquiry into the development of a local occasion.

Carnival's cradle was the Christian-feudal Middle Ages between 1000 and 1300. Its fullest European development took place in the fourteenth, fifteenth, and sixteenth centuries before the double needs of centralizing states and reforming churches led to attempts at repression of Carnival's sinful pleasures and vulgar disorder in the seventeenth and eighteenth centuries. In the nineteenth century some big-city Carnivals were revived and grew enormously: the grand modern developments at Cologne, Basel, and Nice began. But big-city concentrations more often killed than encouraged Carnival, just as they weakened by ricochet many small-town and village festivities. The combined forces of industrialization, bourgeois standards of orderly, respectable behavior, and diminishing Christian traditionalism reduced people's interest in and understanding of the occasion. Except in "backward" eastern Europe, the Alps, and the Pyrenees, where hundreds of villages not only preserved but elaborated the festival, Carnivals, already in gradual recession for two hundred years, decreased in geographical location, in number of participants, and in variety of forms. This double process of general shrinkage and big-city concentration continued until after World War II. Since the war many revivals of Carnival have occurred and in some areas such as the small towns and villages of southwestern Germany Carnival is celebrated today where it never before existed. Among the five phases just mentioned, the Renaissance epoch of development and the nineteenth-century era of big-city concentration are most relevant to Carnival's North American form.

From the fifteenth and sixteenth centuries stem many of the most popular symbols used by the upper-class and middle-class Carnival societies in New Orleans and Mobile. Renaissance humanists with their enthusiasm for classical culture were active in promoting the supposed connection of Carnival with Greek Bacchanals and Roman Saturnalia. Insofar as humanist ideas have remained powerful in elite culture generally, so also has their theory of Carnival. More than half of the societies parading in New Orleans during Mardi Gras in 1987 have named themselves after figures from Greek, Roman, and Egyptian mythology, partly due to tradition (the first societies in the 1850s and 1870s named themselves so) but also due to the humanistically created prestige and seeming relevance of such names.[5]

Carnival celebrations were carried out in glittering style by Renaissance monarchs and their courtiers. Is this why New Orleans' Rex and Mobile's Felix look more like Henry VIII than Richard the Lionhearted or a twentieth-century king? The influence of Renaissance Carnivals on American Mardi Gras runs deeper than costuming and enthusiasm for Greco-Roman paradigms. The ideological meaning of the festival expanded because so many of the period's finest writers interested themselves in it. Cervantes draws a profile of Don Quixote's servant Sancho Panza which plays on Saint Paunch, the incarnation of Carnival in French and Spanish popular plays of the period. Shakespeare's Falstaff has been interpreted as the English version of the same Carnival fat man. Rabelais' Carnival pseudo-king, *Quaresmeprenant*, is the most complexly developed literary incarnation of the festival ever attempted, emphasizing the occasion's relation to Lent.[6]

Humanism and naturalism enriched the meanings of pre-Lenten celebration without submerging its Christian character. These secularizing currents of thought developed the idea of Carnival as the special realm of folly and thus loosened the festival's ties to the logic of asceticism binding it to Lent. Folly may be irresponsible and religiously dangerous, but it is humanly understandable. From the sixteenth century onward Carnival could be rationalized as an expression of the occasional need for carefree silliness rather than seen only as a concession to sinful flesh. The Renaissance ethos of folly has inspired Gulf Coast Carnival more than medieval feast and famine.[7]

The first model for Mardi Gras in New Orleans was the Parisian Carnival during the late eighteenth and first half of the nineteenth century. Here is a brief outline of its main features. The celebration lasted seven days, from Fat Thursday up to and including Ash Wednesday. This apparent defiance of the Roman Catholic rule which begins Lent on Ash Wednesday is found here and there throughout Europe from the time of Carnival's earliest records.[8] There was no overall organization of the festival at Paris, and aside from some police supervision city officials did not intervene. For the elite and well-to-do there were privately organized masked balls and banquets as well as the famous ball at the Paris Opera. Some artisans' gilds marched in procession, most prominently that of the butchers, whose appropriate parade of a fat ox *(boeuf gras)* is said to have occurred nearly without interruption from the 1730s to 1870, except for ten years at the height of the French Revolution (1790–1800).[9]

The fame and popularity of the Paris Carnival, up to 1850, rested on its public masked balls, offered cheaply together with much food and drink at restaurants that were located just outside the gates in order to escape city taxes. Crowds filled the main streets on the last four days of Carnival and the abundant street masking was often performed by informally organized groups: Charlemagne and his court, *commedia dell'arte* figures, a family of monkeys, Don Quixote and Sancho Panza on a single horse. There were raucous orchestras on foot and in carriages and every manner of vehicle, including funeral wagons. One of the regular rituals on the last day of Carnival was the parade of a puppet stretched out on a bier as though dead. Mannequins representing the festival were burned at a number of places in the evening. Satiric references to contemporary events and sharp-tongued insults to those passing by *(poissardes)* were another commonplace.[10]

During the Second Empire (1851–69) of Napoleon III street masking diminished, the Opera balls became more restricted affairs, and the balls at cheap restaurants on the city's outskirts disappeared with annexation of the suburbs and the end of the restaurants' tax privileges. In the years after 1870 large department stores and other commercial enterprises organized parades, sapping the life from street masking and turning popular attendance to commercial ends. By 1910 little remained of Paris Carnival except some neighborhood balls.

Although the Parisian celebration was an inspiration to Louisiana's colonials and continued in the nineteenth century to be a symbol of gaily fashionable behavior in a few elite Creole circles, the main line of development along the Gulf Coast pursued a different path. And while Parisian Carnival waned, the late nineteenth century was the moment when in both American cities Carnival activities acquired the institutional frame and popular support that still sustain them.

Just as these two port cities' size has always been very unequal, so has been the importance of their festivals, seen from a national or international perspective: Mobile's Carnival is very little known. But in terms of local history their Carnivals have occupied from the 1870s an equally extraordinary position. The handful of local histories of Mobile all devote some pages to Mardi Gras as an important local institution. Certainly only New Orleans among large American cities, and perhaps no other metropolis in the world, could or would in 1900 have devoted an entire chapter in a 700-page *Standard History* to Carnival.[11] In 1977 that city's official tourist bureau estimated that 10 percent of the $500 million generated annually by visitors to New Orleans came from the two-week Mardi Gras period. One must add to this $50 million at least half again as much in local spending, which goes on the year round in preparation for the event. In 1981 Mobile journalists estimated that $6 million was generated by Mardi Gras activities; local spending by members of the Carnival societies alone was "well over the million mark" in 1971. Estimates of local residents' participation are difficult to make, in part because some people participate over and over. (One local Orleanian is reported to regularly attend some sixty Carnival balls!) But the anthropologist Munro Edmondson estimated in 1959 that participation in New Orleans was of the order of 50 percent.[12]

Such massive involvement is as extraordinary as people's zany behavior during the season. What is the nature of Carnival, that it should have such a strong and durable attraction for the local people, not to mention the tourists who for over a century have annually attended in tens of thousands? Of the thirty largest urban concentrations in the United States none other has a festival of civic importance which is as old as Mardi Gras, and no large or middle-sized city, not even Pasadena with its Tournament of the Roses spectacle or Philadelphia with its Mummers' Parade, has anything approaching New Orleans' apparent and Mobile's probable 50-percent participation.

There is no single reason why people involve themselves in such great numbers. Much of this book will be devoted to differentiating reasons for it. The ecological metaphor used to open this study was selected because people of such different classes and cultures meet for such diverse causes on the street during Carnival-time. We cannot answer the question, "What is Carnival in Mobile and New Orleans?" without a variety of social and historical inquiries. Before undertaking these, we may conclude this outline of the larger contexts of the festival by sketching the main scenes and calendrical timing of Carnival in the two cities.

Whether in New Orleans or Mobile, Carnival possesses three timing mechanisms, a long-range, a middle-range, and a short-range one. The middle-range timing of Carnival includes the last ten days to two weeks before Ash Wednesday which, it will be recalled, is a moveable date that depends on the date of Easter. During these ten to fourteen days most of the major Carnival societies offer parades, each at a different date and each lasting two to four hours. The climax of the parades on Fat Tuesday includes the parade of the two pseudo-monarchs in each city toward midday and the parade of the two oldest secret societies in the early evening hours, the Order of Mystics in Mobile and the Krewe of Comus in New Orleans.

The parading rhythm sets a smart marching pace for ardent Carnival-goers which leads into the frenzy of the last two days of Mardi Gras with its short-range timing. Street games and informal parties among friends, usually beginning sometime Monday afternoon and lasting until Tuesday's midnight with scarcely a respite, are the main items in this short-range calendar. Whether or not they have partied all night, most true Mardi-Gras folk are up and out and masked by 7 or 8 a.m. on Tuesday and do not stop until their bodies force them to do so.

A long-range timing is provided by the elite societies' masked balls, which begin in a few cases even before Christmas, but generally occur in the period from New Year's Eve to mardi gras. In this respect people's participation is for the most part vicarious, by means of the society pages in the daily newspapers and the gossip of friends. Entry to these functions is with one or two exceptions by invitation only, and invitations are impossible to obtain except for a few favored friends of the societies' members. One may add that there is an even longer, year-round rhythm for that considerable number of ardent Carnival-society participants who, immediately after dismantling this year's floats and ball decorations, begin planning next year's functions.

In New Orleans Carnival-time is like the city's river, big, muddy, ever and again overflowing its banks. By Monday afternoon before Ash Wednesday everyone strolling through the French Quarter wobbles a little, nearly everyone has added to and subtracted from their clothing, and people are painting their bodies in more and more bizarre ways. Spectacular participation: people paint, stripe, or strip themselves to contact others and to join in the mood as well as to solicit the view. Body-paint, spangles, feathers, half-masks, bells and shells, shreds of cloth, ribbons; the murmur of voices, the rumble of rock music, the slosh and nosh of thousands of throats and jaws blends together into a jaunty embroidery on the habits of everyday life. Embroidery, but not yet refusal. That happens next morning. At 10 a.m. on Fat Tuesday (let us leave the reasons for this late hour modestly unexplained except to say that the author ardently participated in Monday's strolls and wobbles) I was out on St. Charles Avenue—too late to catch the Jefferson City Buzzards shuffling in their crazy costumes around the west end of that avenue from watering spot to watering spot. There will be plenty of other walking clubs, many with Dixieland bands alongside, winding their way in and out of the float parades.

This part of New Orleans, which is west of the city's central artery, Canal Street, is the nineteenth-century "uptown" or American section of the city, as distinguished from the older "downtown" French Quarter on the other side of Canal Street with its extensions eastward. St. Charles Avenue is no longer the most exclusive part of town. But the breadth of the avenue, with the only remaining electric trolley in this part of the world running down its middle, and also the big white-columned ante-bellum homes which dot its sides irregularly, give the street a leisurely aristocratic air. There's no trolley this morning, of course. There are no cars on this street either. Rex's parade is coming and people are moving up and down, from side to side, looking for the perfect spot to see. It's a family day. People have brought picnic tables and barbecues, spread out old blankets, and set up stepladders so that they will be in the best position to catch beads above the heads of the others.

Here come the floats, and the pulsing chant begins, "hey-hey-hey-hey-," building to a paroxysm as the parade passes and hands go up to snatch, fumble, tear at, and retrieve the shining pieces of pseudo-money and colored strings of pseudo-jewelry. Individual words, like individual gestures, are indistinguishable. It's a kind of lilting scream which goes together with the imploring gestures to melt people together into one silly sucking desperate need. Rex and his floats go by, and then two hundred and fifty other floats and trucks pass along the route, each with six or twelve or twenty maskers throwing trinkets to the spectators. They are "truck parades": any neighborhood, any group of any kind can get together, choose a common theme, decorate a truck and themselves, each person becoming his or her fondest fantasy. Male and female are about equal in numbers on the trucks.[13]

After twenty-five or thirty trucks have gone by, people's interest begins to be as much in each other as in the show passing by. Black families and black young people are mixed in with whites along St. Charles (the city proper is 60 percent black, but whites are in the majority in this section of the city). Everyone is dancing a little—like this gorilla, for example, in tuxedo and top hat, doing a Fred Astaire turn around his cane. The three-man giraffe and two-man camel make very graceful dancing partners, jiggling along the sidewalk as the "Junkfood Junkies" float goes by with the riders' heads and headdresses made out of root-beer bottles, gigantic hamburgers, and popcorn boxes. It's sunny and hot. A "priest" in long black cassock and round broad-brimmed hat murmurs gravely to us "Ash Wednesday tomorrow," and then shakes his head and laughs uncontrollably at a passing ballerina who, at six-feet-two and two hundred pounds, in tights and ballet slippers shows a little too much hair on "her" chest. A lovely lady frog plops along in yellow tights, her web-feet made of yellow plastic kitchen gloves. "Bugs" are everywhere; half the people on the street seem to use plastic and wire springs to make antennae and eyes waving from their heads or torsos. I stop a pregnant male, dressed demurely in white, and ask when the baby's due, adding that "she" should be careful, for I've seen "women" deliver in the very midst of Carnival. "Oh, that's just disgusting!" her "male" escort screams in a treble. The river flows on.

Things are different in Mobile, less varied in street costuming, but not much less bizarre. The attractive power of the festival on the surrounding country towns is very visible. By five or five-thirty in the afternoon on any day during the last week of Carnival the freeway extension from Interstate 10 which directs cars into the city's center is choked with pick-up trucks for as much as seven or eight miles. Once arrived, the trucks are parked along the city's waterfront boulevard, Water Street, along which the parades will pass. The tailgate is down, there are buns and burgers and a couple of coolers stocked with beer, and patio chairs in the bed of the truck where Mom and Dad lounge while the kids play around the wheels. No masks. These folks drive in from twenty, thirty, forty miles outside Mobile to watch others, not each other. They are there to catch "moon-pies." ("Moon" is probably not a reference to the old associations of Carnival with "moon-fools," or "lun-atics"; this four-inch-in-diameter, two-inch thick cake with a cream filling and chocolate icing was first manufactured by a company named Moon.) As you turn into Government Street, the main thoroughfare of Mobile, the crowd thickens, no parking on the streets is allowed, and soon there will be people wall-to-wall. Government Street, like St. Charles Avenue in New Orleans, is lined with venerable nineteenth-century buildings. But today old facades are cut off from view by stands for popcorn, Coke, and cotton candy, and everywhere vendors are selling beer, beer, beer. You look a little closer, wondering if your beer has been tampered with, because you're seeing people on the sidewalk, men in tails and women in long gowns and white gloves, munching hotdogs and drinking Coke with everybody else. Here are these Beautiful People next to a squawking kid on the shoulders of some guy in Bermuda shorts, all of them standing beside a group of leather-jacketed motorcyclers. "You get your first tails at the age of twelve," I was told by one of the Knights of Revelry. By high school you've been going to formal balls for years. Everybody of importance belongs to a fraternity or sorority in high school: that's how things are organized. The booster buttons ("I like Mobile") on some swallow-tail coat lapels are perfectly in place. These things are proper, essential attire—or satire?

And so the parade passes. First comes the head parade marshal on a beautiful bay stallion, a glorious commander with plumed helmet and spangled tunic. Then a high-school marching band, and the first float, the float with the society's emblem, whatever it may be: for the "Stripers" Society a mammoth tiger, for the Order of Myths a jester chasing death with a pig's bladder around a broken column. The other floats follow, united by some theme, interspersed with marching bands and ROTC units with flags and rifles. Riding the floats are members of the Carnival society, ranged along either side of the float, armed with moonpies and candy which they throw into the outstretched hands of the mass of people which surges around the float in spite of the efforts of police on motorcycles and of marshals on horseback to keep them in line.

The primary Carnivals in the two cities, those taking place in parade form in the main streets, are similar in their tendency to polarize participants and spectators. Carnival here, officially superintended and officially advertised, is well designed to handle masses of people who enjoy similar grand spectacles. The secondary Carnivals, which take place in narrower streets or in black areas, have different functions and a different look.

Interstate Highway 10 is located close to the center of New Orleans just as it is in Mobile. It is a freeway raised on huge concrete pylons above the strip of ground running down the middle of Claiborne Avenue, a broad street which is six blocks northwest of and parallel to Rampart Street, the "back" side of the French Quarter. If you walk along Claiborne Avenue, the swish of cars above melts into the sound of cars and people moving along the thoroughfare below. The street is lined with grocery stores, taverns, and parking lots. The sound is typically twentieth-century metropolitan and it is here that black families are pulling in by 8 a.m. on Mardi Gras with their pick-ups and 1950-model fin-backed American-car grandeur. Soon the whole length of the avenue will be jammed with picnic tables, barbecue grills, beer coolers, fold-up chairs, and people. No whites, unless by mistake or bravado.

Why do people gather here, in the midst of automotive thunder? Because it is a tradition. This is where blacks have met for several generations on Mardi Gras Day.[14] It is toward Claiborne that the blacks' most colorful Carnival celebrants, the Mardi Gras Indians, will sooner or later converge. I will not describe the Indians' masquerade here; they figure in a number of later chapters. The subject here is one portion of their ambiance.

Although there are today a few middle-class "tribes," most Mardi Gras Indians are poor people, like the persons living on central Claiborne Avenue and for blocks on either side. They have little work and are badly paid for it. Many of them, including some of the best dancers and most talented makers of costumes, are illiterate. Their culture is orally and visually absorbed before it is transmuted and transmitted in terms of their traditions. That oral-visual culture is right here, in all its shrill brightness. The din which identifies Claiborne Avenue is cultural raw material. It provides many of the threads from which behavior is woven. Of course, whether you are rich and white or black and poor in New Orleans, you are nourished by the same mediatized capitalist-industrial flotsam and jetsam found anywhere in the Western and Westernizing world. Differences show up when it becomes a question of controlling the flow.

The richer you are and the lighter-skinned you are, the easier it is and the more proper it is to filter the flotsam. If you are poor and dark, then it is not only impossible to purchase filters, it is self-cancelling. Coke and Bud and charcoal grills are accessories, mentally and physically, for the middle and upper classes. For people close to subsistence's edge, who have understood that they can only play with the symbols of twentieth-century well-being and can only enjoy the fine bloom of its commercial images as display rather than as possession, making oneself part of the techno-glitz and thunder of Claiborne Avenue is simply being sociable. You belong. You are part of the system. Its symbols are yours, even if its inner mechanisms are not.

The noise overhead is environmental sound, reassurance that this is the familiar world, everybody's reality, and you are in it and of it. Before the interstate highway was built the din was there on the parkway. It was only a little less enveloping, a little less involving. There is another benefit, too, to the construction of the Interstate: It provides shelter from too much rain and too much sun. It's cool and you can stay cool, doing your picnic. The aesthetics are just about right, in fact. The aesthetics of Mardi Gras are as garish and brash as the Avenue.

The main event of the secondary Carnival in Mobile is the "Mammoth Parade" of mardi gras social clubs: "Maids of Joy, Utopia Club Athenians, Melody Sports, Upsters . . . Krewe of Elks and the Krewettes . . ."[15] The parade moves down Davis Avenue, the central business street for blacks in a city which remains socially and economically segregated. In 1968 the atmosphere was described by a local (white) historian thus:

> Sometimes called the "Harlem of Mobile," Davis Avenue [named for Jefferson Davis] means to the Mobilian not just a street but a whole section. Along with Maysville it is "Colored Mobile."
>
> . . . The parade runs down Davis Avenue, always orderly, with great dignity but in flamboyant style and flashing colors. When the parade finally reaches Central High School, it comes to a halt and the gala affair is over until the next year.
>
> Mardi Gras livens up Davis Avenue during the carnival season but the street is not exactly dead the rest of the year, especially on Saturday night. Club Savoy and the Ebony Social Club are in full swing on that gay evening and the pendulum is a long-time swinging. During the daytime Buster's Eagle Pawn Shop is the scene of some real heart-to-heart swapping.[16]

Claiborne and Davis Avenues are among the main commercial centers of black life in New Orleans and Mobile. St. Charles Avenue and, to a lesser and even more archaic extent, Government Street are centers of less directly advertised, more private power. The stores and taverns along Claiborne and Davis Avenues are, for the most part, open for business. The homes along St. Charles Avenue and Government Street are festooned with the gay colors of Carnival and with distinguished-looking people, standing on porches and balconies, lounging and drinking with friends, watching the parades—and being watched by the people outside their gates.[17]

. . . Joining the throng, or looking at it: the reflexive activity of shouting out your gaiety so that you lose "your" voice in the minglings, or the reflective activity of stationing yourself at a sufficient distance from this gaiety so that you symbolize it, shape it, control it—and make the right contacts.

# Colonial Rites

To enjoy the Carnival at New Orleans and Mobile demands suspension of disbelief. Tourist or native, one does best to enter with alacrity into a world of make-believe. In addition to the heady myths about Carnival-through-the-ages in the media, there are local elements which help one along. The first is romantic history.

The eighteenth century in Louisiana, so runs the tale, was gay and exciting, even if roughhewn. Take the Marquis de Vaudreuil, for example. This Canadian nobleman was appointed governor of the French colony in 1743, some forty years after its founding by two brothers, also Canadian French, the lords Iberville and Bienville. During Vaudreuil's administration (1743–53) the small town of one-story wooden houses surrounded by an earth-and-log rampart became a glittering social center. The marquis' household was a kind of miniature Versailles, where lavish and elegant balls and banquets proceeded apace. The governor had brought his wife, a shipload of furniture, and a dancing master from Paris called Bébé ("Baby") to assist him in the conversion of wilderness into civilization. Bébé, it was intended, should teach the children of the next generation how to behave at that most important of occasions, the *soirée dansante* or ball.

In 1745 eight hundred white males resided in New Orleans. The entire Louisiana colony, which stretched along the coast from Mobile to New Orleans and extended through scattered farms along the Mississippi northward to Natchez and a short distance inland elsewhere, counted four thousand souls. This number included eight hundred soldiers and about three hundred blacks, male and female, slave and free. Although planters had begun to clear the wilderness, no plantation society could yet be said to exist. Those varieties of sugar cane successfully exploited in the Caribbean islands proved inadaptable to mainland conditions. Rice, indigo, tobacco, and cotton were minor crops. Not enough slave ships had yet been summoned to allow excesses of wealth and caste to acumulate. Moreover, the colony's frontiers were not secure. Again unlike the case in the Caribbean islands where Indians had been quickly exterminated or driven to remote mountains, attacks upon scattered Louisiana settlers were still frequent and bloody in the 1740s, even if no major attacks occurred. In view of the insecurities facing the colony, Vaudreuil's balls seem in retrospect like whistling in the dark. Bébé was caught by Indians one day as he rode to a planter's house outside New Orleans, and was mortally wounded while defending himself with a hunting knife.[1]

The obsession with courtly dancing which Bébé incarnated did not die. However absurd for eighteenth-century Louisiana the ideal of Versailles' grandeur may seem, it was this image that the French and after them the Anglo-Saxon upper class cherished. One of the finest fictions sustaining celebration of Mardi Gras is the notion that people here are heirs to a gay and aristocratic French mode of life found nowhere else on the continent. The first ingredient in what became a tradition of Carnival celebration at New Orleans only in the 1830s and 1840s is not the fact but the imagination of colonial upper-class gaiety.

The usual explanation of how Carnival began at New Orleans and Mobile is that the French brought the celebration with them. Settlers continued a Catholic and folkloric custom to which they were accustomed. Carnival grew step by step to become the venerable tradition we enjoy today. The Marquis de Vaudreuil contributed mightily to this tradition through the elegance of his festive affairs.

There are two difficulties with the explanation. Only two scraps of evidence have turned up about the festival before 1781, when an edict concerning Carnival behavior in New Orleans was issued by the governing council of the colony.[2] Both the pre–1781 reports concern Mobile, not New Orleans. Yet there are reasons to suppose that Carnival began, as a regularly recurring, publicly practiced affair, even later in Mobile than in New Orleans, that is, in the 1850s. The second reason for doubt about explanation of Carnival as a French tradition which went on from generation to generation is the checkered history of the colony. If the idea of continuous tradition were true, Carnival would have a more regular history than the colony itself.

The first Carnival for which we have an alleged manuscript description is supposed to have taken place in 1705. Soldiers and settlers at Fort Louis de la Louisiane, located on the Mobile River a few miles upstream from the present site of Mobile, celebrated

Mardi Gras with dancing, eating, drinking, and singing, and "a few exuberant souls . . . donned masks and painted their faces red."[3] Was the occasion prompted by relief at survival from the first yellow-fever epidemic which decimated the colony in 1704, carrying off thirty soldiers and an unknown number of settlers in a total population of about three hundred? Iberville, the leader of the colony, died of the fever in 1706, leaving his younger brother Bienville in command. By 1711 repeated floods of the low-lying ground—one of the causes of the fever—forced abandonment of Fort Louis. Bienville moved fort and capital to the site of present-day Mobile.[4] The following Fat Tuesday is said to have been celebrated by a parade down Dauphin Street, a street which still exists in Mobile, with a "gigantic bull's head representing a fat bull." The parade was improvised by a soldier named Nicholas Langlois and his friends with the sanction of Bienville, we are told in a journalistic account of Mobile's Carnivals. Although Langlois' name is attested in other sources for the period, no historian of Mobile or of the Louisiana colony mentions this event, and the journalist provides no indication of his source.[5]

Whether or not the parade took place is relatively unimportant. There is no doubt that the common folk of the colony, especially soldiers and sailors who had no farming and no family life to establish, sought distraction in the wilderness by recapitulating customs with which they were familiar. Such celebration was as ephemeral as the soldiers' and sailors' term of service. Lack of reference to any regular observance of festivities in the sources for the early and middle years of the eighteenth century is more eloquent than any irregular documentation can be: with the exception of the marquis, his dancing master, and perhaps a few others, people were too concerned with survival to devote time regularly to festivities.

By 1718 Bienville had decided to move his capital again. In the spring of that year he laid out the streets and squares of the present-day French Quarter in New Orleans. He was prompted in part by the arrival in February and then again in June of new shiploads of soldiers and settlers. These people came in search of the bonanzas advertised in Paris by Louis XV's financial adviser, John Law. Law's "Mississippi Bubble" burst in 1720, however, and the stream of new settlers and French financial support subsided. Meanwhile Bienville fought a war against the Spanish in Florida; the two colonial powers disputed rights and territory all along the Gulf Coast (1718–20).[6]

In 1769, after seventy years of French rule, the population of New Orleans was still only 3,190 persons, of whom 1,387 were black (slave and free). The Spanish received Louisiana in 1763, at the end of the European Seven Years War, but they only took effective control of the colony in 1769. Several decades of Spanish rule changed little in terms of population: New Orleans counted 4,016 persons in 1791. Mobile, a tiny village of less than 400 people in Vaudreuil's time (1745: 150 whites, 200 blacks) grew to 746 persons by 1785.[7] The "city" of Mobile, as the botanist William Bartram called it when he made a visit in 1778, was languishing. He found it "chiefly in ruins, many houses vacant and mouldering to earth," although there were still "a few good buildings inhabited by French gentlemen, English, Scotch, and Irish, and emigrants from the Northern British colonies."[8]

Part of the ill success of the colony was due to deteriorating relations with the Indians. In 1729 two hundred French were massacred at Fort Rosalie (modern Natchez, Mississippi). Atrocities followed sporadically on both sides; one and another tribe of Indians were egged on by British, French, and Spanish adventurers who used them to further the imperial designs of the great European powers. French colonists were sufficiently on the defensive to take the extraordinary step in 1739 of offering arms to former slaves or descendants of slaves, when they formed a military company of fifty free blacks to help fight the Chickasaws.[9]

When the colonists at New Orleans learned in 1768 that they had been turned from French into Spanish subjects by the treaty of 1763, they revolted. The Spanish general Alexander O'Reilly (sic) arrived in August, 1769, executed six leaders of the rebellion, imprisoned seven others, and introduced a new, more collegiate form of government called the "cabildo." An Inquisition tribunal was authorized in 1770, although it seems to have remained dormant. Its authorization reminds one of the continual religious intrigues disrupting colonial government, intrigues pitting the Jesuits against the Capuchins in particular. In 1788 the first of many disastrous fires at New Orleans occurred, destroying 856 houses, the cathedral, the Capuchin convent, the arsenal, and the prison. A second great fire took place in 1794. Meanwhile the furies of the French Revolution, stirring all Europe, had repercussions in the Caribbean which brought dangerous refugees to Louisiana. The insurrection at Santo Domingo in 1789, which eventuated in the first black republic in the New World, brought more than 2,000 free blacks, whites, and whatever slaves they were able to take with them to New Orleans over the next decade.[10]

The idea that Mardi Gras was an eighteenth-century French creation in the Louisiana colony is historically absurd. The discontinuities of political and economic life forbid such an explanation. But of course these discontinuities did not forbid occasional observance of the festival in colonial times. If more solid information about Fat Tuesday does one day emerge, it will probably confirm the sporadic character of celebration.

It would be equally absurd, therefore, to maintain that Mardi Gras was never observed before the edict of 1781 confirms its existence. Mardi gras was the prelude to Lent, a Catholic religious obligation enjoined on all residents in the colony by the stipulation that Catholicism be the only legal religion. Church and state formed a single system in the colony, as in Louis XV's France. But the inevitability of some reactive sense of holiday before the austerities of Lent tells us nothing about particular customs, their repetition, and their evolution. Only when these last three elements occur in conjunction do we have a festive tradition. Repetitious yet evolving customs sink their roots into the soil of community life. They become as necessary to the yearly round as the arrival of flatboats on the New Orleans levee eventually did.

If Carnival was not bequeathed to Louisiana by France, how did it originate? By the collision, coordination, and precipitation of five disparate elements: white plantation society's winter festivities, black society's need to adapt African customs in order to preserve them, the Gulf Coast's proximity to and influence by Caribbean festivities, its similar influence by the festive practices of Anglo-Americans migrating westward, and, cutting across all these factors, the Spanish and then American commercialization of leisure time. Carnival's beginnings were composite and slow. The idea of marshland barriers which are hard to see and shifting, richly receptive yet also recalcitrant, is a metaphor for this hesitant, devious process.

In these first pages I have emphasized the difficulties of the first hundred years of the Louisiana colony. Although many of the causes of those difficulties did not suddenly disappear in the 1780s and 1790s, they were henceforth masked by money. The Spanish liberalized the means for foreigners to obtain full property titles at the same time as new technology made cotton and sugar plantations more profitable and the end of the American Revolution sent settlers west from the Atlantic seaboard.

Fifteen hundred Spaniards from the Canary Islands, experienced in plantation culture, arrived in 1788, occupying the delta country below New Orleans. Twenty-one hundred Acadian French ("Cajuns") from Canada came in two waves in 1754–68 and 1785, occupying the territory along the Mississippi above New Orleans. In 1795 the technological breakthrough came which made large-scale sugar plantations profitable in Louisiana. Etienne de Boré perfected a refining process for the kind of sugar cane suited to the southern American climate and showed that it could be profitably employed. By 1805 New Orleans had nearly doubled its population of 1791 to reach the figure of 8,475. By 1810 it had more than doubled again to attain 17,242, of which 10,911 (63.3 percent) were black people.

In 1769, at the beginning of the Spanish era, the black population of New Orleans already constituted 43.5 percent of the population of 3,190.[11] Percentages were probably higher both in 1769 and 1810 in the countryside, although we possess no reliable figures. In any case it is clear that by 1791, when the percentage of "coloreds" to "whites" first takes a sharp increase, the solution to Louisiana's unsteady prosperity had been found. It was not only proprietary and technological but black, morally as well as physically.

Observance of mardi gras was, for the rich and leisure-loving white plantation society emergent in the 1790s and early 1800s, part of the winter festivities extending from Christmas to Lent. Twelfth Night banquets and balls seem to have been equally popular. If Carnival balls had any special meaning, this was not due to some ritual peculiar to that occasion, but rather to the fact that balls would—or should—be prohibited during Lent. Berquin-Duvallon marveled at the universal appeal of the balls in 1802 in his *View of the Spanish Colony on the Mississippi*, a tract based on three years' residence in the colony and calculated to reanimate French interest in Louisiana. Very few places in the entire world, he wrote, exhibited in a narrow space like that of the old French Quarter in New Orleans such "diversity of races, colors, and nations" during the months of January, February, and March, "when the flooding together of people is greater and more varied than at any other time." People seemed to do nothing but dance during this period of cool and generally clement weather and lighter agricultural work: "They dance in the city and dance in the country, they dance everywhere . . . and with not even any variety in the manner. . . ."[12]

This dancing frenzy was not the same as that in the time of Vaudreuil. Engaged in by all classes rather than just by elites, it was based not on imitation of Versailles but on the plantation life and its commercial extensions which were concentrated in port cities like New Orleans and Mobile. To show how plantation prosperity made dancing during the winter season an obsession not only of elites but of the servile class of blacks, requires an excursus.

The life-style of plantation-owning colonials, rather poorly illustrated in eighteenth-century Louisiana, had already been fully developed in the Spanish, French, and English possessions in the tropics, and especially on the Caribbean islands between 1600 and 1700. By the early eighteenth century the system extended from Barbados, Granada, and Martinique in the southeast Caribbean to Santo Domingo, Jamaica, and Cuba in the northwest, not to mention areas farther afield such as Bermuda or the Canary Islands. Caribbean plantations were large-scale operations; a typical planter owned one hundred slaves or more. After 1800 the most prosperous Louisiana, Mississippi, and Alabama plantations reached this scale.

The corollary of large-scale plantation slavery in the Caribbean was the development of a free-black class, the members of which provided managerial and artisanal service for the white planters. Free blacks tended to migrate to cities and towns, where social life was less restrictive and economic opportunities were greater. The same was true in Louisiana. In 1791 the black population of New Orleans (2,751) was 41.7 percent free (1,147). By 1810 the percentage was even higher (45.4 percent) and represented a large community of persons: 4,950. Twenty years later the free-black community in New Orleans, 44.2 percent of all blacks, was a very large group indeed. Free blacks numbered 11,477 persons in a total population, black and white, of 46,082.[13]

This class developed from a double impulse, the effort of slaves to move out of their oppressed position through sexual and personal closeness to whites, and the responsiveness of whites to appeals to blood ties and to personal loyalty. The Spanish government had liberalized the conditions by which masters set slaves free, first set in the French "Black Code" of 1724. American authorities continued the Spanish stipulations during the first years after the Louisiana Purchase. But freedom did not lead to intermarriage with whites by the newly enfranchised; free blacks were consequently led to defend their status by rules of marriage and behavior as rigid as those of the whites. A three-caste system emerged in which free blacks avoided open liaisons with enslaved blacks as much as whites did.[14]

The system was not intended by anyone. The acts creating an intermediate class of free blacks were private and personal, and yet they turned out to have public and social form. The driving force of free-black privilege was hatred of the oppression from which members of that class had recently escaped. And yet they were compelled in greater or lesser measure to engage in that same oppression to maintain their separate position. Many free blacks owned slaves. None were willing to place their privileges in jeopardy by questioning the racist basis for slavery which their achievements nevertheless belied. For the same reason whites had to treat free blacks, with their often considerable wealth, undeniable education, and indispensable technical skillfulness, as invisible. Whites and free blacks found themselves in a doubly defensive posture, vis-à-vis each other and against the enslaved blacks from whom both groups profited.[15]

Mardi gras represented an annually recurring climax to the ironies created by the display of white plantation power in the streets of the city, rubbing elbows—and trying not to—with free persons of the same hue as their slaves. Rubbing other body parts as well. The converse was also true, for Carnival-time was masking time, and who could tell if the man behind the mask was a slave or a free black, a light-colored black or a white man?

The anomalies of the caste system could be bridged in Mardi Gras, bridged at the same time as they were exhibited. Is this why the display in ballroom splendor of females—display of the physical means by virtue of which one belonged to one or another of the three castes—came to be Carnival's cornerstone? Here could be seen in panoramic array "two hundred young beauties . . . rival[ing] each other in elegance, vivacity . . . grace, and loveliness" as one reporter exuded in 1824 with reference to a "society ball" at the Théatre d'Orléans.[16] The dancing season moved to paroxysms of female seductiveness and male rivalry as mardi gras approached. Ballroom conventions allowed both exhibition and violation of the steep social hierarchy, anchored in black slavery, which activated the economy of the city. A series of gradations among kinds of balls was created between the 1770s and 1810 which not only allowed white males at the top of the scale a maximum of social mobility, but allowed for kinds of contact between blacks and whites, male and female, which were unthinkable in the streets.

Three sorts of ball existed by the late eighteenth century. There were private balls, given above all by the members of the upper class for each other. There were "society balls," organized by young men of the upper or middle classes on a subscription basis; subscription meant buying a ticket to a series of six to ten occasions, to which one was entitled to bring three young ladies, or, if one was a married head of household, one's wife and daughters. And there were "public balls," to which admission was charged on an individual basis. Public balls had to be licensed by the city. Some were licensed for whites only, others for free blacks only, still others—the famed quadroon balls, of which the first documented notice is 1805[17]—for white males and free black females. None were licensed directly for slaves, but they contrived to enter the free-black functions.

In 1781 a report to the Cabildo reveals the difficulties—from an official and political point of view—provoked by this way of allowing for intercaste mixing by males. A dangerous situation existed, a Spanish police official, called the syndic, informed the Cabildo council, in that "people of color, both free and slaves, were taking advantage of carnival" at a time when Spanish control over the colony was unsettled by the contemporary American revolt from Great Britain. Under pretext of celebrating the festival blacks were going about "disguised, mingling with the carnival throngs in the streets, seeking entrance to the masquerade balls, both society balls and those charging for admission, and threatening the public peace by introducing enemies of the king into assemblies under mask." Moreover, the syndic concluded, such persons were "using carnival disguises to assist them in the commission of robberies by night." Receiving the report favorably, the Cabildo ordered the commander of the New Orleans garrison to stop "colored people" from engaging in disguises and nocturnal balls (bayles nocturnos).[18]

The political intention of mardi gras masking at nocturnal balls was probably not the revolutionary one imagined by the Cabildo, although such designs cannot be excluded. It was probably a broader intention, at least as far as slaves were concerned, that of using disguise and darkness to have at least a few hours of freedom at the balls. In 1800 during Carnival the Spanish syndic, in another report to the Cabildo, dealt with this problem. Slaves during the 1790s were permitted to attend the public balls given for free blacks, licensed in a ballroom called the Spectacle de la rue St. Pierre, if they could show a written permit from their owners. The syndic protested that this condition was not respected, and that most of the slaves in the city were frequenting this ballroom. Worse still, the ballroom was decorated in such a way as to make it a "ridiculous imitation" of another ballroom, that on Condé Street, which was licensed to give public balls for whites only. The syndic reiterated "the danger of affording such opportunities for slaves to acquire expensive and luxurious habits." The paradox of social barriers, that they invite both imitation and transgression, was noted. It could not be remedied. All the Cabildo did was to abolish the system of permits for slaves. The very next year, during Carnival of 1801, the syndic not only renewed the same complaints but pointed out that the barrier was also being crossed in the opposite direction: seamen, soldiers, and country folk—that is whites—were resorting to the free black ballroom![19]

Most scandalous was the crossing of the racial bar at the "Blue Ribbon" or quadroon balls. One of the most famous descriptions of them is by the duke of Saxe-Weimar Eisenach, who visited New Orleans in 1825. Of the refined affairs at the most prestigious of ballrooms, the Théatre d'Orléans, where the parquet was built up during the Carnival season to the level of the stage so as to provide a continuous dance floor, Saxe-Weimar wrote: "Most of the gentlemen did not remain long at the ball, but hastened away to the quadroon ball, so called, where they amused themselves more and were more at their ease. . . . Like many others, I find the quadroon balls more entertaining. . . ."[20] Psychologically the very existence of a lightskinned black person in a racist society was provocative. It was a physical guarantee that the forbidden could be acccomplished, that illicit, unspeakable intimacy between white men and beings called or compared to savages, apes, and monkeys could and did take place.[21] But it was usually not the women at these affairs who behaved like beasts. Thus Saxe-Weimar described a masked ball at St. Philip Theater:

> There were but few masks, and among the tobacco-chewing gentry, several Spanish visages slipped about, who carried swordcanes, and seemed to have no good design in carrying them. Some of these visitors were intoxicated and then appeared a willing disposition for disturbance. The whole aspect was that of a den of ruffians. I did not remain but a half hour, and learned the next day that I was judicious in going home early, as later, battles with fists, with canes and dirks had taken place. Twenty persons were more or less dangerously wounded.

In spite of this episode Saxe-Weimar returned two more times to the quadroon balls.[22]

It was not only the good duke who was excited by this kind of thing. Ten years later in November, 1835, the acting mayor of New Orleans, Mr. Culbertson, declared to the city council that he "knew of a certainty" that at the latest quadroon ball "there were more white ladies than colored ones." The mayor concluded: "I believe, gentlemen, that such a state of things cannot be tolerated in our country." Ten days later an enterprising reporter of the newspaper the *Bee* affirmed from personal experience the truth of the acting mayor's remarks. At the quadroon ball in the Washington Ballroom "we were certainly surprised to find that two thirds at least of the females present were white women." Moreover, said the reporter, many of them "were usually considered respectable in their sphere of life. . . . It was even asserted that many married ladies were present."[23]

From the point of view of the development of festive custom toward what would become their concentration on Mardi Gras, the shift from French to American rule in 1803 was a non-event. The entire period from the 1770s to the 1830s should rather be seen as the first epoch in the development. It did not begin with the balls of the Marquis de Vaudreuil, inportant as this example was as a French colonial ideal which would live in the imagination. It began when the Spanish colonial government facilitated commercial and agricultural investment in Louisiana, reversing the restrictive politics of the French. This not only led to the sugar-cane experiments which eventually, along with slavery, became the basis of economic prosperity down to the Civil War, but to the commercialization of leisure. On February 22, 1770— that is, on the Thursday before mardi gras—the Cabildo approved a schedule of taxes that licensed taverns, billiard tables, and coffee houses, among other things.[24] We have seen that the 1770s saw the development of the variety of ballrooms criticized by the Spanish syndic in 1781. In 1791 the first acting troupe in New Orleans arrived. Refugees from Santo Domingo, they first performed out of doors and then in St. Peter Street until they acquired a permanent theater in St. Philip Street in 1808.[25] In 1813 a second theater was built, the famous Orleans Theater, which became the scene of many Carnival celebrations.[26]

The merchant's eye perceived the appetite for distraction of a frontier colony which was ethnically too diverse and socio-economically too transient to invest in culture in the settled manner of Boston or New York. Libraries, universities, academies and institutes had little relevance to this milieu. Nothing intellectual or long-term in its benefits could hold the attention, for how could its profits be calculated? New Orleans life, as the architect Benjamin Latrobe observed when he arrived in New

Orleans in 1818, was an eternal bustle.[27] People's sole object is "buying and selling," he wrote in his diary in early 1819; the "occupation of a money making community fills their time, and gives the habit of their minds." The result of this was that although Latrobe was received in New Orleans with great hospitality, he found little opportunity for extended contact with anyone: "The time of a late dinner and a short sitting after it have been the only periods during which I could make any acquaintance with the Gentlemen of the place. As it is now the Carnival"—Latrobe is writing in late January—"every evening is closed with a ball or a play or a concert."[28]

Balls, plays, and concerts: In 1819 there is nothing which distinguishes Carnival from the rest of the winter season except its pace. During the whole period from the 1770s to the 1830s Carnival activities have little particular shape and no enduring form because of the lack of integration of the ethnic and economic forces forming New Orleans and, in smaller degree, also Mobile.[29]

The commercialization of leisure certainly received a quickening thrust from the transfer of Louisiana to the United States. Within six months of the transfer the *Louisiana Gazette,* the first English-language newspaper in New Orleans, appeared with the motto "American Commerce and Freedom." As Latrobe acutely observed, many people of French and Spanish extraction—the white creoles—adapted themselves quickly: "The opportunity of growing rich by more active, extensive, and intelligent modes of agriculture and commerce has diminished the hospitality, destroyed the leisure, and added more selfishness to the character of the creoles."[30]

The Americans, with less sense of etiquette and more of profit, allowed the system of state regulation of ballroom attendance to take its commercial way, to the eventual moral horror of those same Anglo-Americans who had stimulated it, as we have seen with respect to the newspaper commentary on white women at quadroon balls in the 1830s. William C. Claiborne was so bewildered by the place of public balls in the winter season of 1803–4, when he arrived to administer Louisiana as its first American governor, that he wrote in consternation to Secretary of State James Madison, his superior in Washington, as Mardi gras of 1804 approached:

> The Public Ball Room has been the Theater of great Disorder. During the Winter Season there has for many years been a Ball twice a week. Every white male visits it who will pay at the door 50 cents, and the Ladies of

every Rank attend these assemblies in great numbers. The consequence is that the company is generally composed of a very heterogeneous mass.

It seems probable from Claiborne's references to males as white but to females as "Ladies of every Rank" that quadroons and other mulattos were present at these assemblies. Claiborne tries to explain why he should write to Madison about such a matter:

> I fear you will suppose that I am wanting in respect in calling your attention to the Balls of New Orleans, but I do assure you, Sir, that they occupy much of the Public mind, and from them have proceeded the greatest embarassments which have hitherto attended my administration.

Indeed. And it is still so in the 1980s. If the police threaten to strike, as they did in 1979, all New Orleans quakes and trembles. Rex's queen, Comus's queen, still set the social tone for the coming year at their balls. Claiborne did well to do his best "to convince [the people] that the American Government felt no disposition to break in upon their amusements." Governor Claiborne and the military commander in the territory, General Wilkinson, decided that it would be best if they relinquished regulation of the balls to the municipal government of New Orleans, and they endorsed their approbation of the institution by "occasionally" attending the balls in person.[31]

Did Claiborne understand, even if only half-consciously, the classical role that Carnival balls were playing in the early years of the occupation of a hitherto Franco-Spanish empire, the role of acting as a pressure-valve for social tensions? "Would not wineskins and casks break asunder . . . if their bungholes were not occasionally opened? We indeed are . . . half broken casks, wherefore the wine of wisdom, fermenting overmuch . . . would flow forth to no purpose if we did not occasionally recreate ourselves with games and follies." Thus had argued many centuries earlier the heathenish propagators of the medieval "Feast of Fools," to the horror of the Faculty of Theology of the University of Paris.[32] In the same way, but with more effectiveness, the ballroom proprietors of New Orleans in 1804 seem to have convinced Governor Claiborne and General Wilkinson that they were actually public benefactors when they satisfied in a harmlessly gallant manner the sexual fantasies created by caste differences and relieved with games and follies the raw and repetitious life of the frontier.

But of course the matter was more complicated than this. If the extension of the Carnival balls to include popular and even enslaved classes in their compass becomes understandable as a compromise between the needs and desires of commercial-urban and plantation-rural elites, the reason for the appetites of the latter still seem mysterious. What could these rich colonials find so intriguing in the endless round of dancing which usually puzzled and bored foreign visitors? There was of course the traditional component of courtly spectacle. Insofar as slaveholding planters regarded themselves as an aristocracy, a miniature extension of the European courts they had left behind, they had an obligation to continue the masking and dancing which since the sixteenth century were standard parts of royal and aristocratic behavior. The court-as-spectacle was an integral part of policy, a demonstration of princely superiority: The balls and masques which since medieval times were clustered in England and France around the festive times of Christmas and Carnival were part of the colonial memory and the colonial ideal.[33]

The colonial upper class was, after all, caught between contrary compulsions. It possessed the means to establish and display an extensive and sophisticated way of life, a way of life which would distinguish the upper class from the classes below. But in the frontier situation and more particularly in the slaveholding frontier situation, this way of life had not only to be displayed to others but made inaccessible to them. The means of doing this was to imitate the "home" culture, a culture which subordinate classes, especially black people from Africa, could not possibly imitate in any but a laughable, ignoble manner. But insofar as plantation culture became an imitation of the homeland, the place of colonial elites in the new land became transient. Their values encouraged them to regard the colony as exile, and to invest as little as possible in their life in the New World. In a word, the typical cultural attitude of the plantation class in Louisiana, as throughout the Caribbean area, was that of defensive alienation from their surroundings. The purpose of activity could only be to demonstrate their otherness, indeed their lofty absence from the life surrounding them. Thus the duke of Saxe-Weimar wrote about the upper-class "subscription balls" of 1826 in New Orleans: "Most of the women were very beautiful and of excellent French *tournure*. Their dress was extremely elegant and followed the latest Parisian modes." But Saxe-Weimar, eminent representative as he was of the home culture to which New Orleans aspired, was obliged by the very character of what he saw to be deprecating: "The women danced remarkably well and did great honor to their French dancemaster."[34] In terms of mind-set, little had changed since the days of Bébé. American elites were in cultural terms dutiful, precise little children.

Not the powers above but the powerless below proved to be culturally resourceful in the plantation situation. Fredrika Bremer, a Swedish writer who made an extended tour of Louisiana and Cuba and enterprisingly visited slave and also free-black homes, was always surprised at the answers she received when she asked former slaves who had by some means gained their freedom if they did not wish to return to Africa. No, they would reply, usually with amusement; why should they even wish, let alone imagine, that they could exchange their house with its garden in the sun for the unfamiliar place of their ancestors?[35] It was the black people in Louisiana, as in the Caribbean basin generally, who first created festive forms which were an original amalgam of old and new customs, of European and African ways of life. They had to do so in order to sustain themselves in a situation from which there was scarcely any escape.[36]

For the period before 1830 information about these festive inventions is sparse for the New Orleans area and nonexistent for Mobile. The black population of the latter town was too small to leave an impression on travellers (250 of the 500 total population in 1813; 1,200 to 1,400 of a total 2,708 in 1822).[37] This dearth of sources can be alleviated by information concerning Caribbean and some eastern American states. Black customs in places as far afield as Cuba, Trinidad, New York, and North Carolina took forms which shed light on what became black Carnival.

When the slave population could celebrate depended on their masters. But the masters' whims were in turn controlled by two factors: the annual growth-cycle of their crops, above all sugar, and the obligation they felt to offer Christian respite from work. The heaviest work, that of cutting and refining the sugar cane, took place between October and January. During this period slaves might be forced to work eighteen hours a day for weeks. But Christmas, and at least some of the twelve days following it to Epiphany on January 6, were exceptions to this rigor. If mardi gras fell in March rather than February, there was more likelihood that it could be observed in an extended, gala manner, for after the cutting and refining season came the somewhat less burdensome period of planting new cane. For urban blacks, free or slave, both Christmas and the Mardi Gras season following it were times of participation in the festive air sanctioned by the white elites. Along the Gulf Coast the weather was dry and free from the perilous yellow fever. Commercial fever generally did not quicken the pulse until a little later in the year.

Sundays were for the slaves more important than agricultural or business cycles in affording time to maintain their own festive traditions. In 1792 Carondelet, the Spanish governor, proclaimed that Sunday would be reserved for slaves' recreation. In 1795 he further specified that planters should not allow blacks from elsewhere to visit their plantations after sundown. Does the latter stipulation refer to the slaves' practice, documented for the 1790s in British Guiana, of beginning their festivities on Saturday night and continuing all through Sunday and even Sunday night?[38] By 1808 in any case, the city of New Orleans permitted slaves to assemble "for the purpose of dancing and amusing themselves" only on Sundays, "at such places only as may be therefore appointed by the Mayor." The ordinance was reenacted in 1817 with the significant additions that the places appointed by the Mayor be "open or public," and that "no such assembly shall continue later than sunset. . . ." Mixed with the fear that slave assemblies might harbor rebellion was the sense of their unchristian flavor. In 1786 the Cabildo forbade black dancing during evening service on Sundays and holy days.[39]

The most famed place of assembly was the area now called Louis Armstrong Park, on the northwest or back side of the French Quarter, formerly known as Congo Square or Place Congo. It deserves its fame, for it provoked the best descriptions of black African dancing on the North American continent before such dancing died out there in the 1840s. We do not know when dancing began at Congo Square. The ordinances of 1786, 1808, and 1817 do not specifically mention this place. Another area was the built-up bank, or levee to hold back floodwaters, along the river. A boat traveler on the Mississippi in 1799 saw "vast numbers," more than "one hundred negroes of both sexes," and children, too, on the third and fourth Sundays in Lent of that year, "drumming, fifing and dancing in large rings" on the levee.[40] John Watson of Philadelphia similarly reported in 1804 "great masses" of slaves on the levee at New Orleans on Sundays, singing and dancing with merriment.[41]

These generalized references tell us little. The first particular account of black dancing in New Orleans is at the same time the first description of Congo Square. It is by Benjamin Latrobe, the architect whom we have seen commenting in his diary on the city's commercial bustle. Latrobe happened upon the square just two days before mardi gras on February 21, 1819.[42] He calls the place the "Common in the rear of the city." He was drawn to it by accident, having heard during an afternoon stroll "a most extraordinary noise, which I supposed to proceed from some horse Mill, the horses trampling on a wooden floor." Instead of this he found "five or six hundred persons" in the square, arranged in separate circular groups. Latrobe's first shock, it seems, was the performers' racial character: "All those who were engaged in the business seemed to be *blacks*. I did not observe a dozen yellow faces"—that is, mulattos.[43] His subsequent description makes it clear that these singers, players, and dancers, who probably came from surrounding plantations as often as, or more often than, the town, were still very close to their African traditions. This was Latrobe's own conclusion, and it went together with his distaste for the "brutally savage," "dull and stupid" things he saw.[44] His perspicacity as an artist was not entirely dulled by this moral judgment, however. In the margins of his diary he accompanied his interesting and accurate comments on the musical instruments with fascinating designs.

It is the dancing and the general festive ambiance which concern us here. "There was not the least disorder among the crowd," Latrobe admits, "nor do I learn, on enquiry, that these weekly meetings of the negroes have ever produced any mischief." The dancing that Latrobe observed in a few of the many circular groups scattered over the open space was done by women, while the playing was done by men. In one of the largest circles (it was "not 10 feet in diameter") a "dozen women walked, by way of dancing, round the music in the Center." In another, two women "held each a coarse handkerchief extended by the corner in their hands, and *set* to each other in a miserably dull and slow figure, hardly moving their feet or bodies." The music was made by two drums and a stringed instrument, the latter played by a "very little old man, apparently 80 or 90 years old." Women "squalled out a burthen to the playing, at intervals, consisting of two notes, as the Negroes working in our cities"—Latrobe had constructed buildings in Richmond, Philadelphia, and Washington—"respond to the Song of their leader." Here is the African call-and-response pattern, probably exercised in cross-rhythm to the drum-playing. Most of the circles contained similar dancers, writes Latrobe, but the instruments varied. At another spot, "a man sung an uncouth song to the dancing which I suppose was in some African language, for it was not French, and the women screamed a detestable burthen on one single note." In spite of the ordinance of 1817, the dancing was still going on "after sunset near the same spot," when Latrobe returned after continuing his stroll.

Congo Square dancing certainly did not begin in 1818 or 1819, just before Latrobe discovered it. John Paxton's *New Orleans Directory and Roster*, published in 1822, calls the place "Circus public square," and describes it as "very noted" because it is "where the Congo, and other negroes dance, carouse, and debauch on the Sabbath, to the great injury of the morals of the rising generation. . . ." The passage concludes by urging that since it would not perhaps be "good policy" to abolish the custom, the blacks should at least be ordered to assemble "at some place more distant from the houses," which seems to imply that the endangered rising generation was that of white spectators, not black children.[45]

Indeed black dancing was already going on further from the city. Nine years later Pierre Forest, who visited the New Orleans area in 1831, describes the Sunday activities at "The Camp" on Lake Pontchartrain, several miles north of the old city center. In contrast to Latrobe's report of an entirely black milieu, Forest comments on "the strange effect produced by the sight of so many shades of black." "Yet for the most part they are negroes" instead of mulattos, he adds: Forest, like Latrobe, thinks in terms of the three-caste system characteristic of the Caribbean and parts of the southeast United States.[46] "They are gathered in a large number of distinct groups: each has its own flag floating atop a very tall mast, used as the rallying point for the group." These groups, like the circles at Congo Square, almost certainly represented tribal differences, as we shall see when comparing these activities to similar gatherings in Cuba.

The dancing reported by Forest is sharply different from what Latrobe saw: "The negroes dance with extraordinary speed and agility. Actually their dance is rather a pantomime than a dance. The great merit of the exercises they perform lay in the variety of their attitudes and expressions which, further more, are all lascivious. They make their music by beating and rolling their sticks on their drums; a sharp sound is produced, repeated two or three times by the surrounding echoes."[47]

Three areas near New Orleans—levee, common, and lakefront—provided space for the maintenance and development of African festive traditions, three places on the boundaries between contrasting milieus, rural and urban, commercial and plantation, city-edged and water-edged. At the margins there is freedom.

The presence of such contrasts encouraged in at least one case even the mental space requisite for a white man's indulgently philosophical view of such strange dancing. The New England minister Timothy Flint traveled to Louisiana in the early 1820s and was moved to speculate on the holiday behavior of blacks in New Orleans and vicinity because of its strong contrast with that of those other exotics, the Indians. "I have seen groups of these moody and silent sons of the forest, following these merry bacchanalians in their dance, *through the streets*, scarcely relaxing their grim visages to a smile, in the view of antics that convulsed even the masters of the negroes with laughter." [48]

Could this scene have taken place during Carnival? "Every year the negroes have two or three holidays, which in New Orleans and the vicinity, are like the 'Saturnalia' of the slaves in ancient Rome." Two such holidays were almost certainly Christmas and mardi gras. If the inference is correct, then Flint's is the first depiction of black festive behavior during Carnival in the streets of the city, and also the first which reports the Indians' presence at such affairs. Flint describes a new and unexpected figure:

> The great Congo-dance is performed. Every thing is license and revelry. Some hundreds of negroes, male and female, follow the king of the wake, who is conspicuous for his youth, size, the whiteness of his eyes, and the blackness of his visage. For a crown he has a series of oblong, gilt-paper boxes on his head, tapering upwards, like a pyramid. From the ends of these boxes hang two huge tassels, like those on epaulets. He wags his head and makes grimaces. By his thousand mountebank tricks, and contortions of countenance and form, he produces an irresistible effect upon the multitude. All the characters that follow him, of leading estimation, have their own peculiar dress, and their own contortions. They dance, and their streamers fly, and the bells that they have hung about them tinkle. [49]

This sovereign was perhaps a Carnival or Twelfth-Night king of misrule, but if so, his regal role was probably not solely this. It would seem unlikely that the occasion in question was a funeral, in spite of the fact that the figure is called "king of the wake," and that black gaiety at funeral celebrations is well known. [50] The context which Flint cites is that of Saturnalian holiday, and this perception, which we will find in other white observers of black festive customs, was applicable at the time almost solely to celebrations during the twelve days from Christmas to Epiphany and the days leading to Lent.

Colonial Rites       35

Who this king of the wake probably was can be deduced from comparable figures in other parts of the Caribbean, to which we will shortly turn. It is more difficult to imagine who are the following characters "of leading estimation," each with costumes and gestures which Flint does not specify. At least we know from the comments of two German travelers that their bright colors and ornaments, emphasized by Flint but absent from Latrobe's report about Congo Square, were probably typical of the blacks' festivities. J. G. Fluegel saw the Sunday dances at Congo Square in April 1817: "He [Gildemeister, a New Orleans businessman] told me that three of the negroes in the group closest to us were formerly kings or chiefs in Congo. . . . They are richly ornamented and dance extremely well."[51] Johann Buechler witnessed the black dancers in May and June of the same year at "different locations" "behind the city": "The males clothe themselves in oriental and Indian dress with a Turkish turban of various colors, red, blue, yellow, green, and brown with a sash of the same sort around the body to cover themselves; except for that they go naked. The women clothe themselves . . . in the newest fashions in silk, gauze, muslin, [and] percale dresses. . . . They dance in the most wonderful way, form a circle and make on all sides the most wonderful bending gestures with their bodies and knees. . . ."[52]

Black people's sense of Carnival was opportunistic. They had no use for its Christian religious or European seasonal meanings. By 1808 it had become the "custom" of New Orleans blacks to dance even on Ash Wednesday, the sacred day following Carnival's conclusion: "I visited one of those river bamboulas yesterday, Ash Wednesday," noted Pierre Laussat in his *Memoirs*, "where the negroes have the custom of going to do their goodbyes to Carnival. This year the bamboula took place at the river of the Fathers above the canal at Toumazeau's sugar mill. . . . Crowds of negro men and women were scattered about there in groups. Some [were] dancing bamboulas, others contre-danses, and others [were] enjoying themselves around cloths spread with abundant foods [*gros mets*] and black sauces."[53] A picnic scene! Here is the first mention of foods in relation to Carnival in New Orleans. Here also is the first mention of an African designation for one of the dances.

What is a bamboula? The colonial Laussat uses the word both to name a dance and to name a festive occasion. The European Médéric Moreau de Saint Méry, commenting on the Haitian life which he witnessed before the revolution of 1789, calls the bamboula a "short" drum sometimes made from thick bamboo cane.[54] Was it then a certain dance set to this type of drum, which so predominated at certain festive occasions that the latter, too, were called bamboulas? Moreau makes only the connection between the dance and the instrument. For our purposes it is more important to note the breadth of usage than to ascertain its exact meaning and development. The most famous description of the bamboula as a dance is George Cable's nostalgic account of it in "The Dance in Place Congo" for the *Century Magazine* of 1886. But Cable's highly colored words have nothing to do with anything he saw—he admits this—and perhaps nothing much to do with what others saw in New Orleans. His vivid yet vague description of the dancers' movements ("Now for the frantic leaps! Now for frenzy!") has them fainting from "delight" ("the dancers fall . . . with foam on their lips and are dragged out").[55] These excited details are embroidery on what he had learned from Moreau's brief Haitian description, from newspapers and perhaps some travellers' accounts,[56] and also, presumably, from Lafcadio Hearn's description in the *Century Magazine* for 1883:

> Until within a few years ago, the strange African dances were still danced and the African songs still sung by negroes and negresses who had been slaves. Every Sunday afternoon the bamboula dancers were summoned to a woodyard on Dumaine street by a sort of drum-roll, made by rattling the ends of two great-bones upon the head of an empty cask; and I remember that the male dancers fastened bits of tinkling metal or tin rattles about their ankles, like those strings of copper gris-gris worn by the negroes of the Soudan. Those whom I saw taking part in those curious and convulsive performances—subsequently suppressed by the police—were either old or beyond middle age.[57]

Hearn's eyewitness account of a backyard bamboula in the late 1870s or early 1880s indicates that this particular festive dance was a favorite at New Orleans, for the bishop of New Orleans was already complaining about its "hideous gyrations" in 1786, as performed in Congo Square.[58] The connection to Haiti should not be ignored. While some two thousand Haitians—slaves, free blacks, and whites—came to New Orleans during and after the revolution there, contacts and cultural exchange had certainly begun before that event.

The bamboula, then, was played as a drum and danced in African rhythm first at Congo Square and later in semisecrecy in black New Orleans. Along with it was danced the calinda. Pierre Forest, continuing his description of the Sunday occasions at

The Camp on Lake Pontchartrain in 1831, reproduces one of the blacks' "favorite songs" which includes references to both bamboula and calinda. "The original was given to me by a *griffonne* [a mulatto] who was unable to translate it for me," Forest writes. The third stanza runs so:

> Dempé mo perdi Lizette
> Mo pas souchié calinda,
> Mo pas bram bramba boula,
> Quand mo contre l'antre négresse
> Mo pas gagniez zié pour ly,
> Mo pas souchié travail pièce
> Tant que chose à moé mourir.

> Since I have lost Lizette
> My footsteps care not for the calinda
> Nor for the "bram" of the bamboula
> When I meet some other negro woman
> My footsteps are not won over to her
> Nor do they care for work at all
> So much has this thing died for me.[59]

The first line of the first stanza of the song is "Lizette to quité la plaine." Jean-Jacques Rousseau referred to this line as a "Chanson Negre," a negro song, in a manuscript written about 1740. It turned up again in 1811 in a pamphlet printed in Philadelphia called *Idylls and songs . . . by a Haitian Colonist*, and was republished in Louisiana in the 1850's, some twenty years after Forest's time.[60] Similarly, in the oral material collected by members of the Louisiana Writers' Program of the Work Projects Administration between 1936 and 1945 the following words are found among the recollections of an ex-slave from Louisiana named Charity Parker:

> Saturday was our day. Sunday we had to go to church. When I was young I didn't care 'bout no church, but I could sure beat them feets. . . . One day a old man we called Antoine say "I'm gonna make you-all a drum what'll beat, 'Boum! Boum! Boum!' Wait 'til Massa kill a cow." . . . Well he get that hide. . . . He straddle that drum and beat on it. . . . Chile, we dance 'til midnight, to finish the ball we say "Balancez Calinda!", and then we twist and turn, and holler again, "Balancez Calinda!", and turn round again. Then the ball was over.[61]

Does the word "calinda" used in these different documents refer to the same dance? There is reason to doubt it. The earliest account of the calinda seems to be that of Jean-Baptiste Labat, a French priest resident in Guadaloupe, Martinique, and some other Caribbean islands in the 1690s. He describes how blacks danced the "calenda" to the accompaniment of two drums, one large and one small. The small drum was called the "baboula" and was obviously the same as the drum elsewhere called the bamboula. He compares the calenda pejoratively to another dance, the "congo," which he found less "indecent" than the calenda. The calenda, he writes, is an African dance from the "Guinea Coast," that is, from the West African area from which most slaves were taken in the seventeenth and eighteenth centuries.[62] But this dance, which emphasized the women's sensuous swirling of her hips, seems to have been called chica in Haiti, not calenda. The calenda in Haiti, according to Moreau de Saint-Méry in the 1780s, was danced by one or several pairs of boys and girls in a circle, and involved the rapid movement back and forth of each pointed foot in turn. It is more likely that the calinda danced in Louisiana followed this second form, given the closer connections of the Louisiana colony with Saint Domingue (Haiti) than with the more distant Windward Islands (Guadaloupe, Martinique, etc.).[63]

Calinda or calenda, like bamboula or baboula, was very probably an African word broadly adopted in the New World, shifting and expanding its meaning in the different contexts where African dancing developed. There is the additional complication of European misapprehension in all such designations. But for the colonial period one can usually identify what dances were of African as opposed to European origin if some description of costuming is included in the documents.

When black people imitated something European, they generally borrowed the clothing as well. Peter Marsden remarked the difference in Jamaica in the 1780s:

> At Christmas the slaves are allowed three days' holiday during which time they are quite at liberty, and have herrings, flour and rum. The prime negroes and mulattoes pay a visit to the white people during the festivity and are treated with punch; one of them attends with a fiddle, and the men dress in the English mode, with cocked hats, cloth coats, silk stockings, white waistcoats, Holland shirts, and pumps. They dance minuets with the mulattoes and other brown women, imitating the motion and steps of the English but with a degree of affectation that renders the whole truly laughable and ridiculous.

But their Saturday nights (here not Sundays) are another matter. Then "many divert themselves with dancing and singing" in a exceedingly "droll" manner: "They put themselves into strange postures and shake their hips and great breasts to such a degree that it is impossible to refrain from laughing, though they go through the whole performance with profound gravity, their feet beating time remarkably quick. . . ."[64]

By the late eighteenth century black people in the Caribbean had developed a double festive culture, one imitating the whites and the other preserving their own customs. Laussat's comment in 1808 has this significance when he remarks that the Ash Wednesday "river bamboula" of the blacks included some dancing bamboulas and others dancing the rustic European *contre-danses* (i.e., quadrilles) which we know were popular in the white public ballrooms of New Orleans at the time.[65] The same double culture, imitating and defying white standards, was carried forward in the later nineteenth-century black Carnivals at New Orleans and Mobile, as we will see. The establishment of two ritual patterns, one accommodating and the other oblivious to white modes of conduct, created new boundary zones which in turn encouraged still other variants of festive behavior, including some by whites.

"The giving out [of] the Christmas allowances is a very merry scene" in Trinidad, wrote Mrs. A. C. Carmichael in 1833. "They flour each other's black faces and curly hair and call out, 'Look at he white face! and he white wig!'—with many other jokes of their own."[66] Conversely the white belles of New Orleans loved nothing better than to "mask themselves as mulattos" at their private Carnival balls, Laussat reported in describing further the season of 1808. And they were right to do so, he added: "That costume suits them marvelously."[67]

There was thus recognition on each side of the peculiarities of the other, and also what seems to have been an astonishing willingness to display those peculiarities to the other. There is no implication anywhere, for example, that the foreigners who turned up at the black dancing-places around New Orleans caused the performers to hide or otherwise alter their behavior. Conversely, at least occasionally a traveler turned up who was sympathetic enough to join in the blacks' revels, at least when there was a sufficiently reassuring context. Cynric Williams, passing Christmas on a plantation in Jamaica in 1823, was awakened that morning by "a chorus of negroes singing 'good morning to your nightcap. . .'," and entering the house to dance. "I slipped on my dressing-gown and mingled in their orgies, much to the diversion of the black damsels. . . ." In the evening the slaves came with their African instruments, "gombays, bonjaws and an ebo drum," some dancing "a sort of love-dance" before the gombays, and others "a sort of pyrrhic before the ebo drummer." Yet these distinctive African dances were performed in European clothes, "some of the men in long-tailed coats, one of the gombayers in old regimentals, the women in muslins and cambrics, with colored handkerchiefs tastefully disposed round their heads. . . ." Obviously there are limits to the heuristic rule about costuming suggested earlier.

The plantation master, continues Williams, provided liquor freely to all. "Indeed a perfect equality seemed to reign," so much so that "the slaves sang satirical philippics against their master, communicating a little free advice now and then; but they never lost sight of decorum . . . and at last retired . . . to dance the rest of the night at their own habitations."[68]

One of the fullest descriptions of African dancing for the whole Caribbean area was made by an American doctor who visited Cuba four times in the 1830s. His account throws light on the meaning of the flags to which Forest refers in his rural New Orleans description of 1831, and allows one to make a first conjecture about the identity of Flint's "king of the wake." Dr. Wurdemann's description refers to several places on a hill behind San Carlos Alcazar de Matanzas, a town of nineteen thousand persons. On Sunday afternoons the blacks raise flags "on high staffs" there and "indulge in their national dances." The relation of singing to dancing is carefully noted in Wurdemann's description, and the intentions of courtship and prowess are shown to be interwoven. What Wurdemann witnessed is remarkably similar to the "challenges" of black "Mardi Gras Indians" in New Orleans which will be described in a later chapter:

> To the music of two or three rude drums, formed by stretching an untanned cow-hide over the extremity of a hollow trunk of a tree, the crowd of men and women, gaudily dressed, keep time with their hands. Presently a woman advances, and commencing a slow dance, made up of a shuffling of the feet and various contortions of the body, thus challenges a rival from among the men. One of these, bolder than the rest, after awhile steps out, and the two then strive which shall first tire the other; the woman performing many feats which the man attempts to rival, often excelling them, amid the shouts of the rest. A woman will sometimes drive two or three successive beaux from the ring, yielding her place at length to some impatient belle, who has been meanwhile looking on with envy at her success. Sometimes a sturdy fellow will keep the field for a long time, and one after another of the other sex will advance to the contest only to be defeated; each one, as she retires, being greeted by the laughter of the spectators. The

whole time a low song is sung by the crowd, as monotonous as the music of the drums, and composed of the
repetition of four or five words uttered in a more or less
animated tone, as the action [sic] of the dancers increase
or diminish in quickness.

As was the case in New Orleans, the dances were sanctioned
by the civil authorities. But there is a second authority here, un-
mentioned at New Orleans: "Over each tribe the king and queen
presides, and so great is the influence exercised by the former
over his subjects, that complaints made to him of the idle or vicious habits of any particular individual, not infrequently
through his remonstrances correct the evil."[69]

There was, then, some authority internal to the black communities in Cuba. If Wurdemann was correct, this authority was
by no means limited to the festive occasions on which it was
displayed but was exercised in a generally disciplining manner.
Wurdemann makes one other reference to the kings and
queens, this time with respect to a celebration in the small town
of Guines (2,500 persons, half black). The reference suggests
that the royal authority was perhaps not a purely African affair.
On January 6 (Epiphany, "the day of the kings," as it is called in
Spanish custom) "almost unlimited liberty was given to the negroes. Each tribe, having elected its king and queen, paraded
the streets with a flag, having its name and the words *viva Isabella*, with the arms of Spain painted on it."

Wurdemann does not assign a year to his visit. Between 1834
and 1839 Spain was torn by the Carlist war, which pitted Don
Carlos, the brother of the late King Ferdinand, against Ferdinand's regent-widow and her tiny daughter Isabella, eventually
recognized as the legitimate ruler. "Their majesties [the black
king and queen] wore dresses in the extreme of the fashion, and
were very ceremoniously waited on by the ladies and gentlemen
of the court, one of the ladies holding an umbrella over the head
of the queen. They bore their honors with that dignity which the
negro loves so much to assume, which they, moreover, preserved in the presence of the whites."[70]

There were three African "tribes" of this kind in Guines and
many more in Havana, writes Wurdemann. Yet it would be a
mistake to suppose that they represented survival of particular
African tribal traditions. As we learn from an eyewitness report
of 1851 about the Cuban kingdoms or *cabildos*, as they were then
called, the dances, like the dignitaries, were similar in each
group. The anthropologist Roger Bastide has emphasized that
tracing particular American customs to particular African tribes

is usually absurd, because it ignores the important syncretic processes which began among different slave groups as soon as they found themselves together on the ships bearing them to America. Confused again through random sale on arrival, tribal differences were further effaced through intermarriage. More important than tribal origin in establishing the character of local Afro-American cultures was the hegemony of a particular cultural tradition in a given area. The character of this hegemony had as much to do with local leaders and local circumstances of institutional freedom as with the numerical predominance of one tribe over others.[71]

Wurdemann's comments make the tribes of Guines appear more accomodating and more Europeanized than those at Matanzas. Those on the hill at Matanzas are simply described as "gaudily dressed," which may be shorthand for African costumes whose bizarreness was so alien to the observer that he did not attempt to describe them. The ceremoniousness of the parade at Guines, with its principals dressed in the "extreme" of presumably colonial fashion, was closer to white behavior than the formalities of the African dancing at Matanzas with its open male-female rivalry. Is the difference merely because Wurdemann saw a different part of the tribal festivities in the two towns, a parade in one case and a ball in another? Comparison with North American festivities of this kind shows that both parade and ball were usual parts of the black holiday. Is the royalism at Guines, the courtly costumes and display of a flag proclaiming allegiance to the Spanish queen, a consequence of the diminished independence of the black communities at Guines, as compared with that at the larger town of Matanzas? Does the royalism exemplify another hypothesis of Bastide: that these African kings in the New World, when they had disciplinary functions, were descended not directly from African prototypes, but followed "an old Hispano-Portuguese custom . . . practiced by the Negro groups imported to Europe"? One cannot without further information decide among these alternatives.[72] What one wishes to glean from these and other parallel instances to the regal appearances and flag-articulated dances at New Orleans is the general festive structure displayed in them, for this will enable us to fill out our very fragmentary Louisiana sources.

Outside Cuba and Louisiana such royal ceremonials appeared in Brazil, Peru, the Virgin Islands, and the northern United States.[73] Especially well known are the festivities recognizing a black "governor" in a number of towns in Connecticut, Rhode Island, and Massachusetts between 1750 and 1850, festivities which usually took place on a day close to the installation of the white governor of the colony or other local official.[74]

Less well known is the festive sovereign of the black community in Albany, New York, at the turn of the nineteenth century when some white families of wealth still possessed slaves. The black king's leadership was celebrated during Whitsuntide or Pentecost, a moveable feast of the church which falls in May. In Albany, a town first settled by the Dutch, the Dutch word for Pentecost was used: Pinkster. We have a flowery and nostalgic description of the week-long celebration by a white doctor who recalls the scenes of his youth, when the young members of the family, white and colored, were taken to the festival "under the careful guidance of a trusty slave." The culminating ceremonies took place on the second day:

> The hour of ten having now arrived, and the assembled multitude being considered most complete, a deputation was then selected to wait upon their venerable sovereign king, "Charley of the Pinkster hill," with the intelligence that his respectful subjects were congregated. He was tall, thin and athletic; and although the frost of nearly seventy winters had settled on his brow, its chilling influence had not yet extended to his bosom. . . . His costume on this memorable occasion was graphic and unique to the greatest degree, being that worn by a British brigadier of the olden time. Ample broadcloth scarlet coat, with wide flaps almost reaching to his heels, and gayly ornamented everywhere with broad tracings of bright golden lace; his small clothes were of yellow buckskin, fresh and new, with stockings blue, and burnished silver buckles to all his well-blacked shoe; when we add to these the tricornered cocked hat trimmed also with lace of gold, and which so gracefully set upon his noble, globular pate we nearly complete the rude sketch of the Pinkster king.

Eights then describes the dancing which followed on the hill all afternoon and evening. As in New Orleans and Cuba, what struck the white observer was the extreme energy of the dancers and the strange sounds of the African instruments.[75]

Hubert Aimes has pointed out that the North American instances all include two essential elements, some kind of regal or political ceremony and dancing. He also saw that the electoral element was little more than an occasion of reaffirming an authority founded on other bases than annually democratic voting: in most cases the black governors held their office year in and year out, and when they resigned it, they usually designated their successor. This kind of politics was related to African pat-

terns of authority; elections were only an accomodating facade.[76]

The most circumstantial and in several respects the most astonishing account of black festive institutions in the Caribbean
area is by a Swedish woman, Fredrika Bremer, who traveled
through the United States to Cuba, including Mobile and New
Orleans. In April 1851, she was able to visit, along with two
white male escorts, six of the organizations of free blacks in Havana which were called *cabildos*. Unlike Wurdemann, who does
not say whether the festivities he saw included free blacks or
slaves or both, Bremer thus specifies membership in the cabildos
and emphasizes that her entry was exceptional: "The free negroes in general do not admit of the whites in their society."

"These cabildoes are governed . . . by queens, one or two,
who decide upon the amusements, give tone to the society and
determine its extension." Here is a somewhat different world
from the masculine ones of Pinkster Hill's king and of the New
England black governors. "They [the queens] possess the right
of electing a king, who manages the pecuniary affairs of the society, and who has under him a secretary and master of the ceremonies." We are closer here to the presence of a matriarchally
articulated political system, like those found in earlier centuries
in some parts of the present-day nations of Nigeria, Benin or
Dahomey, Togo, and Ghana.[77]

The cabildos of Havana possessed their own clubhouses clustered on a street "near one of the toll-gates," perhaps just outside the city's jurisdiction, like the black meeting-places elsewhere on surrounding hills. On Sunday afternoons the street
"swarmed with negroes, some decked out with ribbons and
bells, some dancing, others standing in groups here and there."
There were whites, too, many of them sailors, who stood near
the gates of the different halls, endeavoring to see inside. But
black men with sticks in their hands kept the doors closed, and
allowed them to open only halfway on entrance or exit. In spite
of this, Bremer repeatedly managed to pass inside with her escorts. In the first of the halls, which she called "the Luccomees'
Cabildo" and which she calculated would hold with ease one
hundred persons, the three whites were presented to the queen
and king and then were offered chairs close to the door.

The place of royalty, opposite to where Bremer was seated,
was indicated by a crown on the wall and by a throne with a
canopy. These perhaps Europeanized accoutrements contrasted
with the dancing going on before it. "One woman danced alone,
under a canopy supported by four people." Bremer supposed

her dancing status to be very high, because, in accordance with the competitive way of dancing earlier described by Wurdemann, "all kinds of handkerchiefs were hanging about her, and a hat, even, had been placed upon her head. The women danced on this occasion with each other, and the men with the men; some struck the doors and benches with sticks, other rattled gourds filled with stones, and the drums thundered with deafening power." Then something magnificent occurred:

> While this was going on, a figure was seen advancing with a scarlet hat upon his head, and with a great number of glittering strings of beads round his neck, arms, and body, which was naked to the waist, from which hung scarlet skirts. This figure, before which the people parted to each side, approached me, bowing all the time, and as he did so the whole upper portion of his body seemed to move in snakelike folds. Still making these serpentine movements, he stood before me with extended hands, I being not at all certain whether he was inviting me to dance, or what was the meaning of his apparently friendly grimaces, and his great, black, outstretched hands. At length he uttered, with other words, "per la bonita!" and I comprehended that all his bowings and bedizenment were intended as a compliment to me, and I made my reply by shaking one of the black hands, and placing within it a silver coin, after which we exchanged friendly gestures, and my friend made a serpentine retreat, and began to dance on his own account, receiving great applause from the bystanders.[78]

Who is this figure? A clue is offered by Wurdemann, for he too mentions an unsettling dancer who appeared following the king and queen in the Epiphany procession through the streets of Guines: "The chief object in the group was an athletic negro with a fantastic straw helmet, an immensely thick girdle of strips of palm-leaves around his waist, and other uncouth articles of dress. Whenever they stopped, their banjoes struck up one of their monotonous tunes, and this frightful figure would commence a devil's dance, which was the signal for all his court to join in a general fandango. . . ."[79]

Every Carnival-goer in New Orleans today knows the Zulus, who until recent years were led by a king who had an immensely thick girdle of grass around his waist, a crown of sorts on his head, and such "uncouth articles" as gilded coconuts in his hands. The Zulu parade was invented in the early twentieth century by a few working-class black men who allegedly saw a theatrical skit about the famous African tribe. Their costumes and antics also say something about the stiffness of the official white monarch of Carnival, Rex. But it is obvious that the deeper sources of the Zulus' festive as well as non-festive behavior lie in African tradition, as mediated by figures like those we are considering.

The Zulus' Carnival parade is only one of their activities, which go on all through the year. Their organization is called "The Zulu Social Aid and Pleasure Club." Like the *cabildos* of Havana which also had more than festive functions, the Zulus' organization is rooted in a communal tradition of mutual aid, of providing money and credit at times of sickness and death. In West Africa this tradition was called the *susu* (sharing group); its forms in Afro-American life have long received attention from sociologists.[80] But its festive side has not been well studied because the semipermanent structural elements have not been separated from the fascinating surface. In all the instances we have considered there is a three-part pattern: elements of ceremony and reverence for constituted authority, elements of parade and prowess in costume, music, and dancing, and elements of communal union, applause and responsiveness. In other words, there are authority figures, heroes, and an audience well enough defined so that members of it may move from the position of audience to that of hero, and indeed to positions of authority.

Performing the pattern regularly produced four positions: a hierarchy (kings, queens, governors, chiefs); stewards and masters of ceremonies to maintain and exhibit the hierarchy (in the Zulus there is a Grand Marshal; on Pinkster Day we observed a master of ceremonies, and the same kind of person could be observed supervising the elections of black governors; at the doors of the Havana *cabildos* are men supervising entry; there were persons setting up the flags at the reunions on the outskirts of Matanzas and New Orleans, and so on); a series of highly athletic, often extravagantly costumed individual dancers; and a group of congruently costumed singers, dancers, instrumentalists, and sundry other accompanists.

But what is there in this pattern and its performance that is carnivalesque, in the sense in which I have developed that term in the Introduction: the removal and escape from social calculations through a variety of costuming and behavioral modes, of which inversion is only one? It is indeed not a pattern that is necessarily carnivalesque. Yet it seems to have moved in that direction. Here is the reaction of one Leon Beauvallet, a European man of the theater, to the parade of a kingly figure through the streets of Havana on January 6, 1856 (Epiphany, the "negro Carnival," as the local people called it at the time): "I saw one with a genuine costume of a king of the middle ages, a very proper red, close coat, velvet vest, and a magnificent gilt paper crown. This negro, who was enormously tall, and had a tolerably good-looking head, gave his hand gravely to a sort of feminine black-amoor who represented some queen or other. He walked by her side with a deliberate, majestic step, never laughed, and seemed to be reflecting deeply on the grandeur of his mission to this world."[81] Like Timothy Flint's "king of the wake" in New Orleans this Havana king has a gilt-paper crown and is excessively tall. But there the resemblance ends. Flint represents his king as a clown, wagging his head, grimacing, and contorting his form. Is Flint's idea simply one more mistaken European perception of a performance whose writhing forms in fact indicated prowess rather than comedy, as Fredricka Bremer concluded about the serpentine figure in scarlet skirts who danced up to her in the cabildo?[82] Or can it be that the context in New Orleans lent a carnivalesque coloring to what was a serious ceremonial in Havana?

The black people of New Orleans did not have the numbers or the political space to develop the regal order based on tribal differences which is apparent in the cabildos of Havana. In Cuba a three-caste system lent a certain dignity to the free blacks who organized the cabildos. We do not know whether the man whom Beauvallet observed was a freeman or a slave, but we can contrast the general effect of this Spanish colonial situation with that of Louisiana, where there was gradual destruction of the three-caste system and its replacement with a black-white dichotomy.

Anyone pretending to regal dignity in the gathering polarity of white and black in Louisiana, as the city burgeoned with the grand new American dimensions of plantation slavery at the same time as it acquired a Protestant Anglo-Saxon sense of order, propriety, and morality, might well be considered carnivalesque. There was less social space here than on the islands to develop autonomous institutions, festive or otherwise. But there was enough such space for the festive practice to exist and to take on the same Afro-Caribbean pattern. Black festive culture was marginal; logically enough, it sought its opportunities for expression in marginal, clown-like, entertainment-oriented ways.

These hypotheses are supported and also given more complex form by examination of black Christmas festivities in colonial Jamaica. There the central figure was not a figure of social power, a king or governor, but instead, at least in the earliest period, a representation of natural power: a man was masked as a bull or wild boar and was called "John Canoe" for reasons which remain obscure.[83] An anonymous resident of Jamaica wrote in 1797 of the puzzling appearance of the "John Canoes": "Sometimes they wear two faces, different from each other; [just] as usually they have but one [face], which is often rendered hideous by beards and boar's tusks." While in former years their aim was a "savage" show, continues this author, it is "now often a polite appearance." Formerly their mask was "ugly" or "insignificant": "a close waistcoat and trowsers, chequered like a Harlequin's coat, or hung with shreds of various colored cloth." Now they "claim attention" with their "modern" clothes, which are sometimes silk and embroidered with lace, and with their careful coiffure, "as preposterously dressed as [that of] some European beaux."[84]

The evolution indicated by the anonymous writer of 1797 is corroborated by Edward Long's description of John Canoes in the mid-eighteenth century. Long, a Jamaican judge of long residence who wrote a history of the island, portrays John Canoes as "tall robust fellows dressed up in grotesque habits" who wore oxhorns on their head, "sprouting from the top of a horrid sort of vizor or mask, which about the mouth is rendered very terrific with large boar tusks." Long's maskers carried wooden swords in their hands. In the anonymous writer of 1797 there is no mention of this. There was evolution, then, both in dress and behavior. There was also some change in the role and character of John Canoe's audience. In Long's account the masker is followed by numerous "drunken women who refresh him frequently with a sup of aniseed-water [a liquor similar to Pernod] whilst he dances at every door, bellowing out *John Connù* with great vehemence."[85] Presumably the households rewarded the dancer with a small coin; early nineteenth-century accounts do specify this exchange. Whether because there was evolution on this point also or because the local tradition was different where the author of 1797 witnessed the figure, there is also no mention in the latter's text of this dancing before particular houses or of receipt of coins (such exchanges will henceforth be called quetes in this book).[86]

In terms of the four roles patterning performance in the black festivities previously considered, what do we have in these two accounts? Is John Canoe a sovereign in some sense, or only a figure of prowess? Let us leave that question open for the moment. Whether hero or sovereign power, John Canoe has been pulled toward European standards within the space of a generation. This is manifest not only in his clothes and coiffure but most interestingly in what surmounts his hair: "a representation of an edifice," writes the anonymous author of 1797, "sometimes very prettily devised and executed in the stile of a baby house, showing different fronts with open doors, glazed windows, stair cases, piazas and balconies in which diminutive figures are placed. They now and then salute with the discharge of little guns placed in some of the buildings."[87] No slave dwelling, this: horns and boar-tusks have been replaced by signs of European civility.

Curiously enough the author of 1797 does not specify the following of this modernized figure. But he does say that John Canoe was "occasionally" preceded by "several fellows . . . with painted sticks or wands, strutting with much formality and grimace": the steward-role has appeared.[88] The fourth role, the participant-audience, is documented less than a generation later in a novel by Michael Scott (resident in Jamaica 1806–22). This novel is, at least with respect to its depiction of "the Negro Carnival or Christmas Holy days," an unexpectedly detailed piece of ethnography. According to Scott the different trades in the larger towns each had their John Canoe. He depicts "the Butchers' John Canoe party" accosting the hero of the novel on a wharf at Kingston, the capital, and capering about him:

> This was the signal for the music to begin. . . . There were . . . two flute players in sheep skins, looking still more outlandish from the horns on the animals' heads being preserved; and three stout fellows, who were dressed in the common white frock and trousers, who kept sounding on bullocks' horns. These formed the band as it were, and might be considered John's immediate tail or following; but he was also accompanied by about fifty of the butcher negroes, all neatly dressed—blue jackets, white shirts, and Osnaburgh trousers, with their steels and knife-cases by their sides, as bright as Turkish yataghans, and they all wore clean blue and white striped aprons.[89]

Already in 1797 the black tradesmen of Kingston paraded at Christmas-time, but the earlier account does not connect them with John Canoe. They are then represented as mimicking their work in such a way as to create for the white author a "disagreeable" hubbub: "the rattling of chains and slings from the wharves, the mock-driving of hoops by the coopers, winding the postmens horns, beating militia and negro drums, the sound of the pipe and tabor, negroe flutes, gombas and jaw-bones. . . ." Among them all the butchers exhibited the most extraordinary masquerade: "The figure exhibited by the Butchers is clad in the hide of an ox with horns, which is held up with a rope and frequently lashed with a cart-whip." Thus the "different trades-men distinguish themselves by the implements of their several employments, and in this manner go through the town stopping at such houses as they expect to receive a gratuity from."[90]

It will be recalled that Long's account of John Canoe, the first document describing him, says that John Canoe was followed by a band of "drunken women." Long's only other mention of women is enigmatic. He says that in 1769 "several new masks appeared, the Ebos, the Papaws, etc., having their respective Connus, male and female, who were dressed in a very laughable style."[91] Does this mean that some black groups were led by a female dancer rather than a male, or does Long mean that some groups *doubled* the principal character, so that male and female led such groups side by side? However that may be, by 1797 the women had developed their own festive activity and they are never afterwards mentioned as being at the side of John Canoe. "It is upon this occasion"—that is, the Christmas holiday—"that the women form themselves into parties which they call sets; distinguishing them by various names, as the Golden Set, the Velvet Set, the Garnet Ladies, etc. They endeavor and often succeed in procuring dresses like each other of the same set. . . . These preceded by a negroe fiddler go through the town singing and marching in a fantastic manner in the streets, or entering into dwelling houses where they have acquaintance or hope to get a present."[92]

What was depicted as a single group of males and females with a male protagonist in the mid-eighteenth century is found with joint male-female heroic roles by 1769 and then by the end of the century has proliferated prodigiously, so that each trade has its version of John Canoe and each section of town, perhaps, has its "set" of female paraders. Twenty years later, in the provincial town of Cornwall, Jamaica, John Canoe has developed a double. Matthew Lewis, an English writer and member of Parliament who visited his Jamaican plantation in 1816-18, writes that John Canoe "and his rival, John Crayfish (a personage of whom I heard, but could not obtain a sight), seemed to act upon quite an independent interest, and go about from house to house, tumbling and playing antics to pick up money for themselves."[93]

We have seen the principle of agonistic competition used in

the dancing of the Cuban cabildos; it is not surprising to see it used in the development of rival characters in the John Canoe groups. A more astonishing use of it is found in Scott's novel. There the butchers' figure of 1797, the man-beast in an oxhide which recalls Edward Long's original version of John Canoe with horns and boar's tusks, is juxtaposed to the modernized, "polite" John Canoe:

> [John Canoe] was a light active, clean-made young Creole negro, without shoes or stockings; he wore a pair of light jean small-clothes, all too wide, but confined at the knees, below and above, by bands of red tape, after the manner that Malvolio would have called crossgartering. He wore a splendid blue velvet waistcoat, with old-fashioned flaps coming down over his hips, and covered with tarnished embroidery. His shirt was absent on leave, I suppose, but at the wrists of his coat he had tin or white iron frills, with loose pieces attached which tinkled as he moved, and set off the dingy paws that were stuck through these strange manacles. . . . His coat was an old blue artillery uniform one, with a small bell hung to the extreme points of the swallowtailed skirts, and three tarnished epaulets; one on each shoulder, and . . . the biggest of the three stuck at his rump, the *point d'appui* for a sheep's tail. He had an enormous cocked hat on, to which was appended in front a white false-face or mask, of a most methodistical expression, while Janus-like, there was another face behind, of the most quizzical description, a sort of living Antithesis, both being garnished and overtopped with one coarse wig, made of the hair of bullocks' tails, on which the chapeau was strapped down with a broad band of gold lace. . . . He made a smart enough pirouette, and then sprung on the back of a nondescript animal. . . . [The latter] was clothed in an entire bullock's hide, horns, tail, and other particulars, the whole of the skull being retained, and the effect of the voice growling through the jaws of the beast was most startling. His legs were enveloped in the skin of the hind-legs, while the arms were cased in that of the fore, the hands protruding a little above the hoofs, and, as he walked reared-up on his hind-legs, he used, in order to support the load of the John Canoe who had perched on his shoulders . . . a strong stick, or sprit, with a crutch top to it, which he leant his breast on every now and then.[94]

It is impossible to know whether such an ox-man as this, previously mentioned only in 1797 as "the figure exhibited by the Butchers," and this John Canoe, portrayed here in a far more detailed and far more anomalous manner than by any previous author, were inventions of the novelist or were truly observed.

Even if invented, one must admit not only that many of the elements of the portrayal can be found as part of black festive costuming at the time, but also that the general idea of such combinations is in accord with others which are documented. If we accept Scott's description as evidence, then it substantiates several ideas suggested by the other documents.

Black festive traditions did not develop in a single "modernizing," Europeanizing line. They were haphazardly syncretic. They adopted some "civilized" features but also on occasion turned again to "savagery," to the powerful naturalist image of a personage with animal features and animal force. One must suppose—that is, one must actively interrogate one's sparse sources to see if one may *pre*suppose—that the same kind of creative process went on along the Gulf Coast. Secondly, one may guess that the absence of any ceremonially hierarchic function in the John Canoe parades (no kings or queens are ever mentioned) has something to do with the fact that it developed in the mixed social situation of the towns rather than on plantations, and something to do with the fact that it developed toward representation of the grotesque.

Wherever the situation in the society as a whole supported a stable social hierarchy, there was a tendency to affirm such stability also in festive terms through traditional African figures of monarchic authority. When the situation was less stable, as in the towns, among tradespeople who were normally mulattos and therefore in a third position between white masters and black slaves not only socially but occupationally, royal decorum had less meaning, while ribald grotesqueness had more. The weird comedy of John Canoe corresponded to the difficult position of free blacks in the town, and exploited the perennial appeal of comic spectacle to relatively large, heterogeneous audiences.[95] Compared to the Cuban cabildos and to the North American governors' and kings' festivals, the steward and hero roles are well developed in the John Canoe tradition, while those of sovereign and participatory audience are weak: this corresponds to the open-ended sociology of the town and the other-directed strategies of the John Canoe players. They were not primarily performing for their own people, as the blacks were in Cuba or at Congo Square.

These conclusions are supported by the appearance and behavior of North American John Canoe troupes found in a few North Carolina coastal towns between 1800 and 1900, probably brought there from Jamaica.[96] As in the Jamaican towns, their performance was for money, and for both blacks and whites:

They were dressed in "tatters," strips of cloth of gay colors sewn to their usual garments and producing an effect of exotic grotesquerie. All were men, but a few wore clothes and acted the parts of women. The leaders of the band and the women actors frequently wore masks known as kuner faces. These kuner faces were painted upon something like buckram and presented features most remarkably distorted, enormous noses, widely grinning mouths, horns, and beards, fierce and terrifying to behold. The leader carried a raw-hide whip with which he prevented interference from urchins in the streets; so he was greatly feared by small boys. The band of Kuners, consisting of ten to twenty negroes, drew up in the street before the assembled group of white people and began their show. The leader stood out in front of his group and sang the verses of his song, the others joining in the refrain while they rattled their bones, made of beef ribs, and made noises upon the cows' horns, triangles, and jew's-harps. The songs proceeded to tunes not remarkable for their melody but of pronounced rhythm. . . . After the song, one of the dancers, performing "chicken in the bread tray" or "cutting the pigeonwing," would approach the spectators with his hat held out.[97]

In these southern American coastal towns, blacks' movements and activities were freer than in the plantation hinterland.[98] But they were still a marginal class in a white-dominated society: is this why they adopted and developed a marginal, half-comic, half-threatening figure like John Canoe rather than an ideal, socially centering figure like a king?[99]

I have pursued analysis of two contexts in order to discover the implications and presuppositions of black festive behavior in New Orleans down to the 1830s, the ambiance of Christmas and New Year's festivals on the plantation, and, in greater detail, the structurally recurrent pattern of festivity among blacks elsewhere in the United States and in the Caribbean. It remains to consider a few further documents from the Caribbean area which express the particular quality we are seeking in these contexts: the carnivalesque.

Epiphany in Havana was "Negro Carnival," as Leon Beauvallet, the visiting French theater-man of 1856 explains: I quoted earlier his description of the gilt-crowned king and queen gravely leading a parade through the streets. The following of the king and queen was anything but grave:

Some had transformed themselves into South American savages, Red Skins, or Apaches. Others had been coquettishly affecting large yellow spots all over their

body. In their hair they generally had magnificent peacock feathers, having destroyed all the dusters in the
city. Most of them had flour on their faces. Myriads
passed through the streets from morning till four
o'clock, screeching out the songs of the country with an
accompaniment of rattles, tin pans and tambourines.

As they were passing before us, several of these crack-
brains, in the hope of getting a few reals [i.e., Spanish
coins], undertook to give a diurnal serenade to Randoux
[an associate of Beauvallet]. . . .

Another negro, dressed in white and pale pink, with
a shepherdess hat and a white and pink mask on his
face, dropped on his knees before the Chéry brothers,
and began to wipe their shoes with an embroidered
handkerchief which he was flourishing pretentiously.

At four o'clock precisely they are prohibited from remaining in the city. They have no right to continue their
procession, except outside of the barriers. There they
riot all night, in the little holes [sic] which swarm in the
lower streets beyond the barriers.

The "little holes" to which Beauvallet refers were probably the
cabildo halls.[100]

The maskers described by the arrogant actor combine the
threatening and the comic in ways similar to those of the John
Canoe troupes: here is an early reference to blacks masking as
Indians, and perhaps even more menacingly, as some African
ritual figure with yellow spots and peacock feathers;[101] here also
is a sweet and excessively servile transvestite, parodying with
his handkerchief flourishes the servant position of blacks in the
city. The symbolism intended by the flour-faced maskers is
harder to determine. From New Orleans sources, we know that
throwing flour on mardi gras had become popular by the 1840s.
Perhaps they simply meant to be clowns. But whitened faces
were also used ritually in Africa, often but not always to indicate
mourning.

Another French visitor to Havana's black Epiphany parade,
Xavier Marmier, saw entirely different maskers only five years
earlier, in 1851: some on stilts,[102] others covered from head to
feet with a fleece coat, "imitating a bear skin," still others bearing on their heads "a forest of artificial bouquets" or "a castle of
feathers." Some again disguised their faces so that they looked
like "a bird of prey or wild beast." Many were "naked to the
waist, tattooed or painted on their cheeks, shoulders, and
chests," or painted with stripes of ochre, white, or waxy black.
Women in brightly colored dresses followed these groups, "a
flower in the hair and a cigar between their lips." The women
formed part of the procession until it stopped in the public

squares or before the homes of prominent people like the governor and admiral. There women stood aside during the first part of the music-making and the dancing which followed:

> The leader on stilts jumps and prances like a monkey. The leader in the bearskin shakes his heavy mane, bends toward the earth, and straightens up suddenly as if about to pounce on his prey; the leader with the plumed headdress rocks and turns. . . [Then] men and women arrange themselves opposite each other and dance.

They dance in that frightfully sensuous African way, whose least figure "would make our town policemen blush." Strange to say, reports the author, no one in the crowd of men and women watching this in broad daylight seemed "embarrassed in the least." [103]

The Havana dances and masks were primarily directed toward audiences of other blacks, not whites. They are less Europeanized than either the Jamaican John Canoes and Set Girls or the extremely varied maskers being contemporaneously developed in the Trinidad Carnival. [104] They are certainly joyous figures and exotic; are they also carnivalesque?

A white man writing about white colonial festivity—that is my case—may sometimes fill in blanks in the sources with intuitions from his own culture and from knowledge of European festive parallels. But this experiential foundation is a handicap with respect to black festive behavior, whose ultimate sources are African cultural traditions and Afro-American social experiences—above all slavery—which are not entirely different, of course, but different in unknown measure from experiences which are part of the white man's heritage. Instead of trusting my intuitions, I must systematically suspect them. I am warned to do so by the misapprehensions of Europeans evident on nearly every page of the sources quoted in this chapter.

Exercising this mistrust suggests the following hypothesis, which attempts to see beyond white Euro-American perceptions of black festive expressions in early New Orleans. In an alien land, in a socially subjugated situation such expressions had to function doubly, and therefore they tended to develop split forms. On one hand they had to provide some continuity with a cultural identity evidently interrupted but by no means obliterated. Slave-masters were interested in their chattels' hands, not their heads. They made little effort to educate slaves, change their language, their motor habits, or their manners except as it affected their work. They encouraged only minimal Christianization. On the other hand festivity for blacks had to function as disguise, to quiet the fears of whites.

Joyful expressions of music, song, and dance obviously had a better chance of assuaging white suspicions, however "lascivious" or "savage" they might be judged, than serious ritual expressions like those, for example, honoring ancestors and the dead.[105] A tacit agreement evolved between these two races over several hundred years of New World coexistence which allowed a system of unabated holiday enjoyment to emerge in return for the suppression or concealment of the deeper ritual, religious, and political roots of African peoples.

Such a development stands in sharp contrast to the social functions originally served by European Carnival. The first of these functions was not expressive enjoyment of an otherwise suppressed tradition but temporary escape from Christian norms generally accepted by all levels of society. It was an escape which was made not in order to deny those norms but to mitigate them. Christian spiritual idealism and its attendant asceticism have moreover always coexisted in European tradition with humanistic naturalism, an idealism of another sort. The second function of European Carnival has been to ritualize material dreams of plenty, of infinite and various food and drink, of limitless sexual pleasure and sexuality of every kind, of dancing, gaming, drinking, and sportive exercising without end. Since this second function is pursued in tandem with the first one, that of mitigating or suspending ascetic spiritual norms which are acknowledged as good and true, Carnival's foolish, escapist qualities are usually expressed with a feverish sense of excess. Carnival escapism is in its European manifestations only spasmodically consonant with happy-go-lucky make-believe and unshadowed sensuous joy. It is gay, but grotesquely so.

Black festivity in the New World had no use for and probably no understanding of such socially grounded grotesqueness. If and when blacks have looked grotesque, the cause has been not acceptance of the rationale of Carnival but either white misapprehension or intentional black disguise—including disguise designed for the whitened eyes of black people. There have always been subordinates who have internalized their subjugation to the point of adopting or identifying with master-race standards.

So the maskers whom Beauvallet and Marmier observed in Havana's Negro Carnival, like the richly ornamented king of the wake whom Flint saw at New Orleans, were not carnivalesque. They were probably dancing with a spirit more closely akin to that Sunday scene at Congo Square in 1834, recorded with rare ethnographic self-awareness by Colonel James Creecy, where he found the same "groups of fifties and hundreds" scattered over the grassy place as in Latrobe's time, and "a variety indeed of queer, grotesque, fantastic, strange, and merry dancers . . . to amuse and astonish . . . the wonder of 'outside barbarians,' un-skilled in Creole or African manners and customs"! Here are the accoutrements of John Canoe and many another festive figure from the Caribbean, "fringes, ribbons, little bells, and shells and balls, jingling and flirting about the performer's legs and arms, who sing [i.e., the bells, shells, etc. "sing"] a second or counter to the music most sweetly." Here is the same competitive prow-ess: "When a dancer or danseuse surpasses expectation, or is particularly brilliant in the execution of 'flings' and 'flourish-ings' of limb and body, shouts, huzzas, and clapping of hands follow, and numerous *picallions* [i.e., *picayunes*, a small Spanish coin] are thrown in the ring to the performers. . . . Here is a more than ethnic apprehension of the values which for sixty years or so found their location at Congo Square: "All is hilarity, fun, and frolic. To witness such a scene is a certain cure to ennui, blue-devils, mopes, horrors, and dyspepsia. Hundreds of nurses, with children of all ages, attend, and many fathers and mothers, beaux and belles are there to be found. . . . Every stranger should visit Congo Square when in its glory, once at least, and, my word for it, no one will ever regret or forget it. It is human nature to love to look on happy, joyous, smiling faces, and there no others are to be seen." [106]

Congo Square was suppressed. The festive traditions to which it lent itself went underground. There the traditions sur-vived somehow and were eventually grafted to Mardi Gras in the late nineteenth and early twentieth centuries, as will be shown in later chapters. The fate of colonially developed black festive culture was not so involuted in other parts of the New World. In Trinidad and in Brazil this tradition of non-carnival-esque gaiety entirely displaced the white colonial Carnival. In Port-of-Spain, in Rio de Janeiro, in a hundred provincial cities of Trinidad and Brazil, this black tradition, centered on Afro-Caribbean music, song, and dancing, is the *first* Carnival, the motor of Carnival's other aspects. [107]

# Meltdown

Epiphany, or Twelfth Night, so important in the cultural life of Cuba, Jamaica, and other English colonies, was of less consequence in Louisiana. More important were Christmas and New Year's Day on the plantations and in the towns.[1] Just as was the case with Mardi Gras itself until the 1820s, January 6 was mainly the occasion for the upper classes to give an especially sumptuous ball.

The "King's Ball" (*bal du Roi*) is so named because of the custom of cutting a cake at a dinner or dance on that day in which a bean has been hidden. The custom dates from the time of medieval royalty: The person receiving the piece of cake with the bean is crowned as an antic, temporary replica of the real monarch.[2] By the time of King James I of England masques or pageants were given to entertain royalty on January 6, which sometimes included personifications of the cake with its bean![3]

An undocumented tradition reported by the usually reliable chronicler of New Orleans' Mardi Gras, Perry Young, maintains that the *bals du roi*, dating from the "remotest time of the colonial regime," served to initiate the series of privately organized Creole dances which would lead to the final ball on mardi gras. The bean king—or queen, if a woman received the prized piece of cake—was given authority at this first ball "to select his mate or hers to reign at the next reunion."[4] Whether or not this delightful manner of proceeding was used at New Orleans and on surrounding plantations, it was certainly not unusual but rather a long-standing European custom to think of the whole period from the end of the Twelve Days of Christmas to mardi gras as Carnival-time.[5]

Perhaps the *bals du roi* were simply the method for choosing the first "king" in a series of balls called by another name, the *bals de bouquet* (bouquet balls). These affairs were described by a British officer, Captain James Alexander, as he learned about them during a visit to New Orleans in 1831. Alexander does not explain how the king of the first bouquet ball of the season was chosen, but he specifies that this king is a bachelor "invested with the sovereignty at the beginning" of what he calls, without any dating, the "gay season." The bachelor king's "first care" is to choose a queen whom he designates by sending her a crowning wreath of flowers. "At her house and in her name is the ball then given." After two or three dances she is conducted to the middle of the room by the king, where she bestows another wreath of flowers on a new king, "another bachelor of the party." The new king in turn chooses a new queen, "the band plays a march, and followed by the rest of the company, they polonaise round and round the room." Then authority reverts to the king and queen, and dancing continues "until day breaks, when the first king and queen cease to reign."[6]

This system of ball-giving exchanges, already documented in 1808, together with the bouquets for the tiny town of Saint Genevieve on the Mississippi below St. Louis,[7] is important in two ways for the distinctive style of what will become Gulf Coast Mardi Gras: There is a "grand march" of the guests; that is, an element of spectacle and pageantry is added to the dancing. And the chain of balls circulates eligible young men and women among the distinguished families; perhaps the chosen queens were young ladies whom the bachelors were considering matrimonially. Both these elements have their place in the later system of choosing Carnival-society queens and maids of honor as a function of their social status and entry into marriageable age as debutantes.[8]

Down to the 1830s, at least, holiday meant for both whites and blacks, above all else, music and dancing. They were conveniently physical, wordless ways of forgetting the reasons people had for hating each other in a slave-based world and a world of sharp political and economic competition between Creoles and Anglo-Americans. The timing of holiday, however, insured that slaves and free men rarely danced at the same places. Slaves danced throughout the year on Sundays and in some places also on Saturdays. The Christmas holidays and the days before Lent provided a little extra festive time. White festivities were more concentrated in the cool, clement winter season and above all in the period from New Year's Day to Ash Wednesday. In New Orleans and Mobile as on the surrounding plantations Christmas and New Year's seem to have had more particular usages attached to them than Mardi Gras.

In the 1820s this began to change. We learn more about Carnival street-parading. There is a concerted campaign to officially allow more masking between January 1 and mardi gras. The newspapers begin to notice Carnival in a regular manner. It becomes possible to provide some chronicle-like history of the festival, at least for New Orleans.

These changes came about in part because of the city's continuing growth. New Orleans' population doubled between 1803 and 1810, and grew by nearly 60 percent between 1810 and 1820. It grew 70 percent more between 1820 and 1830, and then in the next decade took the most gigantic leap of its history in terms of percentages. In 1830 New Orleans' population was 46,082, of which 56.3 percent was black (slave and free). In 1840 its population was 102,193, of which 41.8 percent was black (slave and free). New Orleans had become the fourth-largest city in the United States.[9] These changes were more than quantitative. In the 1830s and 1840s New Orleans ceased to be that strange mixture of sophistication and rawness, of pretentious colonial grandeur and small-town squalor delineated in the previous chapter. Whatever its continuing problems of political integration, whatever the horror of its recurrent susceptibility to the ravages of yellow fever, New Orleans had become a metropolis, a burgeoning center of possibilities, a lodestone for thousands of immigrants, year after year.

The immense new white immigration put pressure on the existing laboring classes in the city, which were largely black. The free blacks, especially, who had achieved solid positions as artisans of many kinds, were looked on with envy by the arriving hordes of Irish, Germans, and Anglo-Americans. New Orleans' fast growth and enlarged civic possibilities also put new strains on the relationship between older white Creole families and the new Anglo-American business elite.[10] For a long time white Creoles were able to capitalize politically on the willingness of the American government to allow local Franco-Spanish legal systems to continue. Between 1805 and 1812 there were two non-Creole mayors, but after the latter date white Creole mayors were regularly elected to 1846. Creoles also dominated city commissions and much of the judiciary. That situation could not last. In 1836 the Anglo-American community, which had concentrated itself west of the French Quarter, succeeded in obtaining approval in the Louisiana state legislature for a plan dividing New Orleans into three nearly separate municipalities! Although the city continued to have a single mayor and a general council with jurisdiction over some common problems, such as poor relief, between 1836 and 1852 each municipality had its own board of aldermen and taxing powers. The westernmost municipality, where Anglo-Americans clustered, soon manifested better transportation, schools, and fire protection. The central municipality, which included the French Quarter, and the eastern municipality (the Faubourg Marigny and northward) had severe financial problems and few municipal facilities. The political division led people to accentuate differences in habits and mores precisely when, as Virginia Dominguez has pointed out, "more and more Creoles began to speak at least some English and more Americans interspersed their speech with words and phrases of French."[11]

The strife between white Creoles, with strong attachments to plantation agriculture, and American business leaders, whose power came from commerce, did not interfere with their common interest in repressing the Afro-Americans. Their chief irritation, especially in New Orleans, was the free blacks, who not only arrogated nonservile positions to themselves but corrupted the slaves. Louisiana slaves wanted nothing more than a chance to reside in the metropolis, where contact with people of every kind "generated the corrosive acids" of freedom.[12] Between 1820 and 1852 a series of laws further restricted conditions of slave manumission, of free black employment, and of juridical representation (free blacks never had the right to vote in antebellum New Orleans). The aim, achieved after the end of the Reconstruction era following the Civil War, was to eliminate the three-caste system and to replace it with a simple dichotomy, in which any tincture of African blood made a person "black."

Antebellum political repression of the free-black class in places like New Orleans was accompanied by the forging of a new instrument of ideological repression, the minstrel show. Thomas "Daddy" Rice, a skilled white dancer, introduced his "Jim Crow" song and dance act to New Orleans at the American St. Philip Street Theater in 1835, and also performed it in French "at the leisure of several French families." In 1841–42 another white performer in blackface, "Jim-along-Josey" Diamond, and a "Mr. Sanford," were billed at the St. Charles Theater from December through early January as "two celebrated Professors of Niggerology."[13] The whites had learned to turn to racist profit the gradual maturation of black festive dancing. Perhaps that was a reason for blacks to abandon their Congo Square performances in the late 1840s.[14]

The three developments just outlined constitute the conjuncture in which New Orleans' Carnival tradition took form: the attainment of metropolitan size, the intensification of rivalry between white Creoles and Americans, and the attempt to limit the effects of the stimulating atmosphere of the city on black people's appetite for liberty.[15]

It will be recalled that the first certain notice of Carnival in New Orleans was an edict by the Spanish cabildo which prohibited "colored" people from masking (1781). As mardi gras approached in 1806 a special meeting of the city council was called which enacted an even more sweeping prohibition; all masking and disguises of whatever kind were prohibited in the streets and public places; moreover, no public or even private masked ball was to be permitted, under penalty of heavy fines both for those offering the ball and those attending. In theory these two prohibitions were kept in force for the next twenty-one years. But in practice masked balls were given not only privately but also by the early 1820s in some of the public ballrooms.[16] Finally on December 29, 1827, masked balls were permitted from January 1 to mardi gras, and in November 1835 the masked ball season was extended to include the whole time from November 1 to May 1 each year. Like the edicts concerning masks, the city's regular attempts to control access to balls were between 1781 and the 1830s no less regularly honored in the breach. Complaints continued about white women who went masked to the quadroon balls after the scandals of 1811, and in 1837 heavy fines were reiterated for those "giving masked balls who allowed white and colored women to be admitted together."[17]

In theory the ban on street masking was still in force in 1835 as in 1806. Here again popular practice defeated legislation. James Creecy, so delighted with the dancing in Congo Square in 1834, also found much to admire in the Carnival which he presumably witnessed in 1835:

> Men and boys, women and girls, bond and free, white and black, yellow and brown, exert themselves to invent and appear in grotesque, quizzical, diabolical, horrible, humorous, strange masks and disguises. Human bodies are seen with heads of beasts and birds; . . . snakes' heads and bodies with arms of apes; man-bats from the moon; mermaids, satyrs, beggars, monks, and robbers, parade and march on foot, on horseback, in wagons, carts, coaches, cars, &c., in rich confusion up and down the streets, wildly shouting, singing, laughing, drumming, fiddling, fifing, and all throwing flour broadcast as they went their reckless way. . . .[18]

The helter-skelter parading was double in meaning. It was certainly popular and egalitarian in its open, public social tone. But it was elitist in its cultural rivalries. Individuals in their masks might seek to lose themselves among the crowds. But each group strove to outdo the next with vivid allegory and unusual actions. In this same season of 1835 elaborate floats like those in contemporary large-city European Carnivals appeared. Creecy reports one drawn by four horses "uniquely caparisoned and draped with fiery dragons . . . [which] was the moving prison of his most satanic majesty . . . blowing from his volcanic mouth flames of fire and fumes of sulphur, surrounded with his familiars, imps of the most infernal appearance conceivable, 'cutting up' and playing antics . . . whooping, yelling, groaning, grinning, and gibbering. . . ." Such terrifying and yet comic displays were an old feature of European Carnivals, found already in sixteenth-century Florence and Nuremberg.[19]

The street maskers whom Creecy observed certainly did not appear in the street in 1835 for the first time. But it is impossible with the present documentation to determine when such street masking began. Newspaper and tourist-guidebook writers in the late nineteenth century, referring now to 1827 and again to 1835 or 1837, fabricated the story that the first masked processions were due to the efforts of "a number of young Creole gentlemen, some . . . just returned from finishing a Parisian education." The legend assuaged the smarting egos of the Creole faction in the city, for by the time of its invention in the 1870s Carnival had become more of an American than a Creole celebration.[20]

The first time that local newspapers described street processions, as opposed to masked balls, was in 1837 and, more fully, in 1838. The initiative was taken by the *Daily Picayune,* whose first issue appeared less than one month before mardi gras in 1837. The *Picayune* was designed to sell more cheaply and to attract a wider readership than other local publications. Was this why it turned its attention to what was going on outside the ballrooms?[21] Although founded by Anglo-Americans and published in English, the newspaper was generous in attributing the brilliance of the 1838 mardi gras procession to the Creoles. "Yesterday was a jolly time in our city. The grand cavalcade which passed through the principal streets was an entertaining sight. A large number of young gentlemen, principally Creoles of the first respectability, went to no little expense with their preparations.[22] In the procession were several carriages superbly ornamented—bands of music, horses richly caparisoned—personations of knights, cavaliers, heroes, demi-gods, chanticleers, etc., etc., all mounted. Many of them were dressed in female attire, and acted the lady with no small degree of grace."[23]

Only three years after the first description of street masking, we have documented here the main elements of Carnival parades as they are still done in New Orleans and Mobile today: men on horseback accompanying ornamented carriages (which will later become floats), bands of musicians, and masking centered on pagan mythology and on the impersonation of animals, clowns, and the opposite sex. These elements were commonplace both in contemporary European Carnivals and in the earlier versions of the festival from the fifteenth century onwards. It required no education in Paris to imagine such a parade. But perhaps it was true that these diverse elements were first consciously pulled together in organized fashion in 1838. The reports of the 1835 and 1837 street masking and parading, cited earlier, give a helter-skelter impression and do not mention the bands of musicians who perhaps defined the pace of march and its pauses, as well as its beginning and end. The *Commercial Bulletin*, in any case, claimed that real parading began in New Orleans in 1838: "The European custom of celebrating the last day of the Carnival by a procession of masqued figures through the public streets was introduced here yesterday, very much to the amusement of our citizens." [24]

Not only had a parading recipe emerged, but the bridge between masking in the streets and masking in the ballroom was in place by 1840. That year, reported the *Courrier de la Louisiane*, "after parading in the streets until nightfall many of the maskers went to the Orleans Theater, where they joined in the galopade of *Gustave*," a French opera by Auber whose final scene takes place at a masked ball and includes a grand march and brisk dance called a galopade. [25] It became the fashion for maskers from the street to join the maskers on stage in the finale, and then for all of them to retire to a chosen ballroom to dance the night away.

Carnival had begun to take shape as a coherent custom by the late 1830s. But the elements that eventually constituted its white, elite form emerged at the same time as the holiday was joined by a vast number of new revelers, including laborers and recent immigrants, who had no idea of and no access to such affairs as *Gustave* and the exclusive ball following it. Founding a viable Gulf Coast Carnival was not only a matter of interesting the upper classes in a spectacle in the streets but also one of containing the enthusiasm of nonelites so that the event did not dissolve in random violence.

Thus during the 1840s and 1850s, as street masking burgeoned, public opinion ebbed and flowed over the practice. All three of the conjunctural causes of Mardi Gras development had their role in this: fear of lower-class violence as new masses crowded into the city; ethnic rivalries and hatreds, particularly those of the white Creoles, watching their social preeminence slip away along with political and economic supremacy; and white resentment of the black people who lived and behaved in this city in such an unusually free manner. The division of New Orleans into three almost separate cities facilitated the expression of these differences.

Carnival was seen by the Creoles as "their" custom: "God be praised," sang a staff writer of the French newspaper *The Bee* in 1838; "for we still have a day to ourselves, and what a day! Mardi gras . . . mardi gras such as you have never seen, a mardi gras which promises to be sublimely extravagant. . . ."[26] No wonder that Louis Tasistro concluded after his visit in 1841 that "The celebration of the carnival in New Orleans is almost exclusively confined to the French Creole population: The Anglo-Americans act only as spectators, leaving all the burden of performance in the mummeries of the day to their more mercurial brethren." Spectators perhaps they were, but they were interested ones. Tasistro goes on to point out that the Anglo-Americans were present in force at the costume ball of the chief band of paraders in 1841, where the "customary black and blue colors" of their clothes, "cold emblems of the marble age," scarcely fit "the splendor and magnificence of the magic scene."[27]

The New Orleans newspapers were as ambivalent about the presence of non-Creole elements as was Tasistro. By the 1840s the great joy of the masses on mardi gras was to throw flour. This was an old custom in Europe, and seems to have been a clean substitute for the tossing-about of ashes, dust, and even excrement in the fifteenth and sixteenth centuries as gleeful symbols of the approaching end of winter's drying fires and interior confinement. In New Orleans it had other overtones. "The blacks of the city were principal objects for flour attacks, and on occasion the editors found all their joy in telling how the kinky heads and lively faces absorbed the white flour, to transform the 'little niggers' into ghostlike specters."[28] In 1845 a reporter from St. Louis wrote that flour, dirt, and brickbats were used in such quantities in the second municipality (the western Anglo-American, but increasingly also the Irish, section of the city) that the carts and carriages in the Carnival procession hurried through St. Charles Street "as though they wished to get back into the First Municipality as soon as possible."[29]

"It was a great day with the boys," wrote James Coleman about the Carnivals of the 1850s. "Clothed in old dominoes and masks, with a stout hickory club in their hands and a bag of flour by their sides, [they] would march around the streets, looking for an available victim on whom they could throw their flour and whom, if they resisted, they would punish with their shillelaghs."[30] The use of an Irish word for the clubs perhaps identifies these boys as Irish. They, and those others who substituted quicklime for flour, made celebration not only disorderly but dangerous. Every Mardi Gras man had his pockets filled with flour which he threw on the well-dressed stranger in 1847, declared Albert Pickett. Anyone on foot was likely to fare badly, since gangs of boys would gather and pelt him with sticks and mud. Yet the beauty and fashion beheld on the gallery of the St. Charles Hotel near Canal Street in the second municipality made it all worthwhile for Pickett: this was "the grandest sight my eyes ever beheld."[31]

The newspapers, echoing public opinion, seesawed between vituperation and exaltation, which reflected the fluctuations in preparation for the event. One year might see extremely elaborate costuming and parading and the next nothing at all. Yet the *Daily Picayune*, after declaring in 1851 that the masquerades were a failure and "should be put a stop to hereafter," also reported on the occurrence of new Carnival balls at places in the American sector for the first time.[32]

This ambivalence in the press is not surprising, for the growth of street parading confronted the city with problems it had never faced before. Masking in the streets required not only preparation but crowd control, at least in the burgeoning situation of the 1830s and 1840s. Masked balls have parameters which are easily surveyed: the walls of the hall make it easy to control entry and exit, often with police examination for weapons, and at New Orleans also for racial color beneath the mask (city regulations in the 1840s still required momentary removal of the masks at the entry to public balls). Streets, on the other hand, are open in all directions. If there is to be crowd control, it must come largely from internalized standards of behavior. The police can only supplement, not supply, such restraints. If there is a spectacle, however, which draws eyes to it and orients communication among merrymakers toward passive gazing, the problem of public order is greatly reduced.

From the mid-30s to the mid-50s of the nineteenth century New Orleans Carnival-goers stumbled blindly toward a mode of behavior that would reconcile public abandon with public order.

Carnival was becoming a general custom in these years, something with a broadly popular side as well as an elite side. To the public of those days it meant both street masking and an intensification of the dancing fever which seized Orleanians at Christmastime. The masked balls could obviously be welded to the street parades, as the galopade at the Orleans Theater showed. But no one as yet had discovered a manner of giving such unions a stable form.

By the 1820s a winter season of festivity with distinct black and white sides to it had emerged all over the Caribbean basin, including New Orleans and the plantation country surrounding it. Within the lengthy period from November to May the French and Spanish colonies tended to place primary accent on Carnival, with a secondary accentuation on the "day of the kings," Epiphany. The English colonies developed festivals more during the twelve days from Christmas to Epiphany. This English accent seems also to have shaped the early history of Mobile festivals, for as we learn in the next chapter the first stably recurring winter celebration in Mobile took place not on mardi gras but on New Year's Day. At present there are no known documents about Carnival in Mobile during the period considered in the present chapter except for one or two instances at the beginning of the eighteenth century. The Latin accent to festivity in Mobile died out, or retired to private rooms, when the town relapsed toward wilderness. It returned only after the Civil War.

The social parameters of this pre–Mardi Gras period along the Gulf Coast (1699–1830s) were largely determined by colonial politics and plantation economics. In terms of the history of festive culture the political turning-points of 1803 for New Orleans (the purchase of Louisiana by the United States) and of 1813 for Mobile (the capture by the United States of Mobile and southern Alabama from Spain during the War of 1812) were unimportant. The critical events in the formation of a distinct festive tradition took place not at the beginning of the century but in the 1830s, when masked balls, street masking, and organized parades were first drawn into connection. Shown with respect to New Orleans in this chapter, this story will be told for Mobile in chapter 4. First, however, let us try to understand this formative process at a deeper level.

The three building blocks of Carnival's white American style had long existed separately in Europe and in other parts of the Caribbean basin. A season of masked balls lasting from New Year's to Ash Wednesday was aristocratic custom in seventeenth- and eighteenth-century France. The violence attending them indicates that it did not take a slave society to make the ballroom an ideal place for transgression. "Quarrels, duels, robberies, pillage of the banquet tables, aggressions by valets"; such things happened at every grand ball during the Carnival season.[33] Nor were New Orleanians inventive with their system of semiprivate subscription balls. They are found at Paris from 1786, at Nice from the 1760s, and they expanded tremendously in number and kind after the French Revolution. Public balls, where anyone might enter for a price, date from 1715 in Paris.[34] It would be an error to suppose, therefore, that the dancing fever at New Orleans among all classes was just a frontier phenomenon, endlessly indulged for lack of something better. It was also a democratic phenomenon and a capitalist phenomenon, and as such characterized French, English, and other Western European areas where a broad and enterprising middle class attained in the late eighteenth and early nineteenth centuries the means to develop their notions of leisure time. Louis Tasistro was amazed to count as many as eleven balls on a single Carnival-time evening in New Orleans in 1841.[35] But the Parisian prefect of police counted on mardi-gras night of 1836 182 public balls and 874 private balls within the city, and he did not even attempt to enumerate the balls going on at the inns just outside the city gates where most of the lowest classes congregated.[36] Even the idea of converting the final scene of Auber's *Gustave* into an occasion for street maskers to storm into the theater and join the actors in a triunphal masked ball was also realized at Paris.[37]

As for parading in an organized manner, sometimes around a carriage with a large symbolic figure like Satan (1835) or an outsized rooster (1839)[38] and sometimes simply as a procession of masked figures on foot and horseback, this was not only common in European Carnivals from the fifteenth century,[39] but was also familiar as unmasked but symbolically costumed practice in patriotic celebrations. Both the American Revolution and the French Revolution had encouraged tradespeople, for example, to parade with the symbols of their trade and under banners of adhesion to revolutionary ideals.[40] The transfer from serious to merry motifs was easily made: the necessary vocabulary of behavior was already in place among nonelites no less than among elites.

Did all the masking themes explored in the streets and at the balls have their European precedents too? Generally yes; specifically no. To mask as Amerindians was a New World affectation;

to mask as "savages" of some kind was an eighteenth-century custom. "Powdered aristocrats" appeared in early nineteenth-century Paris as bizarre as in the New Orleans of 1852. If the Grand Turk expressed exotic power at the Grand Salon ball of 1812 in Paris, the Bedouin represented much the same thing in the streets of New Orleans in 1841. The Parisian "Chicard Balls" were especially famed for their inventive social inversions: here the rich played at being poor. In New Orleans rich Creoles masked as poor "Irish paddies" already in the 1820s.[41] At a private ball in 1808 New Orleans women amused themselves by "masking as mulattos," so well indeed that Laussat, the diary-writer reporting the event, confesses that he recognized no one.[42] On the other hand, I have found no instance of whites masquerading as blacks in the New Orleans streets during Carnival before the Civil War. From the 1830s this game was nevertheless enjoying immense success on stage in the minstrel show. Throwing flour was in vogue in Paris as at New Orleans, without (at Paris) the noisome addition of quicklime and with the sophistication of an accompanying baker's costume.[43]

These surveys of Gulf Coast dancing, parading, and masking impel one to conclude that while there was much range of expression, it followed no single pattern consistently. The imitations and inventions alike needed to be melted down in the crucible of a local cultural style before Carnival could become Mardi Gras. The first step in that direction had gained momentum by the 1830s: de-Catholicizing the occasion. In 1808 Pierre Laussat, the French prefect who had delivered the city to the Americans in 1803, wrote about the Carnival balls of that year in his diary. It is he who reported the mulatto disguise of upper-class Creole women mentioned in the previous paragraph. After dancing until dawn on Saturday, Sunday, and Monday, these same women had determined to continue all through Tuesday night—mardi gras itself—and on into Ash Wednesday until it was time to go to mass.[44] Well might the "Turkish spy" report—as Louis-Sébastien Mercier writes amusingly about late eighteenth-century Paris—that although the French, both male and female, go totally mad during Carnival, they return suddenly to calm and reason on the morning after mardi gras by the simple application of a grayish powder on their heads.[45]

By 1825 even ashy powder no longer availed in New Orleans. The duke of Saxe-Weimar observed that year that "Balls continued through Lent, but were little frequented."[46] In March 1831, the council authorized the mayor to permit masked balls to continue to Saint Joseph's Day. This saint's day, March 19, often fell toward the middle of the moveable season of Lent. "Mid-Lent," the fourth of Lent's seven Sundays, was in some parts of Europe since at least the sixteenth century a traditional moment of relief from the church's austerities. It allowed a momentary resumption of Carnival games. In New Orleans' custom Saint Joseph's Day became the equivalent of European Mid-Lent, with the important difference that for many, including the mayor's council, the exception became rather a substitute for Ash Wednesday as the terminal date for the enjoyment of dancing.[47] Again, as Henry Kmen has remarked, "Washington's birthday usually falls during Lent, a fact which perhaps contributed as much to the popularity of Washington's Balls as did patriotism." In 1837 balls in honor of Washington were given on February 18 and 25, as well as on the twenty-second, lightening a whole week of Lent. "For the rest, there were always worthy purposes to justify a Lenten ball, . . . helping a widow . . . aiding destitute orphan boys."[48] Moralism conditioned and finally undid the liturgical commandment. This de-Catholicization of the Lent-Carnival relationship did not mean that New Orleans Catholics became generally apathetic, let alone that the Protestant segment of New Orleans' opinion, which grew steadily with the evergrowing migration of Americans from the Eastern states, had no more reason to quarrel with Catholic "frivolity." But Carnival behavior was disconnected from religious behavior by the gradually growing interest of Protestants in the balls and parades and by the urge to do more than observe among the blue- and black-suited gentlemen on the edge of the ballroom floors and among the richly attired ladies on the verandas and balconies of St. Charles Street.[49]

Carnival by the 1840s and 1850s was becoming what *Orleanians* did and not what Creoles or Catholics did, at least to the eyes of outsiders—and not just to remote outsiders, such as the British and German travelers often quoted in these pages. Reminiscing in 1866 about bygone "village balls in the Carnival season" outside New Orleans, an anonymous contributor to the New Orleans newspaper the *Crescent*, paid tribute to the renown of the festival and its identity as a metropolitan peculiarity. "Folk wore little at other times, but they would lay out almost any amount of money [during the Carnival season] in order to make their appearance in the ballroom saloon . . . like the fashionable people from the city of New Orleans."[50]

Not only what Orleanians did but what they thought about it was different in the 1840s and 1850s from what they did and thought about Carnival in 1810 or 1820. Public consciousness had changed. The editor of the Louisiana *Gazette* announced in 1824, after the Carnival season was over, that the "silence preserved by the newspapers of this city" concerning Mardi Gras activities "leaves a void which can usefully be filled". The ensuing article seems to be the first attempt by a local organ of public opinion to generalize about what was becoming recognized not simply as winter festivity but as a distinctly carnival time, "from Epiphany continuously to Ash Wednesday." But after his apparent decision to review the season's "shows, banquets, concerts, balls, fetes, [and] masquerades" generally, the editor limits himself in fact to examination of privately organized "society" (non-costume) balls and masked balls, the most elite and exclusive Creole functions. "The [society] balls . . . presented a gracious blend of beauty, good taste, and decorum. The allure of our ladies owes little to the glitter of gold. . . . It is due rather to the clinging tulle that sets off their slender figures. . . . In our spacious, richly ornamented ballrooms . . . two hundred young beauties rival each other for grace, elegance [etc., etc]." As for the masked balls, "each masker affected a scenic dress from the theatre's [Theatre d'Orleans] property rooms . . .; here one meets Mahomet, Brutus and Montezuma . . . and savages dancing with the shepherd girls." The account concludes with only a nod in the direction of everything else: "Many other public and private fetes took place; all classes of society and all colors had their bacchanals." [51]

By 1839 such a narrowly conceived notion of Carnival was becoming impossible. We have quoted the exultant tone of the Creole-oriented *Bee* (*L'Abeille*) on mardi gras of the year, predicting that mardi gras, "our day," would resuscitate with its "extravagances" and "follies" the old Venetian Carnival, a celebration renowned more for its street games than for private balls. The other French-language newspaper of the time spoke more specifically of the now-prominent street masking in its Ash-Wednesday assessment: "The end of Mardi Gras was celebrated yesterday with almost Venetian pomp. . . . A numerous throng of maskers, composed of extraordinarily grotesque groups, paraded through our streets. The entire population, which hastened to follow, was happy to find that the masks provoked mirth among even the most morose." [52] In the 1824 article the accent is on beauty and decorum. In 1839 the key words are "grotesque" and "mirth" (*l'hilarité*).

If New Orleans black people participated in these urban street mixtures —and no doubt they did—they did so with such circumspection that we can only guess at their activities. Yet this same slavery-dominated period produced a festive tradition which at the end of the nineteenth century would reemerge in arguably more innovative forms than anything going on at that time in white Carnival. From the point of view of cultural power, the power to create symbols of significance to all humanity, slavery for black people in this country turned out to be a point of transfer, not a dark, impenetrable wall. It was a frontier which set special conditions for the transformation of African festive behavior. It was not a dead end.

The following chapters will amply illustrate this. But an indication of what was happening can be given by recalling the discussion above of what seemed to outside observers of Christmas and Epiphany celebrations the "Saturnalian" equality of those celebrations. The slaves, given entrance to the plantation mansion and plied with good food and drink, did not content themselves with effusive thanks but performed sly satiric songs and skits about the lords' and ladies' behavior. The bar between master and slave blinds the master; the slave is obliged by this same barrier to become a sharp observer and an adept manipulator of appearances. Black people thus gravitated toward performances that amplified their sense of ambivalence and grotesqueness: would not these qualities be put to use one day in Carnival?

White people, meanwhile, were lured toward visions of grandeur. This too had its Carnival uses . . .

Indeed, is not the delicately dislocated feeling that you experience after strolling a few hours near Jackson Square, enjoying a dozen fresh crayfish, dealing with the mask-vending street pedlar, and settling down for one more cup of chicory coffee by the fountain near the Café du Monde—is not this strange and satisfying remoteness from reality precisely the "Carnival" feeling for which you came to New Orleans? Are you not feeling positively grand?

Visions of grandeur: they tended, whatever their origin, to circle back to cluster in the space where you are sitting now. . . . That cooling sensation which you experience here, even on a breathlessly heated day, comes from the long, abolished, colonial past.

It was a past too thin in men and deeds to weigh upon the city when it became American. It was a heritage to dream about. New Orleans had no time between 1800 and 1850 to develop a vision of itself. It was growing too fast, in too many directions, with too many kinds of population. Politically and economically it was becoming something entirely new. But it still looked like any too rapidly growing child might appear to its elders, a gangling specimen of something gone before—right down to the time in 1845 when the Baronessa Pontalba, daughter of Don Almonester y Roxas, governor of the once-Spanish city, built the arcades and iron balconies of the long red brick buildings across the street from where you sit: these superb Pontalba Buildings which in earlier days flowed from the Cathedral and the Cabildo on the north down either side of Jackson Square directly to the levee and the Father of Waters.

The finest fruit of the colonial heritage of Louisiana is this city's provision for occasional removal from duty, its checking of the Yankee call for hard-nosed practicality, purposiveness, and work. In this city there is *time*—time for conversation, time to put some sparkle in it, time to stop and stare at every unlikely occurrence ("He will dance on the tight rope divers steps. . . . He will appear on the rope in men's clothes; an empty bag will be given him into which he will enter . . . he will then be seen to come out in the character of an old woman of eighty and in that dress will dance to the tune of "Yankee Doodle"—New Orleans handbill, 1815), time to enjoy the most jejune of operas and most frivolous of farces ("A Representation of Brisquet and Joliecoeur, A Farce in One Act, to be followed by Rouge et Noir, Or the Chances of Gambling, An Opera in One Act by Tarchi. The Whole to Conclude With The Innkeeper, Judge, and The Hairdresser Lawyer, a Farce in One Act"—Playbill, November 20, 1823)[53]

Intoxicating fruit! The visitor from the north bites into it voraciously; no more thoughts about the next move, not even much desire to measure, morally, the lapse between one bite and the next. . . . This cultural quality, this strange sprout, was not found in the bayous. It had European origins. It came from a vast and old system of colonial exploitation. If the colonists found it easy to establish a slave-and-master society, that was not least of all because their models, the courtiers at the royal castles and watering-places of France, Spain, and England, had developed over a long preceding period the conventions of a hierarchical society built on peasant exploitation.

The fruit, then, comes from transplantation. It takes its rich colors from centuries of inequity in the Old World, colors then enhanced by ripening in a Caribbean social climate which encouraged even harsher contrasts between high and low, between tended gardens and their untended dilapidated environs. Yet to hurl away this fruit in rage at its oppression-nourished sweetness would be as absurd as to ignore or deny the plant's conditions of growth.

Carnival is not a colonial inheritance. But without the colonial air exuded from the windowsills and patios of this place, without the pomegranates of leisure-time offered with a smile from so many of its doorways, Carnival would be something else entirely.

# Civic Festival

The Mobilians are right. Gulf Coast Carnival's "modern" form, a healthy century and more old in the 1980s, was born in Mobile, not New Orleans. But it was not born on Mardi Gras.

The element that has given continuity to the festival is the so-called "mystick krewe," a private society dedicated to the preparation of parades, balls, and banquets. Private groups organized for festive purposes began to appear in the 1840s in New Orleans, but they did not endure. The first such enduring organization was established at Mobile in 1831; its purpose was to celebrate New Year's Eve, not Carnival. In fact most festive fun at Mobile was concentrated during the Christmas holidays until after the Civil War. Only gradually, in the late 1860s and 1870s, in conscious imitation of New Orleans, did Mardi Gras become Mobile's prime festivity.

Rivalries and imitations, sometimes friendly and sometimes rancorous, marked the relations of the two once-French and once-Spanish cities in the middle and late nineteenth century. This was to be expected. Mobile, too, became an important city in the 1830s. The two communities established their American identity during an era of civism, a time when American life was articulated by the rapid growth of regional collecting-points of production and exchange, economic and social. During the period preceding 1830, American life, with the partial exception of the northeastern seaboard, was lived in communities whose connection with each other was tenuous. People depended on their own local resources; most economic production was locally consumed, and the transactions of social life, the connections among family, friends, and local notables, were articulated by sentiments of neighborliness. Conversely, since 1900 the sense of neighborhood has been displaced by awareness of national and international controls over local issues.

Between the two eras of local and national concentration of socioeconomic power came the period of civism. The largest population centers became more than large towns and overgrown villages. Neither stalwart yeomen like those at Concord Bridge nor the oil men, steel men, and financiers of a nationally articulated system of power symbolized American endeavor in this period. It was the era of "city fathers," gravely black-frocked, bearded gentlemen whose portraits line the walls of city halls and libraries across the country. It was the golden era of Boston, New York, Baltimore, Philadelphia, Chicago, St. Louis . . . and New Orleans and Mobile. Cities had become indispensable points of passage toward whatever was more local or more national than they seemed to be, and at the same time they thought of themselves, precisely because of the exchange function, as the very embodiment of local peculiarities and national goals.

Such civic-centered consciousness is not surprising in a period when transportation and communication were revolutionized by steamboat, railroad, and telegraph. Before the era of automobile and airplane, after the period of strict dependence on horse, wagon, and sailing ship, regional centers drew upon local production and local knowledge with unrivalled power. For New Orleans the whole Mississippi Valley became its barnyard; Mobile supplemented the dimensions of the Alabama-Tombigbee river basin with a railroad line joining the resources of the Ohio River valley to the advantages of Mobile Bay as a seaport.[1]

Of course the three periods sketched here are not exclusive. Locally self-sufficient features do not all disappear either from practice or from ideology when regional cities become lodestones of power. Localism and civism have not, even in the nationalizing twentieth century, entirely relinquished their hold upon habits of thought and behavior, nor will they in the foreseeable international era. The less successful a community is in adapting itself to the contours of social life in succeeding eras, the more it tends to hold and cherish features of earlier periods. This phenomenon has occurred in several ways at different times at New Orleans and Mobile. Carnival practice has been sometimes an instrument and sometimes an opponent of such reactions.

Consciousness follows prowess. The terms in which the festive private societies were first founded at Mobile and New Orleans were not expressly civic in the way that they *became* so by 1900. Civic-centered values proved with time to be the means of the private societies' growth, and through them of Carnival's fascination for the Gulf Coast generally. In sociological terms Carnival does not begin with the formation of these societies, let alone in any earlier era. It begins when the Carnival-society idea is linked on the one hand with civic self-consciousness and on the other hand with elements existing disparately in previous decades: street masking, balls, banquets, and parades by groups. This double linkage developed after the Civil War.

In 1813 the Gulf Coast area east of the Mississippi River, including Mobile, was ceded by Spain to the United States. In 1818 the Bank of Mobile was founded. In 1819 the town was incorporated under the laws of the newly admitted State of Alabama. In 1820 Mobile's first mayor (who was also first postmaster, first bank president, and first collector of customs) presided over a community of 2,672 souls, white and black. If Bernard Reynolds, one of Mobile's early newspapermen, is to be trusted, this population shrank by half during the sultry and feverish summer months. Even in 1830 Mobile's winter population was only 3,194.[2]

These circumstances not only remind us that it took several decades before Mobile made its profit from the joint effects of cotton, slaves, rich black earth, and great numbers of migrants from the eastern American states. They also tell us that the setting for the foundation of what became the first durable "mystick krewe" was not the same as that which saw its growth, fame, and eventual transfer to New Orleans. The demographic and economic take-off of Mobile took place in the 1830s. In 1840 Mobile's population was 12,700, a nearly 400 percent increase in ten years. In 1850 it was 20,500 and in 1860 29,300. At the latter date the metropolitan area of Mobile counted 41,131 persons, including 11,376 slaves and 1,195 free blacks.[3]

These statistics also tell us that, however spectacular the growth of Mobile between 1830 and the Civil War, it remained a regional center constructed on a different scale from New Orleans, which in 1860 had a population of 168,000. If Mobile became a city in this period, New Orleans became a metropolis. The problem of swallowing such immense numbers had different parameters for the two cities, however comparable they were in terms of proportionate growth and in terms of their ultimate arrival at civic self-consciousness. Mobile's commerce was more strictly tied to one crop, cotton, and to one way of producing it, large plantation slavery. "Cotton was truly king. Every man and woman of the city's population was in some way dependent upon it. Doctors, lawyers, merchants, ministers; all dabbled in cotton. Bales piled high on the quay dominated the waterfront as the power they represented did the social and political circles of the city."[4] This also meant that, for all of Mobile's century-old Spanish and French existence, the materials, mental and physical, used in constructing civic institutions in the 1830s and afterwards were largely American and Protestant. Little remained of the eighteenth-century town but a few streets and stores, and the bodies in the Church Street Cemetery. The City Hospital, Barton Academy, Presbyterian Church, and Episcopal Church were constructed in sober, monumental Greek-Revival style rather than in the more delicate and decorative iron-balcony fashion of Spanish days, although the latter did influence the appearance of private residences.[5]

On Christmas eve of 1831 a cotton broker named Michael Krafft allegedly supped with Captain Joseph Post in his ship, "one of the Hurlbut Line, lying at the Government Street Wharf." His subsequent behavior suggests that he and the captain toasted the occasion repeatedly. Krafft was anyway, according to contemporary account, "a fellow of infinite jest and . . . fond of fun of any kind," besides being "cockeyed, which gave him a peculiarly quizzical appearance." Leaving the ship and wandering uptown in a light rain after dinner, Krafft apparently stopped to collect his wits in the doorway of a hardware store. Gathering up a string of cowbells and attaching them to the teeth of a rake, he then went on, clattering the bells. "This extraordinary spectacle of course attracted the attention of 'the boys' and by the time he had reached Royal Street, he had a crowd around him. Someone passing along and observing his grotesque appearance, with the crowd following him, exclaimed, 'Hello, Mike,—what society is this?' Michael, giving his rake an extra shake and looking up at his bells, responded, 'This? This is the Cowbellion de Rakin Society.'"[6]

These incidents constitute what usually passes as the story of the origin of the first Carnival society in Mobile. Their implication is that the society was the invention of one waggish fellow, Michael Krafft. But in fact the same contemporary, Charles Kennerly, who records these particulars also points to the real origins of the society when he explains the consequences of Krafft's escapade. Krafft went on the rounds of the town with his rake and cowbells and fell in with James Taylor, "a commission merchant who had his own peculiar eccentricities. . . ." Finding "an old half-starved mule," they mounted him and, after some drinks at a "drinking house" in Exchange Alley, "they made much sport for the lookers-on," writes Kennerly. The antics of Krafft and Taylor found their way into the newspapers during the following week, together with intimations that there would be a "display" on New Year's Eve. "Everybody," Kennerly continues, "was agog to see it, quite as much as they are now." On New Year's Eve Kennerly's friend and roommate in a local boarding-house, John Haynie, persuaded Kennerly to go with him to a clothing store on Dauphin Street "where we found a number of men arraying themselves. Being thus brought in contact with 'the boys', I could of course do no less than affiliate. . . . The study of each one was to make himself as grotesque as possible."

Something, it is evident, had been organized during the week since Krafft's escapade. What was organized was in some sense already familiar to the participants: they knew that they would be participating in a "display," and that "grotesque" masking was the way to display themselves. "I have always had a notion that Jim Taylor was progenitor of the New Year's Eve display," Kennerly continues. "He led the party that night and dismissed it at the close of the show." If heroization of Krafft is misleading, however, it would be just as mistaken to substitute Taylor for Krafft as the organizer of the first festive society. It was certainly not Taylor alone who was responsible for the character of the second outing. Forty to sixty people had assembled into a line of march by 9 P.M. on this New Year's Eve. "Having got into the street we were met by a messenger from the Mayor, John Stocking, Esq., who invited us to call at his residence and partake of a collation. We had too much respect for our municipal chief to decline such an invitation. . . ." After partaking "in most hospitable profusion with everything nice and gustable to eat and drink," the maskers passed the residence of George Davis, "an eccentric old citizen well known in Mobile," where they found more edible hospitality. They also dropped in on "one or two other citizens"; Kennerly does not remember the circumstances exactly.

New Year's good cheer was a feature of colonial society. It was also a custom—including calls on the mayor—in the cities and countryside of the eastern United States, from which the majority of Mobilians probably stemmed by 1831.[7] The mayor and George Davis and whoever else offered hospitality that night already possessed a festive vocabulary appropriate to the occasion. They provided, along with the throngs in the streets,[8] the audience whose responsiveness insured repetition of the spectacle in following years.

Who were the forty to sixty men in the parade? Kennerly names six persons, several of whom attained later prominence in the city. The most important clue to their identity is his mention in quotation marks of "the boys." In Europe ever since the thirteenth century Carnival and other festive demonstrations engaged above all the enthusiasm and fraternal inclinations of the young men of a community, and this was probably the case in Mobile. It was a youthful male group which was most responsive to the Christmas capers of Krafft and Taylor. Probably many of them, like Kennerly and his friend Haynie, were young men in business, not yet fathers and husbands, for whom the holidays were less a time of family-oriented celebration than a time to get out and have fun in the streets.

To these two ingredients—the tradition of New Year's well-wishing and open-house hospitality, and the presence in fast-growing Mobile of numbers of young men, eager for bachelor fun—were added the shenanigans of Krafft and Taylor, and Taylor's "spirit . . . inclined to lead." Leadership by one or a very few persons has proved crucial to the continuing prosperity of festive societies from these early days to the present. Just as important has been the invention of ambivalent symbolism. The cowbells and rake, which Kennerly says were used to lead the procession on New Year's Eve, are eminent examples of this. They were symbols of a local, prosaic farming ambiance which Mobile by 1831 was leaving behind. They were comic because of that past in relation to the opening commercial future. Krafft's invention of a French-sounding name built superbly on this ambivalence about Mobile's identity. "Cowbellion de Rakin" suggests French dignity and frontier impudence at once: rebellion and cowbells, rakin(g)/raisin(g) a ruckus. Allusion to the grand old Creole element of Mobile society is made in the same breath as reference to homely implements that dethrone and undo the French pretentiousness of the name.

There is more to it than that. Michael Krafft, the merchant reveler, migrated to Mobile from Bristol, Pennsylvania, a community a few miles northeast of Philadelphia on the Delaware River. His name indicates German ancestry. In areas with large German communities in Pennsylvania as well as in North Carolina, Virginia, Nova Scotia, and other areas up and down the East Coast, a custom called "belsnickling" took place on Christmas Eve. A "belsnickle" was a man disguised in a furskin coat or cap impersonating a demonic version of Saint Nicolas. "Bels" (German *Pelz*, skin) "-nickle" means "a furry Saint Nick." Amply recorded in eastern Pennsylvania from the 1820s to the early twentieth century, the belsnickle is a variant of the wildman figures who, in some places during the Twelve Days of Christmas and in others at Carnival, haunted and still haunt households in the Alpine regions of Switzerland and Austria. Shaking cowbells at his waist or smaller bells attached to his garments and brandishing a club, whip, or other menacing instrument, the belsnickle goes queting from household to household, frightening the children but also bestowing small gifts.[9]

Several specific details associate Krafft with these Christmas Eve celebrations with which he may have been familiar from childhood. Kennerly appends to his account of the Cowbellions "another source"unidentified by name—which, while differing in date and some other details, still deserves "entire credence," in Kennerly's opinion, insofar as "thoughtfulness and intelligence" are concerned. This source says that Krafft tied cowbells to the rake on Christmas Eve "for music," and that a fife and drum were also used.[10] Making "rough music" of this kind was a still more widespread custom among merrymakers at Christmas and Carnival than the wild costumes of the belsnickles. Susan Davis has recorded the use of mock instruments and raucous music among the lower classes in Philadelphia where, she says, the terms "fantasticals" and "callithumpians" replaced "belsnickles" to describe holiday masking after the 1830s. On New Year's Eve in 1847 a "callithumpian band . . . accoutred grotesquely and with blackened faces . . . rams horns, bells, and kettles . . . shocked the very moon with their enactments."[11]

Krafft's invention seems to memorialize the "callithumpian" aspect of Pennsylvanian revelry more than its wild-animal form. The *Pelz*/bel has turned into a cowbell which makes a racket with the rake. Such linguistic slippage is commonplace in folk custom. S. S. Haldeman's *Pennsylvania Dutch,* published in 1872, comments on this very case in its definition of "bellsnickle": "A noisy party accompanies him [the bellsnickle], often with a bell, which has influenced the English name."[12]

The Cowbellion de Rakin Society prospered. It met regularly on Christmas Eve to drink eggnog, sing, and march about in costume inside the "den" before appearing in public on New Year's Eve. A document which allegedly concerns mid-century meetings describes the parties, at which members quaffed eggnog from a bull's horn instead of cups, as follows:

> When all had assembled the knight of the Bowl in his
> robes of office sang:
> > Come Cowbellions hear me tell
> > How much we love the old cowbell
> > Bring up and fill the old bull's horn
> > And keep your bells in tune!

As each member entered the den, the same source states, he "donned his domino, put a leather collar around his neck . . . [and] covered his face with a cowhead."[13] The Cowbellions' use of rough music, animal masks, and bells connect the Mobilian society with Pennsylvanian and German European customs. They disconnect it from white holiday behavior as we have heretofore found it along the Gulf Coast.

What can have prompted this extraordinary change? Although the answer to this question can only be speculative, the question must nonetheless be posed along with the following one: how in heaven's name did this group pass from being the first to becoming the most venerable of festive societies in Mobile, a collection of "old married gentlemen," revered by all when they finally ceased to exist in the 1890s? The answer to the second question may lie in Kennerly's explanation of why he participated in the second annual parade of the Cowbellions: "Being in port during the last days of the year, I saw in the papers a notice calling the Cowbellions together at the appointed time. And in obedience thereto as a member of the previous turnout, I could do no less than appear and report for duty."

No organization, then, had been formed by 1832. You were a Cowbellion by right of participation. But participation was a kind of jocund "duty." Would a Creole-created activity have prompted such expression? There is nothing less likely. *Voir et paraître,* observe closely and then do it yourself, even more spectacularly! Such was the unspoken rule of Creole celebration, founded as it was upon imitation of European aristocratic court spectacles. The emphasis upon glittering beauty at the balls and in the theaters at Carnival-time in New Orleans expressed a highly developed sense of social rivalry and by the same token a disdain for any show of cultural strain. The first assumption upon which Creoles acted was their absolute superiority to Anglo-Americans in manners. To maintain that assumption made impossible not only grotesque behavior but also any adhesion to prescribed order, to any "report for duty."

It is always risky to invoke the nebulous concept of ethnic or class "character." And yet in anything less than a cultural history as long and wide as the development of Euro-American societies, some resort to such shorthand is indispensable. I have emphasized the lack of continuity between the Franco-Spanish era at Mobile and the period of rapid expansion which the city enjoyed in the 1830s. The expansion was due to the influx of Anglo-American and European newcomers. Mobile was culturally inchoate in the 1830s; everything was changing, anything seemed possible. In that situation some sense of orderliness was appealing; it was also a habit of behavior to nonelite classes and to persons reared in the more unyielding climates of northern as opposed to southern climates. Festive tradition at Mobile acquired its steady footing due to the rough antics of a group of men who had made their way in the world not through family connections and politico-social privilege but through daily, dutiful work.[14]

From Krafft's day to the present a note of formal stiffness, largely absent in New Orleans, characterizes Mobile's celebrations. Balancing this quality, however, have been surges of comic absurdity which have overturned the formalism and refreshed festivity in ways equaled in New Orleans only by black participants. If the grotesque defines the carnivalesque, then it was in Mobile that Carnival truly began. Michael Krafft's perhaps apocryphal answer to the friend who asked about his society on Christmas Eve in 1831, as he wandered through Mobile after a late and bibulous dinner, is emblematic of the blend of order with grotesqueness created there. The friend presumably meant something loose and general; his question might be paraphrased as "what kind of strange company are you keeping tonight, to wind up with cowbells and rake?" Krafft's answer changed "society" into "Society," a specific organization with rules and rituals, however comic. It was as a Society that the Cowbellions survived.

The uncommon reconciliation of opposed qualities found in the Cowbellion de Rakin Society reflects the unsteady development of Mobile, the difficulties it experienced in moving from the Franco-Spanish past to an American future, and the difficulties individuals had in adjusting their assumptions to the bonanza consciousness of a burgeoning mercantile center. It seems likely, then, that in spite of the grand response to the first parade, there were vicissitudes during the early years of the organization. James Taylor died in the autumn of 1832, even before Charles Kennerly returned to "report for duty." Michael Krafft died of yellow fever, aged thirty-two, at Pascagoula, Mississippi, in 1839. When and how did the Cowbellions realize the shift from a society to a Society?

By 1840 the deed was accomplished. The Cowbellions paraded that year, it seems, for the first time with a specific subject and with floats. Six horsedrawn tableaux on flat-bed wagons presented the theme "Heathen Gods and Goddesses."[15] The parade was followed by a masked ball, which was opened, according to Bennett Wayne Dean, one of the local chroniclers of Mardi Gras history, with a poem read by the secretary of the organization, William Holt. Dean could not verify the exact poem read on that occasion, but he did discover a poem by Holt that may have been the one in question. Since it was written by an officer and long-time leader in the organization, its first stanza, at least, is worth quoting in order to give some idea of the homely atmosphere of those early days:

Cowbellians [sic] de Rakin
(The Cause)
The wine was red and the food was good
The boys at the board drank all they could
They ate and they drank till most midnight,
Then started for home, which was perfectly right. . . .[16]

If the Cowbellion de Rakin Society caught on in Mobile, it was because the idea suited the needs and the taste of a sizable and significant group in the community, not because it expressed the particular personality of Michael Krafft. Heroization of Krafft by Mobile's civic-minded historians has tended to obscure both the sources that Krafft probably drew upon from his youth, small-town and lower-class sources which stimulated immediate response from the young men of Mobile, and also the larger cause of the Society's growing appeal, which was the new—*too* new—business success of Mobile in the 1830s. The Cowbellion de Rakin Society with its bathetic camaraderie provided stabilizing as well as fanciful reassurance in those fast-moving times.

The formula engendered imitation. In 1843 an organization which still exists today paraded on New Year's Eve, the "Strikers Independent Society." Like the Cowbellions, they seem to have been young men engaged in the cotton industry. Their name, the "Strikers," is said to refer to their activity in marking cotton bales after weighing and before shipping them. In 1845 still another group paraded on New Year's Eve, the "Tea Drinkers Society" or "The Distinctive Society"—neither version of the name can claim exclusive early documentation. It is not known whether these societies used themes like the Cowbellions of 1840. Their early records, like their membership, were kept privately.[17]

By the 1850s the societies had become elite. "The Cows had money to burn in those days, and a matter of four or five hundred dollars for an eggnog bowl [of sterling silver] was of no consequence. They ordered one from France. . . ." Holding five gallons, the bowl bore the Society's insignia: owl, rake, cow's head, and torch.[18] The Strikers, instead of indulging in eggnog, apparently struck an elegant French pose by drinking champagne. The Tea Drinkers, belying their name or nickname, "served lager beer in kegs."[19]

Mobile society had matured a good deal in twenty years. These halcyon days are warmly depicted by the Swedish traveler who provided so many precious details concerning the black cabildos in Havana. Fredrika Bremer was invited in 1850, just before her Cuban visit, to stay with the family of Octavia Le Vert, wife of a prominent physician and hostess of Mobile's most elegant and intellectual salon. She went to the theater, strolled through magnolia gardens, and luxuriated in the company:

> I have . . . seen at Mrs. LeV's a great number of the grandees of Mobile, and more lovely young ladies I have never met with. . . . I remember . . . with pleasure some elderly gentlemen, men of office in the states, who were wise and clear on all questions with the exception of slavery. And among the young men [there was] . . . the young, gifted poet and dramatic author, Mr. Reynolds . . . who has afforded me many an agreeable hour by his excellent heart and genuine conversation. . . . [As for Octavia Le Vert] that little worldly lady, whom I had heard spoken of as a "belle," and as the most splendid ornament of society wherever she went, has yet become almost as dear to me as a young sister! . . . With this young lady have I conversed of Transcendentalists and practical Christians, of Mormonism and Christianity, and have found it a pleasure. . . . We have been involuntarily and naturally attracted to each other.[20]

Fredrika Bremer's enthusiasm for Mobile and in particular her sense of attachment to Octavia Le Vert indicate how the institutions of local life had by mid-century conspired to produce figures whose attitudes and consciousness were comparable in most respects to those of older, larger centers of European and American society. A slightly more whimsical but nevertheless similar impression is conveyed by a fictional account of Mobile in a novel by J. T. Wiswall, published in London in 1864. There is no mention of the Civil War (1861–65); in fact the author, who was a Mobilian, studiously avoids any reference to slavery. Wiswall gives the only extended description of the early New Year's Eve parades in Mobile which is presently known.

The floats and masks which he describes in the Cowbellions' parade reflect the theme of 1840, "Heathen Gods and Goddesses," but since Wiswall's parade takes place in never-never time, we cannot be certain that the actions he depicts correspond to any real occasion. Jupiter in a chariot, driving four white horses; Diana followed by "her beautiful lover, the drowsy Endymion"; Neptune with marine gods and sea-nymphs; Bacchus drawn by tigers and accompanied by Pan and satyrs; Aphrodite, Cupid, Aurora, and so on—"the whole a voluptuous cavalcade of immortals" who hurry through the streets to the theater, where the parquet, floored over on a level with the stage, provides an arena for "*tableaux vivants*, taken from the traditions of the gods." "When the last tableau was duly represented, the throng of gods, obeying the signal warble of Mars' whistle, formed in a line and slowly marched around the parquet to one of the weird and solemn marches of Mendelssohn." After the grand march, the band played a polka and the Cowbellions invited ladies to the floor. After the first set, the dance was opened to the guests who crowded the surrounding boxes, dress-circle, and galleries.[21]

This extraordinary fantasy of the "honorable and ancient Society of the Cows," as they are humorously called in the novel, corresponds remarkably to the manner in which Mobile's Carnival societies conduct their celebrations today.[22] The author does not go on to describe the "splendid" parade of "the Goats," as the Strikers are called in the novel,[23] and the Tea Drinkers are not mentioned. Reference is made, however, to a society called the "Indescribables" who according to Bennett Dean paraded in 1846, and Wiswall also says that a society called the "Rising Generation" participated.[24]

Neither the cultural activities displayed in these New Year's celebrations nor the social functions of which they were the vehicle were peculiar to Mobile. However homespun their imitation, the Cowbellion de Rakin Society and the others were associations, like many others before them, of young business elites. Private societies, organizing Carnival and New Year's activities to make sure that the right people get to know each other and maintain their ties, were half a millennium old by the time the Mobilians reinvented the idea. The Limpurg Society in the great German trading center of Frankfurt, for example, flourished in the mid-fifteenth century. Annually it celebrated Carnival with a banquet and a costumed parade through the streets and around and through three ecclesiastical establishments, including on some occasions a convent where the unmarried daughters of the city's elites were wont to be sent.[25]

The Cowbellions' festivity was a mixture of aristocratic and popular elements. It soon became elite in membership but in other ways it maintained Krafft's and Taylor's belsnickle obstreperousness. A ticket to the Cowbellions' ball in 1853 shows an engaging combination of cupid-like figures in the border decoration with a simply sketched cow and bell as pictographic sub-

You are respectfully invited to attend the

**FIRST FANCY DRESS & MASQUERADE BALL,**

Of the                IONS.

To be given at Union Hall, Fourth District,

On Saturday, Christmas Eve, Dec. 24.

Invited by

5. Invitation to Cowbellion Ball, Mobile, 1853 (photo, Norman Magden, from Zuma Young Salaun, *Mardi Gras Facts and Fancies*)

stitutes for the society's name in the center of the ticket (see plate 5.) It is as if the makers of the card wished to undercut the occasion, "First Fancy Dress and Masquerade Ball," by recalling the un-fancy costuming which first made their fame.

Aside from belsnickling, the closest thing to an organized, masked procession on New Year's Eve in colonial America was the raucous custom of "shooting in the New Year," documented in the 1650s for Dutch New York and also recorded half a dozen times between 1750 and 1800 in or near Philadelphia and on through the nineteenth century in rural Pennsylvania.[26] There was also costumed "mumming" on New Year's Day in a variety of places along the eastern seaboard.[27] In most cases these activities were carried out by small groups of less than a dozen people, and were not supported by ongoing organizations.

It seems likely, at least, that such games constituted the informal festive vocabulary upon which the forty to sixty young men drew when they turned up at a clothing store to accoutre themselves for the first Cowbellion parade in 1831. During succeeding decades such expressions were amalgamated with the older elite customs of plantation society for the Christmas holidays, the balls and banquets, to form the oldest still enduring civic festive tradition in this country with a distinctive style—homespun, slightly comic, even grotesque on occasion, and withal very orderly and ceremonious.

Some Mobile Cowbellions came to New Orleans on mardi gras in 1837 to repeat their New Year's mascarade of 1836. They did so again, it seems, in 1838.[28] The impulse must have been something like that leading famous Carnival masking groups today to appear a second time in costume, performing their dances, at summertime folk festivals.[29] In 1852 the *Daily Orleanian* again reported their coming: "It is thought we will have an accession to our maskers in the 'Cowbellions' from our sister City of Mobile. . . . It is only those who have seen, in Mobile, the Cowbellions, on the eve or night of New Year, who can form any conception of their almost unearthly grandeur. . . . Under the homely and rather odd name of Cowbellions ranks one of the most picturesque societies imaginable."[30]

By the 1850s some Cowbellions had moved to New Orleans. In 1853 the *Daily Picayune* reported that they had formed their own organization: "Our Mobile friends are not ahead of us so far as might be expected. . . . We too have a Cowbellion association flourishing in our midst. They get up things in style, too, with all the appropriate metallic and quadruped insignia, and private, mysterious letters, names, etc." The New Orleans Cowbellions gave a masked ball on mardi gras.[31] Given the evident attractiveness of the Mobile organization to many Orleanians one might have predicted that it would not be long before the Mobilians' street parades were imitated as well as their secret society.

What was it that attracted them? Certainly not the mere idea of marching as a body with an exotic name. A group of "fashionable and handsome young men" called "the Bedouins" paraded alongside the Cowbellions in 1852. They had already moved as a company through the streets in 1841 along with another group—masked as clowns?—called "the American Circus Company" (*La compagnie du Cirque Américain*). Still another group, styled the Mardi Gras Rangers, marched in 1842. Street parades organized by private societies already existed in New Orleans.[32]

One difference between these groups and the Carnival society organized by six young former Mobilians in 1857 was ethnic. None of the six who issued the first call for an organizational meeting of a new society in January 1857 were from Creole families, nor were any of the thirteen who replied to that first call. The Bedouins, Cirque Américain, and others seem to have been mostly Creole.[33] The former Mobilians and their friends who founded the Mistick Krewe of Comus were, however receptive to French ideas of fun, in practice possessed of an Anglophile and Protestant sense of festivity. The verbal choices which they made in choosing their name and the subject of their first parade express this: "mistick krewe" is a half literary, half archaically English way of saying "secret society"; "Comus" was an ambivalently seductive and devilish character in courtly masques written by Ben Jonson (1573?–1637) and John Milton (1608–74); the theme of the 1857 parade, "The Demon Actors in Milton's Paradise Lost," expresses a sense of trespass which for Americans of Protestant background is nearly inseparable from merrymaking.[34]

The Comus society was a way of outdoing the Cowbellions, even as they imitated the latter.[35] Gone were the homespun symbolic references to rakes and cows. The society issued three thousand invitations to the ball following the parade in the Gaiety Theater, and the mayor led the first quadrille. All the elite of "fashion, taste, and beauty"—at least of Anglo-American origin—was present from this burgeoning city of over 150,000 people. At midnight the members marched in order from the theater to a nearby address where they banqueted into the wee hours. From its inception the Comus society expressed ambitions of grandeur, and was able to call upon ample resources to that end.

Newspaper response was generally enthusiastic.[36] The following June the society drew up a constitution, and stated its purposes: "Holding it to be a self-evident truth that man at his creation was so constituted that social and intellectual enjoyment should ever be the accompaniment of labor . . . we . . . desiring properly to celebrate the Carnival as one of the occasions afforded for Relaxation and in the true spirit of Charity desiring to benefit our fellows . . . do hereby . . . establish the following Constitution." The rhetoric of civic-spirited democracy and pious benevolence, imitated from the American Declaration of Independence, encircles the key phrase, "desiring *properly* to celebrate the Carnival. . . ."

The society's present-day estimate of its importance, in the brochure which it published a century after its foundation, repeats this emphasis almost like a syllogism: because the members of Comus were "socially important," their celebration was necessarily "orderly, educational and cultural." The social function of elites is not simply to preserve order but to celebrate it; the key to doing so is to lift people's ideals. "Comus brought to the Carnival of New Orleans the refinement which it lacked before, lending tone and dignity to the festivities."[37]

In fact it was not refinement that made Comus successful but its happy combination of order with disorder, of pretentious gaiety with organizational pragmatism. Comus's parades were "grotesque" and "motley," as the newspaper said, and at the same time "magnificent" and "brilliant." The nighttime torch parades of the society provided a centering element in relation to which the street games, the random violence, the hucksterism, and the escapism could cluster, adjust themselves, and also be controlled by the forces of order. New Orleans in the 1850s was a roiling, rollicking city fairly flooded with civic strife, corrupt in administration and police, incapable of dealing with its most basic physical problems, such as the sewage and swamps which led to repeated yellow-fever epidemics, and swollen with ethnic groups—above all the Irish—who clamored for the destruction of the 20,000-strong free-black community with whom they competed for jobs in the trades and on the wharves. Carnival in the later 1840s and 1850s became a theater for these discontents, and so public opinion wavered between affirming and denouncing it. Whenever the organized parades of Bedouins, Cowbellions, or others provided some restraint—or some forgetfulness—of the brickbats and quicklime thrown by some of the more ruthless revelers, it was lauded to the skies. But when there was not such distraction, then the editors denounced "this miserable annual exhibition," which "originated in a barbarous age, and is worthy of only such."[38]

Recent study of Philadelphia's festive traditions has shown remarkably similar public reactions to festive behavior during the same decades, 1830–60, although the Philadelphians did not create so effective a solution as that of the Carnival societies. The same complaints about violence—in Philadelphia centered during the Twelve Days of Christmas—were voiced in the newspapers, and were directed similarly against the behavior of blacks and Irish.[39] The mechanism generating this discontent was neither ethnic tradition nor lower-class barbarism. It was rather the very system that had produced the elites who vociferously denounced violence. The "manic-depressive rhythm" of capitalist-directed markets sucked into the large and ever-larger cities "an underlayer of surplus labor, fitfully employed, that the new capitalists managed [in order] to depress wages and meet any sudden demand in production."[40] This unstable and insecure mass of people, expressing on occasion its vulnerability in violence, was the precondition at the time of commercial and industrial profit. The greatness of New Orleans was inseparable from its savagery.

The organizers of the Comus society can thus be said to have addressed themselves, presumably in a largely unconscious manner, to two major social problems which existed only on a smaller scale in Mobile. The first was how to provide for the stable concentration—that is, recirculation—of power among elites. The second was how to render such elite concentration attractive to the discontented and dangerous underclasses. With respect to the second problem the Carnival-society idea proved to harbor practically unlimited resources for insuring public tranquility and thereby also distraction from the city's serious problems and the serious solutions needed to deal with them.[41] In its first, civic phase these resources were displayed as a power to attract masses toward passivity by engaging them in admiration of a dazzling spectacle. In the second, twentieth-century phase, to be examined later, these resources consisted in the capacity to stimulate imitation by all classes, not just the elites, of the idea of a private society for public festive display. For increasing numbers of Orleanians and Mobilians over the past century the excess of energy beyond that engaged by their jobs has been absorbed by festive productivity rather than by rudderless leisure behavior.

The Carnival-society idea also revealed two differing capacities with respect to the first problem, the circulation of elites. The Anglo-American origin of Comus was ambivalent: it declared American independence from the French way of participating in Carnival, but at the same time it incorporated the Creole practices of masked balls and sumptuous banquets into its parade-centered activity. The prestige of Comus confirmed in the cultural sphere what had already happened in the economic and political spheres, the replacement of Creole by Anglo-American elites.[42] But the transfer was conciliatory. The self-evident truth of man's right to relaxation was spelled with a French accent: Carnival, not Twelfth Night, Christmas, or the Fourth of July, became the center of festive life in New Orleans. Comus very soon attracted and admitted prominent Creoles to its membership. Both elites were satisfied. Later in the century the other aspect of the problem of elite circulation, that of preserving power in the same hands even while moving from generation to generation, was worked out by incorporating another old Creole custom into the Carnival-society system, the selection of queens of the balls.

The Comus-Cowbellion concept was also successful in engaging the approbation of officialdom for its part in augmenting the city's orderliness and its renown. Tourists had long come to New Orleans for the winter season and the Carnival. Now the attractiveness of Comus's spectacular display supplied a new motive. Already in 1858 the *Illustrated London News* covered the event and reproduced an engraving of the society's nighttime parade.[43] In 1859 the mayor and his wife received the krewe members in his parlor at City Hall when they reached that point in the parade route. Evidently the floats already included some female participants because the contemporary report continues: "An immense bowl of champagne punch had been provided for his guests by the liberality of the Mayor, as well as a bouquet for each of the lady members of the procession."[44]

The long-term factors which favored preservation and extension of the private Carnival society, organized on a permanent, year-round basis, were probably not clear to the founders of Comus or even to those city officials who welcomed them. Least of all was it clear at first that the new parades solved the problem of rowdy reveling. Yet the newspapers, at least, seemed inclined now to view the latter with bemusement rather than angry denunciation. In 1859, the third season of Comus's appearance, the *Daily Crescent* reported the general masking which preceded the night parade as follows:

> All the "vagrom" boys were out in all sorts of cheap harlequin and clown disguises, with bags of flour, whitening each other and the negroes, and leaving their floury tracks on the banquettes in all parts of the city. The grown-up jolly boys galloped on horseback up the town and down, dressed and painted as Bedouin Arabs, Indians, Turks, Chinese, Venetian cavaliers, and African negroes. Groups of ludicrous maskers of all conceivable descriptions went flying around in cabs, buggies, furniture wagons, and carriages. All the courtesans in town appeared to be out; many in male costume of all kinds, from that of the primp Canal Street dandy to the rollicking drunken sailor of Gallatin Street.[45]

Comus was not welcomed because it solved the social problems displayed in Carnival. It was heralded because it distracted people from them, much as the Mardi Gras Rangers or Bedouins had been congratulated. What, then, were the elements that differentiated Comus from these other groups, enabling it to act as an organizational paradigm which gradually produced the long-term effects mentioned above?

The formula adopted by the society included no innovations. It simply applied to Carnival what the Cowbellions had been doing at New Year's in Mobile: parade, masked tableaux, ball, and banquet. With the exception of the masked tableaux each of the four elements had been separately practiced for years. Although New Orleans street maskers had long since taken the habit of joining the actors in Auber's *Gustave* in their grand finale scene before beginning their ball, Comus was the first to organize a theatrical inauguration to the ball which was independent from what was going on at the opera house. The "mistick krewe" presented four scenes associated with the theme of their parade, Milton's *Paradise Lost*, on the stage of the Gaiety Theater in 1857. After the final tableau the maskers "marched several times around the floor, which had been thrown over the parquette, thus giving the spectators an opportunity of observing the actors in the evening's entertainment more closely."[46] After this grand march the dancing began. Comus's ball ended on the stroke of midnight when an official called the "captain" blew his whistle and the members of the society retired to their banquet.[47]

The social feeling which prompted this smoothly articulated celebration was shared oligarchic feeling and a penchant for privacy, qualities that contrasted with Creole inclinations. The Creoles' desire for public glitter was undercut by their inability to work together. Like their honored Parisian cousins, these Latin upper-class revelers regarded streets, other people, and finally the theater as scenic backdrops for their individual pleasure. It never occurred to them to put on a theater-like show in the streets for these other people. The Anglo-Saxons aimed at a collectively created vision which would polarize actors and spectators, impressing people with its distant grandeur rather than with its individualistic splendors and helter-skelter rivalries.

Americans, as the Frenchman Alexis de Tocqueville pointed out in his book about the transatlantic democracy which he observed in the 1830s, do everything by forming "associations," whether political parties, trading companies, or club committees.[48] They seem always to be capable of compromise because it is more pragmatic. Such was the instinct of the men who formed Comus:

> At the first election Charles Churchill was chosen captain. Captain Joseph Ellison was appointed chairman of the "Dress Committee." . . . Ellison with his committee went to Mobile to borrow or to secure costumes and to get some ideas. . . . The invitation committee worked day and night getting out the invitations. The members met nightly . . . [and] were instructed in the part that

they would take in the tableaux. Each man was numbered and would take his place on a chalked circle on the floor, moving only when the captain's whistle blew. In this manner they rehearsed the tableaux to be given on the stage of the theatre.[49]

How strange it seems to prepare a festival whose essence is excess with such rote strictness! Yet this was just the idea that was needed. The same efficiency is exercised by tens of dozens of Carnival societies preparing their parades, tableaux, balls, and banquets today. The committee system functions in rapport with habits of obedience to leadership and with selective admission to membership to insure the regular realization of the societies' goals, which indeed have more to do with mutual social recognition than with the unbuttoned pleasure-seeking commonly associated with Carnival.

The members of Comus formed a social organization, the Pickwick Club, some months after their first parade. The club rented rooms on St. Charles Street. Henceforth "the Krewe would continue a myth," while the private club would perform the functions of other such groups in the city, like those of the equally elite Boston Club, formed in 1841 for "gentlemen who desire to pass the leisure hours, when at their disposal, agreeably and pleasantly, in comparative privacy and retirement. . . ."[50] By these means the private interests of the most socially eminent males in the city were made coherent with the very public system of pleasureful display which, in the form of gala balls, had long been the character of upper-class Carnival in New Orleans.

The restrictive, obedient, decorous quality of the new organization was expressed in its antique, learned name and symbols. But these elements also expressed something more. The front page of the *Daily Picayune* on mardi gras of 1857 (February 24) referred to Comus thus: "'M.K.C.'—As will be seen by referring to another part of this morning's Picayune, these mystic initials have a meaning, 'if one could find out.' The most interesting facts the public have to deal with are that those 'misticks' are to give a most amusing fete tonight. . . ."[51] The Mobile societies had already adopted the habit of referring to themselves by initials, and they continue to do so in Mobile to this day. Secrecy is less sought than mystification. The use of initials and an antiquated spelling of "mystic" in Comus's name go together with the mysteriously burning square stone pyre depicted on their invitation card to the ball of 1857 (see plate 6).

6. Invitation to Comus Ball, New Orleans, 1857 (photo, Norman
Magden, from *One Hundred Years of Comus*)

The cultural ambiance of mid-nineteenth-century America was strongly imbued with Gothic-romantic elements. Rationalism and classic clarity, so important to elite culture in colonial times, had been displaced by the ardent emotions of enthusiastic religion, the lights and shadows of passionate love, and attention to seemingly involuntary attraction, like that drawing Madame Le Vert of Mobile and Fredricka Bremer of Sweden toward each other. Was it simply some general complicity with this cultural atmosphere that led the invitation committee to emboss a bat on the side of their burning pyre? What can it mean? At the top of the card, as if to emblemize a chaotic intention hidden behind its well-geared elegance, the society placed a bat with widespread wings, grasping a grinning Carnival mask by its clawlike toes.

Was there some influence of Freemasonry on the founders of this and other Carnival "mystic" societies? Freemasonry was highly popular with the American founding fathers (Franklin, Hancock, and Washington were Masons). The secrecy and elaborate ceremonialism of its rituals parallel those of the Carnival societies, although of course the latter are performed in jest, and this is no doubt how one was expected to understand the stone pyre and the bat: as mysterious nonsense.[52] "When Comus was the Pickwick Club [1857–84]," the society's commemorative brochure explains, "new members were initiated with a serio-comic take off [sic] of the ancient mysteries. The darkened room and black veil, the death's head and the owl (the bird of wisdom), the solemn voice of the captain, the administering the oath [sic] were all a part of the ritual."[53]

From the point of view of European Carnival customs Comus's parading symbols were no more original than the elements of their celebration. After the parade of Satan and his devils in 1857 came depiction of the "classical pantheon" in 1858 and the "English holidays," such as Christmas and Twelfth Night, in 1859. Themes similar to these had been presented in float parades from Renaissance times. The art historian Giorgio Vasari (1511–74) attributes to the painter Piero di Cosimo in Florence, about 1500, the development of nighttime torchlight Carnival parades, which displayed men on foot and horseback richly dressed "in costumes adapted to the subject," surrounding a "car or triumph full of ornaments, spoils and curious fancies which enchanted the people and instructed their minds." Vasari describes with particular detail one of Piero's darkest inventions, as threatening as Comus's parade of devils. It included a "car of Death," from which a gigantic figure holding a scythe stepped out at intervals, accompanied by others costumed with "the complete skeleton painted on their draperies."[54] In 1601 at Palermo, reports a contemporary, the jousts habitual in Carnival were preceded by a parade including a float with twelve musicians dressed as sirens, surrounding the figure of Neptune.[55] At Paris in the early nineteenth century it was already customary to associate Comus, his putative father Bacchus, and the god of mockery, Momus, as a Carnival trio:

> Momus shaking his bells
> Comus lighting his furnace fires
> Bacchus drunk atop his barrel
>    And Athena losing logic
>    Apollo singing out of tune
> Disorder divine! Infernal racket!
> That's what it is to go to Carnival![56]

But the guiding ambition of Comus was never originality. Orderly magnificence was their aim and they achieved it, integrating elements near and far in time and space to the earlier Carnival customs of New Orleans. Their success with the public, as with their own class, was due to the cross-cutting influence of several factors, positive and negative: rivalrous imitation of the successful New Year's Eve celebrations of the Cowbellions, confiscation of the decaying cultural leadership of the Creoles, and disdain for anything resembling the disorderly Carnival of the lower classes.

Just as the new formula was being worked out which would make Carnival central to the Anglo-American city, the Civil War intervened. The war and its consequences added to Comus and the other Carnival activities in New Orleans an element of grotesque verve which had been largely lacking.

Louisiana had already seceded from the Union in 1861 when Mardi Gras arrived. One of the newspapers reported that during the Carnival "a band of nigger minstrels, playing nigger music,"—presumably whites in black-face—"marched around, having at their head a comical effigy of Old Abe Lincoln, riding a rail of his own splitting." To ride a rail was a variant of the old Europeen custom of charivari, often conducted in Carnival, in which males who contravened the unspoken laws of the local community were held up to ridicule by being paraded about on an ass, a hobbyhorse, or its equivalent (here parts of a wooden rail fence) in a manner manifestly opposite to the accepted heroic image of a man on horseback.[57]

Between April 1862 and May 1865, New Orleans was occupied

by federal troops and governed by Union generals. In spite of a political situation in New Orleans so unsettled that it erupted in bloody riots during the summer of 1866, in which thirty-four blacks were killed and over two hundred were wounded, Comus resumed its Mardi Gras parades in 1866. By act of Congress in March 1867, Louisiana was reoccupied by federal troops who supervised creation of a new constitution, enfranchising blacks, and providing for equal access to public schools and public transport. Governmental expenses and taxes soared over the ensuing decade until the troops departed for the final time in April 1877. Whites blamed the blacks and formed White Leagues which in September 1874, rioted in New Orleans against the governor-appointed metropolitan police. Twenty-seven men were killed and one hundred wounded. In this situation Comus, which had paraded every year from 1866, suspended its activities in 1875. The lengthy attempt to supervise reconciliation between the races from outside the state had proved a failure. Led by the predominantly white-owned newspapers, which fanned racial hate to inflammatory heights, most whites wished to believe, as the *New Orleans Bulletin* put it on December 16, 1874, that "The white race rules the world—the white race rules America—and the white race will rule Louisiana—and the white race shall rule New Orleans."[58]

Mobile whites, like those of New Orleans, had solidly supported the Confederate cause. They took defeat just as bitterly and inconsolably, but the city was not quite the object of such concentrated repression by Northerners nor quite the stage for such new black opportunities as New Orleans. Mobile was occupied by Federal troops only on April 12, 1865, three days after Lee's surrender at Appomattox. In 1874 carpetbag government dissolved without resort to bloody riots like those in New Orleans.

In February 1866 a local market clerk named Joseph Cain, born in 1832 of Irish parents in Mobile, disguised himself as a legendary Indian chief of the Chickasaws, against whom the French had conducted inconclusive wars in the eighteenth century.[59] He was a member of the Tea Drinkers Society; he knew and enjoyed festive play. He is said to have also been to New Orleans and to have observed Carnival there. Most relevantly, he was an ex-Confederate soldier, and this was probably known to many in the still relatively small city of 40,000. The point of his disguise was surely not lost upon his fellow Mobilians, when he drove through the streets in a decorated charcoal wagon on mardi gras, advertising himself as the undefeated Chickasaw, "Chief

Slackabamorinico" from Wragg Swamp on the outskirts of the city. He was accompanied on the wagon by six other veterans, all of them also members of the Tea Drinkers Society, and all but one of them, like Cain, of Irish origin.[60]

The next year "Old Slac's" following multiplied. Sixteen Confederate veterans marched behind Cain, each playing an instrument "without regard to the efforts of the others."[61] Such incongruous, raucous antimusic was a traditional element of both New Year's and Carnival festivity. It was grotesque and disorderly, a contravention of propriety, which is exactly what the veterans wanted to suggest.[62] They called themselves unambiguously the Lost Cause Minstrels. Their number included on this second occasion in 1867 a future newspaper editor, a future sheriff, and the son of a confederate hero, Admiral Rudolf Semmes. Motivated by political resentment, Cain's new manner of celebration effectively shifted the main occasion of public festivity in Mobile from New Year's Eve to mardi gras.[63]

Times of disaster are often times of heightened festive abandon. The 1870s were no exception. As the effects of military defeat and economic decline penetrated Southern life more deeply, a festival which celebrated the supremacy of Southern white culture became more and more desireable. In 1873 Comus chose for the subject of its parade "The Missing Links to Darwin's Origin of Species." The first wartime military governor of New Orleans, Benjamin Butler, was paraded as a hyena with the general's face, President Grant himself was portrayed as the "Tobacco Grub," and many carpetbaggers were similarly caricatured. The *Daily Picayune* described the last link in the chain of creation leading to Man:

> [As the] last link . . . appeared the Gorilla; a specimen, too, so amazingly like the broader-mouthed varieties of our own citizens, so Ethiopian in his exuberant glee, so at home in his pink shirt collar, so enraptured with himself and so fond of his banjo, that the Darwinian chain wanted no more links . . . He passed; a few rag-tag trailed behind, like the smell of dirty dishwater after a feast. . . . We shall not kill the effect by pinning on a moral, having a steadfast faith, however may be the impressions of the night, in the Survival of the Fittest.[64]

Although *Scribner's Magazine* included a report on and illustrations of the Mardi Gras parades of 1873 in its November issue, these daring representations were not commented upon. The gorilla/black man appears in an illustration of Comus's ball, bearing a crown to indicate his usurpation, presumably, of the white man's place as the king of creation (see plate 7). The scene

7. Comus Ball, New Orleans, 1873 (photo, Norman Magden, from *Scribner's Monthly*, November 1873)

of the gorilla's crowning was enacted at the ball as the second of Comus's tableaux.[65] In the illustration there is also a gentleman in swallowtail coat standing opposite to the gorilla-king. "Some of the more hasty spectators seemed inclined to think he was put there to represent Darwin himself," wrote a local reporter. The gentleman has the head and feet of an ass.[66]

Times of disaster are also times of social withdrawal, social self-protection, social pretension. Elite societies multiplied and other organizations too began to give masked balls on mardi gras, the Young Men's Benevolent Association at the National Theater and the Young Men's Dress Society at the Odd Fellows' Hall in 1870, for example.[67] The Twelfth Night Revelers, who paraded under the leadership of a Lord of Misrule on January 6, organized a permanent society in 1870, and in 1872 the new Knights of Momus introduced a parade on New Year's Eve.[68] In 1877 Momus presented the most daring caricatures yet devised of President Grant, General Butler, General Sherman, and a host of other national and local Reconstruction-era figures, picturing them all as denizens of hell. The parade was called "Hades, A Dream of Momus," and culminated with a representation of the sinking "Ship of State," foundering in a sea of fire. Unlike the Comus parade, this produced angry telegrams from Washington. The local newspapers were divided in their reaction, some of them feeling that Momus had indeed gone too far. But the affair blew over without punitive actions being taken.[69]

In 1987 the annually published *Guide* to New Orleans' Mardi Gras asserted that: "Scholars agree that the most important parade of all time was the 1877 Momus production entitled, 'Hades, a Dream of Momus.'"[70] Most important? That depends upon one's ideology. It was certainly the most vehement political parade ever seen in Carnival along the Gulf Coast. Its sharply etched satire helped fix the image of Southern resistance to Northern and national interference and certainly aided in the construction of civic pride peculiar to New Orleans; but it also retarded participation in the shifting currents of national culture.[71] "Judging from conversations with a number of persons, there is not much hope in the present condition of affairs," the *Scribner's Monthly* journalist concluded in 1873, "that the equality of races will be thoroughly recognized by the white man in Louisiana."[72] That was putting it mildly. It would be a hundred years before anything resembling James Creecy's joyful "king of the wake" (1835) would be seen again in the central streets of New Orleans. Carnival during the first decade after the Civil War was used to dig still deeper the chasm between the races.[73]

Was this chasm the precondition for making Mardi Gras an emblem of civic pride and attractiveness? To nearly all whites good citizenship could only be constructed upon their racial superiority. In New Orleans and Mobile at this period civism implied, rather than conflicted with, elitism. This was true not only with respect to race. To maintain the notion that the South, with its one-crop economy, and the South's cities, with their lack of energy in developing industrial and railroad capacities, were nevertheless blameless for their problems, the civic spirit had to develop a historical elitism as well. The greatness of New Orleans was in its past, when the grandeur of France and Spain shaped the city. By the same token the grandeur of New Orleans' elite Carnival societies lay in their superiority to present circumstances and in their allegiance to predemocratic symbols like Comus, Momus, and the Twelfth Night Revelers' Lord of Misrule. To use these signs was a compensation for and refuge from current economic and political decline. These reincarnations of ancient glories raised their adherents above the vile standards of the day, if only for the space of a festival.

Between 1865 and 1900 New Orleans first developed its vocation for tourism by billing itself as "the city that care forgot." The city was carefree because of its gaiety, which stemmed from its Latin heritage and was best expressed in its celebration of pre-Lenten Mardi Gras: thus ran the tale. But in fact its gay carelessness also grew from discouragement about the present, and its "Latin" veneer developed in good part from nostalgia for the slave-based prosperity of the past. As for the origin of its Carnival, this Catholic occasion became a significant occasion for the city generally only after it became predominantly Anglo-American in population and irreligious in its sense of celebration.

Mardi Gras became an important tourist attraction in the later nineteenth century by the intermingling of two desires: the reactionary nostalgia of native whites and the need for a model of otherness by Northerners who were prospering while New Orleans decayed. In 1872 the intermingling produced, as if by accident, the creation of Rex.

> If ever I cease to love, If ever I cease to love,
> May oysters have legs—And cows lay eggs,
> If ever I cease to love.

> If ever I cease to love, If ever I cease to love,
> May the Grand Duke Alexis—Ride a buffalo through Texas,
> If ever I cease to love.

The theme song played each year during New Orleans' Mardi Gras parades was played for the first time in 1872. Grand Duke Alexis Romanov, after hunting buffalo in the West under the guidance of General George Custer and Buffalo Bill, stopped in New Orleans. Inspired in part by the presence of Russian royalty, a group of businessmen and civic leaders invented a king of Carnival named—with a nod in the direction of the festival's supposed Roman origins—"Rex." Alexis saluted the monarch from reviewing stands and was serenaded with the song above, taken from a local musical comedy of which he was said to be fond. Whether or not the last two verses were truly sung in the grand duke's presence, they are of a piece with the other lines, mixing sentiment, bad verse, and comic hyperbole to silly perfection.[74]

Like most other elements of Gulf Coast Mardi Gras, the idea of a monarch incarnating the festival was first tried out during the European Renaissance.[75] Limited personification already existed in New Orleans in the shape of Comus, but there is little evidence that the Greek god actually paraded in the streets in the early years of this society.[76] More important than the idea of a monarchic symbol of the festival was the political fantasy. Rex—hastily organized less than two weeks before the Grand Duke's arrival—issued a flurry of proclamations expressing comic sovereignty over New Orleans. This too was European custom, and indeed had been tried out in a limited way many years before by the Bedouins in New Orleans.[77] In the current situation of "carpetbag" government the proclamations carried specific reference and relevance. "Edict 12," issued the day before mardi gras, included incredibly high prices for cotton and sugar to please the merchant community; it also suspended "the Registration Law . . . Election Law . . . Taxes . . ." and a congeries of other hated stipulations. Edict 2, issued earlier, had ordered the governor to "disperse that riotous body known as the Louisiana State Legislature" from 3 P.M. to sundown on mardi gras. No offense intended, of course! Another provision of Edict 12 declared "all quarrels, hatreds, jealousies, and vendettas . . . hereby cancelled. . . ."[78]

In 1882 one of the founders of Rex, J. Curtis Waldo, wrote a *History of the Carnival in New Orleans*. The eighty-seven-page book was published by the Chicago, St. Louis, and New Orleans Railroad and urges its readers at many points to take this railroad line to New Orleans for the festival. The extended advertisement offers a different explanation of Rex's foundation, scarcely mentioning the Grand Duke's visit. According to Waldo, the reason was that more and more Mardi Gras visitors had been returning home disappointed, not having obtained cards to the evening's tableaux balls. In fact the problem, according to the local newspapers, was not only touristic. For several years the crush of would-be gate-crashers at the door to Comus's ball had been so great that even the authority of General Beauregard, commandeered for the occasion, had not entirely succeeded in eliminating gentlemanly dismay and unladylike disarray in entering.[79] The Rex ball was open to "strangers," that is, to elite nonresidents of New Orleans. The device satisfied the tourists' voyeurism, the old elite's self-satisfied exclusiveness, and a new, more youthful business elite's ambitions.

The success of the first Rex parade prompted its founders to seek more permanent association. A group of "merchants and bakers entrusted with our city's welfare," Waldo writes, formed an organization called the "Royal Host" and pledged money to the founders. "To the members of the Royal Host splendidly designed patents as Dukes of the Realm were issued, emblazoned with the seals of the State of Louisiana, city of New Orleans, and the King of the Carnival." These patents can be found, Waldo assures his readers, "framed in the offices of our most prominent business houses." [80]

From the outset, then, Rex was based on principles other than those of Comus. They were the familiar principles of middle-class America, identifying the public welfare with business welfare. The symbols used by Rex in its parades and balls were more stolidly Anglo-Saxon than those of Comus. The king was accompanied in 1872 by the "Earl Marshall of the Empire," and by "yeomanry." "New [auxiliary] organizations were formed; the King's Own, a splendid squadron of cavalry of four companies, the Oxonians . . . the Lights of St. George. . . ." In 1877, when Rex presented "the Military Progress of the World" as its parade, "Our Sovereign, the all-potent Rex, returned to us as Charlemagne, attended by his Twelve Peers. . . ." [81] Given the military character of government in Louisiana over the preceding fifteen years, it is not surprising that this imaginary monarch looked so frequently like a general. In 1874 his "arms, weapons, banners, etc. . . . were those of the time of the valiant Totila," a Germanic ruler of Italy in the sixth century (see plate 8). [82]

In the first years of the Rex parade many advertising vans followed the parade: Carré's Plantation Cabin, Singer Sewing Machines, Warner's Bitters, etc. The thematic floats were sometimes rudimentary, more emphasis being placed on the military-aristocratic entourage of His Majesty. Most important, however, was the tendency of other groups of all kinds and also individual maskers to follow in Rex's train. In 1873 these groups were organized under the supervision of the Lord High Sheriff of the Guilds and the Lord of the Unattached, the British titles reminding those familiar with the history of European spectacles of the London Lord Mayor's parade. [83]

As in the case of Comus's parade, the Rex procession included a stop at City Hall, making to the mayor and receiving in turn appropriate gestures of acknowledgment. From the beginning, too, it was perfectly good form to go to the Rex ball unmasked. Proper attire was well regarded and comic costuming was accepted, within limits. As Edward King wrote in 1873, commenting on Rex and Comus and the atmosphere which they had generated by that date, "comparing the Carnival in Louisiana with the Carnival in reckless Italy, one might say that the Americans masqueraded grimly. There is but little of that wild luxuriance of

8. Rex Parade, New Orleans, 1873. "Totila?" (photo, Norman Magden, from *Scribner's Monthly*, November 1873)

fun in the streets of New Orleans which has made Naples and Rome so famous; people go to their sports with an air of pride, but not of all-pervading enjoyment."[84] Pride more than enjoyment: that was indeed the aim of Rex and Comus and their early imitators. The conjunction of Confederate resentment, social despair, and withal a sharp eye for touristic appeal explains the style.

Comus appears today in a mask which has a benign, insipid expression. Used for centuries in European Carnivals, this mask-type is often found there in tandem with those displaying grimacing features, such as those of devils or witches.[85] Comus's mask is that of the good-natured fool, aloof from life and politics. Rex, on the other hand, does not wear a mask. He has always been immediately recognizable as a man of distinction and propriety. The group behind the new monarch called itself not a "mystic crew" but the "Rex Organization" or "Rex Association."

Its motto was "Pro Bono Publico," "for the public good."[86] "The Rex Association was conceived and brought into being through the wisdom and patriotism of some of the public-spirited citizens of our city," declared the aged Colonel George Soulé in 1922 (he had been Rex of New Orleans in 1887). "For half a century the Rex Association has presented its Royal Pro Bono Publico Balls and receptions at its Imperial Palace, without a dollar's expense to the city or state. The funds are supplied by the dues of its members and by a few subscriptions from business men who receive souvenirs and are commercially benefited by the visiting public."[87] The connection of business to civic good could not be put more clearly nor more imperially, unless it be expressed by a relative of the king of 1887, Edward E. Soulé, Rex of Carnival in 1931, speaking in 1950 to the officers, captain, former kings of Carnival "and other worthy gentlemen of the organization":

> Now Gentlemen before we proceed with the introduction of the King, let us pause for a brief moment to consider the present much mooted question of whether or not we are overdoing the Carnival business in New Orleans. . . . The older parade organizations have full membership. It is a difficult matter to join any one of them. . . . It follows then that other organizations must provide for other pleasure seekers. . . . Remember this is a democratic form of government and every good citizen has the same personal right as you have and I have.[88]

George Soulé's references to Imperial Palace balls "for the public good," Edward Soulé's insistence that "other" Carnival societies be formed on the democratic principle of exclusion from older organizations like Rex and Comus, express with clarity the important part which the Rex Organization has played in transforming Carnival from an aristocratic peculiarity, accompanied by annoying street extensions, into a flexibly expanding and civically responsive elitism. The hierarchic drive to power which provides so much of the steam of social aspiration in democratic polities has in New Orleans found a proper organization, a publicly recognized form. Comus was incomplete without Rex. The private-society idea needed a civic dimension in order to survive in a democratically organized polity.

Rex has become over the years the common denominator and at the same time the enlargement of the other parading societies' pretensions to grandeur. It anchors and legitimates them with a vague communitarian rhetoric. Its symbolic vocabulary is commonplace, expressing the typical populist dreams of monarchic heroism, so that its inventions, for all their frequent splendor, tended to pale before those of Comus, Momus, or Proteus in the late nineteenth century, and they remain less daring than the extraordinary floats of Bacchus and Endymion today. The Rex parades are a reassuring center-pole, around which other extravagances can flourish.

In the same year that Rex was invented in New Orleans, Emperor Felix was created in Mobile by a group of fourteen men. Organization and intentions were parallel.[89] By 1875 the "emperor" was also being referred to as His Imperial Majesty King Felix. Unlike Rex, King or Emperor Felix—his title continued to vary[90]—did not accompany his procession with thematic floats. In later years it became the custom for one of Mobile's elite societies, the Knights of Revelry, to follow his parade with their pageant. In the 1870s and 1880s, however, Felix's parade was a magnet drawing behind it the same miscellany as that in the Rex parade: after the "uniformed bands of music, heralds and bodyguards and marshals in glittering garb . . . [and] mounted nobles and cavalry" came "various 'day clubs,' temporary organizations representing odd designs," and finally "individual maskers, mounted and on foot—some grand and stately, others bizarre as the members of the Witches' Sabbath. . . ."[91]

Parallel to New Orleans, too, was the formation of new elite societies in Mobile during the economically and politically disastrous period following the Civil War. When New Orleans' Twelfth-Night Revellers chose in 1870 to parade on January 6, they snobbishly upstaged Comus by reminding Orleanians of the old colonial Christmastime celebrations with their *bals du roi*.[92]

In a similar elite manner the most exclusive festive society in Mobile today, the Order of Myths, chose upon its foundation in 1867 to reverse the Mobile tendency to concentrate festivity around New Year's, the time of the Cowbellions, Strikers, and T.D.S. society balls. They established their celebration on the date that the plebeian but patriotic Joe Cain had chosen: mardi gras. Presumably they had an eye to the prestige of Comus in nearby New Orleans as well. The emblem chosen by the five youthful organizers of the society was appropriately ambivalent. To many of the city's elite it became generally symbolic of Mobile's Mardi Gras, as Comus's goblet did in New Orleans. The central part of the emblem is a broken Corinthian column, that Greco-Roman ornament used on the facade of so many early nineteenth-century Southern mansions. In the earliest published version of the emblem two figures, a skeleton and a jester clad in traditional cap and bells, are seated on opposite sides of the base of the column. No one knows the intentions of the designers or the interpretations of early members of the society. But later commentators see the column as the "broken hopes of the Confederacy" or "life broken off at its apex," interpretations appropriate to white Mobile in 1867.[93] In a representation of the emblem in 1878 the jester, called Folly today, seems to be encouraging the skeleton, now called Death, to dance a jig with him, but Death pulls away.[94] It has become the custom for Folly to pursue Death around the column on the float and to strike him with gold- and silver-colored bladders attached to sticks. According to Bennett Wayne Dean, the first to impersonate Folly on the lead float of the society was none other than Joseph Cain.[95]

In 1870 the Order of Myths was joined by a group calling itself the H.S.S., the initials in this case standing for a Latin motto which proved less than satisfactory, so that they changed their name to "Infant Mystics" in 1873; they paraded on mardi gras evening. The Knights of Revelry, another elite group which still parades today, was formed in 1874.[96]

What goes up most often comes down, sooner or later. Pretentiousness in Carnival has always called forth satire. The H.S.S. in 1871 devoted its parade to the theme, "Burlesque of Secret Societies in Mobile." One authority argues that the T.D.S. society acquired its deflationary name, the "Tea Drinking Society," on this occasion. On this interpretation the initials were originally supposed to stand for "the determined set," and to represent an attempt to distinguish this group from the earlier Strikers and Cowbellions.[97]

With Mobile's Carnival one is never sure about how much is due to provincialism and how much to a well-tuned sense of the grotesque. "Infant Mystics": was the name propounded as a subtle undoing of the story—apparently unfounded; in any case, undocumented—that the carnival societies emanated not from Krafft's disreputable antics but from the activities of a grave and spiritual "Spanish mystic society" existing in Mobile's dim eighteenth-century past?[98] Or is "infant" an honorific rather than satirically puerile term, vaunting the society's lineage? The old emblem of the society, when it was known—mystically?— as H.S.S., was a cotton bale with the letters H.S.S. ("Hoc Signo Sustineat") imprinted on the side. The new emblem of the Infant Mystics includes the old, but the H.S.S. cotton bale (now emblazoned "I.M.") appears as a kind of circus stool for an elephant rampant, "symbol of unfailing remembrance"; the elephant faces a knight, part of the old H.S.S. coat of arms, "symbol of undying chivalry." Between the two is a cat, "symbol of all things inscrutable." Is this delicious hodgepodge of signs and countersigns seriously meant?[99]

By 1874 Joe Cain's group advertised itself in the local newspaper as led not by an unconquered Indian but by "the King of the Carnival," "Old Slac." The accompanying illustration, made according to the announcement by the "Lord High Pictoriographer of the Minstrels," shows a man in a high fur hat like those worn by Her Britannic Majesty's guards outside Buckingham Palace today, beating with drumsticks on a large bass drum on which the words "Lost Cause Minstrel Band" are written. "This year Old Slac invites all maskers, horse, wagon, cart, foot and dragons to join him in one grand procession through the city," concludes the announcement.[100] (See plate 9.) Whether there was an Emperor Felix that year or only the remembrance of the personage from the two preceding years' parades, Slackabamorinico's pretensions undercut that inflated emblem in an amusingly uncouth way which recaptures the homespun manner of the early Cowbellions.[101]

The Lost Cause Minstrels disappeared from Carnival in the late 1870s. The penalty of continuous inventiveness is exhaustion; only the uninteresting can be conveniently repeated. This

9. Advertisement in Mobile Weekly Register, 1874 (photo, Ray Tallow, from Museum of the City of Mobile)

is true even of Gulf Coast Carnival's most long-lived subversive society, the Comic Cowboys who in 1984 commemorated their hundredth anniversary. They were founded by a Jewish shipping clerk in a dry-goods store with some vaudeville experience on the side. Dave Levi was certainly influenced by the style of Cain's shenanigans. But he widened the sense of what could be pleasurably lampooned. His first parade was a simple satire of circus spectacles, a direct reference to the Carver Wild West Show which had performed in Mobile a few weeks before mardi gras. Levi issued a circus broadside in four sheets, perhaps thrown from the floats in his parade, which read in part:

The Greatest Novelty for Ten Centuries!
The Wildest Westest Gang. . .
The Evil Spirit of Mobile with his Book-keepers, Oyster Openers [oysters were a favorite cheap food in Mobile] and Dry Goods Clerks, etc. will surely astonish the natives of Mobile with their splendor. . . .
Part 1st.
Grand March of the Yahoos, introducing Dr. Cutter of the Gulf City Gun Club, who will . . . with his Scatter Gun shoot Watches, Diamond Rings and such other trifles as the ladies along the line may furnish.
Part 2d.
Grand Match Race between two Boss Oyster Openers
Part 3d.
Three Red Toy Balloons to be let go at once.
Part 4th.
Recitation by one of our most prominent Beer Saloon Keepers, (entitled)
"Vy do dey klose me on Sundays." . . .
Part 9th.
The Wonderful One Horse Drag making the time from Commerce street to the Steamboat Landing in one hour and forty minutes which on an average would make it twice around the public square.[102]

The local newspaper was ecstatic: "In all the years of day parades . . . nothing funnier has ever been seen than the burlesque pageant of 'Doctor Cutter's Wildest Westest Show'. . . ." Dr. Cutter rode first with a man in Chickasaw costume at his side called Eagle Eye, followed by scores of cowboys and Indians, a mule-drawn stagecoach, a float with a papier-mâché wild boar garnished with vegetables, a squaw hauling an Indian cradle with a red-feathered chief drinking from "the Little Brown Jug" planted between his feet, and so on.[103]

The parade combined appeal to widely known clichés of popular spectacle common in late nineteenth-century America with many references to local places and people. Levi's sense of humor localized Carnival rather than basing it on flight to the remotely exotic and mythological. The nicest touch was the illustration on the back side of the broadsheet, which made gentle fun of the white-tie formality of the upper-class Carnival-society balls. In a vaguely rustic setting under leafy trees a number of rabbits are shown holding each other's paws and dancing in a ring. Some are wearing long gowns and others are in swallowtail coats. The accompanying inscription reads:

> [At the top] We are so glad we are going to the Circus. [At the bottom] This card will admit you to the grand performance which takes place immediately after the parade.

In 1886 a similar satire was distributed to the Carnival crowd:

> M____, the felicity of your company is urgently desired to enjoy a soul-stirring Reception, Crazy Quilt Party, Mikado Bazaar and Ice Cream Festival which will be held this day at the airy, elegant, and spacious Mobile and Ohio Railroad Sheds. . . . To prevent any jam or sweet confusion the Police Board has decided to allow access via Conti, Dauphin and Government streets to the wild scene of revel. The Bottle Corps has been detailed at the request of 782 of our best citizens, including the Comic Cow Boys, and will discourse sure enough music, the See-Saw Waltz exclusively. . . . [104]

The 1888 parade of the Cowboys was announced by a card with a large cow-head engraved at the top, slaver dripping from its jaw, and the words:

> C.C.B.'s: Their Fifth Anniversary, A Big Boom in Local Satire! Mixed Pickles!

The ninth float in that year's parade was entitled "Dream of a Mobile Coon." It showed a bed with a black man dreaming unhappily. Above his head was suspended a black angel with outspread wings, holding a sign with the cabalistic number 4-11-44. At the foot of the bed was a huge opened razor with the inscription "Bad Man." The Comic Cowboys were ready to undo the pretensions of would-be aristocrats, but they also played their part in keeping black people in their place. [105]

As the features of Carnival and local life evolved, so the Comic Cowboys shifted their targets. Although they had their own special cookbook of satiric recipes, they finally depended on the actions of others to provide the ingredients for their witty clambakes. [106]

In New Orleans a parallel to the Comic Cowboys became a standard part of the parade, following Rex, between 1878 and

1885: the Phunny Phorty Phellows. The group was first organized by members of New Orleans' Mississippi Fire Company
No. 2, but was subsequently supported by "businessmen," according to the chief chronicler of New Orleans' Mardi Gras,
Perry Young.[107] In 1880 the parade was especially long and replete with references to local politicians and social issues. The
third section of the parade, entitled "Our Guests the City Fathers," consisted of a line of dilapidated carriages housing "The
Lord Mayor and Boss of the Finance Department," writes
Young, "clothed in ermine [and betopped] with immense heads
of papier maché (each principal character in the entire procession was in heroic caricature and of unmistakable resemblance);
the Lord of Assessments and Keeper of Accounts; the Chief
Clubber (administrator of police); the Engineer of Shanties and
Plugs (administrator of waterworks and public buildings); the
Jack of Spades (administrator of improvements); the Proprietor
of Levee Privileges (administrator of commerce)." Ethnic groups
were caricatured with costumes and stereotyped accouterments:
Ye Ancient Order of Hibernicons, The Deutscher Verein, the
Italian de Macaroni Christo Colombo Societee.[108] Developing
similar satiric and caricatural themes, a second group joined the
Phunny Phorty Phellows in the Rex parade after 1881. It was
called the Independent Order of the Moon. In that year both
groups parodied prominent women. Sarah Bernhardt, who had
appeared in New Orleans, was lampooned on one float. A
prominent feminist, Dr. Mary Walker, who had served as a sur-
geon in the Union Army during the Civil War and had adopted
men's clothes, was depicted as chief of police, leading a group of
her "officers," all in bloomers and ruffles. These locally oriented
satires, it is reported, were as popular as those in Mobile. Like
the latter, they also parodied the high-toned gatherings of the
older Carnival societies, as in 1881 in the couplet poeticizing the
theme of the Phunny Phorty Phellows ball: 'Music hath charms
to soothe a savage/To bust a rock and split a cabbage."[109]

Gulf Coast Carnival has its peculiar traditions. Their peculiarity
is due not simply to the special history of that part of the world
but to the mixture of local conditions with more general ones. In
a previous chapter I emphasized Caribbean-African influences;
in this chapter I have until now emphasized Anglo-American
ones. But the deepest roots of Gulf Coast Carnival are European.
In the Introduction the idea of the carnivalesque, as developed
over some eight hundred years and given particularly full

expression during the European Renaissance, was said to revolve around ambivalence. This ambivalence is itself ambivalent. It refers not only to the notion that in Carnival any symbol will always prove to have two sides, both of them sooner or later exploited. It also means that the gestures of Carnival move in two directions: toward trespass and toward totality, toward expression and indulgence in excess and toward encompassing enlargement of every sort of limit.

The Infant Mystics with their cat and elephant and Latin motto may have been and may still be very serious about their undying chivalry. But this chivalry is exercised during Carnival, the moment when all things also mean their opposite. Infant or mature, the members of the society have no control over that ambivalence, that enlarged framework in terms of which their actions are seen. The same larger framework applies to the activities of Comus. Their first parade was darkly or lightly ambivalent, depending upon the spectator's own attitude, since it juxtaposed in its two floats the quintessential Protestant judgment of Carnival—the festival as the work of the devil—to the quintessential Catholic one—the festival as a time of pagan release, of Comus-jolly excess before the sobrieties of Lent. Comus's succeeding shows became less interesting. They exploited the society's reputation for splendor and abandoned its attachment to carnivalesque ambivalence . . . until after the Civil War when, prompted by anger and political opportunity, Comus briefly resumed the genuinely carnivalesque role of satirizing officially endorsed norms. But if the Darwin parade enlarged the boundaries of contemporary consciousness, giving exotic, excessive form to current ills, it also narrowed them, giving amplified form to racism and a know-nothing anti-intellectualism. It is absurd to attach any moral quality to Carnival beyond the very general virtue of ventilation.

Carnival is so ambivalent in nature that it produces its own opposite, which is mechanical, spiritless, drab repetition. If applause greets a Mardi Gras gesture and it feels good, its success encourages its incorporation in a traditional repertory. Since it worked this year, why not do it again? Inevitably, then, Mardi Gras parades exhibit many loads of dead wood, antique traditions blindly repeated from year to year until they are knocked off the float-wagons by the genius of excess and enlargement, which has inspired someone else's inventions and drawn from the crowd bigger yells of glee.

The contrast between invention and repetition, between the

carnivalesque and the traditional, gives a dynamic pattern to Carnival's unfolding qualities over the years. After several seasons Joe Cain and his friends abandoned the guise of the Chickasaw chief to lay more emphasis on lost-cause minstreling, as we have seen. After the minstrelsy wore thin and no new ideas occurred, the group simply stopped parading. The destiny of the main subjects of this chapter, however, has been different: The elite societies, however stilted their repertory, have maintained themselves. From time to time, coerced by others' inventions, they have refreshed their pageantry. But their power has been their continuity, that is, their conventionality. There are many reasons for this, most of which will be explored in a later chapter. One of them can be suggested and exemplified here.

In the developing mass society of the later nineteenth century, in a New Orleans which had lost its earlier moorings in the aftermath of the Civil War, Carnival-as-pure-disorder was an impossible option. Anchorless throngs, less and less connected by ethnic or neighborly ties, required an image of convention within Carnival in relation to which they could exercise their debasing verve and comic excess. The elite Carnival societies came to play that stabilizing role, first in New Orleans and later in Mobile as well.

The origins of the Mistick Krewe of Comus were nearly as waggish as those of the delightfully grotesque Cowbellions, but they were quickly erased by success and self-consciousness. We can measure the change and the move toward assumption of a stabilizing role by the elimination from consciousness of the meaning of Comus's name. We have noticed that the first element of that name, "mistick," was probably related to Gothic-Romantic style and feeling, parodied in the initiation of Comus's new members "with a serio-comic take off of the ancient mysteries." This element of Comus's carnivalism remained conscious and consciously imitated by other Carnival societies until at least the 1920s when, for example, "The Mystic Club" was founded in New Orleans. And it is still common today to speak of "Mobile's mystics" in reference to the ensemble of groups participating in Carnival.[110]

In New Orleans the more usual term for the Carnival societies is "krewe"; the popularity of the word bespeaks the prestige of Comus, which was first to use it. But what does "krewe" mean? No one, it seems, has bothered to inquire. The society's commemorative brochure does not explain either "mistick" or "krewe" but instead concentrates on the elegant appropriateness of the Greek element of its name:

> On the 8th of February, 1857, at a succeeding meeting
> [after the first organizational meeting on January 10],
> Mr. J. H. Pope [owner of a local drug store and one of
> the original six founders from Mobile], well versed in
> the classics, suggested as a name for the organization,
> The Mistick Krewe of Comus. Comus, from the Greek
> Komos, meaning revel or a company of revellers, was in
> the later Greek mythology the God of Festive Mirth. . . .

Ben Jonson, the history continues, included Comus in one of his masques and Milton did, too, "whose Comus is a more refined creation."[111]

By the twentieth century, when this account of Comus's history was written, the leading sense of "crew" was a ship's body of men. This sense was already prominent in the 1850s, but it coexisted with older meanings. The word crew is recorded from the mid-fifteenth century onward in the sense of a band or company of soldiers used to augment a regular force. From the mid-sixteenth century this sense was extended to mean any number of persons gathered in association. It was used by Lyly, Spenser, Shakespeare, and Milton both positively and negatively to describe such groups: "a noble crew of lords and ladies"; "a vulgar crue"; "a joviall crew"; "this monstrous tattered crew." But never before Comus's nineteenth-century invention, it seems, was the word spelled "krewe."[112]

There is only one relevant meaning of crew, insofar as its selection by J. H. Pope as the name for the Carnival society is concerned. That is the meaning which Milton gave to it in his hardly "refined" portrait of Comus in the masque *Comus*, presented at Ludlow Castle in 1634 for the earl of Bridgewater.[113] Comus is a demon, as ominous as the devils in the poet's *Paradise Lost*, the very subject, we recall, of the new society's first parade. The meaning of crew as J. H. Pope saw it was presumably determined by its association with this Comus, for it is Comus's action in Milton's poem which creates, out of scattered individuals, a distinctive association of persons, a "crew."

Comus is not merely a reveler like his father Bacchus but a sorcerer like his mother Circe. Indeed he

> Excels his mother at her mighty art,
> Offering to every weary traveller
> His orient liquor in a crystal glass. . . .[114]

Comus's goblet of "orient liquor" still plays an important role in the society's ceremonies.[115] In Milton's masque whoever tastes the liquid is changed in countenance "into some brutish form of wolf, or bear . . . or tiger, hog, or bearded goat, all other parts

remaining as they were." The group of monstrously transformed wayfarers in Comus's magic forest

> Not once perceive their foul disfigurement
> But boast themselves more comely than before,
> And all their friends and native home forget,
> To roll with pleasure in a sensuous sty.[116]

Such is Milton's vision, and such was J. H. Pope's and the society's first vision of themselves. The list of dramatis personae at
the head of Milton's poem refers to them so: "Comus, and his
Crew."[117]

The same grotesque sense of humor which led the Cowbellions to march about their hall garbed in cows' heads and drinking from a bull's horn presided at the founding of Comus. Their
first parade and subsequent tableaux, in which the krewe impersonated "the Fates, the Furies, the fallen angels, Sin, Death,
[and] all the vices poor humanity is subject to," was, we may
surmise, not merely an extension of and extrapolation from Milton's *Paradise Lost* but also from Milton's *Comus*.[118]

How did this demonic Comus and his crew turn into the Mistick
Krewe of Comus, and why did the word become the generic
term for carnival society? The archaic spelling of "mystic" and
"crew" lent to the words the glow of England's most glamorous
epoch, the age of Elizabeth with its great seafarers like Walter
Raleigh and Francis Drake.[119] Was it J. H. Pope again or some
other member or members of the society who suggested the
Elizabethan patter used on the banner of the first float of 1858,
introducing their parade presentation of "Mythology"? "Marry
but you travellers may journey far and look not on this like
again. Here you do behold the Gods and Goddesses, presently
you shall see them unfold themselves."[120]

The archaism was fashionable: it was part and parcel of the
Romantic era's enthusiasm for the bygone and the exotic. Contemporary audiences may also have caught a phonetic resonance to which the late twentieth-century ear is perhaps less
sensitive, a resonance of k-sounds. The English-language part
of the New Orleans newspaper *L'Abeille* reported two days after
the first parade of the society: "For what purpose the strange
'Krewe of Komus', as they style themselves, have . . . set their
vessel at sail over a sea of mystical ceremonies . . . [is some-
thing] to be answered only within the widest limits of vague
conjecture. A kurious Kompanie of four skore or more seem to
have set sail for this with a rare kargo of mysticisms, kollected

under the direction of a kritical superkargo, kurioso, supernu-
merary virtuoso of Komus, an island as yet unlocated. . . ."[121]

"Krewe" became popular because it was mysterious and yet
understandable, connecting an English seafaring past to an
American commercial present. (The name designating the person who became the chief officer of this and later krewes, the
"captain," carries these associations further.) The word became
popular because the krewe of Comus was prestigious. And the
krewe of Comus, having become prestigious, forgot its Milton.
When the society celebrated its fiftieth anniversary in 1906 by
presenting as its parade theme "Comus, A Masque by Milton,"
the title float reduced the theme to an innocuous image of gaiety.
This is how the title float is described in the "Comus edition" of
the *Carnival Bulletin*, a handbill published in February 1906 (see
plate 10):

> This masque [by Milton] . . . in honor of whose titular
> deity the Mistick Krewe of Comus is named, was . . .
> given at Ludlow Castle, Shropshire, England. . . It was
> a magnificent spectacle worthy of the time and occasion

10. Title Float, Comus Parade, New Orleans, 1906 (photo, Norman
Magden, from *Carnival Bulletin*, Mardi Gras day, 1906, courtesy of New
Orleans Public Library)

and ended with a dance or ball of equal splendor. . . . [The title float of Comus is then illustrated in a drawing.] Surrounded by an enormous mass of luscious, royally tinted grapes that seem well-nigh bursting with juicy fruitiness, a life-like mask, beribboned at either side, rests against a chiseled goblet of precious metal. In it is to be seen that liquor so deliciously red and exhilarating. A jovial and merry look glints from the eye spaces of the smiling mask, the reflected look of the whimsical god himself.[122]

In Comus's goblet there is no mysteriously transforming "orient liquor." There is just red wine, and the most that one can expect to extract from it are smiles and whimsy.

# Sex

It was almost as if men had decided to take the place of the ladies. Once upon a time, "in our spacious, richly ornamented ballrooms, where the glitter of a thousand candles is multiplied a thousandfold by mirrors, two hundred young beauties" had rivaled each other "for grace, elegance, vivacity and youthful ardor."[1] After the Carnival societies were founded, Comus and Rex and Chief Slackabamorinico and the Phunny Phorty Phellows replaced these beauties in the public eye. Did this have to do with the gathering thunder of Victorian morality, enjoining modesty and homebound retirement on the feminine sex? Was it the difference between Latin and Anglo-Saxon notions of proper male and female behavior? Or did it signal the coming to maturity of a raw Western town, where the scarcity of women and family life had led temporarily to an unusual amount of female display at the balls and in the theaters? There was a certain consistency between such changes as these in the sexual boundaries of the public and private spheres in mid-century New Orleans and the privatization through the Carnival societies of that hitherto most prominent symbol of Mardi Gras in New Orleans, the masked ball.

Male dominance in Carnival did not last long. In the early 1870s the custom of choosing queens to reign over the societies' balls began. The innovation was in one sense a revival, for the balls at Christmastime during colonial and early American times had frequently involved selection of kings and queens to reign over the festivities. It had been a traditional part of Twelfth-Night celebration, too: if a male received the slice of cake with the bean, then that evening's ball or banquet was ruled by a king; if a female, then by a queen. When the Twelfth Night Revelers celebrated their first ball in 1870 at the new Opera House there was supposed to be a bean in the huge cake, but in the exuberance of the Revelers' distribution of the cake to the ladies seated around the parquet, it was lost. In 1871 the society prepared affairs more carefully. The Lord of Misrule, knowing which slice contained the bean, observed with care the lady who received it and proceeded to crown her queen of the ball with a wreath of oak leaves.[2]

The women of New Orleans were not above the most boisterous tactics when it came to seeking admission to the exclusive balls. As the anonymous authors of the brochure chronicling activities of the Krewe of Comus drily comment, after citing the commendable service of General Beauregard at one of the portals to their ball, "Again in 1869 at the old French Opera House, uninvited ladies actually formed a 'flying wedge' and tried to push themselves through the entrance. Six of them fainted and others had their clothes so torn that they had to go home."[3] The incident verifies our metaphor for the social process displayed in American Carnival: setting up an elite measure of festivity in a society whose larger ideology is democratic sooner or later converts a barrier into a crossing-point. In the years after 1870 women widened their wedge into a position of dominance at the balls.

Rex originally had no consort. His first queen, chosen in 1873 on the occasion of Rex's first ball, was not told of her coming honor in advance. She was the wife of a diplomat who had served as a colonel in the Confederate Army. His royal highness, after marching around the ballroom with his attendants, halted before the astonished lady and persuaded her, in Perry Young's revealing words, "that the cushion at his feet was for her knees." For the moment at least males were still in control. Having received the royal diadem, Rex escorted her to the throne and the Earl Marshal announced that king *and* queen would jointly receive their subjects.[4]

The next breach in the male-managed system was the publication of ladies' names in the newspapers. This was shocking. As late as 1881 the editors of the *Democrat* had proclaimed that "The principal beauty of woman is modesty, and the ladies we know and admire would blush to see their names and accoutrements published in the public prints." The *Democrat's* rival, the *Picayune*, had nevertheless delivered the name of the first Queen of the Twelfth Night Revelers to all and sundry as early as 1871, and in 1878 it described the elegant costumes of half a dozen young maidens at the Revelers' ball. In 1879 both the *Picayune* and the *Times* began to publish regular features written by women, discussing social affairs. In the early 1880s all the newspapers began publishing lists of the women selected by members of the "krewes" to dance with them on the first occasion after conclusion of their tableaux, a custom named "callout" which still persists at the societies' balls.[5]

In 1880 Rex made known his choice for a consort during his parade rather than more privately at the ball. He presented one Miss Rathbone with a bouquet. By this time his queens were unmarried young ladies. Momus and Proteus both selected queens at their balls after 1882, but Comus resisted. In 1884, however, Comus's Krewe invited five daughters of Confederate generals and of the Confederate president, Jefferson Davis, as honored guests. Comus paid Miss Mildred Lee special respect by escorting her to the floor for the first quadrille. In later years, when it had become customary for Comus also to select a queen and maids, this occasion was recalled as the moment when Comus chose his first court. Meanwhile Rex and his queen and court had begun in 1882 to visit Comus's ball, and Comus's krewe had begun to prepare the left-hand proscenium box at the opera house to receive them. Thus in 1884 the right-hand box was filled by the "daughters of the Confederacy," as they came to be called, and by several high Confederate officers and members of the daughters' families, including the former president, Jefferson Davis, while the left-hand box, decorated with a floral tribute labeled "From Comus to the Queen," housed the Rex group.[6] (It is still the custom for Rex and his court to come to Comus's ball. Today this is done at midnight on mardi gras. The two courts meet, Rex and Comus escort each other's queens in a grand march, Rex waves his scepter, and Carnival is ended for another year.)

By the mid–1880s the Carnival societies' spectacles were becoming less a place for successful men to strut than for their wives, daughters, and fiancées to display their charms. It became impossible to attend the balls without high hat and tails for the men and long gowns for the women. Only the parading members of the krewe appeared in masquerade. From the 1890s the women to be honored in the first dance with krewe members were placed in a special seating section so that everyone might see them as they were "called out." The newspapers passed from naming names to including photographs of the pseudo-kings, pseudo-queens, and their courts in 1898, beginning with the Proteus court. By 1900 it had become the custom for Rex to salute his queen publicly when he passed the reviewing stands in front of the Boston Club on Canal Street.[7]

These traditions developed in a parallel but more halting and modest way at Mobile. The first consort of Emperor Felix seems to have been honored in 1893.[8] By the early twentieth century a system of circulating the imaginary honors of royalty among young women of the best families by displaying the debutantes of a given year in the courts of the Carnival societies had emerged here as also in New Orleans.

Connecting the fun and games of Carnival to the more serious business of showing off eligible young women to the right people was not the intention but the result of the gradual elaboration of the Carnival societies' rituals. But the idea had certainly never been absent from white elite celebrations. In fact it was inseparable from the decorative manner of life prescribed for all Southern women of the upper classes until well into the twentieth century. As a Mobile queen explained in an interview in 1981 at the age of seventy-five, "In those days [the 1910s, the 1920s] it was different. Girls didn't go back to school after making their debuts. My father [a grain merchant] didn't believe in women having too much education." "Mobile was a wonderful place to live. There were always balls, parties, and things going on at the Country Club."[9] For such people Carnival was not an inversion, not even an enlargement, but simply an extension of everyday life.

The organizational efficacy and perfectly geared social functions of Carnival contrasted then and still contrast now with the cultural discontinuities displayed in the celebration. The ambitiously grand symbols which are employed clash with the balls' frequently commonplace ambiance and the gestural awkwardness of kings and queens for a day. I was struck by this in 1982 at Mobile, when I witnessed the ballroom scenes staged by one of the top-ranked societies.

Most parades, like that of this society, pass through the main streets and halt at the 12,500-seat Municipal Auditorium, a cavern of concrete where the balls of the parading societies are usually held. I had been given a ticket to sit in the stands above the floor and observe affairs. Some non-parading members ("honorary" memberships are available for the elderly in the society who have ceased to ride floats in the parade, and "associate" memberships exist for those who do not wish to ride) moved to a special boxed-off space at one end of the dance floor. At 9:00 p.m. sharp the lights went down (which made the "Have a Bud" neon-light sign up near the roof of the auditorium sparkle more brightly); the band played the Marine Corps Anthem. A master of ceremonies stepped to a microphone and stage curtains opened to reveal the leader of the ball and the queen seated in a fairyland atmosphere (puffy clouds of white smoke floated mistily around their thrones).[10] The MC announced to this grandeur and to us the names of each member of the Carnival society and the lady he was escorting, as they came forward couple by couple. After a bow and curtsey to leader and queen these couples marched proudly or dance-stepped their way (the band was playing) in a spotlight across the vast dance floor to the opposite side of the arena, above which we visitors were seated. The women were dressed glitteringly in bejewelled and fashionably modern gowns while the men were still clothed in their parade costumes, so that they stood out in sometimes bizarre contrast to the ladies (see Plate 11, a similar scene.)

Then the Great Moment arrived. All lights were concentrated on the leading pair, who were in fact—and this is frequently the case—father and daughter. With few exceptions the balls' leading ladies have not been married women. The queen was accompanied by her peers, a half-dozen other elegantly gowned young ladies. Until the night of the ball a young woman was supposed to know only whether she had been chosen to be in this court. Only when the "royal" limousine arrived at her door a short time before the ball

11. Masked ball, Mobile: Knights of Revelry, 1972 (photo courtesy of Dr. S. P. Dowling)

was she expected to realize that she had been chosen as queen. A wealthy man, if he is prepared to spend sufficiently, can insure his daughter's queenly status when her debut occurs. As the band played a stately piece of mush ("This is the best of times . . . Oh, honey, we have made history here tonight," the singer crooned), the proud father escorted the lovely girl slowly around the ballroom while she benignly nodded.

Social ambition and a naive delight in spectacle have been made congruent here with a variety of local complacencies. These balls are not for dancing, but for showing who belongs.[11] One needs to experience it in order to believe. Just visiting the rows of costumes, classified by year, in the showcases of the city museum of Mobile or in those of the Louisiana State Museum at New Orleans is not enough. Or perhaps the art of the novelist is needed to illumine the manner in which, from the late nineteenth century onward, a place in a queen's court became a new reason for focusing social energy and cultural activity on Mardi Gras. Consider these scenes evoked by Edward Tinker, scenes along St. Charles Avenue and Canal Street in the Carnivals of the 1940s and 1950s:

> Little bands of maskers overflowing with happy anticipation begin to appear on St. Charles Avenue along which the Rex parade is to pass. . . . The galleries are draped with bunting in the gay Carnival colors, and large flags, diagonally divided by single broad golden stripes with solitary crowns in the middle, leaving triangles of green above and purple below, swing lazily in front of every house in which a King or Queen of past Carnivals lives. That is a prerogative of royalty! By nine o'clock groups of old ladies are gathered in front of the Boston and Pickwick Clubs, waiting patiently, and, when the doors are finally opened, they surge forward. . . . Up the stairs they hobble and pant, across the slippery ballroom floor and out through the tall French windows to settle down with sighs of satisfied exhaustion in the front seats of the grandstands erected across the second stories of the two clubs. . . . Every old lady . . . is just as excited as though she were herself a debutante; each has her stake in the spangled game: some daughter, niece or cousin; or, lacking that, the child of some old family friend may be Queen of Rex or Comus, or among the Maids; and they are sure to have relatives on the floats.[12]

In the late nineteenth and early twentieth centuries women of proper society in New Orleans and Mobile reserved their power for the semiprivate sphere of the ball, with the exception of Rex's queen, who briefly appeared in public. But from the gay nineties onward they found ways to use that sphere in more dominant, less decorative ways. The "first women's organization in Mobile composed of society ladies," writes B.W. Dean, gave a ball several weeks before Carnival in 1890, a ball at which the women all dressed in "pink domino costumes." They called themselves "M.W.M.," which Dean translates as "masked ladies and mystified gentlemen." [13] Were the men perhaps "mystified" because they were treated like those at New Orleans in 1896, where women gave a ball at which the queen and maids were masked while the king and dukes sat unmasked before them, waiting to be called out? The pretext in the latter case was the folkloric tradition that in leap year women, not men, may take the initiative in heterosexual contact. The second tableau ball of Les Mysterieuses, as this female Carnival society called itself, occurred during the next leap year in 1900, but after that the organization ceased to exist. [14]

In the 1920s, age of the flapper, roles changed further, although women still avoided parading publicly. Ihe Krewe of Iris, founded in 1922, was headed by a woman impersonating the goddess. Arthur La Cour's description recaptures the founding atmosphere: Iris, Goddess of the Rainbow, "directed the fair matrons of her comely Krewe through rhythmical movements under the myriad hues of the rainbow. The golden vessel at the end of the colourful spectrum overflowed with happiness bestowed upon the prominent beau of the period, J. Marion Legendre, who beamed as the first king of the Krewe of Iris." [15] Just as the queens were supposed to be unmarried young women, displaying their charms to a select but maritally interested few, so King Legendre would seem to have been selected for his attractive availability. It was not until 1923 that a married woman could become queen of one of the Carnival societies in New Orleans, and wedded pairs were first selected for a Carnival court in 1948. [16] A further step for middle-class white women's role in Carnival was taken in 1941, when the first parading women's group appeared, the Krewe of Venus; a second parading women's krewe appeared in 1959. [17] As for men and women parading together on the basis of equal prestige, that had to await the 1960s. [18]

From 1870 to the present male dominance has been slowly eroded, first in the ballroom and then in the streets. Women's pretensions have not gone unsatirized. The queen of Mobile's Comic Cowboys, who seems to have appeared for the first time in 1917, has always been a transvestite male. Beginning in 1930 this queen has been a female version of the traditional fatman figure in Carnival.[19] Charlie Blanchard, weighing some three hundred pounds, performed the role until 1937, and was then replaced by Johnny Loris, who rode in a wagon drawn by a double team of horses. Its placard read: "Eva, A Quarter Ton of Queen."[20] In 1981 Queen Eva's placard defiantly declared her to be "not the prettiest but always the biggest."[21]

But the subject of male and female ideals and counterideals in Mardi Gras is only grazed if it is limited to women's participation in Carnival societies. There are two reasons for this. One is the general character of Carnival and the other is the particular character of sexual relations at New Orleans.

Sex has always been as central as food to Carnival expressions of excess and enlargement. This was inevitable. The Catholic church's ban on fleshly indulgence during Lent enjoined from the earliest medieval times not only no meat but no sexual activity. Whether the latter was ever preached, let alone practiced, along the Gulf Coast is another matter. But the tradition and its ritual consequences were there, coercing people's subconscious sense of the festivity. Equally deep-seated in Western culture is the association of lovemaking with the turning of the seasons toward the renewed exuberance of spring, that turning which Carnival heralds, especially in southerly climates. From the earliest records of Carnival in the twelfth century, the festivity has therefore been seen and practiced as strongly sexual; that is one reason for all the male preening and prancing.

Until the 1860s there were many more white males than females in New Orleans. The opposite was true of black people.[22] White females during the early colonial period were so scarce that they were imported like manufactured goods from the "mother" country; they were a commodity like textiles and slaves, essential to the success of the male-directed enterprise. During the succeeding American period of rapid expansion, New Orleans was a city of transients. Young men in business— not to mention the flatboatmen, sailors, and steamboatmen— were reluctant to establish families in a city of repeated yellow fever epidemics. Rich planters came to town during the winter season and departed during the unhealthy late spring, summer, and fall. This fostered among other things the quadroon-ball system which in turn augmented the half-caste population and undermined stable family life for people of every shade.[23]

These peculiar conditions of sexual illegitimacy and unstable family life developed during a period in which Western familial and sexual ideals took a sharp turn away from the older courtly and aristocratic ideals encouraging large families and extended sociability. In the course of the eighteenth century the small nuclear family became the dominant ideal among Western European upper classes generally for the first time. Henceforth the ideal male and female paired off to construct not a grand manor but a warm home, a loving place of privacy which was to be centered less on the exchange and extension of adult interests than on nurturing children. The model community ceased to be a collection of hardworking cottage workshops and farmhouses clustered around richer but still locally rooted gentry. Productivity was no longer based on such organically interconnected households and communities but on larger, impersonal networks of marketing, consumption, and finance. Cutting the productive tie which made households the basis of communities gave powerful impetus to the substitution of private, family-centered sentiments for the old communally oriented social ideals.

Is it surprising, then, that men and women developed strange customs of sexual companionship in places like New Orleans, where it was very difficult to live up to the new domestic ideals? The simple thing to do, if you were male, white, and well-off financially, was to combine marriage with concubinage. The combination was sanctioned by the old courtly-aristocratic ideals which had flourished in colonial days and continued to be easy to sustain in a big city characterized by slavery and transience. Yet the longer this lordly way of leading a sexual double life was carried on, the more it was belied, both by the new ideals of sexual behavior centered on private family life and by the growing power of capitalist modes of production, which came to dominate the production of sexuality no less than of cotton or sugar cane. Females were packaged to sell in an ever expanding, ever more impersonal market system. This affected high and low, white and black alike. Respectable white women's insistence on secretly visiting the quadroon balls in the 1810s and 1820s, which so scandalized the newspapers, was no less inevitable a response than the frenzy of elite young women to be constantly dancing, that is, to be on view, openly and pleasurefully.

New Orleans' famed sexual indulgence was due not simply to its status as a large seaport and frontier town nor to its Latin and aristocratic heritages but also to the new model of male-female relations as exclusively domestic, which so enclosed and privatized the legitimate expression of sensuous and sexual feeling that it produced, as if in retaliation, a greatly expanded market and show-place for perversities. "Vice in every shape," wrote

Captain James Alexander in 1833, "seems to hold high Carnival in this city of the great valley."[24]

To epitomize the peculiarities of the city's life in this way and call them Carnival was no accident, nor was it a manner of speaking confined to foreign visitors or to stiffly Protestant local residents. The Carnival spirit thrives on moral denunciation. The more doubtful people are about the wisdom and probity of their daily lives, the more they are disposed to allow themselves a moment of total ambivalence, where they let it all hang out. Comus's bubbly sweetness is one face of the festival; the devilishness of his crew is the other.[25]

These are male faces, one insipid, the other with a leer.[26] Carnival societies after 1857 *did* drain off some of the male sexual energies once lavished upon the counterpoint of quadroon balls with society affairs. Further sexual ventilation was provided by the queens, courts, and female-directed krewes, inventions which came at the same time that economic decline and a diminution in immigration made settled and modest family life more reasonable. But it was not enough. Even as the quadroon balls and other less savory public balls declined, even as the Anglo-Americans with the Carnival societies appropriated leadership in celebrating white elite Carnival, the Creoles replied by instituting a new and more elegant "French Ball" at the Opera House, beginning in 1861. The *Bee*, principal voice of the French-speaking element in the city, insisted in its report of the occasion that every beautiful, gracious, and witty Creole woman in New Orleans danced and banqueted in the foyer until four in the morning. But this French ball, still called by the Creole press "the gayest and most brilliant of the season" in 1870, after its resumption following the Civil War, was after all a public affair. By 1870 it offered free admission to any and every "lady" while requiring a three dollar fee from "gentlemen"; the ball slid toward identification as a commercialized showplace. In 1882 the French ball shifted its location to Odd Fellows Hall, away from the French Quarter; it was now sponsored by "two well-known gentlemen of this city."[27]

The prostitution trade, limited for some decades to the sidewalks during Mardi Gras, had found a new refuge. From this date until the closing of New Orleans' licensed red-light district in 1917, the balls of the "Two Well-Known Gentlemen" became an ever more notorious alternative to the grand affairs of the Carnival societies. The two gentlemen in question were tavern-keepers. One of them, Tom Anderson, who served two terms in the Louisiana legislature before 1908, became undisputed lord of the bawdy houses in the red-light district called Storyville, located northwest of the French Quarter from 1898 to 1917.[28]

The rhetoric was well chosen to exploit the old sexual dislocations in the city. Here were two "gentlemen," unidentified yet "well-known"—well-known for what? To ask the question was to fall prey to a prurient joke, to be drawn into leering male companionship if you were male, to be thrown into blushing confusion if you were female. The parallels to the old voyeurist system of the quadroon balls are obvious. They have simply acquired a more capitalistic and "democratic" setting, if democracy is given its then-usual racist definition, as Henry Rightor noticed in his summary review of Mardi Gras activities in 1900.

> The balls are essentially democratic in respect of the personalities of those who attend, the test being only Caucasian blood and a reasonable degree of decorum. . . .
> It is a common thing for the *jeunesse dorée* who have spent . . . earlier hours. . .at some of the exclusive balls of the patrician class, to wind up the night at these easier affairs. . . . The men do not, as a rule, mask. . . .
> [The women usually do, as] at one of these balls given during the Carnival of 1900 . . . [One] represented Mephistopheles, and was garbed in flame-colored fleshings with a hideous mask and horns. Two little women, disguised as clowns, advertised a brand of champagne. . . . There was also a Marguerite and a Faust, . . . an empress, a dozen flower girls, a Red Riding Hood, a Dolly Varden, a Pocahontas. . . .[29]

Quadroon balls imitated society balls. French balls imitated the Carnival-society balls—including the sometimes highly literate masquerades; on occasion, they even elected a queen. Thus reported the Mardi Gras, 1906, edition of the *Sunday Sun*, a tabloid regularly publishing stories about the houses of prostitution:

The French Balls
And the probable candidates
for the Queen Title

> The event of the Mardi Gras season in the four hundred social circles of which our dear girls represent a large percentage will be those warm french balls given at Odd Fellows Hall on Saturday and Tuesday night respectively. These strictly local affairs, which have long since become famous will exceed all former balls and a grand time of high revelry will be given those attending. These great events will be conducted as in the past by the two well known gentlemen which means a whole bit. The topic of conversation among landladies and leading girls of the district during the week has been rel-

ative to the queenship and much speculation has been rife among them. Among those spoken of are the Misses Josie Arlington, Margaret Bradford, Hilda Burt, Margaret Miller, Jessie Brown, Ray Owens, Florence Leslie, Flora Meeker and following all-star boarders Myrtle Burke, Eva Standford, Daisy Meritt and many others too numerous to mention.

Storyville and Carnival were in the late nineteenth and early twentieth centuries perhaps the only certainly profitable businesses in New Orleans. Their linkage was inevitable. The same issue of the *Sunday Sun* carried such suitably veiled advertisements as these:

> Thousands have seen her and millions have heard of her; such are the expressions of many regarding the extensive popularity of Countess Willie Piazza, who operates a swell house at No. 317 Basin Avenue. Carnival visitors should visit this establishment if they want a swell time.[30]

Just as in the case of the early nineteenth-century balls, too, respectable white women found the lure of the illicit affairs irresistible. One of the madams, irate at this useless presence of nonprofessionals at the ball of the Two Well-Known Gentlemen, arranged for the police to raid the ball on mardi gras in 1906 and to arrest any woman not carrying the card registering her as a Storyville prostitute. An unnamed number of ladies of high society were taken to the police station, unmasked, and sent home.[31]

Carnival has always been sexy, but in earlier European times the sexuality tended toward the grotesque rather than the illicit. Prostitutes, when they paraded—as they did at Venice in the 1520s or at Rome in the 1580s—pretended to be the opposite of what they were: the laws against wearing jewelry, for example, were lifted and so the courtesans at Venice in the instance just cited looked to an English traveler "as if they were queens."[32] Prostitutes were thus "honored"; they were also abused. In some Italian and French cities in the fourteenth, fifteenth, and sixteenth centuries they were forced to run footraces, frequently along with Jews or pimps or hunchbacks, sometimes at Carnival and sometimes at other springtime festivals. At Avignon during Carnival in the seventeenth century young men prowled the streets and entered brothels in order to catch prostitutes and exercise their "right of butt-beating" (*droit de bataccule*), lifting and letting fall the women upon the pavement repeatedly.[33] In sixteenth- and seventeenth-century England artisans customarily invaded brothels on mardi gras and sacked them.[34]

These women, whether entertained or rejected, whether in Europe or at New Orleans, were on display: they were there in Carnival, as in everyday life, for the use of males. The difference is that prostitutes in later nineteenth-century New Orleans were no longer objects of collective rituals of public exposure; this served the better to conceal the fact that they had become the objects of private rituals of subordination, anonymously organized by the working of economic and social institutions.

Prostitutes as a class, in contrast to their fate as individuals, have enjoyed relative freedom at New Orleans from the 1880s to the present day. The tensions of post–Civil War economic stagnation interacted with the city's traditions of commercial transience and Creole leisure to require the kind of escapist outlets that Storyville, like Carnival, afforded. Carnival sexuality, like sex-for-money, is sensuousness without responsibility, sex cut off from reproduction, from family life, from the ardors of passionate love. It is gaily irresponsible sexuality and a little crazy. As long as Storyville lasted, you—that is, you white males—could come in here at the railroad station, walk a few steps across Canal Street and drop into Anderson's saloon on Basin Street for a couple of well-laced beers, and be ready for a "swell time," no questions asked, as long as your money belt did not run dry or otherwise disappear. The best time to do it was Mardi Gras.

Prostitution prospered for many of the reasons that Carnival prospered: one was the crevice between gaiety and morality, ineradicable from the city's dual Creole-Catholic and American-Protestant heritage, rendering slightly suspect every pleasure and richly adventurous every deviance; others were the connections between escapism and profit, and between the maintenance of respectability and the necessity of corruption to make things run smoothly; there was, finally, the barrier between black and white, requiring repression even in the provision of pleasure, and requiring equally its circumvention in the name of that same pleasure.

Blacks were segregated from whites in Storyville, informally at first and finally by law in 1917. Not only could black men not set foot in the bawdy houses as customers, but after March 1, 1917, lewd women of the "black race" could not live or work on the "downtown" side of Canal Street, the area directly adjacent to the French Quarter. Nevertheless it was black men who provided the music in nearly all the "swell" houses of the prostitute district. There was intense competition among black musicians to secure these jobs during a period when they were being displaced by means legal and illegal from their traditional jobs as skilled tradespeople. Through this competition Basin Street and the prostitution district unexpectedly nursed, although they did not create, jazz.[35]

They also nursed, although they did not create, new modes of Carnival participation. Jelly Roll Morton, one of the three or four most important early innovators of the music that became jazz, was a frequent piano player in Storyville between 1905 and 1910. In the memoirs he taped in the 1930s at the Library of Congress, he speaks about the atmosphere in the District: "Hundreds of men were passing through the streets day and night. The chippies in their little-girl dresses were standing in the crib doors singing the blues. Then you could observe the fancy Dans, dressed fit to kill, wearing their big diamonds—sports like Willie the Pleaser, Bob Rowe (the kingpin of the District), Clark Wade (who took over after Rowe went to California). . . ."[36] Morton's interlocutor and biographer, Alan Lomax, did not do research to determine which of these men strutting through Storyville were white, mulatto, or black. Some of them were almost certainly less than pure Aryan, in spite of the racist laws. There are many stories about the sometimes white and sometimes black sexual tastes of Storyville's madams.[37] But the part of Morton's reminiscence which interests us here is the reference to the "little-girl dresses" of cheap whores in their "cribs."[38]

A journalistic account of New Orleans' Carnival activities in 1940 quotes the words of a black woman in her fifties who paraded as a "Baby Doll" that year. According to Beatrice Hill the "Baby Dolls," a group of prostitutes who paraded in Mardi Gras from at least the 1930s to the late 1950s or early 1960s, and sporadically since then, began in 1912:

> We was all sittin' around about three o'clock in the morning in my house. A gal named Althea Brown jumps up and she says, "Let's be ourselves. Let's be Baby Dolls. That's what the pimps always calls us." . . . And we decided to call ourselves the Million-Dollar Baby Dolls, and be red hot. . . .

If Beatrice Hill's story can in some measure be trusted—there are internal inconsistencies—then the Baby Dolls, as a feature of New Orleans' "second," black, lower-class Carnival, dates from the days of Storyville. In 1940 their costume consisted of "tight, scanty trunks, silk blouses and poke bonnets with ribbons tied under dusky chins. False curls framed faces that were heavily powdered and rouged over black and chocolate skins. The costumes were of every color in the rainbow and some that were not." "Let's be ourselves," Beatrice Hill said: black prostitutes were already wearing "little-girl dresses" in the cribs before 1910, according to Jelly Roll Morton. After 1910 they took the dresses to the streets (see plate 12).

Beatrice Hill was not from Storyville proper but from the black section on the other, "American" side of Canal Street, one of the toughest and grimmest sections of New Orleans. She was an "uptown nigger," darker of hue than those living "downtown," who claimed the prestige of living closer to the French Quarter or of being of old Creole free-black ancestry. "Liberty and Perdido Streets [uptown] were red hot back in 1912 when that idea [Baby Doll parades] got started.. . .You didn't need no system to work uptown. It wasn't like the downtown red-light district, where they made more money but paid more graft."

The Baby Dolls, then, began as a mode of competition with higher-caste downtown women:

12. Baby Dolls, New Orleans, ca. 1940 (photo, Norman Magden, from L. Saxon et al., *Gumbo Ya-Ya*)

We was all lookin' sharp. There was thirty of us—the best whores in town. We was all good-lookin' and had our stuff with us. Know what? We went on downtown, and talk about puttin' on the ritz! We showed them whores how to put it on. Boy, we was smokin' cigars and flingin' ten- and twenty-dollar bills through the air. Sho, we used to sing, and boy, did we shake it down. We sang "When the Sun Goes Down" and "When the Saints Come Marchin' Through I Want to Be in That Number." We wore them wide hats, but they was seldom worn, 'cause when we got to heatin' we pulled 'em off. . . . We showed our linen that day, I'm tellin' you. Man, when we started pitchin' dollars around, we had their mens fallin' on their faces tryin' to get that money. And there you have the startin' of the Baby Dolls.[39]

Whether they began in 1912 or a decade later,[40] the creation of the Baby Dolls is an important moment in the development of Mardi Gras. Almost a generation before respectable white women began parading in groups, here are women marching in Carnival. Obviously they could do so because, however disrespectable they might seem to the community at large, their milieu supported them. The Baby Dolls represent, among other things, that social urge which desires on this day of freedom to exhibit its neighborly mores to one and all. "And that Mardi Gras Day came and we hit the streets . . . We went to the Sam Bonart playground on Rampart and Poydras and bucked against each other to see who had the most money. Leola had the most—she had one hundred and two dollars, I had ninety-six dollars and I was second, but I had more in case I ran out." The women have their homes, their meeting-place, their camaraderie, and their following: "We had all the niggers from everywhere followin' us."[41] And so they went downtown to challenge their rivals.

Besides being women from a particular neighborhood who were challenging those from another, they were black. Some black individuals participated in Mardi Gras after the Civil War: they can be seen waiting for the parade at the Clay Statue in 1873, for example.[42] But only one organized group of black maskers seems to have preceded them in the streets: the Mardi Gras Indian "tribes" which, like the Baby Dolls, were neighborhood organizations, in this case male, and which, also like the Baby Dolls, had no inclination or opportunity to relate their celebration to that of the "first" white Carnival.

Baby Dolls are like the Mardi Gras Indians in another respect: contrary to their own sense of local origin, their costumes and antics are borrowed from the Carnival customs of blacks in other parts of the Caribbean area.[43] Lafcadio Hearn, observing Carnival in St. Pierre, Martinique, in 1888, saw the following in the parade of black and brown revelers (whites are mentioned only as spectators) in the little city's main streets:

> The sight of a troupe of young girls *en bébé*, in baby-dress, is really pretty. This costume comprises only a loose embroidered chemise, lace-edged pantalettes, and a child's cap; the whole being decorated with bright ribbons of various colors. As the dress is short and leaves much of the lower limbs exposed, there is ample opportunity for display of tinted stockings and elegant slippers.[44]

The name is absent but the Baby Dolls' costume is there. How did they walk? What were their social origins and occupations? Of these matters Hearn says nothing. At about the same time as they appeared in Martinique the Baby Dolls were noted in nearby Trinidad, where they regularly marched until the 1930s. There the Baby Dolls, lower-class black women, paraded with "Jamet bands," men of the underworld who sported bright-colored silk handkerchiefs, open shirts, low-slung pants and Panama hats.[45]

The Baby Dolls were rough women; in that also they resembled the early Mardi Gras Indian tribes, who were usually led by a fighter, and sometimes a murderous one. Mardi Gras Indians and Baby Dolls are straightforward examples of Carnival-as-inversion: on the day of their parade, they turn round their oppression as the lowliest of city residents. Singing and "walkin' randy," the Baby Dolls inverted the usual relations between client and whore: men, not the women, "fall on their faces" to get the money they fling; women, not the men, smoke the cigars.

Their action inverts their business relations and it subverts their social position in the marginal world of prostitution by advertising the absurdity of one of the great world's symbols of sweetness. What was so attractive about this all-too-experienced flesh parading with a sexually blatant strut in the guise of pretty, pre-pubescent children, dolled up like babies? Dressing with preternatural innocence is still a cliché in the business, but in the atmosphere of late nineteenth- and early twentieth-century America, an era in which traditional patriarchy was buoyed up by the ideal of domestically enclosed families, images of girlish innocence exercised special power over the male libido.[46] However unconsciously it was done, these "Jezebels'" adoption of the very emblem of happy family-centered sexuality in a public parade of their venal charms mockingly exposed the illusory origin of their desirability.

Prostitution is a constituent system of commercial societies. The quickness and superficiality of paid-for intimacy simply carries to its zenith the idea of venal pleasure which is the mode of being of all desire, from a commercial point of view. In this sense the perennial presence of prostitutes in New Orleans' Mardi Gras is no surprise: it exhibits rather than invents social reality. The Baby Dolls' public, collective presence forecasted the place of deviance in Carnival today. As social forms have become more standardized, democratized, and nationalized, the need for inversion, with its revolutionary overtones, has decreased and the desire for mere escapism, for deviance as a supplement, has increased. Fleshliness has a dozen competing forms today: what was in European Carnivals and in earlier New Orleans an ambivalent otherness, provoking tolerance and aggression by turns, has become as anodyne as the similarly once-shocking transvestism.

Our subject in this chapter has been the way women were inserted and also inserted themselves into a holiday traditionally commanded by men. There is more to say about this. To say it we must widen our focus to relate the present subject to the questions raised in Chapter 4 about the construction of Carnival as a civic festival.

In a sense the use of Mardi Gras as an emblem of civic identity was an admission of economic and social bankruptcy. Along with Southerners generally the people of Mobile and New Orleans refused to countenance joining the forces of Northern industrialism which had defeated them in war. Dependence on largely one-crop agriculture, largely river-oriented transport, and largely raw-material brokerage continued for decades. Population stagnated. In Mobile it hovered around forty thousand from 1860 to after 1900. In New Orleans, due to a large influx of freed black people after the Civil War (24,074 in 1860; 50,456 in 1870) and moderate increases in the black population thereafter, stagnation was less obvious. There were 168,675 people in New Orleans on the eve of the Civil War and 287,104 people in 1900. In national terms, however, the metropolis was losing its place among the great cities of the country. In 1840 it was third in population; in 1900 it was twelfth. Slowly the city's leaders accommodated themselves to new roles as custodians rather than makers of greatness.

They did so by outfitting New Orleans as a tourist city, a role which the city's writers furthered with alacrity: culture replaced economic power. The romantic picture of New Orleans, a place of ironwork balconies, trailing wisteria, and vivacious mulatto street-vendors, was created in this period. The moment was well chosen. Precisely because New Orleans' leisurely way of life accorded so ill with the nation's late nineteenth-century exuberant capitalism, it was infinitely attractive as a place of cultural consumption for people from elsewhere. Exotic black African and Caribbean ways, scorned in fact, were glorified in story: George Washington Cable, Lafcadio Hearn, and others created a national audience for the unique qualities of New Orleans by artfully interweaving a condescending compassion for blacks with a sharp eye for the multitude of picturesque ways in which this caste-ridden society coped and compromised.[47]

Just as conspicuous consumption, once a mode restricted to nobility, became proper and even expected behavior for the successful middle class, New Orleans began advertising itself, and especially its Carnival, as the world's greatest spectacle. From their beginning in the 1850s the lavish Mardi Gras parades were described in the national and international periodical press, publications such as *The Century Magazine* and *Scribner's* (the latter had 150,000 monthly readers in the 1880s).[48] The first book entirely devoted to the New Orleans' celebration, *A History of the Carnival at New Orleans*, was published in 1882 by the Chicago, St. Louis, and New Orleans Railroad "for gratuitous distribution." Special trains brought tourists directly from Chicago and St. Louis to New Orleans for the extravaganza. In 1906 a train of fifteen coaches was made up in Cleveland to bring visitors to Mardi Gras. Tourists were estimated at 60,000 in 1881 and at 100,000 in 1900.[49]

This of course was the reason for presenting such conciliatory spectacles as the Northern and Southern white soldiers shaking hands atop a float in Comus's parade of 1877, the "Military Progress of the World."[50] It was the reason for shaping Carnival generally as a spectacle rather than as participation. The Carnival-society system, which had begun as an effort of one elite to co-opt the cultural authority of another, and which had first functioned to centralize Carnival activities enough to make them more easily controllable from a civic point of view, created by means of its very success a new objective, that of attracting tourists.

The latter was a goal which everyone could share in an era of economic uncertainty and social vindictiveness. Spectacle supports illusion. Already in 1877, exuded J. Curtis Waldo in his *History of the Carnival*, on occasions like the parade of Momus, "thousands of people, especially women and children, turn out early to secure good seats, just as they would do if they were going to attend an opera.[51] Crowds formerly rioting in black, Irish, and other immigrant neighborhoods accepted passive roles as Rex's subjects and Comus's or Momus's worshipers. Some blacks adopted the "darkie" role of being flambeaux (torch) carriers for the nighttime parades of the societies while others formed their own Carnival societies.[52] Ethnic enmities and racist repressions slumbered: the statue of Henry Clay, "the great Conciliator," at the junction of Canal Street with St. Charles Avenue in the 1870s, "served as standing and sitting room for a thoroughly Democratic crowd of men, women, boys and children, white and colored. . . . An amiable Chinaman standing up beneath the shadow of Henry Clay's coat tail . . . quietly allow[ed] a fat old colored woman with a gay madras handkerchief tied around her head, to sit sleeping, leaning against his (John Chinaman's) lower extremities for an hour at least." The physical scene, if not all its interpretation, bears the mark of exact observation[53] (see plate 13).

The civic sense, never very strong in New Orleans, was pulled awry by the needs of tourist advertisement toward expression in the philistine displays of Carnival-parade magnificence. Educational institutions, public works (yellow fever was still a menace due to inadequate sewage- and waterworks), police-insured security were inadequately funded; the city's richest and most capable classes found ways to transfer the burden of such responsibilities to those below them, and for those below, the burden was too great.[54]

Civic pride fulfilled itself through the Carnival, "the most extensive and magnificent in all the world and in all history": this is no quotation from a tourist advertisement but from the sober and reliable *Standard History of New Orleans* written by a team of historians under the direction of Henry Rightor and published in 1900.[55] The boast was based on a now comfortable complement of three elements: wealth, order, and exoticism. By the late nineteenth century the "exquisite order and organization with which the Americans have endowed [Carnival]" had a good deal to do with the sapphire-studded scepters, ermine gowns, ducal decorations, and richly embossed ball favors which were whispered about for months before and after Carnival: Mardi Gras' activities had become not only attractive but nearly indispensable to the city's would-be as well as actual elites.[56] The relation

13. Street Maskers, New Orleans, 1873 (photo, Norman Magden, from *Scribner's Monthly*, November 1873)

between the exoticism and the wealth and order was more subtle. Carnival's lascivious side, always present, was now contained and controlled by its elite elements. The ethnic clichés which attributed a slightly wicked gaiety and sophistication to the descendents of the "French" and a careless wildness to "Negroes" could be used as cultural capital instead of repressed as social disturbances.[57]

Thus we return to the subject of this chapter. A "French Ball" is a sexy party; if mulatto and black prostitutes are not directly present, they are in the shadows just beyond. Carnival has a low-life side which the out-of-towner should see. After Storyville was closed down in 1917 the low-life side was relocated in

"Frenchtown," the northwest end of the old Creole quarter from which the richer people of French descent had long since emigrated. Latent perhaps in the Anglo-Saxon mind from the beginning, a slippery, seductive association of symbols took shape which joined the decline of one ethnic group to the denial of the other's cultural heritage by means of the old association between filth and lucre: French is sexy is black is dirty is money is glitter is fun is French.[58]

Once upon a time there was a little boy from plantation Louisiana whose grandfather lived in the old French Quarter of New Orleans. In 1900 the boy, about eight or ten years old,[59] visited his relative and the city for the first time. The visit took place on mardi gras. His chaperon for this visit, as it happened, was a young black male named Robert who served in the house of a friend of the grandfather. Grandfather and the friend, it seems, had other things to do, and so they delivered the boy into the hands of the servant for the whole day. "As the door closed behind us a great change came over Robert. His meekness fell from him as though it were a cloak thrown aside. He began strutting down the street as though walking in time to silent music: 'Us is goin' tuh have us a time!' he said."

The little boy grew up to become a gifted writer about Southern customs. I have drawn upon Lyle Saxon to tell the story of Bébé, the Marquis of Verneuil's dancing master. If Saxon did not himself write the chapter including the interview with the Baby Doll Beatrice Hill—it is unsigned—he was nevertheless one of three writers who supervised the research and writing which went into the book in which the interview appears. About 1925 Lyle Saxon began work on a book called *Fabulous New Orleans*, published in New York in 1928. The first sixty-seven pages contain the longest description of what purports to be a single Carnival day ever written: these pages tell the story of the little boy and Robert.

A somewhat abbreviated version of the same story was published almost simultaneously in *The Century Magazine*, a monthly miscellany of public affairs, light philosophy, and belles lettres somewhat like *Harper's Magazine* today. *The Century Magazine* had long shown its receptivity to Louisiana topics: George Cable's evocations of Congo Square dancing had appeared there in the 1880s. The place of its appearance helps one understand the story and its character, for Saxon's account of Mardi Gras in 1900 is as interesting for its ideologies as for its facts. The two are mixed together, and that is surely due in part to Saxon's awareness of his predominantly white, Northern audience. He was a professional writer. He wrote not only for truth's sake but for the sake of sale, and the magazine's editors in turn bought with an eye to their circulation figures.[60]

The reason the magazine bought the story is probably due to the writerly advantages which Saxon derived from using *two* eyewitnesses, white and black. The witnesses are congruent: the boy is too little to do anything but agree to Robert's suggestions; Robert is too dependent upon his occupation as servant to carry the boy very far beyond a boy's understanding. But more importantly the double eyewitness allows Saxon to carry his readers back and forth over the line between what I have called the first—elite and white—and the second—popular, both white and black—Carnivals in New Orleans in ways forbidden to any single person at that time, let alone to a pair of comrades of the same age and same hue. Robert and the boy mask themselves as devils, and they play the very devil with the color line, each lifting or lowering his mask, depending on where they are in the city and who happens to be their interlocutor. They are always taken by other revelers to be of the same race. They always "pass." It was a brilliant idea, this masquerade of Robert's, and it was brilliant of Saxon to turn it to account.

So we trot along through the streets with little Lyle, as eager as the little boy to participate by proxy in manners and motions entirely inaccessible to us, and indeed to nearly all of Saxon's readers in 1928. I emphasize this inaccessibility because I think that Saxon counted on it. When his account is closely examined, it turns out to have two aspects, and hence, unconsciously or not, two intentions. The first aspect, related to the story's representation of itself as an authentic memoir, is intended to inform readers about the essential features of New Orleans Mardi Gras. Any reader who *did* know or attend the festival would recognize many familiar things. The memoir surveys very well the grand variety of events which happen during Carnival. That is so, however, because Saxon has connected his impressions of later Carnivals with his boyhood recollection. This can be demonstrated in one case discussed further in the next chapter: the parade of the Zulus and their king, who, although they were invented only toward 1910 or later, are represented in full regalia in this Carnival of 1900. In how many other cases can similar anachronisms not be shown, while nevertheless being the case? The perennial quality of Carnival behavior may be Lyle Saxon's invention in 1925 rather than perception in 1900.

The second aspect derives from the use of Robert. The little boy's naiveté allows Saxon to strip the black man naked, physically and psychologically. As Robert takes off his clothes to don his devil costume, the boy sees a body "unbelievably black," arms "knotty with muscles," legs "thick and bent slightly at the knees," his hands hanging "down like the paws of some gigantic gorilla"—Darwin's origins of species again. The boy, dressed like Robert as a red devil, trails along after his companion, supporting his spangled tail.[61] In Rampart Street they pause before a drugstore while Robert examines the articles in the window intently. "Here was piled blue powder, yellow sulphur-like powder, black chicken feathers . . . black candies, small spirit lamps. . . . These things were voodoo accessories . . . ingredients for conjuring . . ., the dark factors in a darker magic. I remember Robert's respectful interest, his rolling eyes, his intent scrutiny."[62] The scene, as we shall see, later turns deadlier than this, more hidden, and more sinful. The second intention of Saxon's account is to *imagine* how black people participated in mardi gras, and to make this a symbol of how they understood life generally. The voyeurism that white people felt in the segregated society of the later nineteenth and earlier twentieth centuries, whether they lived in North or South, is given satisfaction. Here is Storyville, not only its white streets but its darkest back alleys, here are the uptown slums out of which swirl the Mardi Gras Indians and the Baby Dolls, out of which come eventually the Zulus too.

"The negroes," wrote Henry Rightor in 1900 in the *Standard History of New Orleans,* "preserve in its truest essence the primitive spirit of the Carnival." Rightor can only tell you approximately where the primitivism is located and generally how it looked; he speaks of it as "mad and rollicking."[63] Saxon pretends to take you by the hand and push and shove and dance and weave with you among these sweating, grinning beings, so strange, so loathsome, so marvelously unabashed and sympathetic.

We must use Lyle Saxon's rich descriptions. We must use them with the utmost caution. The elements of Carnival which he describes, on and off the streets, are not surprising: he mentions parading societies and masking types visible since midcentury. But he offers the "geography" of these elements, their mutual relations, as they were first fully integrated at the end of the century, in the fullness of what I call the civic phase. This geography has not changed much since 1900. It has a four-fold pattern. First, there is the division between masking and parading, acting and looking. Street masking, with its informal drunken and ribald confrontations and also its formalized masking contest, is already located in the French Quarter. Parading is concentrated along St. Charles Avenue and Canal Street, and the two essential parades, never to be missed, are those of Rex toward midday and of Comus just at nightfall. Other parades trail along in their wake.[64]

Second, there is the division between white and black Carnival:

> We dodged through groups of maskers, we ducked under ropes, and finally after traversing several squares, turned from Canal Street into another thoroughfare where a group of negro girls were dancing under an arcade while two negro men picked on banjos. I saw no white maskers here, but there were many negros in costume who seemed to be holding a Mardi Gras all their own. And here I found that the crowd was moving in another direction, away from Canal Street.

The center of this Carnival is Rampart Street, on the uptown side of Canal Street, "the Broadway of New Orleans negroes," full of shops, of eating houses, and on this day also full of street maskers: "yellow girls dressed as Spanish dancers . . . negro men dressed as Indians . . . men dressed in their everyday clothes or even in overalls, but wearing grotesque masks; negro children of every shade from velvet black to the lightest *café au lait*, screaming and romping in the streets. . . ."[65]

The third pattern which weaves its way through Saxon's narrative—more literary man than social scientist, he of course does not state the patterns explicitly—contrasts the central streets with the neighborhoods. Robert drags the boy to the so-called "Irish Channel," far south of Canal Street, toward the river. "Here drunken men lay about in barrooms and many fights were in progress. Robert informed me . . . that 'White mens up thisaway would jes' as soon kill a nigger as eat dinner!'" Little has changed here since mid-century.[66] "We saw a street dance in progress, with a portion of the roadway roped off and many couples bouncing about in the street to the music of a band of coatless and sweating musicians." Saxon's pretext for this unlikely survey of neighborhood carnivals wears a little thin, as the boy and Robert forage more and more afield. Little Lyle is tired and wants to go home. "But when asked why he had brought me to such a place, he said that he wanted me to see everything"—that is, the *reader* must see everything. "We must have visited half a dozen markets, I am sure, and before each of these markets a neighborhood celebration was in progress. Here was none of the grandeur that I had witnessed in Canal Street, but it was the carnival of the masses."[67]

Lastly Saxon contrasts the functions in the streets with the behavior of people indoors. He not only describes the expected scenes at the masked ball of Comus at the French Opera House, but offers the more unusual vignette of a lavishly gowned white woman at the Ramos bar in the old St. Charles Hotel, unescorted, one foot on the brass rail, sipping gin fizz. "Later I learned that on Mardi Gras all police regulations regarding barrooms were put aside." Women on this day—"fashionable women"—might "go into these places. . . ."[68]

Sex and liquor and Carnival: it has its white side, and its black. The most lurid scene in Saxon's story occurs at the back, black end of Storyville, behind a bar-room with its "jangling piano" and its "yellow girls and their dark-skinned boy friends . . . at tables drinking," down an alley and into another house beyond, where a room, "tightly closed," shone with "electric lights [in the black slums of 1900?] and I saw that the ceiling was a mass of red and green streamers of paper, rather reminiscent of Christmas." The place was thronged with black people "pressed together so that they seemed one, and many dancing with closed eyes and lunging hips."

According to Saxon, this was the Zulu ball:

> It was then that I saw the Zulu King again. He was lolling on a throne on a sort of dais at one end of the room. He was laughing very loud and showing all of his magnificent white teeth. He lay back in a chair, and upon his knee was a mulatto girl with a short red dress. . . . The room smelled of unwashed bodies and stale beer.

Seating the boy, Robert joined the gyrating throng. Then the music stopped, a space was cleared, and "To the center of the floor came a woman, a thin quadroon. She began to shake in time with the drumbeats, first a shoulder, then a hip. Then she began to squirm and lunge. At each beat of the drum her position would change, and as the measured beating continued she moved her body with each beat. At last she was shaking all over, head wagging, hips bobbing back and forth." Saxon makes no comment on the performance. His words record in this case only the physical movements. They are close enough to some of the descriptions of Congo Square and Caribbean colonial dancing for one to recognize an authentically maintained tradition.[69]

For Saxon, for Saxon's audience of readers, and at least as he would have us believe, also for the black people present, what was important was not the tradition nor even the sensuality but the sexuality:

> As the drumbeats became more rapid, her gyrations became more violent. At the end of a few minutes the drumming stopped and she stood limp in the center of the floor. There was wild applause. She retired and another girl took her place, this time a black girl. Her movements were more suggestive, more animalish—and pleased the crowd more extravagantly. When she had finished a third girl took her place. I could not understand why the negroes thought this entertainment so fine.

At last a winner of the shimmying contest was announced, and the couples' dancing resumed. The boy fell asleep in his corner—until he woke with a start to witness "a general fight," with women knocked down and chairs flying.

> And it was at this minute that I saw the Zulu King—a razor in his hand. He was slashing at some man who held a glittering thing high in the air . . . and a moment later I heard a man's scream that ended in a gurgling sound . . . and there in the open space stood the king, the razor red in his hand.[70]

It is just possible that sometime in the early days of the Zulu Social Aid and Pleasure Club a scandal concerning the king did take place. If so, it has been carefully kept secret. And it certainly did not take place in 1900. This picture of drunken violence in the most exploited area of the city is misleading in general, in addition to its questionable details. The concentration on sexy dancing and murder by a black version of Carnival's king, together with the presentation of Robert as pulled in his Carnival behavior toward the quest of this dangerous scene, steers the reader toward complacent reaffirmation of simple-minded racial stereotypes. It identifies the sinful complement to Carnival's splendor with the black underclass.[71]

Between 1827 and 1917 the federal government expended well over three million dollars in order to deepen the ship channel between the mouth of Mobile Bay and the city. The expenditures were in the interest both of city business and national security, and Mobile's importance as a port city grew greatly, especially during the two world wars in the twentieth century. During the second half of the nineteenth century, however, Federal aid was not decisive enough by itself to give strong impulse to the town.

Mobile slumbered. By January 1902, when the bicentennial of the founding of Fort Louis de la Mobile at 27-Mile Bluff was commemorated, the city's past had come to seem something less than brilliant, at least to the Comic Cowboys who, during Carnival that year, celebrated the occasion with their own special kind of satire. There were two parts to their Float Number Six that year. On one part of it, symbolizing Mobile Present, lay two signs trailing long chains: the city government had just enacted an ordinance requiring removal of all swinging signs. The other part of the float symbolized Mobile Past: here was an old haystack at which a mule was eating away; scattered around and in the haystack were relics and trash "supposedly saved over the last two hundred years," according to the report of the parade in the *Mobile Register*.[72]

Mobile was a small town with a comic conscience. The role that Carnival played there during the civic era was different from that in New Orleans. New Orleans was eventually able to turn its festive heritage to tourist profit, but it paid a price for the conversion, installing a group of myths and stereotypes which sanctioned large amounts of elite and official indifference to the social welfare of all citizens. Perhaps this was inevitable. Certainly the public-spiritedness of city elites elsewhere in the United States during the Gilded Age is not especially impressive. But in New Orleans it became right and even necessary to construe civic welfare as social escapism.

That of course was not the view of contemporary opinion. Carnival, having become an essential part of the civic identity of the two cities, had to be defended. Rightor's estimate of New Orleans' festival is most eloquent: "The Carnival is not a commercial expedient . . . It is the expression of a genuine emotion. It is the embodiment of care thrown to the winds. . . . Yet it sets in motion powerful commercial activities. If it did harm it might not endure. It not only does no harm, but on the contrary is productive of much good; so it is supported heartily . . . by those who, from motives of philanthropy or public spirit, perceive in its perpetuation a benefit to the city and its people."[73] The Mobile writer and impresario Thomas De Leon went even further in generalizing about the happy effects of Mardi Gras and especially of the Carnival societies in the two "Creole cities":

> These give their people a distinct and distinguishing feature; possessed by none other, yet possible only to a race susceptible of sentiment and of culture. This alone

has doubtless fostered a civic pride which did something to hold up the heads of many who, without it, would have hung them in desponding doubt, in the long era of poverty and trial. . . .

The educational result also must strike all who reflect upon the subjects illustrated by these pageants. The public eye is educated to harmony of color and form; to artistic contrasts of cause and effect. The public mind is stimulated, memory refreshed, or curiosity and ambition waked in many departments of history and poetry. . . .

Such is the aesthetic side of mystic mummery; where intellect, culture, imagination and experience combine with artistic taste and tireless industry, to aid the very lavish use of money. And this last suggests that, even doubting any higher good, there may be a practical one in the hard realism of dollars and cents.

. . . Wherever the money comes from, it certainly goes for the benefit of the whole community. The vast crowds, pouring in to witness the Carnival, have been noted. Some of these are visitors on direct excursion for Mardi Gras. . . . But the vast body of the influx is of smaller merchants and business men, from the proper trade-territories of the two cities. These bring not only their wives and children, but literally add their sisters, their cousins and more distant kin. They not only disburse large amounts personally, but they also buy larger bills of goods from wholesalers than at any other season. Thus all interests benefit mutually. . . .[74]

The commercial benefits at least did not escape observation elsewhere. De Leon himself was hired to reproduce a "Creole carnival pageant" for the bicentenary celebration at Albany, New York, in 1886, and, wrote De Leon in 1890, "almost as I write, Augusta [Georgia] has been crowing over a carnival out of season, which brought strangers by the thousand and rattled the nimble dollar of the daddies [sic] into pleasantly receptive tills."[75] Pensacola, Memphis, Vicksburg, and Baltimore (the last-named also supervised by De Leon) imported Carnival in the 1870s and 1880s, and Ogden, Utah, welcomed New Orleans' Rex himself to "Rocky Mountain Carnival" in July, 1890; Birmingham, Alabama, and doubtless other cities also produced local versions of Mardi Gras in the 1890s.[76] But of all these commercially motivated attempts only one succeeded, that of the Veiled Prophet parade and ball in Saint Louis, begun in 1878 and still continuing today—on the fourth of July.[77]

Both Mobile and New Orleans were wise enough to ban advertising vans from the Carnival parades by the end of the nineteenth century. Commercial success remained a side effect, and guaranteed that other motives would determine the character of Carnival. Sociopolitical, not economic factors, underpinned the cultural impulse. By sociopolitical factors I mean causes of tension, not consensus. Carnival became a central civic event first because Anglo-Americans wanted to rival Creole cultural prestige, second because the occasion could be used to express Southern resentment at Northern interference after the Civil War, and third because, once women were brought in by means of the queen-and-maids system, Carnival could be used to discriminate socially, and at the same time to advertise, an elite's importance. Each of these victorious elitizing elements had its negative side: Anglo-American orderly spectacles tended to counter and diminish the vivacity and inventiveness of street masking; blacks ceased to participate in the white man's Carnival except as employed servants; the rigidities of social elitism provided a secure place for its moral opposite, prostitute "gaiety," which is to say female exploitation at a number of symbolic as well as real levels.

Carnival's duplicities flourished. This account has endeavored to discern the unexpected positivities resulting from such illusions and clashes. Civil War resentments insured Carnival's enduring nostalgic, utopian features, and at the same time by the absurdity of such features it opened up space for satire. The "mystic krewes" marched toward the production of ever more preposterous fantasies; the satiric counter-societies found more and more scope for their buffoonery, leading Carnival ever and again back to its democratizing, helter-skelter street forms.

Until the 1870s Carnival was one among many expressions of exuberance, escapism, class distinctions, and caste differences. Between 1870 and 1900 it became the umbrella beneath which and by means of which these contrasts could coexist. If by 1900 it had become the central event among those exemptions from seriousness which every social group allows itself, this was not just due to the factors considered one by one in the last two chapters. It was due, beyond them all, to the cumulative effect of these two cities' nineteenth-century experience.

Quite to the contrary of the Comic Cowboys' bicentennial invention, history was no accumulation of hay and trash which could be munched away by the mulish citizens of 1902. Not just ethnicity or sex or economic hardship or regional politics, but the accumulated weight of opportunities which were dealt with and of opportunities which were missed revealed itself as a barrier for elites as well as for the people. The sense of life as a rich and easy flow from past to future, so plausible to early nineteenth-century whites, and to all who aspired to their condition, turned out to be something that only seemed real on one—happily recurring—occasion of utter unreality.

# Wildmen

After 1850 that inevitable measure of pleasure, sexual display, was given double representation in Gulf Coast Mardi Gras: the splendor of kings and dukes in their courtly leggings and curls, accompanied and then eclipsed by queens' and maids' satins and pearls, was juxtaposed to an orgiastic ballroom scene replete with dirty, black, "French" pleasures. The site of the latter was imagined in the back streets of New Orleans; the vision flickered, in any case, at the back of most people's minds. The Main-Street representation of Mardi Gras was equally ubiquitous, preoccupying people's egos as obsessively as the "French" vision did their ids. Life as a perfectly high, ethereal, filmy dream, and life as a perfectly low, sensuous indulgence without let: one extreme called for the other.

No less inevitable than sex in Carnival is the presence of male competition, rivalry, violence. It has been pursued from the beginning of the history of Carnival as if for its own sake, as gratuitous as springtime with its prompting exuberance. The first known ritual concerning mardi gras centered upon marching groups of men, who ritually killed bear, bulls, and cock (Rome, about 1140); the first recorded Carnival playfulness consisted of ballgames and cockfights (London, about 1150). All during the thirteenth and fourteenth centuries church councils and bishops inveighed against the participation of clerics in the stick fights and ball games pitting parish teams against each other on mardi gras.[1]

In Mobile and New Orleans such traditional displays of pseudo-knightly bravado take sublimated forms. Like all else in these two cities, including the sexual symbols surveyed in the last chapter, the forms split into high and low modes, although they do not break along racial and ethnic lines quite so rigidly as do the sexual displays. The high form includes the roles of king and dukes whose formation has been traced; the fantasy of prowess is most obviously exercised in the throwing game along the parade routes which, coupled with the bizarre masks of the men, sometimes affords images of nearly insane concentration

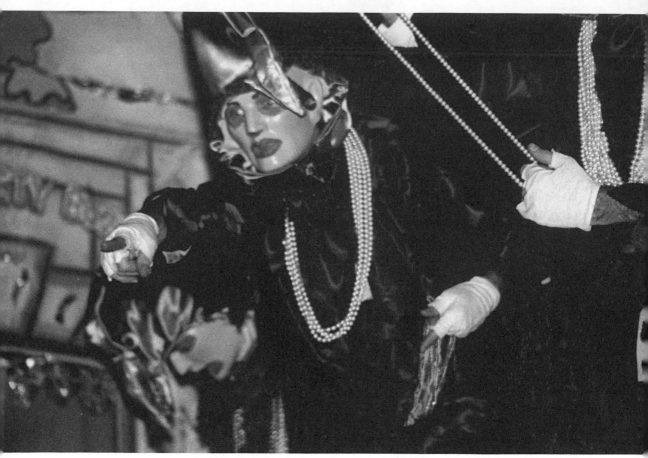

14. "Duke" in nighttime parade, New Orleans, 1987
(photo, Norman Magden)

and imperiousness (see plate 14). It is equally expressed in the apparent necessity of including in nearly every parade, punctuating the floats along the line of march, a galaxy of U.S. military contingents, national guardsmen, ROTC groups, marchers from military academies, and the scarcely less militarily disciplined high-school bands. Beyond these strikingly visible emblems of male control is the slightly less apparent but still more powerful one of the "captain," the real leader and organizer of the parade, a man on horseback who rides at the beginning of the krewe's floats and whose face is ominously veiled in a silken, bejewelled piece of cloth. His lonely, preeminent place, his unique costume, the powerfully archaic symbolism of his seat upon a superb stallion evoke, in conjunction with the yelling throngs lining the streets through which he moves, the image of the Conqueror.[2]

The low form of male physical rivalry in Carnival is our subject in this chapter. Its central symbol is the wildman, a special being, indeed a separate race. Carl Linnaeus, whose genus-and-species system remains the basis of biological classification, listed him in 1758 as one of the six variants of Homo sapiens, along with European, Asiatic, African, American (Indian), and Monster.[3] Quite to the contrary of the dukes, kings, and captains, the wildman as a species exhibits perfect lack of control.

Every culture has its counterculture, every civilization its wilderness. For as long as people in the group of societies called Western European have thought about themselves, they have also hypothesized their opposite. They have compulsively tried to imagine the life of people who could have no legitimate location within the boundaries of "civilized life as we know it." In medieval times the wildman and woman who lived somewhere in primeval woods and mountains occupied this space of the imagination. Such people lived with—and like—wolves and bears. Bespeaking his still half-human authority, the wildman in medieval myths is often made the master of the wild animals among whom he lives, like Tarzan, his modern avatar.

For Europeans the discovery of equatorial Africa, the West Indies, and soon afterwards the North and South American continents located the wild people elsewhere, and gave them new names; above all others, those of "Indian" and "Negro." In the course of the following three centuries these wild people were by turns brought in, driven out, killed off, and finally freed—at least in terms of formal civil status—as the hybrid societies of the New World emerged. But different stages of the New World sociopolitical development were not automatically followed by the imagination, as if each epoch could wipe away the memory of the wild peoples' previous condition. Images of wildness predating as well as postdating discovery, slavery, and emancipation—children of Ham, of the devil, of darkness; children of innocence, wild, simple folk, noble savages—continued and still continue to permeate representations of black people and red.[4] The Indian, the black person, is the Other. On the streets and in the white Carnival parades of Mobile and New Orleans the two appear again and again—in headdress and warpaint, in blackface with banjoes—as exotically marginal figures who on this topsy-turvy day of excess can and should be exhibited at or near the center of things (see plate 13 above).[5]

The psychologically automatic association of black man with wild man turned up in Rex's second parade as part of the *boeuf gras* ensemble (1873). A contemporary engraving of it in *Scribner's Magazine* groups together a fat ox with three curiously garbed persons (see plate 15). Striding along in front is a bearded white man with naked legs and a close-fitting, long-sleeved, hairy but flesh-covered tunic covering his upper body, a ragged pelt wrapped around his torso, leather sandals, and a Roman-looking, warlike helmet. He carries a club over one shoulder. Two ropes are attached to a halter on the ox's head, one on each side of the ox. The man holding the rope on the ox's right side has a bear's-head mask, an ax on his right shoulder, a white cloth wrapped around the head, white gloves, a white apron over dark clothing covering the body, and dark shoes. On the left side is a black man, probably someone in masquerade because the facial features are preternaturally large, like those of the bear masker on the other side. The rest of the black man's clothing is the same as that of the bear-man, except that he grasps the halter rope with both hands and carries a basket or pouch strapped to his waist and filled with a number of implements which are probably butchers' knives. His dark tunic pos-

15. "Boeuf Gras," Rex Parade, New Orleans, 1873
(photo, Norman Magden, from *Scribner's Monthly*, November 1873)

sesses pleats around the neck, unlike the clothing of the bear-man. His hands are white and do not seem gloved, which may be a clue, like the facial features, that the person is a white man masking as a black.

The symetrical placement of bear-man and black man implies that they belong to the same subhuman level of creation. It was in this very year of 1873, we recall, that Comus presented its parodically Darwinist proof of this proposition, only a few hours after the Rex parade depicted in plate 15 had passed through the streets.[6] The role of the bear and the Negro is to serve the white man with the club over his shoulder who precedes them. These three will perform the sacrifice of the fat ox, which explains the presence of knives, ax, and white aprons and headdresses. Bear-man and black man are butchers.

The white man striding along in front is a somewhat anomal-ous representation of the medieval wildman who lived in the woods. His hairy skin, felt-like clothing, and huge club were standard symbols for this figure as he was represented in Car-nivals of the fifteenth and sixteenth centuries.[7] But his Roman-looking helmet was not. The latter is a symbol of disciplined martial prowess, and thus seems incongruously placed along-side the wildman's club and his hairy nakedness. Was the hel-met added in order to make clear, like the fact that this white

16. "Boeuf Gras," Paris, 1852 (photo, Bibliothèque Nationale, Paris, France)

man precedes the ox and its subhuman butchers, that he is the conqueror, the "master of animals," to whom rulership is reserved?

The ox paraded by Rex was customarily butchered on the day after the parade and its meat distributed to the queen and to members of Rex's court. Such a parade and sacrifice were supposed to represent a last indulgence before Lent, but since the butchery took place on Ash Wednesday the symbolism seems a bit askew.[8] The idea of leading along an ox in Rex's parade—he was included from the parade's first occasion in 1872—has no doubt something to do with the occasional presence of a *boeuf gras* in previous Gulf Coast Carnivals.[9] But its specific form—an ox accompanied by three wildmen—is a direct imitation of the way it was paraded in Paris during the Second Empire of Napoleon III, as an engraving of the procession in 1852 shows (plate 16).

The parallels are obvious. Did someone among Rex's organizers see this broadside or the Paris parades of the 1850s? The differences are just as evident. Here the bear-man beats a drum, leading the procession. He has no fellow black man; there are no blacks in this parade. One wildman guides the befeathered and garlanded *boeuf gras* by a neck-rope. Two others, one in front and another on the far side of the ox whose headdress and lower legs alone are shown, carry large clubs. They are bearded like the Orleanian club-bearing man and similarly wear tunics around their otherwise naked torsos, but they also have cloaks on their shoulders. They are not butchers; there is no sign of the coming sacrifice, unless the clubs are supposed to indicate it. Above all, they wear festive feathered headdresses of a kind used elsewhere in European popular prints to signify American Indians. The similarity, not the difference, was the reason to associate wildmen with the fat ox here. The pseudo-Roman crested helmet appears on the head of a pipe-smoking man who strides along after the bull. In the Parisian print a variety of clownish maskers are shown running before, after, and alongside this central group. Most curiously, the ox is accompanied by two little cupids carrying baskets of flowers.[10]

Carnival celebration in the French capital in the 1850s and 1860s centered upon the parade of the fat ox. But the popularity of this figure had begun earlier, and from Napoleon I's time (1799–1815) had been regulated by police statute to include an extraordinary number of persons in uniform, in addition to a select number of master butchers: "ten mamelukes, six wildmen, six Romans, four Greek swordsmen, six French knights, six Poles, two Spaniards, a drummer, twenty musicians," etc.[11] It seems probable that the wildman with the pseudo-Roman helmet in Rex's parade is a scrambled and condensed version of Parisian precedents, whether taken specifically from a model like the 1852 parade or more generally from its military accents. Obviously the New Orleans idea of amalgamating wildmen, military symbols, and the fat ox was a commonplace long before Rex made use of it.[12]

The Rex parades in the 1870s were particularly concerned with military symbols, as we have noticed. From the broader iconographic perspective used in the present chapter, it would seem that images such as that of Rex as Totila (1873: see plate 8), riding in chain armor, on horseback, and flanked by mameluke foot soldiers bearing rifles, were adopted not only out of civic rancor but because of long-existing, internationally shared traditions which defined male grandeur in military terms. Such traditions were of course not particularly carnivalesque; if anything, they moved Mardi Gras away from its ludic qualities toward officious seriousness, however absurd the costuming.

A generation later everything had changed (see plate 17). Rex

BOEUF GRAS.

17. "Boeuf Gras," Rex Parade, New Orleans, 1899 (photo, Norman Magden, from *Carnival Bulletin,* Mardi Gras day, 1899, courtesy of New Orleans Public Library)

was seated on a flower-like throne atop a float in light-colored Elizabethan costume.[13] The ox, too, no longer ambled along on his own four feet and his escort includes no one who looks like a wildman. There are several other striking adjustments in this drawing of the Fat Ox float in the parade of 1899, a sketch published on mardi gras in the Carnival Bulletin which at the time was annually published by local newspapers and served as a guide to the parades. A person clad in a long robe and turban-like headdress holds the halter of the horses pulling the float (a transformation of the mamelukes?). The butchers are seemingly Caucasian, apparently without face-masks and wearing tunics which leave legs and arms bare, like those of the other two figures on the float. Instead of an ax, one man carries a huge cleaver. The other butcher has no knife-case at his waist. The man in front is a vaguely Greco-Roman soldier with a long spear and winged helmet. He has lost all vestige of wildness. There is, however, a second soldier, also with spear and winged helmet, who has large rings in his ears and wears knee-high boots. A touch of exoticism has, after all, been preserved—or is this only an artist's whimsy which did not actually appear in the parade?[14]

The eclectic quality of the 1873 *boeuf gras* had given way by 1899 to a unified presentation of pre-Christian sacrifice. The folkloric idea of Carnival as a pagan rite, involving sacrifice, is reinforced by the addition of a square pedestal with a burning urn on it to the back of the float. Perhaps the founders of Comus, too, embossed their early ball invitations with a pyre to intimate the pagan origins of their celebration (plate 6). The sacrifice of the fat ox, situated thus among antique symbols, required the disappearance of medieval and modern mythic elements. Civilized military protection for the docile ox and a clean, four-square sacrifice performed with a properly sharp steel implement has been substituted for the primitivist symbolism of an earlier day.

The move illustrates a general evolution, one which we have already noted in the Carnival societies. Frequently they begin on a parodic note, but with time their success inculcates conservatism and symbolic flatness. Wildness and satire are eliminated or softened. There is one honorable exception. According to B. W. Dean, the first Carnival society of them all, the Cowbellions, herded a pack of live Jersey purebred cattle, heifers and bulls, through the streets of Mobile as their parade in 1884. If the heifers were followed by the bulls, one can imagine that the occasion was lively.[15] Again in 1889 the Cowbellions revived their old private initiation ceremony. Parading on foot, they donned cows' heads and, carrying torches and cowbells, marched through the streets.[16]

We have seen that the Cowbellions' invention is probably a Southern adaptation of the Pennsylvania and Old World belsnickle. We have similarly noted that the cow's-head wildman, a man in ox-hide and horns, led with a rope, was a figure in the eighteenth- and nineteenth-century Christmas celebrations in Jamaica called "John Canoe," celebrations carried out by blacks who were butchers, which reminds us of the black man with his knives who escorted Rex's ox in 1873.[17] Was Rex inspired in its 1873 eclecticism by the Cowbellions, the Jamaicans, or some other unknown source which also supplied the idea of a bearman? We shall perhaps never know the answer to that, anymore than we will be able to determine the inspiration for the half-wildmen, half-cupids peeking from amongst fronds on early Cowbellion and Comus ball invitations (plates 5, 6).

Wildmen belong to Carnival.[18] At the very epoch when the white man eliminated them for their uncouthness, they became the soul of the second Carnival's two finest inventions, the Mardi Gras Indians and the Zulus. Black Indian groups in Carnival are now about one hundred years old; the Zulus have existed seventy or eighty years. The social, economic, and cultural factors which brought about these inventions are not only different from those involved in the creation and endurance of the Carnival societies considered up to now. They are also more unfamiliar to most readers of this book or to anyone accustomed to reading, because they emanate from a nonliterate culture. The Carnival games and rituals of the Indians and Zulus are embedded in ways of life which during the nineteenth century folklorists believed were on the verge of extinction, preserved in only a few isolated pockets of archaism far away from the ruinous uniformities of industrializing mass societies. New Orleans' black Indian groups are not organized in clubs with elected officials, constitutions, and committees. Their stability is based not on this kind of instrumental organization but on ritualized habits embedded in a particular mode of everyday life. Quite to the contrary of the folklorists' prediction, this mode of life still flourishes, and indeed may be inseparable from the way capitalist-industrial society functions to create an "underclass." What follows in the remainder of this chapter is a study of the feature commonly considered the most "folkloric" phenomenon in Gulf Coast Carnival, the Mardi Gras Indians of New Orleans. The study requires explanation of far-flung social and cultural factors which in the case of other groups could be considered as intuitively understood by most readers. This does not mean that the Mardi Gras Indians are unique, as some have maintained. What will distinguish the approach here is again the search for comparative materials, not only in the Caribbean and in Africa but also in rural European areas.

Costuming oneself as an Indian was one of the most popular disguises in nineteenth-century Carnival. For both white men and black, the aboriginal American was a suitable alter ego.[19] The Indians, after all, had been defeated but never quite vanquished. They lurked on the margins of the Southern imagination just as they continued to be a sporadic menace on the western margins of American expansion until nearly the end of the nineteenth century. They were despicable and dangerous, formidable and unconquered, remote enough to be stereotyped in the Wild West shows which came into vogue in the 1880s, close enough both in actual residence and in the collective memory to constitute powerful tokens.[20]

Use of the Indian mask is always related to the cultural theme of male rivalry and prowess. It is always related to the social theme of struggles for power; an Indian masker symbolizes, actually or virtually, confrontation with the white man, the victorious civilization, the dominant community. Use of this mask at once allows—and compels—the masker to acknowledge defeat in some general social way and yet to express defiance here and now.[21] Although this masked Indian is below, he is also beyond the white man's sanctioned power. He thus becomes at one and the same time superior and inferior, noble and ludicrous in his uncivilized otherness. As such the Indian mask served resentful whites in the aftermath of the Civil War at Mobile.[22] As such the masquerade was developed by black revelers throughout the Caribbean area, from Trinidad to Haiti, Cuba, and finally New Orleans.[23]

The first written notice of New Orleans black groups masking as Indians, it seems, is part of Henry Rightor's survey of Carnival, published in 1900:

> The favorite disguise with the negroes is that of the Indian warrior, doubtless from the facility with which it lends itself to a complete transformation of the personality without the use of the encumbering and embarrassing mask; and in war paint and feathers, bearing the tomahawk and bow, they may be seen on Mardi Gras running along the streets in bands of from six to twenty and upwards, whooping, leaping, brandishing their weapons, and, anon, stopping in the middle of a street

to go through the movements of a mimic war-dance, chanting the while in rhythmic cadence an outlandish jargon of no sensible import to any save themselves.

Since Rightor speaks of jargon that cannot be understood, it would seem that he was personally present at one of these performances. His subsequent reference to evening activities, including an extraordinarily precise spatial description of the hall where the Indians' balls were held, almost guarantees that we have a firsthand account:

> With undiminished spirit and energy, and with the utmost good humor, these negro maskers continue their pranks and capers till night falls, when they repair to the hall they have selected for their ball, where they are joined by their women, and new accessions of maskers and dance away the hours till the Carnival spirit has died within them from sheer fatigue.
>
> At such a ball the hall is usually decorated with garlands and festoons of colored tissue paper, which contribute a very animated appearance to the scene. Near the entrance is to be found a kind of bar, at which are dispensed liquid refreshments of various kinds—lemonade, beer and more ardent liquors. At the rear or on the floor below is located a primitive kind of café communicating with a little kitchen, in which enormous cauldrons of gumbo are boiling, platters of which with a liberal allowance of boiled rice, are served to the bucks and their wenches for a small sum.[24]

It is possible that the relatively complex all-day sequence described by Rightor had only recently been worked out, but it seems unlikely. If groups of a half dozen or two dozen males were capable of capering from morning to night, if they had learned to chant in call-and-response patterns the songs which—judging from an example which may have been sung as early as the 1890s or early 1900s[25]—had at first some Creole dialect words mixed together with other elements and adapted rhythmically so that they seemed an "outlandish jargon" to Rightor, then it is probable that this Mardi Gras behavior was long in gestation.

Perhaps inspired by the black-power movements of the 1960s, a few students of the Mardi Gras Indians have in fact maintained that these Carnival maskers are the finest flower of a long-hidden "subculture" in New Orleans, a flower whose roots lie in black-Indian intermarriage from the earliest days of the French colony. It is more than likely that blacks and Indians lived together and raised families on occasion as early as the eighteenth century. It is less likely that such contact provided cultural or racial inspiration to the Mardi Gras Indian groups. And it is altogether impossible that from the eighteenth century until 1900, when Rightor published his description, no one would have noticed such an elaborate subculture, integrating song, dance, and costumes in an all-day festival on one of the hegemonic culture's main holidays.[26]

There is an alternate version of this racially based idea of the origins of the Mardi Gras Indians, more circumscribed in time but just as misleading in its simplification of a phenomenon engendered by complex and by no means isolated sociocultural contexts. In this version the foundations are familial. They have the kind of seeming time-place precision already encountered in Beatrice Hall's story about the Baby Dolls' foundation in 1912. In a recent book about black music in New Orleans the chief author is the willing victim of such a family story, as told by the "chief" of one of the black Indian tribes in 1982, Tuddy Montana: "The Creole Wild West [tribe] originated from that house on 1313 St. Anthony Street. That's where the Indians got their start, from my family."

In the house lived Tuddy Montana's "granduncle," Becate Batiste, who "had Indian blood." Tuddy, born in 1922, knows this because his grandmother told him so: "Well my grandmother, she always said that we had Indian blood. . . . I have some cousins . . . man, they look just *like* an Indian. My grandmother died at ninety-eight. In those days they didn't keep birth records like they do now." Jason Berry, coauthor and presumably the chief writer of the book in question, concludes that "the first black to mask as an Indian, Becate Batiste, founded the Creole Wild West Tribe in the early 1880s." After Batiste came Henri Marigny, who formed a new tribe in the Seventh Ward (a Creole area with black and white residents north and east of the French Quarter), while the Creole Wild West Tribe moved "uptown" and was led by Robert Tillman, Senior, etc.[27]

This account, with its nice coordination of time-and-space moves from one family and one part of New Orleans to another, is a construction based on taking at face value the statements of participants in solicited interviews. The problem is familiar to oral historians. Representatives of orally transmitted culture, who have no record-keeping instruments except memory and ritualized behavior, are quick to sense and accommodate the expectations of their literate interlocutors. Berry's apparent desire to establish time, place, and names leads him to mix third-hand accounts with firsthand memoirs without discrimination. Tuddy

Montana learned of Becate Batiste at some time or other from his grandmother. His grandmother was speaking about her brother's actions forty years before Tuddy was born. More useful is the written account of one Elise Kirsch, presumably a white woman of German parentage, who was born in 1876 and lived on Robertson Street near the French Quarter. Her memoir of her childhood and early days was published in 1951 and includes, according to Berry, an account of Mardi Gras in 1883:

> At about 10:00 A.M. that day there was a band of men (about 60) disguised as Indians who wore the real Indian costumes and their chiefs had turkey feathers running down from around their heads way down in the back. They came along from St. Bernard Avenue on Robertson Street, shouting and screaming war whoops, and carried tomahawks—on their way back would stop and perform war dances, etc., and would run for a block and begin again. Though we were frightened when very young, we always waited for the passing of "the Indians."[28]

Kirsch's description coincides in details with that of Henry Rightor: the war whoops, tomahawks, and pauses in the street to perform war dances are mentioned. Instead of precision in names and family connections which serve the ends of clan pride, Kirsch offers details about a child's vision of these maskers when "very young." Here too the over-precision of recalled memory ("10:00 A.M."; "about 60") need not be taken literally, but the general mood, appearance, and sequence of actions can be trusted. They indicate that the chief elements of Mardi Gras Indian behavior existed by the early 1880s.

Black Indians chanted and danced in the Carnival streets at the very time when Lafcadio Hearn, writing in November 1883, reports that he had seen bamboulas danced and played in "the backyard of an abandoned property far out on Dumaine Street," that is, in an area slightly to the west of Kirsch's residence. Hearn's dancers, chanters, and instrumentalists, however, were "either old or beyond middle age," and their gatherings had already been "suppressed by the police" before Hearn's memoir was published. Did the suppression of what seemed to Hearn to be African dances, African songs, and African "tinkling metal or tin rattles about their ankles," cause younger men by repercussion to adopt and adapt Indian disguises as a way of continuing what was by the 1880s a century-long tradition of Afro-Caribbean music-making?[29]

The written accounts of whites help situate the beginnings of black-Indian masking and suggest its connection to the suppression of the more frankly African forms of festive merriment traditional until then. But they are of no aid in illuminating the semiotic sources. We have already indicated that these sources are Caribbean in many details; others probably represent a much adapted African heritage without any necessary Caribbean intermediary; others still seem to be adapted from white images of Indians. Another black Indian interviewed in 1982, Paul Longpre, gives an example of the latter and its inventive combination with everyday materials and casual conversation. Longpre, explaining the name of the Yellow Pocahontas Tribe (probably a late nineteenth-century organization), said that they took Pocahontas "from a history book." "Yellow" was added "'when one guy had on a suit with this yellow fringe from an old-time lamp shade' and a white woman asked 'Yellow Pocahontas?' Thus, says Longpre, the name stuck."[30] Longpre was seventy-nine years old when he recalled these incidents in 1982. If, as he and Berry maintain, the Yellow Pocahontas existed in the 1890s, then Longpre either has the date of the tribe's foundation wrong or he merely heard these stories rather than being present at their fabrication. Their tenor, not their truth, is what counts. Black Indians participated in and reacted to the white man's tales of "good Indians" like Pocahontas. White women watched the black Indians, and talked with them about their performances. Like Rightor's testimony, this incident suggests that Lyle Saxon exaggerates when he pretends in the memoir of his first visit to New Orleans that his experience of black Mardi Gras was unique for a white of that day. It was not only in Storyville or after hours at the Frenchman's Club that black and white met.

Saxon on his rounds with the black servant Robert on that mardi gras in 1900 saw "negro men dressed as Indians with faces painted and feather headdresses." But since Saxon situates this sight in the train of the Zulu King, who did not exist in 1900, this reference to the black Indians may not be trustworthy.[31] If the reference is accurate, however, it is generally coherent with the two written reports which we possess from the late nineteenth century, which show performances taking place in the black Creole sections of the city for hours on end, in street after street.[32] These performances seem to have been peaceful. They were centered on the display of male bravado but not necessarily of male belligerence. The simplest view of these activities might be that the performers were simply having Carnival fun with the wild west clichés of contemporary popular culture.[33]

Between 1900 and the early 1930s black Indian tribes multiplied in number and variety, and as they grew they began fighting. The tribes developed a ritual of confrontation. This is how Jelly Roll Morton remembered in 1938 the way the game went in his boyhood, about 1910: "They would send their spy-boys two blocks on ahead . . . and when a spy-boy would meet another spy from an enemy tribe he'd point his finger to the ground and say, "Bow-wow." And if they wouldn't bow, the spy-boy would use the Indian call, "Woo-woo-woo-woo-woo," that was calling the tribes—and many a time, in these Indian things, there would be a killing. . . ."[34] No one has explained very well why this period ended during the Depression era. It was certainly not because blacks found more jobs or benefited from less racial suppression and had fewer scores to settle: the social matrix in which the tribes took form did not change until the 1960s, and even then it did not change much. Paul Longpre, who "masked Indian" in the 1920s and 1930s, thinks it was because police surveillance increased, perhaps due to some notorious acts of violence. Equally interesting, but hardly the whole story, is Jason Berry's idea that fights subsided because the line had been effaced that had marked social difference among New Orleans blacks, the uptown-downtown line between those who had Creole affiliations and those who didn't.[35]

The third phase of black Indian masking, still current today, substitutes aesthetic for fighting prowess. Its expression is verbal, kinetic, visual. Although the different roles of chief, spy boy, queen, and—yes!—"wild man" seem to have existed in the 1920s and 1930s, they have since been elaborated and differentiated, so that there are second chiefs, third chiefs, trail chiefs, and so on. There are many ordinary Indians in costume also. Moreover, the tribe is accompanied by a large group of uncostumed friends and associates of the tribe, the "second line," who dance and make additional rhythm with tambourines, congo drums, cowbells, and other simple percussive instruments.

Today's tribes begin moving through the streets of their neighborhood around nine or ten o'clock on mardi gras, bending their knees and swaying from foot to foot while turning in a circle with arms outstretched. The movement shows off their costume, which is dominated by an immense headdress modeled in part on that of nineteenth-century Plains Indians with its showy crown of eagle feathers. Some decades ago eagle feathers yielded pride of place to still more ostentatious ostrich plumes, so that the headdress may now extend in a gently waving rainbow-colored aureole for a meter or more beyond the masker's face, which is unpainted and unmasked (see plate 18).

18. Mardi Gras Indian Chief on Parade, New Orleans, ca. 1978 (drawing by Toan Le)

Each dancer weaves his own costume, which means reweaving it: the costume is annually dismantled after its appearances on mardi gras and one or two other occasions. Costuming talent is chiefly exhibited in the plaques at the center of the headpiece and skirt or apron: pictures of Indian heroes, animals, birds and flowers, or elaborate geometrical designs are woven from glass beads, sequins, velvet rhinestones, lace, and ribbon. Early "suits," as they are called, included bottle caps, bits of glass, and eggshells. The plaques are often not dismantled but are given new settings and arranged in new association with each other another year. The suit is kept secret in the neighborhood until the moment of its appearance in the parade. Eventually the Indian chiefs compete for a "best costume" award. It would not do for a rival to steal your ideas. Chants consist of a call, usually initiated by the chief, so abbreviated by the elisions and ellipses of shared memory that it is nearly unintelligible to the outsider. The tribe's members respond with an echo of part of the line or a seemingly "nonsensical" line like those characteristic of folk music the world over (cf. the English "As I was out a-walking, a-taking the morning air, Lolly tu-dum tu-dum, Lolly tu-dum day"). Some of the words are probably of African derivation, and the call-and-response mode is definitely an African musical inheritance.

> Hey-an dan dalu wild mamboula!
> Handa wanda o mama [or mambo]
>
> Said uptown rulers and downtown too!
> Handa wanda o mama.[36]

The behavior of the maskers includes two ritual elements in addition to the sparkling vision and auditory glory of sometimes more than three dozen dancers chanting and swaying in brilliantly intricate costumes. One is the specialization of songlines to indicate purpose or action. For example, the verse "Big Chief like plenty-a fi-yuh wa-tuh," may be the signal for some Indians to move among people in a bar or along sidewalks to take up a collection with which to buy wine, an age-old Carnival tradition in a new form.[37]

The second ritual element has to do with the march of the tribes. It is more than a song-and-dance show-off of costumes. When spread out down the middle of a street, the tribe may extend over five or more city blocks. The spy boy comes first, looking for other approaching tribes. Then comes a flag boy, bearing the tribal banner which indicates the Indians' name: Wild Magnolias, Wild Tchoupitoulas, Golden Eagles, White Eagles, Flaming Arrows, White Cloud Hunters, Hundred and One Tribe. The most important figure, near the center of the procession, is the Big Chief; there may also be second, third, and fourth chiefs, each of them accompanied like the Big Chief by a queen. The average number of maskers today is fifteen to twenty-five people, but Jason Berry affirms that in 1965 the Golden Blades tribe included 125 braves.[38]

Sooner or later a confrontation takes place in dance and song with other tribes. The spy boy, seeing another group, gives a signal to the flag boy and the flag boy passes it on to the chief. "No other Indian can meet our chief but a chief. The wild men [described by this same source as the "craziest acting" members of the tribes] . . . meet first and they do their dance." The respective spy boys, flag boys, and chiefs confront each other in turn. "Then after that we go one way and they go another. We go and meet other gangs."[39] Echoing the jargon of an earlier era a meeting with other tribes was still in the 1960s conceived less as a friendly display of talent than as a "war." "The war is carried on mainly through singing and dancing about the greatness of each tribe's respective chiefs, but occasionally the . . . war becomes physical and one chief will demand that the other humbah [humble] himself to him. If the other chief refuses to humbah, which he invariably does, a humbug follows. A humbug is a fight. In the old days when one chief defeated another, the victor took the loser's crown."[40] The fantasy of political inversion, heard in the white Indian Chief Slackabamorinico's informal title as "Old King Carnival of Mobile," carries a component of neighborhood rivalry in the black sections of New Orleans: "Indians comin' from all over town/ Big Chief singin' gonna taken 'em down/ Chocka mo feny hey de hey/ Indians the ruler on the holiday."[41]

Through the three phases of Mardi Gras Indian development runs a unity of signifying activity which is based on the peculiarities of orally centered culture. I use the term "orally centered" to make it clear that by nonliterate culture I do not mean one in which no one can or does read, but one in which meaningful action is primarily shaped not by written but by oral modes of communication. In orally centered culture, meaning arises most often from face-to-face, interpersonal exchanges. The call-and-response pattern of Mardi Gras Indian music is an aesthetic example of this. In letter-centered culture, meaning arises from reference to impersonal, broad networks of institutions, texts, and systems of knowledge. Face-to-face encounters tend to refer beyond the immediate occasion to more abstract and general systems which the present moment of communication serves. Roles in letter-centered cultures consequently tend to be more meaningful than personalities: the opposite is true in orally centered cultures.

Orally centered cultures prize performance above the exchange of views. Exchange of views is a testing device: it not only allows issues to be sorted out in their frequently long-term, long-range complexity; it also allows the chief players in a given game (of politics, of business, of city planning, etc.) to see whether some reordering of status and roles can and should be attempted. Exchange of views determines the relative value of roles in a given situation; performance in letter-centered culture is merely the execution of what has already been determined by such probing and rearrangement of roles. The performance of a Mardi Gras Indian chief, on the other hand, is crucial to his retention of the role. His ability to create a beautiful costume and to execute with finesse a series of dance moves are important, but what counts most is the chief's ability to judge when to make the moves and how to use the costume: his most important talent is discretion in initiating songs, verses, and new rhymes to fire up and cool down the members of his group, so that the tribe remains in collective control of themselves and the street occasion. The chief's power is circumstantial. This is no less true in recent decades when violence has been virtually banned as a part of performance. Violence remains around the edges of the performance; in the poverty-soaked areas of New Orleans which today as for the past one hundred years are the seedbeds of this Carnival, the difficulties of daily life engender such insoluble conflicts that acts of passion which maim and kill are inevitable. On Mardi Gras day the chief must feel the approach of such passion and thwart it before it arrives. "Otherwise," as one chief confided in 1987, "they just be shuttin' us all down. They be no more maskin' Indian at all." Carnival is very big business in New Orleans today. The Indians, for reasons to be explained presently, are part of that business, knowingly or unknowingly.

Orally centered culture is polyvalent, while letter-centered culture strives toward unity of purpose; toward single "essences." This quality has to do with what the structural anthropologist Claude Lévi-Strauss has analyzed as the principle of *bricolage* ("make-shift construction").[42] People who are part of orally centered cultures construct their lives and their cultural activity from interchangeable parts, parts with which one can make do in many different situations. Since resources are so limited, everything must serve six purposes. Soda-pop bottle caps were once used to make part of the sparkle in the Indian's costumes; now they may be used, by punching holes in the center, to provide substitute rattles around the edges of tambourines. The Indian suit must never be the same from year to year; but its constituent parts are pulled apart, traded, and used again and again—just like the yellow fringe from an old-time lamp shade.

Such use and reuse develops an eye and an ear for the polyvalence of symbols and materials: given another setting, nearly anything changes its meaning. Things have no essence, no hard, unyielding permanence. Things must be played with to find their meaning, which is relative to circumstance.

The inventiveness of the Indians, ever different and yet reassuringly similar in the variability of their costumes, their dance steps, and their songs, derives from this necessity and this willingness to play with the elements of meaning.[43] Letter-centered cultures, obsessed with universals, have less flexibility. The mythic figures exhibited on the floats of the white Carnival societies, whether profound or trivial, high or low in sentiment, share qualities of fixed ideation. The kings and dukes and queens and maids, smiling from their thrones according to the rank and degree of their roles, are stuck there. Each of them is just right, and if a hair is out of place, that is quite a fault. The fantasy of orally centered culture is infinite flexibility. The fantasy of letter-centered culture is well-arranged perfection.

Polyvalence, personality, performance: these qualities are integrated by what Mikhail Bakhtin calls the sense of the "lower bodily stratum," by what philosophers might call naturalism, by what the Baby Dolls call "shakin' it on down," by what I shall call a search for the sensuous continuum. The slithering, rippling dance which shocked observers at Congo Square and which fascinated Fredrika Bremer in the cabildo at Havana, which puzzled little Lyle Saxon when—so he claimed—he saw it repeated with such obsession by the blacks in a hidden hall in Storyville, is there in another form with the Indians in their dances through the streets. "Masking Indian" is not costume art; the performance is unified by the rhythmized body, to which all else—sequins and gestures and tambourine sound and chants—are subordinated. Letter-centered culture culminates in the Visionary Word. The other culture is rooted in the body's down-flowing, gravity-centered kinetic feel. "Getting real low": the rock-and-roll dancer and singer Jerry Lee Lewis offers still another formula for the way this culture aims at unifying reality from the bottom up rather than from the head down.[44]

"Orally centered culture," then, is as limiting a term as "nonliterate" is nondescriptive. This mode of invention is not always or essentially verbal, musical, oral. But to say "bodily centered" is to speak too generally. Even Bakhtin's notion seems too limited, the idea that carnivalesque culture weaves its signs upon the body's foundations, its belly, guts, and genitals, its downward-dropping, earth-directed parts.[45] What is sought is *directness* of communication no less than integrated expressiveness and earthiness. "Willie Tee" Turbinton describes the experience of his band meeting the Wild Magnolias and developing a music appropriate to these Indians' chants:

> They came out and started doing their thing. . . . So we just kind of started jamming. And it was so hip and natural that, you know, when you strike a groove musically with somebody, it's almost like knowing 'em. You pass up the barriers of getting to know somebody.

To understand the Carnival societies' floats, to fathom the meaning of their ballroom decorum requires eight steps of knowledge and nine of imagination, so as to reconstitute the codes which make them more than mutually mirroring clichés. In the case of the Indians, you only have to pick up some sticks, beat in time, and move with the others in order to begin to understand.

From participation to inspiration, however, is still a long road. With musicians like Turbinton, who had himself masked Indian before meeting the Wild Magnolias and their leader Bo Dollis, there was mutual interaction, sparking new inventions, and changing the valence of old tunes:

> They were singing "Iko Iko" and "Handa Wanda". . . . But it just stayed in one key and didn't change. . . . Bo and them, just having a raw thing, they didn't know where they were going technically—well, wherever we went, man, Bo could just naturally hear how to sound.[46]

Letter-centered, bodily indirect culture; and orally centered, bodily direct culture share the notion of inspiration, however differently they construe its source. For the first culture, meaning, symbols, words, and music typically arise somewhere deep "inside" the organism as a complex, hidden product of immaterial thought, emotion, and intuition, afterwards sent "outward" through the senses and other material instruments.[47] For the second, meanings and signs of all kinds arise on the boundary between the organism and its environment: the world itself, and not just its mental equivalents or the soul's "super-natural" parts, is numinous. With musicians, Turbinton said—but should we not say it about anyone sharing this culture?—"You pass up the barriers of getting to know somebody. . . . It's a closer look at a person's spirit." And, I would add, the world's.[48]

Black culture is "soul" culture, but this spirituality has little to do with the ineffable supernaturalism of white Western traditions. How can it be that black Christian people allow themselves to clap and sing, jump and cry, writhe and fall to the floor in the house of the Lord? The Spirit accosts black worshipers, it moves them totally, without and within. The path to God is no quiet removal from the world's temptations in silent inward prayer. Inspiration comes directly to the true worshiper, and it moves from one believer to another. The trancing possessed ones share their glory with the congregation. This embodied sense of soul and spirit explains why black people can speak of "soul food," of "soul music," of the politics of "soul" with no sacrilege and no devaluation of words. In terms of this culture, where could soul and spirit possibly be if they did not move through and with the world?[49]

In a remarkable essay called *Spirit World*, the New Orleans photographer Michael P. Smith has shown the parallels between many of the Mardi Gras Indian rituals and the peculiar healing, baptism, and prayer practices of "Spiritualist Churches" in that city: the Faith Temple Church of God in Christ, the Beauty of Holiness Church of the Lord God in Creation, Saint Daniel's Spiritual Temple, the Holy Family Spiritual Church, the Guiding Start Spiritual Church, and so on.[50] Smith found not only parallels in the manner in which soulful participation rises in rhythmic force over the course of a lengthy meeting but also many specific Indian references.

A large number of the spiritual churches trace their foundation to the work of a woman named Leaf Anderson who moved to New Orleans from Chicago in 1920. This woman was "half Mohawk," according to the present-day leader of the Eternal Life Christian Spiritual Church. Her "spirit guides," continues this informant, were Queen Esther, White Hawk (?), Black Hawk (the famous Sac Indian who in 1832 resisted whites in a war in Illinois), and a Father Jones or Father John.[51] One of Smith's photographs shows a statue of Black Hawk, decked out with a Mardi Gras Indian-like headdress of eagle feathers and ostrich plumes, being used in a "Black Hawk ceremony at the Israelite Universal Divine Spiritual Church."[52] At a service on Halloween evening in the Infant Jesus of Prague Spiritual Church, Reverend James Anderson, wearing a Mardi Gras Indian costume belonging to the chief of the Wild Tchoupitoulas, functioned "as a medium for Black Hawk, the . . . warrior whom the church connects with peace and justice."[53]

So, too, black Indian tribes have their spiritual side. During the 1930s and 1940s, according to some of Jason Berry's informants, the tribes set out on mardi gras morning after reciting the Lord's Prayer and singing a song called "Indian Red." The song is still sung by most tribes at the beginning or end of practices and just before parading on mardi gras. It functions to introduce the role-names (not individuals' names) which are included in the group: spy boy, flag boy, and whatever may be the number and kinds of chiefs, as well as to vaunt the name of the particular tribe. "In earlier years it was called the 'Indian Prayer Song.'"[54] The only person who was acknowledged—at least for some years in the 1960s and early 1970s according to some informants—as an authority above or between these sovereign unconquerable nations was the Indian Chief Counsel, a person designated to "keep down trouble." He did so not by virtue of any pseudolegal authority but because he was "like a pastor."[55]

> I bring my gang all over town
> Drink fire water till the sun go down
> Get back home we gonna kneel and pray
> We had some fun on the holiday.[56]

Embodiment, spirituality, pleasure: they are one.

It is true, then, that New Orleans possesses a black subculture. But it has taken form only slowly. The old black culture of colonial and pre–Civil War days was broken. New forms emerged slowly between 1860 and 1900. They were not based exclusively in or around "black Indian" groups. The creative force of the emergent subculture derived as much from black Christian practices as from contact with popular images of Indian heroes such as Black Hawk, as much from the rich development of black music in this Southern city, the "cradle of jazz," as from familial traditions of black-Indian intermarriage, as much from the necessities of poverty and racial repression as from the opportunities of Carnival.[57]

This subculture is not by any means synonymous with black New Orleans. It is a special, and from the economic, demographic, or political point of view, a negligible part of the larger black community which in 1900 numbered more than 80,000, in 1950 182,000, and in 1980 308,000 persons. The historians of New Orleans' black musical community, Al Rose and Edmond Souchon, have counted about one thousand professional jazz musicians who were active between 1900 and 1925. The total number of black people masking as Indians between 1880 and 1941, the beginning of World War II, probably did not exceed that same number of one thousand. Today in a city population of a third of a million black people and a metropolitan population of over 400,000 blacks, only three or four hundred people belong to tribes.[58]

We are speaking of a "micro-climate," spawned in uniformly black, uniformly poor, congested neighborhoods which are no longer representative of the living situations of most black people in this city. For most blacks, as for most whites, "masking Indian" is a phrase, a rumor, a picture in the newspapers. But this very smallness and imperceptibility, along with the racking preoccupation with basic problems of existence which leave little margin for reflection or individual initiative, are what preserve it.

The central city, where most black Indian tribes are located, remains today, as it has been since the later nineteenth century, the main staging area for the leisure time of all New Orleanians. In the 1920s, as tribes grew in number and popularity, the area seemed to hold countless places of enjoyment. Danny Barker, a banjo player who has done much to preserve the jazz history of this era, recalls: "There were balls, soirees, banquets, weddings, deaths, christenings, Catholic communions and confirmations. . . . There were hayrides, advertisements of business concerns, carnival season (Mardi Gras). Any little insignificant affair was sure to have some kind of music and each section engaged their neighborhood favorites: Joe Oliver, the cornet player around the corner, or Cheeky Sherman and somebody's piano, or Sandpaper George whose pockets were always loaded with different grades of sandpaper and who said, 'Good music must have variety; different music, different grade of sandpaper.'" In those days, Barker continues, "there was a caste system in New Orleans." The black-white line, which to whites cast everyone with a tinge of African ancestry into darkness, produced a fantastic array of color types among blacks: "Mulattos, Quadroons, Octaroons, all those different people . . . had different halls. You went to them according to your family standing or your background. . . . They had these speakeasy peekholes at the dance hall. . . . The man was watching and if you didn't belong, you didn't get in."[59]

The caste-like social situation which lent strength and violence to the tribes' sense of selfhood was the result of at least four kinds of social barriers *within* the black community: The black/white line was translated into many shades of lightness.

Non-whites in New Orleans did not simply accept the two-part caste system instituted by whites after the Civil War; rather, they tried to adjust this new exigence to the continuing existence of a third caste with its own elaborate marital rules, the "free blacks" with their miscegenetic origins. The whites might prefer to ignore this, but light-colored blacks saw the profit in maintaining the older difference. Thus, first of all, the more sharply whites enforced a simple black-white line, the more light-colored blacks fought back by creating a galaxy of intrablack racial prejudices, expressed in separate institutions, in schools, "social aid and pleasure" societies, benevolent organizations, neighborhood bands, Carnival societies. The inspiration to have another party, to march down the street, to start another tribe did not simply come from "the city that care forgot." It came also from mulatto racism, from Creole pride, from family traditions. Secondly, and as a consequence of erection of the first barrier, segregation in New Orleans reinforced the desire to claim Creole French descent among those blacks who could: the Creole/non-Creole line was inextricable from the assertion of superior social status within a politically and economically declining community. Third, the Creole line in turn was related to an informal pecking order which Danny Barker calls "family standing"—they were typically large families, with many uncles and aunts and close relations among three generations—and the influence of that sense of family status on the character of neighborhoods.[60]

Beyond these three lines of difference was, finally, the larger fact of living in a city with no tradition and no intention of acquiring a tradition of providing basic social services to its black citizens.[61] One cannot understand the way Mardi Gras Indians celebrate Carnival, preparing for it all year long, unless one realizes that tribal ties fulfill a whole gamut of social no less than cultural purposes. To disconnect the Indians' performance on mardi gras day from its social setting obscures the meaning of that performance far more fundamentally than disconnecting literate culture's theatrical presentations from the lives of the actors. However, up to now the Indians have not attracted the attention of sociologists. The generalizations which precede and follow in this text are based on the reading and personal contacts of a cultural historian and are no substitute for sociological research.

19. Headdress and its extension, Mardi Gras Indian Chief, New Orleans, 1987 (photo, Norman Magden)

> My principal informant, the leader or Big Chief of the White
> Cloud Hunters tribe in "uptown" New Orleans, is a sign painter
> in his forties. Most black Indians are drawn from the laboring
> class and are often marginally or completely illiterate. Chiefs of
> the tribes may retain their position ten, twenty, or more years,
> often until death.[62]

I walk from the French Quarter down Dumayne toward Claiborne Avenue
with my friend who will take pictures. Charles has said he and his "gang"—he
doesn't say "tribe"—will be out at "seven or eight" this morning, mardi gras
day, March 3, 1987. It is beautiful weather, crisp and clear. It will be hot at midday in the main streets. But right now at a few minutes before seven in the
morning all is calm . . . too calm. We are at the gang's meeting-place, the
chief's sister's house. Nobody in sight. . . . Now it's 7:15 . . . 7:30, how curious that nobody at all has shown up. We're feeling pretty uncomfortable,
standing a little away from the house, as this person and that comes in or out
of the houses in the all-black neighborhood. We must have the wrong house
number, maybe even the wrong street. . . . And then, quite suddenly, the
door to the house opens and we are invited in. Here after all is the Big Chief,
stooping over his costume, sewing, sewing. Yeah, it just isn't ready. Of course
everyone in the gang knows the parade will be two hours late. There's mardi
gras music playing on the radio, and there is the "suit", as the Indians say,
propped for the moment against the wall, eight feet or so tall (plate 19).

What a vision! It changes everything I had seen in the way of Indian costumes. There seems really nothing Indian about it at all, little beadwork, no
eagle feathers, except that this flight of fancy recognizably began from the
common Indian style of recent years, with its gently waving broad aureole
wreathing the face—in this case, the whole body. "Flight" is the right word.
The Chief will be a bird; the costume is the plumage of a peacock. The bird's
body will sit directly on the head; the lifted feathers of the male peacock's fan-
tail have turned into jewels.

It is a study in white and black, with other colors, faint blues, rose-whites,
yellows, greens and violets, concentrated in the crisp raised triangles of the
fan-tail, studding the bird's neck and the sides of its body (plate 20). The head
will glow with light, sparkling in the sun, gathering energy there, sending it
out in black-and-white waves from the floating, dancing body. The outer
double row of white furry softness is interrupted every twelve inches or so by
a real "eye" peacock feather, glued to the fur. So the stony jewels and the textile softness are punctuated by reminders of the natural bird's incomparable
iridescence.

Charles is crouching on the bedspread, pulling his needle through the thick
fabric with a pliers. He's been sewing with only brief breathers since 5 A.M.
the previous day. "It gave me trouble," he sighs. Toward one o'clock this

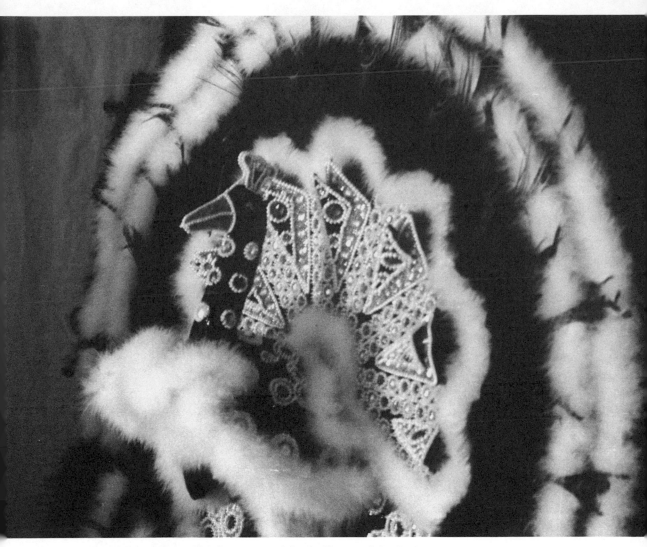

20. Peacock headpiece, Chief's costume (photo, Norman Magden)

morning it seemed that all was in place, and then the peacock perched above his head came loose. A whole elaborate reinforcement had to be inserted. Several other folks stand around, quiet, respectful, no one venturing to do anything till Charles directs. The last adjustments must be his own . . . (see plate 21).

Two days earlier, on Sunday night at the Candlelight Inn, the White Cloud Hunters held their last practice. The members of the tribe who, as is usual with the black Indians, have been meeting here for four or five months irregularly, once every one or two weeks, will get it together this evening, try out their

moves, practice some confrontations, some "challenges," and generate the energy they will need to dance all day in their heavy costumes. Practices are usually scheduled to last a couple of hours; they take place at bars which are the regular forum for men in the neighborhood.[63] No description of the moment-to-moment unfolding of such practice sessions, where invention and preparation are interwoven, has appeared in the literature about New Orleans Carnival. Michael Smith's photos, taken at many different practices over a ten-year period, provide fine documentation on particular points but, like his commentary, do not offer a sense of the continuities involved in such sessions.[64] The description which follows is that of an outsider and probably contains misunderstandings. But the outsider also sees freshly and relatively: the discipline involved in elaborating the description helped me to determine the generalizations about this subculture that have just been discussed. The descriptive particulars, aside from their intrinsic interest, are also offered to readers to help them specify the parallels with Caribbean and African Indians and wildmen which will subsequently be introduced.

My photographer friend and I, invited to the practice by Charles Taylor in the course of a previous interview, arrive at the Inn about 7:15. The practice is scheduled "from about 7 to 9." The room is twice as long as it is wide, perhaps forty by eighty feet. The bar runs forty feet long on the left side, toward the back end of the room. People are ordering mostly beer in bottles from four bartenders. Pint bottles of bourbon are ranged for sale along the counter behind the bar; there are, too, some fifths of various liqueurs and liquors for drinks by the shot. There was only desultory drinking by anybody, least of all by the gang, throughout the evening. You go to the bar, get your drink, pay, and sit down at one of the fifteen or so small tables arranged irregularly on the right side of the room and up near the door on the left side.

It is no tourist joint. Would we have found it if we had not been brought there by friends and relatives of Charles Taylor? No big sign out front, only a beer sign in one window, a nondescript building on a nondescript street of one-story residences. What signals the place is the group of young men standing near the door, leaning on the cars parked at the curb, talking animatedly, sipping beer.

21. Working on the headdress (photo, Norman Magden)

Rightor in 1900 noticed "garlands and festoons of colored tissue paper" in the Indians' dance hall. There they are in 1987, some of the colored streamers reading "Happy Birthday White Cloud Hunters." There are also some balloons and two white, blankly staring face-masks attached to a pole in the center of the right-hand side of the room toward the back. In this rear area on the right there are no tables and the space is evidently reserved for dancing—and the practice? (See plate 22.)

Yes. It is 7:40 now. With no announcement, no evident hush or other preparation, a group of ten or a dozen people, mostly men, a couple of women, all in their twenties or thirties in appearance, have moved into the farthest back corner of that space, at the farthest extreme from where we are sitting near the door. The place is by no means crowded, there are maybe sixty or seventy people in the room, and the fifty or so who aren't in the corner just go on chatting at the tables and along the bar. They're saying something to each

22. Mardi Gras Indian Practice, Tavern, New Orleans, 1987 (photo, Norman Magden)

other in the corner, bent into a loose circle, there's a tambourine shake, giving a shiver sound, stopped with a thump on the tambourine drumhead. More soft talking, repeating the shakes and thumps, and then quickly but smoothly a rhythm takes over, one guy beating on the side of a little bell. They are all in everyday clothes. The only sign of festivity is the garlands of crepe paper, balloons, and the two masks. Casual and cool.

Then quite soon one man starts weaving, turning, moving faster and faster, he has some kind of squirrel tail in his hand, there's a heaving up and down around him, bodies bobbing in rhythm with that fellow in the middle. He holds up both arms, balancing, as he goes down with deeply bent knees. Then without anyone giving a signal that I can see (I am moving right up there now, no one seems to mind), they all move in close, standing up, nearly still, and Charles is in the middle, shouting something, everyone else responding (plate 23). It's a variant of one of the songs I've heard on the record of the Wild Tchoupitoulas tribe, with the Neville Brothers performing with the tribe; they're saying "White Cloud Hunters gotta golden crown." I flash on the old

23. The chief gives the call (photo, Norman Magden)

pseudo-King traditions of Carnival —is it that? Is it a Christian reference (all those hymns, my mother murmuring, "oh my, he deserves a golden crown!"), a reference to Big Chief George Landry of the Wild Tchoupitoulas with his golden headdress (I can see it: it's on the album's slip cover)?

Others take over. Charles steps out. There's another song—where have I heard it? "In-dj-unn, heh dey come. . ." (later I find it: also on the Wild Tchoupitoulas record).[65]

Some further incidents follow, but I've lost a little interest. It seems repetitive of what I've seen. . . . And then, unexpectedly, a new guy turns up, he wasn't in the group before. He's dressed differently, snappy, neatly, white shirt, wild tie, some kind of silver amulet swinging over the tie, tan suit coat and trousers, sharply shined dark shoes. My god, he can dance. He's at the side at first, there's some kind of channel forming between him and Charles.

24. Dancing, male style . . . (photo, Norman Magden)

Is this then the famous challenge? The fellow is super, lunging, quick, looking this way, now that, all the way down, lower body tense as a spring, torso loose as a cat's, fingers snapping, smiling, moving in toward Charles now, all eyes fixed on him, grinning, watching the feet, watching the hands, fascinated, Charles is wide-eyed too (plate 24).

No, it's not really a challenge because Charles isn't trying any counter-moves. Who is he? They've got arms now around each other's shoulders, going all the way down together, bobbing back up, hips in perfect undulating closeness (plate 25). O.K., maybe he's not even part of the tribe, he's just doing his male thing. A virtuoso.

A practice is like jazz music, improvisations. Each performer when he gets the feeling takes a riff, struts, moves to the center

25. With the chief (photo, Norman Magden)

26. Dancing to the queen . . . (photo, Norman Magden)

and does his stuff. That will stimulate somebody else, they may play then together. But it's all done with a guiding rhythm; the chief, the leader of the gang is always there.

A challenge is a break in the rhythm, making strong dance moves, getting the tambourines to follow your moves, stopping the rap of the other. It happened several times during this practice but it didn't seem to develop very far—is that because these people are all White Cloud Hunters or their "second-line" sympathizers? Michael Smith writes that during the winter season, when they meet from week to week for practices, one tribe may visit another at their tavern and the challenges may be for real.[66]

27. And for the queen (photo, Norman Magden)

As the confrontation gathers, people who are standing around, letting their bodies move with the tambourines, start throwing up fists, flail their arms, open wide their bodies, go away and go back toward the conflict.

I had asked Charles in an earlier interview: what happens in a challenge? "You get hot," he said, "you get too close. Challenge

is talking about yourself, boasting. You talk 'til you're cut."—
What did that mean, "cut"? I did not dare ask.

It happened. The group straightened out from its bunched-together way, there was a double line, forming a channel six or eight feet across, twenty or twenty-five feet long. Charles is moving down it. Someone at the other end is doing his own moves, to his own rhythm, his own tambourine. Charles moves backward, inviting the guy out, out to the middle of the channel. The two are there. The music stops.

Charles says something, his gang yells approbation. Charles speaks again, he shouts, he points. But the guy is there, six inches from his nose, screaming. Charles throws both arms up, the crowd around is interfering, yelling. I can't hear single words. Who could? Are they words? No one needs words. No one needs to hear anything but these gushing, enveloping screams, and the sudden, ominous pauses. The words and the pauses—they must be prescribed, I tell myself, my heart beating a little bit much. They're formulas.

Then it's over, very suddenly. What happened? I am glad. They're back to a new chant. Whee-ee. I look at my watch. Twenty minutes zipped in that challenge.

They're back to "White Cloud Hunters Wear a golden Crown," starting to build the energy again. They've gone over an hour now, no stop; though the same singer, same dancer is never all the time in the center, none of them has backed off for a beer either. By this time all of us at the tables have come up closer, we're all ringed around, moving around. There's a kind of easy in and out among us, and we are doing some boozing.

Where are the women? There's Charles' queen, small like him, not so wiry. Charles is in his forties, his teenage daughter is here, a head taller than him, playing tambourine. The queen is not his wife, not his girlfriend. How did you get your queen? I had asked in the interview. "She came to me . . . She came recommended." Reputations. You are always already known. You start masking Indian at 3 or 4! (Smith has some crazy photos of these little kids in their Mardi Gras Day Indian costumes.[67])

The queen wears a blue sweatshirt that says "Big Queen." The way she and Charles dance to each other is more like that with the guy I call virtuoso, but it's not exactly that either. The queen seems to be there to bring out his dancing. They are dancing down the channel toward each other now. Charles eyes her warmly. Now he's really into it, dancing really funky. Queen is throwing out her arms, swinging with it, attentive . . . (plates 26 and 27, a closely shot sequence).

I begin to think about the sexual politics, the sexual kinetics. When the energy begins to build, the centripetal beat pulling people into an intense circle, generating some kind of merciless intent, it excludes the women, however they pound the tambourines.[68] It's machismo, this intensity, this absorption of

28. Into the rhythm (photo, Norman Magden)

each one in his ecstasy, even though they're doing it together, dependent on doing it together. That's the function of polyrhythm then, the way the yell will go up and be punctuated by a tambourine shake which is off-time, syncopated, cutting across the main beat without weakening it, just complicating it. Unison and dis-unison, all together and none together. The cooperation of the men absorbed in their bodies, the cooperation done so often and so long that you can play all you want with it, just like a jazz theme which seems to evaporate in the riffs and yet is always there, fully in tune with the individualism. When the circle pulls tight into the middle, the women aren't there, they give a little way, they're too conscious of themselves, of the others, to isolate themselves in closeness like that, paradoxical as that sounds. The men cooperate, they want the chief's chief-ness because that allows them to imagine themselves, too, in that spot. (I exit from my raw notes a moment and ask the reader to look carefully at those ten faces in plate 28, each one going every which way, and to compare it with the queen's attitude in plate 27, and the spacing and stance of her movement there vis-à-vis Charles.)

. . . Well, it's not entirely like that. There's another woman here, a queen from another tribe who summons this macho intensity, who has the moves, the theatrical flair, the sudden hard looks which stop you dead, which make you move off in a confrontation. And she was "hot" tonight, her chief so drunk there'd be no practice on this last-chance occasion of perfection before The Day. At a certain point she moved toward the chief from the other end of the room, during a lull in the action. It looked like a real challenge coming. But the chief of the White Cloud Hunters responded easily. They did some hard looks and some strong steps up to each other, but there was no shouting match. They know each other well. Later, after the practice, in a pickup truck with this woman and an older man with whom she had masked Indian for years, I overheard the man say to her: "What you think you doin' back here?" "Wha . . . ?" "I tol' you already, you nevah dance to the chief!" Silence.

It is a male scene. Women are there to decorate the males, and not vice-versa. They are certainly not there to challenge them. Charles again: "The Chief is the flower." But Charles also said: "When I was a boy I saw two queens split open each other's heads with hatchets." I believe it. And after this evening I don't believe so much that stuff about the violence being all ended.

. . . The dancing seems to be winding down. I notice lots of stomping now, with highly raised knees: does this imitate some kind of movie-Indian dancing and whooping in the war dance? Two men go to the center, dance around each other, a little clumsily. One of them is huge. "Who is he?" I ask someone. "The wildman," I am told. And then I remember an incident near the beginning of the evening, before the dancing had moved to its first peak of chanting. I had seen the tall, begrizzled wildman (plate 29) arguing with people outside the door. And then he had strode into the middle of the gang, breaking up the early rhythm, arguing and shouting. He had stomped off, back toward the door, and then had returned again to the still loosely formed group with their tambourines, shouting and waving his arms. Then before I could follow the sequence (I was still near the door) there was the chief, pulling him by his sweatshirt, down about navel level, gently, not too fast but firmly, out of the group and all the way outside where they had a talk. I asked Charles about it. "He was goin' too fast," he said. So the behavior was expected, but not at that point opportune or well enough controlled, one or the other or both. So that's how the chief operates too.

> Thinking about the pattern of the practice (it ended almost precisely on the stroke of nine), I see its up-and-down, wave-like motion. The way up was toward the challenges, after the magnificent dancing of the tan-suited man, after the early distractions of the howling wildman. Then on the way down came that distraction of the queen from elsewhere. But it didn't stop any-

29. The wildman (photo, Norman Magden)

thing, really, the practice went on in little waves carried on the big wave, went on with this core group of ten or twelve, others having joined and then left as emotion gathered and waned. And then this core group, without any hitch in the motion or emotion, just stopped. The event had had scarcely any real beginning and its ending was too abrupt to be called a finale. Its curve was a sensuous continuum.

Thinking about that conclusion in turn, and its relation to the sexual dimension which caught my fancy in the middle of the performance, I saw more clearly that these naturalistic continuities of performance, the way the practice is shaped in an easy unconscious way, avoiding sharp transitions, must have developed in counterpoint to the discontinuities of what the gangs used to call "war," the fights which were so big an attraction in the earlier part of the century. Machismo and violence are still here, they're even essential to the groups' modern attractiveness, but they're here between individuals. The goal, then, is double: the ease of skilled moves, the excitement of confrontation. The performance unfolds in sensuous continuity, but it also leads, it *should* lead, to a rift in the unfolding. The smoothness is there to carry you up to and away from this sparking, this "slanging each other,"[69] this clash and discharge. In the "old days" the smoothness and the discharge might be practically assured through ritual. "The night before 'Fat Tuesday,' the members of the tribe would gather at a bar or in one of their homes, smoke their 'peace-pipes' and drink a mixture of gin and gunpowder" before beginning the final practice.[70]

The clash or moment of discontinuity in the continuum has an aesthetic more than compulsive quality today. The black Indian, like his Caribbean cousins, demonstrates his prowess through "signifying" in the contemporary black-slang sense and also in the semiotic sense of that term.[71]

> Hoon-don-da-ay
> Low-down, dirty wa-ay . . .
>
> We de uptown rulers, we de
> Wild Tchoupitoulas . . .
> We de Injun rulers now
>
> Hoon-don-da-ay: Meet everybody
> Hoon-don-da-ay: Nobody goom bow [going to bow]
>
> . . . Let 'em come now
> . . . I got the knife boy
> . . . I got the gun now
>
> Hoon-don-da-ay: whoop an' holler now
> Hoon-don-da-ay: what we holler 'bout
>
> . . . Set 'em on fiyo [fire]
> . . . Fiyo on the bayou
> . . . Run 'em in the rivo[72]

Weapons cannot be displayed openly in the parades. But they can be sung about. The singing is both a boastful warning and also—an essential function in oral cultures—a way of carrying forward the memory of the past. Another song, performed by the Wild Tchoupitoulas in 1976, includes the story of a battle on Magnolia [Street] Bridge, a bridge which had not existed for several decades at that time. It crossed the New Basin Canal, a waterway now paved over:

> Big Gang standin' on the Magnolya Bridge
> Early Mardi Gras mawnin'
> Here come de gang from Metry Ridge
> They struck without no warnin'

> Hey, hey give 'em no warnin'
> Hey, hey give 'em no warnin' [73]

And songs commemorate fallen heroes, in this case a singer and black Indian stabbed to death outside a bar in central New Orleans "just after Carnival":

> Well I remember the mawnin', remember it well
> Brother John is gone
> Well I remember the mawnin my Brother John fell
> Brother John is gone
>
> He sang mighty-kootie-fiyo on a Mardi Gras day, yawl
> Brother John is gone
> An' whoever wasn't ready had to git out the way
> Brother John is gone
> He was a mighty brave with a heart of steel
> Brother John is gone
> He never would bow and he never would kneel
> Brother John is gone
>
> Hey keep singin' bout: brother brother brother brother
> Brother John is gone [74]

People who are communicating in nonliterate and sensuously continuous rather than in intellectually or mechanistically discontinuous ways, pull those who want to share time with them toward similar modes of behavior. This pull influenced the rhetorical mode adopted in the preceding section, just as it probably affected the words which came to mind at the time, conserved in the nearly illegible jottings from which I have constructed the account. Nevertheless there is a hiatus—a hiatus which I would like to emphasize rather than obscure with the smoothness of discourse—between a resolutely unwritten or even *anti*-written enterprise like the Indians' practice and the written simulacra which try to evoke it.

But beyond the incommensurability of different instruments and different modes of communication—a relative rather than absolute matter—there lurks the social scientist's bugbear, objectivity. The reporting social scientist is painfully aware that no experience, however directly sensuous its claims and appeal, ever arrives at the cranium, let alone at the pen's nib, uncharged with an ensemble of ideological, institutional, and personal preoccupations. He—or she, but I can't pretend to be much more than autobiographical here—must introduce a series of filters to reduce the residue of his predilections and to refine his apprehensions of the seductively simple, straightforward behavior that he witnesses.

Some filters have already been introduced: the Mardi Gras Indians' history, its embeddedness in circumstances of segregation and of black racial rivalries, and its larger adherence to a mode of cultural development based on nonliterate modes of knowledge-seeking and pleasure-seeking. Now I want to employ the filters of comparative semiotics, by analyzing differences in visual and performative components of the Mardi Gras Indians with those of similar festive groups—some within the Caribbean area and others further afield, in Europe and Africa.[75]

# Africa

The pages that follow do not attempt rigorous semiotic analysis. Only a few initial steps have been taken, using a rudimentary set of costume semes and performative semes.[1] The analysis does move beyond the observation of one-to-one parallels in costuming and behavior which has been the normal manner until now of explaining black Indians' behavior: their music sometimes approaches calypso rhythms, the beadwork imagery seems to be taken from movie Westerns, the call-and-response pattern of chanting is African, and so on. Single-factor comparisons are helpful but inconclusive. Such associations can only be affirmed as influences or borrowings if their analysis leads to discovery of an associated ensemble of traits, or if it leads to establishment of a step-by-step evolution over time and space from one kind of performance to another. Without such verification seeming similarities must be classified as interesting parallel evolutions without consequences.

As I shall show, both associated ensembles of traits and a probable evolution of performance forms can be traced by means of the comparative method in the case of the Mardi Gras Indian. Carried further, this kind of combined semiotic and historical analysis will certainly yield further insights. On the other hand, a limitation to what may be expected is already visible. Implied in the previous section, which describes an Indian practice session, is the notion that verbal and rhythmic elements—more precisely, verbo-gestural-percussive rhythms—are the central semiotic elements of black-Indian performance. Apprehension of such elements is hardly possible without experiencing an actual performance or possessing highly detailed descriptions of it. We cannot obtain either the experience or the detailed description of actual performance for most of the parallel cases to black-Indian behavior investigated here. Therefore less attention will be paid to musical, verbal, and dance components than to the costuming, the masking roles, and the "plot" of performance in these comparisons.

First we may compare the Indian maskers in Trinidad with those at New Orleans. In 1847 "Spanish peons from the Main"—

that is, working-class people, allegedly of partly Indian ancestry, from the Spanish-speaking area of what is now Venezuela, just across the strait separating Trinidad from the mainland—came "daubed with red ochre" to participate in Trinidad's Carnival as "Indians of South America," according to an eyewitness.[2] But there is no demonstrable connection between these early maskers and the later companies of "Wild Indians" (called red, blue, black, and white, according to the predominant color of their costumes), "Fancy Indians," and "Indian Warrior Bands" that paraded in the gigantic Carnival festivities of the 1950s in Port of Spain.[3] In 1888 an engraver for the *Illustrated London News* made a print of Carnival revelers in the streets of Port of Spain which included one black man masking as an Indian; there is no sign that he was part of a group.[4]

Red Indians claimed, like some New Orleans black Indians, to be of mixed, partly Indian blood, and were supposed to have originated in Venezuela. But "in recent years" (those just preceding 1956) the Red Indian group was led by two blacks from Grenada and included "Trinidadians of every shade, including East Indian." Red Indians sang traditional songs, using archaic words in what they called the "Red Indian language." Daniel Crowley, who has considered these texts together with others in the "black Indian language," suggests that knowledge of "Spanish, Creole patois, English, and South American Indian languages" would be needed to unravel their meaning. Black Indians were said to also include African words in this "language." Red Indians performed short, play-like skits in the streets and also elected a queen who was crowned amid pageantry, singing, and dancing. The other Indian maskers oriented themselves toward spectacular parading. Those closest in organization to New Orleans' black Indians seem to have been the warrior bands, who possessed kings, queens, chiefs, medicine men, "ambassadors from other tribes and other dignitaries" among their very large groups ("several hundred" men and women).[5] But there is no way at present to determine whether the Trinidadians were influenced by the Orleanians (whose first groups certainly date no later than the 1880s), or vice versa. What is certain is that by the 1950s these two geographically distant areas had converged in their idea of how to "mask Indian."

In Trinidad slavery was abolished in 1833. From the 1840s large numbers of East Indians began to arrive as indentured laborers, and sometime later Chinese arrived in the same way. The racial mix was thus enriched at the base of society. A two-caste system like that in the American South never developed.

Since Trinidad's independence from England (1962), blacks (but this means every shade of mulatto color) have dominated politics. Carnival, a holiday in which blacks had participated with joy and great numbers from colonial times, acquired the prestige of a national celebration. Thus the public status of Indian maskers in Trinidad has long been and still is higher than that of their counterparts in New Orleans. Crowley writes that most of the Fancy Indians, who have developed the high headdresses and costumes most similar to those of the Orleanians, were "artists." Although he does not define this term, he presumably means that these maskers gained their living not in menial jobs like those of most New Orleans black Indians, but in the national media or in commercial-art positions. "Fancy" Indian maskers of Trinidad are presumably not nurtured in the nonliterate, sensuously direct culture which is the matrix of the Orleanian groups.

Trinidad's "Warrior Bands" seem most similar in organization; the "Fancy Indians" are most similar in costume. Fancy Indians may parade in small groups of three to ten people: "in recent times" they have joined themselves to the Warrior Bands "so as to have a more appropriate retinue."

These sociopolitical and organizational differences need to be kept in mind when comparing the Trinidadians with the Orleanians. The situation of relatively high social prestige for Indian maskers, indeed the positive stimulus to develop elaborate fantasies in dress and performance for the purpose of winning government-sponsored parading contests in Carnival, is quite unlike the situation in New Orleans.[6] Parallels in costuming and performance thus suggest some deeper level of continuity, some common cultural imagination whose structural coherence can only be noted in its outward effects at this point.

Costuming parallels are readily seen in drawings of a Mardi Gras Indian chief (ca. 1978) and a Trinidad Fancy Indian (ca. 1956) (plates 18 and 30).[7] Both have developed the headpiece out of proportion to all other elements of the costume, by means of a lattice-work of wire covered with feathers, sequins, and beads in the case of the Indian chief and dotted rather than entirely covered with colored paper, ribbons, mirrors, and bits of tooled leather, and so on, in the case of the Fancy Indian. The headpiece comes down low upon the brow of the Orleanian Indian, and there are beaded extensions on each side of the face, obscuring the chief's visage. The Fancy Indian's face is left more visible and so can be effectively decorated with warpaint.[8]

Growing emphasis on the headpiece correlates in New Or-

30. Trinidad Fancy Indian Chief on Parade, Port of Spain, about 1970
(drawing by Toan Le)

leans with the decline of violence and the rise of tourism. This huge and unwieldy costume immobilizes the chief: he cannot participate in or effectively direct an "attack" on a neighboring tribe from within this encasement. But he can be a man-of-words, boasting about and showing his prowess with the grand display of his crown. In Trinidad too the headpiece's height and extension were obviously correlated with desire for grander spectacle.

The headdress is an altered crown, mainly derived from the eagle-feather bonnets of Plains Indian chiefs. But the use of feathered headdresses is also African. The Ashanti of Ghana (formerly Gold Coast) adorned their war-captains with "immense plumes of eagle's feathers."[9] A fan-shaped spray of long feathers spreads upward and outward for a half-meter from the head of the "State Sword-bearer" of the Ashanti and from those of swordbearers of some of the states subject to Ashanti overlordship in the 1940s.[10] Thus in some African as in Amerindian traditions the use of feathered headdresses is particularly associated with the power of the polity in war.

The figurative elements in Mardi Gras Indian headdresses, on the other hand, were not derived from black people's observation of Amerindian customs. No native American ever wore a peacock perched upon his head in front of an outsized display of feathers. This kind of headpiece "sculpture" occurs both in New Orleans (plates 19–21) and in Trinidad.[11] It also was used by Jamaica's "John Canoe" figures, who carried "baby houses" on their heads in the 1790s, "showing different fronts with open doors, glazed windows, stair cases, piazas, and balconies." Twenty years later the headpieces carried miniature "house-boats."[12] One researcher has associated the latter with the paper-and-wood houses called *fanales*, carried in night processions (with lighted candles within the "houses") in Senegal, Gambia, and Sierra Leone at the present day. Some other paraders carry model sailing ships upon their heads in the same way.[13] One cannot in this case anymore than in the case of the relation between Trinidad and New Orleans conclude anything about an exact and specific source for the costume of nineteenth-century John Canoes. But it seems clear that some aspects of John Canoe costuming and of Mardi Gras Indian costuming can be traced to generally present elements of African ritual art. For example, much fine African headpiece sculpture—the well-known Gelede cult masks of the Nigerian Yoruba people, often whimsically realistic in the John Canoe manner—develops the headpiece in this fantasmatic way, loading it with birds and humans and human implements.[14] Documented *direct* contact has up to now not been established between African festive practices and Gulf Coast Carnival ones. But a common semiotic proclivity seems to be present, orienting the work of the imagination.

Like the headpiece, the rest of the costume of the Mardi Gras Indian chiefs invests the body closely. Little or nothing of the body's own contours remain; they are hidden behind the colorful swirl of dyed feathers, bead paintings (geometrical or representational), and imitation rabbit fur. An overloaded, heavy look is cultivated. The costume is spectacular not simply because it is brightly colored, not only because it makes the masker superhuman in size, but because it is extraordinarily intricate, both in its overlapping skirts, blouses, and sleeves, and in the motifs which decorate these elements of costume. These costumes are baroque rather than classical. There is a bright but dense materiality about them. They excel through excess.[15]

The direction of Trinidadian development seems to have been slightly different. The Fancy Indians' costume is borne lightly above and adjacent to the body, rather than heavily piled upon it. There is seemingly more use of miniature mirrors, and more latticework is left empty for air (and the eye) to pass through and around. Is this because the climate in February-March there offers more leeway, more chance of warmth and sunlight to glint upon mirrors than in New Orleans? Certainly there can be no question of slavish imitation of either kind of Indian costume by the other, whatever the paths of borrowing may have been.[16]

A comparison of the main features of performance in Trinidad and New Orleans requires introduction of another kind of popular participant in Trinidad's Carnival, the stick fighter or *batonyé* (from French *batonnier*). In the 1860s and 1870s the most prominent Carnival groups were young men going about in bands of five to twenty, bearing stout sticks with which they engaged their rivals in fights. When two antagonists encountered each other, they tried to flick off a heart-shaped panel of cloth decorated with swansdown, rhinestones, and mirrors, loosely sewn on the shirt.[17] For days and weeks before Carnival the stick fighters practiced their art in the areas called "barrack yards" in Port of Spain. The population of this city increased nearly 80 percent between 1860 (16,457) and 1880 (29,468); most newcomers were crammed into long wooden structures constructed behind the streetfront shops and houses. These barracks were subdivided into single rooms, each of which might contain a family. There was little privacy, water and toilets were for the use of everyone in the yards before the barracks, and so strong feelings developed in the yards, for "us" and against "you." Leaders among the stick fighters, champions in the yards, were thus expected to insult and provoke rival bands in Carnival songs or "carisos." When they were good fighters and good boasters, they became heroes.

Like some parts of New Orleans in the nineteenth century, this barrack-yard society was not a ghetto in an isolated poor section of town but existed back-to-back with upper- and middle-class houses. In the front houses many of the barrack women were servants. Out of this mixed situation—which, also like New Orleans, frequently produced liaisons between the women and middle-class men—evolved the *jamette* subculture to which reference has already been made.[18] "Skill and bravery in . . . stickfighting, sharpness of wit and repartee in conversation and in song, talent in dance and music, indifference to law and authority, and great [male] sexual accomplishments" were its vaunted features.[19] They parallel the mores in the late nineteenth- and early twentieth-century quarters of New Orleans in which Mardi Gras Indians seem to have formed.

What is the relation between the Indian bands so prominent in twentieth-century Trinidad and the batonyé groups who from about 1860 set the tone of Carnival with their flashy fighting and showy clothes? Pearse, Crowley, and Hill do not pose that question. Trinidad's English colonial government placed restrictions on stick fighting from the early 1880s after a major riot took place in Carnival. By the 1950s batonyé persisted, writes Crowley, only in a few country villages. On the other hand, he says that the Red Indians "in the past" held classes in their special language, because an Indian who could not "brag . . . ornately" about his prowess might be beaten "by the clubs and staves of his challenger and followers."[20]

Comparative materials supply a missing link which suggests that the Indian bands of Trinidad were once intimately connected to the batonyé. In Jamaica sometime in the twentieth century new roles were added to the John Canoe troupes which have continued to perform in towns and villages in many parts of the island. Among these new roles was Wild Indian, who carries a long cane and crossbow, bears a feathered headdress in which playing cards, pieces of glass mirrors, and other items have been inserted, and wears a foil-covered heart on his chest and strands of beads.[21]

Contacts between Trinidad and Jamaica have long been frequent and rivalrous. They did not cease with the end of British rule over both islands, nor with the failed Federation of the West Indies which briefly united them (1958–62). It seems likely that the high prestige of Trinidad's Carnival after World War II had something to do with the public resurgence of John Canoe masquerades since 1951, after a long period during which it was thought that the tradition was dying or had indeed disappeared.[22] If that is so, then it is not surprising that the Jamaicans added the Wild Indian role to their troupe, given its prominence in the Trinidad Carnivals of the 1950s, and certainly for a considerable time before the 1950s, since at that time the Wild Indians had already developed their special "languages" and the rituals to go with them. What is surprising is that the Wild Indian costume, with its headdress so similar to Trinidadian—and Orleanian—creations, also includes the heart-shaped decoration distinguishing Trinidad's batonyé.

One costume seme such as the heart does not establish a connection between two ritual figures. But the heart, coupled with the three costume semes that are parallel to those of Trinidad Indians (bow and arrow, headdress, and strings of beads are all mentioned by Crowley),[23] and with the name "Wild Indian," certainly argues strongly in favor of Trinidad's influence. Perhaps it was the Jamaicans who synthesized the batonyé costume with that of the Wild Indian. But why did they do so, if there was not some similarity, some common ground of wildness, uniting the two?

If the Indian bands of Trinidad are descendants or at least first cousins of the batonyé, then the connection between Trinidad's Indians and those of New Orleans becomes closer because the sociohistorical conditions producing the early Trinidad Indians can be seen as parallel to those producing the batonyé, which in turn are akin to those in which the Orleanian Indians emerged. Parallels in performance are then less surprising. The warrior-like batonyé groups, like the Orleanian Indians, spent months preparing for their Carnival appearance in boastful but also cooperative, communally bound practice sessions. At the same time the differences are obvious. New Orleans black Indians developed group fighting only after 1900, it seems, when the batonyé were already in decline in Trinidad. The weapons used by Orleanians were knives, tomahawks, and guns, not the rapier-like sticks of the batonyé, although it is said that in the 1930s and 1940s the New Orleans tribes used "sharpened mosquito rods" as weapons.[24] New Orleans Indian "practices" today are devoted less to fighting moves or boastful declamation (like the

31. Stick dancers in Carnival, Haiti, ca. 1883 (photo, Norman Magden, from A. Orloff, *Carnival, Myth and Cult*)

Red Indian "classes") than to chanting and dancing.[25] Both these similarities and these differences are at the present time based on too little information. Our feelings about the parallels must be held in abeyance, but at least this bit of information should be added, which does not seem to have been noticed before. Plate 31, a drawing of Carnival in 1883 somewhere in Haiti—an island halfway between Trinidad and New Orleans— shows a stick fight going on between rival bands. The fighters apparently wear white masks over their faces, cowled, skirted tunics, and what seem to be colored kerchiefs strung through their belts like those of the batonyé in contemporary Trinidad,[26] except for one man, flourishing his stick in the air on the left and wildly dancing: he wears an Indian-like—or is it African-like?— headdress of feathers. Here is still another missing link.

Any of the three following hypotheses may be the case: Black Carnival revelers in New Orleans learned of Trinidad—and Haitian?—stick-fighting practices and Indian-masking groups separately, and then developed their own synthesis of the two, combining them with a variety of features from American popular-cultural presentations of the Indian which had already been part of the vocabulary of street masking in New Orleans for decades. Or the idea of group fighting and Indian masking, already amalgamated in other Caribbean Carnivals, was imported ready-made to New Orleans.[27] Or there was no connection at all between the Indian masking and group rivalries on different Caribbean islands and those at New Orleans. The three—but how many other cases may comparative analysis eventually reveal?—developed in parallel but autonomous ways.[28]

If the last hypothesis is true, then the similarities of Orleanian to Trinidadian and some Haitian black masking derive from common social and cultural conditions rather than from direct contacts. They derive, for example, from the appeal of Indian wildness to people of African ancestry in situations where the paradigms of civilized behavior are uniformly white, as they largely have been in the Caribbean and Gulf Coast areas until very recently, after as before slavery, after as during colonial rule. They derive from the logic of festive play proper to Carnival, which urges libertarian play with serious life and stimulates remembrance of long suppressed norms of behavior; in this case, African norms. An African component of black Indian behavior is strongly suggested by the special role allotted to the wildman within the New Orleans tribes.

There are few references in Trinidad's Carnival literature to anything like the Orleanian black Indian wildman. Trinidad "Indian Warrior Bands" included medicine men among the special roles allotted members of their groups, but Crowley, our source for this information, does not describe their costume or their behavior.[29] Medicine men—that is, healers with shamanic powers of communication and even identity with the spirits which cause human malady—were common features of both Amerindian and many African traditions. Amerindian "medicine-men" and African "witch-doctors" had congruent functions and similar powers. It is not surprising to discover that the "witch-doctor", so frequent a part of New Orleans' Zulu Carnival fun, wears furs and buffalo horns in the same way as the "wildman" among the Mardi Gras Indians.[30]

The wildman is the only black Indian who wears animal horns. What is the reason for creating a role within the group which intensifies the sign separating that group from other Carnival revelers generally—that is, the ferocious, terrifying, and oddly beautiful lack of "civilization" of Indians—first by *naming* the sign ("wild"-man), second by signifying it visually with the invention of a costume which assimilates the human to an animal, and finally by playing it out through the development of especially aggressive behavior? (The wildman, we recall, was once described by a tribal member as the "craziest acting" fellow in the group; his behavior at the White Cloud Hunter practice bore that out.)

Taking on the powers of a spirit is an awesome thing. The medicine-man/shaman/witch-doctor is a being possessed, someone with more than human powers. As Michael Smith has shown, the Spiritualist churches in New Orleans have conserved in a mildly Christianized form the African sense of healing as a spiritual, shamanic process, and in at least the instance of one such church they revere the Plains Indian Black Hawk as just such a superhuman mediator. But this general atmosphere of spiritualist possession accepted within black orally centered culture in New Orleans does not explain its animal-oriented features. Why clothe the wildman with horns and furs more than with feathers?[31]

We have already met this man-beast among black revelers: in Jamaica in the eighteenth and early nineteenth centuries "John Canoe" wore horns and animal skins, and twentieth-century John Canoe troupes include a character called Cow Head who wears a cow's horns but no fur or skins.[32] But no line of historical evolution, no borrowing of John Canoe's various costumes by New Orleans blacks, has been traced nor does it seem plausible to suggest that it occurred. Just as in the case of the parallels between Mardi Gras Indians and Trinidadian Indians and stick fighters, one may more plausibly argue for the independent, parallel development in Jamaica and in New Orleans of a similar *pattern* of signs. This pattern would have been elicited by the same causes as those to which we referred concerning the Caribbean Indians and stick fighters: the cultural effects of black subordination and the restimulation of suppressed African norms by Carnival's logic of libertarian play.

By "African norms" I refer neither to allegedly pan-African cultural traits nor to traits possessed by one tribe alone. The mixing of tribes on slave boats, slave auction-blocks, and colonial plantations forced cultural amalgamation on this side of the Atlantic, so that tracing particular pieces of behavior to particular tribes is not only very difficult but pointless in most cases.[33] Afro-Caribbean culture is best explained in terms of the process of assimilation which occurred in the New World, insofar as that is possible. But of course this process too can only be indicated in general terms because it took place orally, not literately, and because it was mostly ignored or despised by those who were literate. What we can know about it is that which we know about cultural processes in orally centered cultures generally or that which we can establish by judicious comparison of African festive practices in areas which might have influenced Caribbean and American slaves. These areas are overwhelmingly located in West Africa, from Senegal to the old Gold Coast and Niger River basin and also the Congo River basin. I shall also make reference to one tribe from southeast Africa, the Swazi. This people, like other tribes in the very large subfamily of Bantu peoples, speaks a Niger-Congo language like the West African groups, and, while part of a culture area today which is far from West Africa, probably developed out of the same linguistic, ethnic, and cultural configuration as the major West African groups.[34]

In many areas of Africa the sovereign has been at the same time a priest, performing the shaman's role of mediation with and assumption of supernatural powers on certain critical occasions. One well-known example of this is the New Year's festival of the Swazi people who live in southeastern Africa adjacent to the Zulu. During an annual six-day ceremony which follows closely upon the December solstice, the Swazi king is first ritually separated from his people and "doctored" to absorb demonic powers. A pitch-black castrated bull from the royal herd is forced to the ground, it is named *incwambo* (a muscle near the testicles), and then the king sits naked upon it while tasting a medicine "related to part of the liver which is supposed to cause disorderly, confused behavior."[35] T. O. Beidelman supposes that this name *incwambo* is given in order to emphasize the sexually anomalous, symbolically intermediate status of a bull which has been castrated, a status which the king, seated upon it, takes upon himself. The "ox-bull" is slaughtered, and the king-priest subsequently emerges from his isolation hut, having been ritually painted black, covered with bright green grass, and wearing a headband of lion skin. He dances "demonically," that is, as *silo*, "a monster," expressing reluctance to rejoin his people. He has absorbed the power of the oxbull. "He is said to present an extremely fierce and terrifying sight."[36] Later he casts away the greenery, kindles a fire with friction-sticks, and burns a series of articles selected to represent "filth" which must be burned to end the disturbed state of the king and that of the nation which he also embodies at this turning of the old toward the new year.

He then washes off his "medicines," that is, his ritually required blackness, and sprinkles cleansing medicines on himself and the royal herd (the Swazi raise cattle; they are prime symbols of the nation's wealth). People gather and rain is supposed to fall, quenching the flames of the filth-fire and blessing the rites.[37]

Let us recall in more exact detail the features of "John Canoe" as reported between the 1770s and 1820s in Jamaica.[38] In the 1760s and early 1770s he wore oxhorns, sprouting from a mask that had boar tusks at the mouth. In the 1790s he no longer possessed oxhorns, while retaining the boar tusks and adding a beard, but another group of Christmas revelers, the butchers, conducted a figure "clad in the hide of an ox with horns." Twenty years later, in the novel by Michael Scott which may or may not represent a realistic description of Kingston's festivities, we have a John Canoe who appears thoroughly human except for his wig of "bullocks' tails," his Janus-like double mask, looking forward and backwards at once, and his sheep's tail. This John Canoe, it will be recalled, rode upon an unnamed second figure who seems to have absorbed the bestiality which John Canoe had cast off, "clothed in an entire bullock's hide, horns, tail . . . and the whole of the skull. . . ." These John Canoe figures, like the wildmen among the Mardi Gras Indians, are unpredictably aggressive, rushing up to bystanders, cavorting and colliding, and importunately asking for coins. In both the case of the Indians and the John Canoes, the ambiance of this aggression is festive, which allows it a certain leeway and lends it an air of parody.

Are the John Canoes, as has been suggested, merely an awkward, debased version of European mumming practices like that of the *belsnickle*, the beast-man led from house to house in Germany and in German Pennsylvania to frighten children and amuse adults at Christmastime?[39] There were many such practices in sixteenth- and seventeenth-century England which could have been brought to Jamaica after the island became British in 1670. I have not located an exact replica from England itself, but consider this extraordinary parallel from the small town of Hof in what is now East Germany, which occurred in the year 1566:

> The butchers for their customary Carnival drinking party [*ihr quas zu fassnacht*] . . . dressed one of their number in a raw ox-skin [i.e., with the hair left on] and in horns on his head. He ran around from one street to the next [in Hof] like nothing else than a living devil,

and he vexed the peasants particularly by knocking into them. Then . . . in the evening [all] the butchers ran out again through the streets, and danced with their cowbells, sheepbells, and clubs. . . .

Later in the evening the butchers laid an ambush for their rivals, the textile workers, who were enjoying their own Carnival dance in another part of town. Bringing their clubs and also daggers into play, they attacked the textile workers "in such a wild way [*in solchem wilden wesen*]" that one man was killed.[40]

The costumes here run parallel to those of the John Canoes; the behavior moves from a dancing display to a murderous confrontation like those involving the Mardi Gras Indians in the old days of violence. The confrontation between butchers and textile workers at Hof, however, was not ritualized. It happened only on this particular mardi gras, unlike the case with the Mardi Gras Indians where "challenges" remain today, in altered form, an essential part of the demonstration of the powerful superiority of the group. Even so, is there not some common core of motivation here, operating across centuries and across very different cultural and social circumstances, which would explain these similarities and, more importantly, would explain how an occasion of gaiety can turn so easily into a matter of life and death?

There is, no doubt, such a common core. The butchers at Hof, like the John Canoes and the Mardi Gras Indians, possessed the psycho-physical mechanisms of all members of Homo sapiens, responding to unusual spectacles with awe and defensiveness. By the same token they were inclined to provoke such spectacles for amusement's sake. The butchers like the others were part of an urban lower class; their culture, too, was orally and sensually centered, and it existed as a subculture, in social and political subordination to the dominant culture's superior privileges. Is that all there is to it? From the point of view of the ruling classes then and now, yes: for them, the rest of the story is that of the brutishness and stupidity which makes it appropriate for lower classes to be lower. But such dismissal of the spectacle and the violence glosses over too many details to be satisfactory. In addition to the common human and common nonliterate factors of motivation there are culturally specific ones. I am not pursuing here the cultural factors specific to Hof which would explain the particularly infuriating character of equipping some urban dwellers with rural symbols like cowbells, sheepbells, and clubs, costuming a group leader as an ox-man, and attacking peasants by predilection in the streets.[41] I am rather concerned with the more difficult because more composite cultural heritage of Afro-American lower-class urban dwellers.

Part of the cultural specificity of this heritage derives from the African norms exhibited in such rituals as the New Year celebration of the Swazi. Here are three tenets exhibited in that ritual which operate at a semiconscious level in the behavior of the John Canoes and Mardi Gras Indians, but do not operate in the same systemic, mutually implicatory way at Hof or in any other of the many European Carnival practices where men mask as animals. First, within the pattern of thought exhibited in the Swazi ritual, animals are not seen as existing on a lower scale of being than humans, nor still further below saints, angels, or gods. The bestial—the ox-bull, and then the ox-king—is powerful because it is as supernatural, as *excessive*, with respect to what is human, as is the high sun. Animals are predictable in some ways but in others they are manifestly beyond human control. The "super"-natural lies outside whatever is normal in a tribally centered universe; it lies both above and below the earth, it lies in whatever is beyond the human. It is not situated, as in Western literate cultures, uniquely above the human and natural sphere.

Second, in this thought-pattern mixed substances and mixed beings represent power, and therefore danger. (Blackness in the case of the Swazi symbolizes such a mixed substance and mixed position, powerful, dangerous, filthy because mixed. Although this is a widespread symbolism, it is by no means pan-African; color symbolism is notoriously variable within particular cultural traditions.) Beasts with their dark unfathomable power, animate like men, similar in many of their needs, are mixed beings. The African sovereign is "the bull of his nation" in the Swazi case;[42] more generally he is always a potential link between the natural and supernatural worlds, embodying the nation to the gods and to foreigners, embodying godlike power to the nation. This mixed status of kingship is what allows the king under proper ritual guidance simultaneously to take on himself the collected "filth" of the old year, its failures, its used-up opportunities, and at the same time to carry it away and to acquire supernatural force for the nation as it enters a new year.

Maximal power is given to those who exist in mixed, ambiguous ways, as the king briefly does during the New Year ritual. Being wild—living on the margin between cultivated and uncultivated territory or living in a ritually removed state from ordinary life, partaking of both human and animal qualities—offers a person this power, but only at the risk of being "crazy," that is, of being possessed by powers beyond the human.

The wildman is an awesome being because of these connections with the natural world, a natural world which *is* "supernatural." Such a system of signification as this, it seems to me, works at a subliminal level to pattern the appearance and behavior of John Canoe, that of the wildman among presently black Indian tribes in New Orleans, and to some extent also that of the black Indian tribe as a whole, all of them taking on the body and spirit of the exemplary wildman of American folklore, the Indian. The same system even determines some of the traditional feeling about that apparently innocuous figure of fun in New Orleans' second Carnival, the king of the Zulus (see plates 35, 36, and 38). In 1964 one of the oldest members of the organization, lamenting what he considered to be a kind of "gentrification" of this previously working-class black group, gave voice in the most naive and hence also most powerful way to the conviction that power for humanity lies in its connection to this supernaturally natural world of beasts:

> *Now* they're trying to ape after Rex. Before that, we had something original. Before, you'd look at that king, with moss on his head, then horns like a cow, and a body like a rabbit, and as you went down his body, it would change animals. Man, that was a terrible-looking sight.[43]

Alex Rapheal did not simply look at the king of the Zulus in their annual Carnival parade: he "read" the body's signs. White men, and perhaps most black men—for most blacks are in present-day New Orleans part of literate culture—saw something incongruous when they beheld the old-time king, and they laughed. That incongruous, ludicrous element was there in the costuming, and by design, as we will see. But the nonliterate black man, like this participant in the group's life over decades, looked at the organization's emblem and embodiment and saw *also* something marvelous because it was dreadful. This black man's eye moved down the king's body, *constructing* its meaning as a mixed, monstrous, wild being, an anomalous man-animal, a terrible-looking sight—as "something original" because its composite parts had a unitary meaning which he grasped. Was this not the unity it expressed as an image of sovereignty, that African sovereignty which possesses power over the community because it unifies natural with supernatural, human with animal force?[44]

There can be few more impressive examples of this kind of

sovereignty, at least as seen by Europeans, than that witnessed by the English trader Bowdich in 1817, when he was received at Kumasi (central Ghana) by the king of the powerful Ashanti empire, accompanied by an estimated 30,000 warriors. Bowdich's description, however, is useful to this inquiry not simply in a semantic way, showing the tendency to signify power by joining human to animal symbols. It is also relevant in a formal sense: the densely intricate manner with which the Mardi Gras Indians crowd their costumes with richly replicating beads, spangles, and colored stones, totally overwhelming the natural contours of the body, is in Bowdich's description a prime feature of this royal display.

Such is the third aspect of the African thought-pattern. Power, when it is concentrated, does not take the form of some glimmering, ethereal light, some representation of immateriality, as in Western elite tradition; it rather appears as an intensification of the material, natural world. This intensification frequently has the form, as in the Swazi ritual and in the Ashanti reception now to be considered, of glistening and bedazzling, yet very weighty, materiality. (The king-priest emerges from his isolation hut painted an uncanny black, covered with excessively green grass, naked, with a lion-skin headband.) Elements of the natural world cluster together to produce an unnatural materiality, a kind of glittering thickness which assaults beholders and weighs upon them, extinguishing their sense of autonomy and separateness.

Bowdich was received as the representative of an important foreign power which, like the Dutch and the Danes at the time, held forts on the coast of the Gold Coast, while the Ashanti dominated the interior. He and his retinue passed in procession before the king, his ministers, and his chief warriors. They were then seated, and the king, ministers, chiefs, and their retinue subsequently passed in turn before them. Like a black Indian performance, this procedure took the whole day, ending slightly after nightfall with the visitors totally exhausted from the extraordinary spectacle.

The categories of costume semes listed in the Appendix allow comparison of Bowdich's description with the typified costume of a Mardi Gras Indian (plate 18) at eleven points.[45] The Indians place no emphasis at four of these points and the Ashanti place no emphasis at three. The seven points where costuming is emphasized both according to Bowdich and in most Mardi Gras Indian suits are as follows:

First, the headpiece: "The dress of the captains was a war-cap, with gilded ram's horns projecting in front, the sides extending beyond all proportion by immense plumes of eagle's feathers." Later in the description Bowdich comments further on the emphasis on feathers in these headpieces, which were perhaps propped up behind the seated chiefs whom these captains served: "The war-caps of eagles' feathers nodded in the rear and large fans of the wing feathers of the ostrich played around the dignitaries."[46] (Here the parallels are to the cow horns of the Orleanians' Wild Man and to the eagle's feathers and/or ostrich plumes worn by the Big Chief and other Indians.[47])

Second, the face: "The sides of their [the warriors', not the war-captains'] faces were curiously painted in long white streaks, and their arms also striped, having the appearance of armour."[48] ("Warpaint" was used by the Orleanians until at least 1940.)

Third, the upper torso: "Their vest [the war-captains'] was of red cloth covered with fetishes and saphies [Muslim amulets] in gold and silver, and embroidered cases of almost every colour, which flapped against their bodies as they moved, intermixed with small brass bells, the horns and tails of animals, shells and knives; long leopards' tails hung down their backs over a small bow covered with fetishes [packets of hair and other animal parts, plant substances, etc., with occult properties]."[49] (The Orleanians wore vests covered with beadwork, bits of animal fur, birds' feathers, sequins, colored stones, etc.)

Fourth, fifth, and sixth, the lower torso, legs, and feet: "They [war-captains] wore loose cotton trousers with immense boots of a dull red leather coming halfway up the thigh . . . ; these were also ornamented with bells, horses' tails, strings of amulets, and innumerable shreds of leather. . . ."[50] (The Orleanians' torso, legs and moccasins are covered with the same kind of shiny and/or figurative pieces of artwork as the upper body.)

Seventh, materials carried: A small quiver of poisoned arrows hung from their [the captains'] right wrist, and they held a long iron chain between their teeth, with a scrap of Moorish writing affixed to the end of it. Small spears were in their left hands, covered with red cloth and silk tassels. . . ."[51] (Until the 1930s black Indians openly carried tomahawks and some other weapons. Today none are flourished, and the chiefs usually carry instead—or have carried for them—side panels which are extensions of the headpiece design. The headpiece is periodically set upon these side panels, so that the chief is freed temporarily from its weight.)

These highly ornamented costumes were calculated to bedazzle the English agent, and they had their desired effect, especially in conjunction with the other elements of the reception. A war captive was led past, who was being horribly mutilated "by men disfigured with immense caps of shaggy black skins, and drums beat before him" (a parallel to the Orleanian Wild Man's furskin headpiece which, however, also carries horns). Bowdich and his companions were brought toward the king, seated at the far side of a field "nearly a mile in circumference," which was crowded to surfeit "with magnificence and novelty."

> . . . A hundred large umbrellas or canopies . . . were sprung up and down by the bearers with brilliant effect, being made of scarlet, yellow, and the most showy cloths and silks, and crowned on the top with crescents, pelicans, elephants, barrels, and arms and swords of gold; . . . the valences (in some of which small looking-glasses were inserted) fantastically scalloped and fringed; from the fronts of some the proboscis and small teeth of elephants projected, and a few were roofed with leopards' skins. . . .[52]

In addition to taking note of the miniature mirrors also used by Orleanian and other New World wildmen, one observes here leopard skins—often part of the Orleanian Zulu's "witch doctor" costume and sometimes of the king's (plates 4, 37)—and the employment of parasols: these and regular umbrellas are favorite ornaments of the black Indians' "second line" (the friends and neighbors who dance with the tribe along streets and sidewalks) who swing them up and down, opening and shutting them, in rain (as often happens) or shine.

When the Englishmen had finally succeeded in passing "this blazing circle" and had greeted the king, whose clothing and ornaments differed from those of others chiefly in golden worth and artistic elegance, they were seated to receive the greetings of the company which they had just reviewed, beginning with the parade of the king's several chiefs.

> One chief . . . under his umbrella, was generally supported round his waist by the hands of his favorite slave, whilst captains holloa'd, close in his ear, his warlike deeds and (strong) names, which were reiterated with the voices of Stentors by those before and behind. . .

This boasting was followed, again in remarkable parallel to what would emerge as a Carnival performance half a world away, by extraordinary dancing:

> A band of Fetish men, or priests, wheeled round and round as they passed with surprising velocity. Manner was as various as ornament; some danced by with irresistible buffoonery, some with a gesture and carriage of

defiance; one distinguished caboceer performed the war dance before us for some minutes with a large spear, which grazed us at every bound he made. . . .[53]

Just as in the case of the black Indians, too, with their sense of the order of confrontation, in which the most furious dance, that of the wildman, occurs first, and the most efficacious and dignified dance, that of the Big Chief, occurs last, so at Kumasi we see that in the first half of the ceremony the approach of the Englishmen to the king takes place only after what seems to have been several hours of progress through the ranks of all the war-captains and state dignitaries. The Englishmen's progress toward the king is initiated by a fearful outburst: "Upwards of 5000 people, the greater part warriors, met us with awful bursts of martial music . . . horns, rattles, and gong-gongs were all excited with a zeal bordering on frenzy to subdue us by the first impression. . . . The captains . . . discharg[ed] their shining blunderbusses so close that the flags were now and then in a blaze, and emerg[ed] from the smoke with all the gesture and distortion of maniacs."[54]

Here then are all three parts of the pattern: the same use of wildness as an aspect of spectacle and as an attribute of power, the same sense of joining the power of men to that of birds and animals, the same emphasis upon material glitter and material density as the essence of splendor.[55] These general qualities, as much or more than the evident parallels of particular symbols, suggest the African roots of the black Indians' masquerade.

It is easy to wax eloquent about cultures not one's own. I reemphasize that my suggestions about the parallels between African and Afro-American festive behavior are hypothetical. The hypotheses, as presented, may turn out upon further testing to be untenable. But the problem provoking the hypotheses is as real as the maskers whose behavior I am trying to explain: These costumes and performances, with their Caribbean-wide parallels, are not explicable when dealt with simply as locally impromptu inventions.[56]

# Grotesques

Exploring the connections of black Mardi Gras wildmen in New Orleans with analogous figures in the Caribbean led to Trinidad with its bands of Indians, to Trinidad a second time and to Haiti with their stick fighters, and to Jamaica with its Wild Indian figure among modern John Canoe groups. At this point I suggested a move away from comparisons at the level of phenomena (costumes, performance, words, dance, music) to comparisons at the level of "norms," of performance patterns, of ritualistic, ceremonial expectations. On this level the signs exhibited by the most archaic Afro-American festive figure documented for the Caribbean area, the eighteenth-century John Canoe, could be associated with African rituals of kingship and annual renewal, and the pattern could then also be seen in the Mardi Gras Indians.

The obvious objection to this association of African norms with the New Orleans maskers is that the African examples are serious; the black Indians, like John Canoe, dance for fun. This difference is crucial to my argument.

The Swazi ox-king *must* succeed in his yearly renewal or his nation is considered ritually doomed. The Ashanti king, chief, and warriors must bedazzle and indeed terrorize the Englishmen; this is how they had established and maintained their overlordship during many generations. But for John Canoe the most that is at stake is an extra shilling or two; as for the Mardi Gras Indians, no matter how ardently they battle and boast, on Ash Wednesday morning they will still be at the bottom of the political and economic heap. African rituals in Africa had the weight and necessity of officially endorsed cultural behavior. African rituals in the New World were not only unofficial, they were from the point of view of the dominant culture positively evil.

The consequences of being at the very bottom of society, with no claim to status and hence with little stake in the success of one's cultural endeavors, and of possessing as an ancestral inheritance religions and customs considered both barbarous and evil were over the long term strangely liberating in the cultural sense. Wherever black people lived together in considerable numbers among themselves—as was the case on large plantations—they conserved their culture by disguising and transforming it. A favorite form of disguise, because it appealed so easily to whites, was the carnivalesque. John Canoe's ludicrous side is probably due to this. The Mardi Gras Indians' use of the white man's festival as a mold within which to develop the complex dynamics of their communal festival exhibits the same creative opportunism.

This does not mean that blacks created these figures with the intention of giving them a double meaning, one to the initiate and another to the innocent. African ways were genuinely lost and forgotten due to the necessity of adaptation; the negative judgments of the master culture were internalized to a very considerable degree. But this triple process of cultural disruption, creative subterfuge, and willing acceptance of alien norms was carried on within the framework of nonliterate modes of communication. Loss, creation, and co-option, taking place by big steps and little, were all assimilated to the soft-edged contours of a continuously interwoven "folk memory." It is for this reason that African norms, only dimly retained and subconsciously felt, could be welded both to the "high" spiritualism of Christian worship and to the "low" enjoyments of European holidays, and that Chief Black Hawk can today be revered both in churches and in Carnival with no cognitive dissonance.

In the 1810s and 1820s, the very period in which Michael Scott sets that strange double-figured performance of a half-civilized John Canoe seated upon the back of a preeminently savage ox-man,[1] a quite different variant of the same masker developed in Jamaica's capital, Kingston. This alternative figure is an excellent example of the plasticity of black festive practice. The "Koo-Koo or Actor-Boy," a drawing of whom is shown in plate 32, developed the John Canoe figure toward the portrayal of little street plays. Shakespeare's *Richard III* was excerpted; a contemporary source adds that "Pizarro was also one of their Stock Pieces; but whatever might have been the performance, a Combat and Death invariably ensued. . . ." After death came dancing: "there was always a general call for music—and dancing immediately commenced—," which proved to be death's medicine, for the slain man then "became resuscitated and joined the merry throng."[2]

Those familiar with the mumming play, performed in farming communities in the British Isles and in more fragmented form in some parts of the eastern United States and Canada between the

32. "Koo-Koo" or Actor Boy, Variant
of "John Canoe," Jamaica, 1830s
(drawing by Toan Le)

seventeenth century and the present, will have recognized its pattern here. Evidently even Shakespeare's play was adapted to the standard plot of a hero and his adversary who come into conflict and fight until one dies. After lamentations, a more or less comical resurrection very often concludes these rough theatricals, performed from house to house for small coins and a holiday bowl of cheer.[3]

But the mumming play was only the European side of this figure's behavior. Equally or more important to the Koo-Koo boys, with their elegantly embroidered riding coats (and accompanying whip), fine white neck-cloths, grandly flowing wigs, beribboned shoes, and gaily flourished fans, was a kind of informal costume contest which took place "on the Parade, a large and much frequented thoroughfare in Kingston, near the immediate scene of business, or in front of one of the principal Taverns." "Gentlemen," as they passed, were "requested to decide which is the smartest dressed." Those who lost such contests set upon the victor with blows and much rending of garments.[4] I. M. Belisario, who records these circumstances, concludes by saying that the dramatic skits, popular in the 1820s, were already being set aside in favor of this kind of ostentatious parading in his time (he wrote in 1838). Belisario himself prepared a lithograph of the figure from which the drawing in plate 32 is taken, with its extraordinary headpiece of "pasteboard trimmed round the edges with silver lace, surmounted with feathers" and inlaid with sequins, mirrors, and stones, so similar in the richness of materials and complexity of geometric design to the headpieces of Mardi Gras Indians.[5]

Thus, although the Koo-Koo boy with his skits, European clothes, and white smiling face-mask developed first as an even more direct imitation of European festive practice than the other John Canoes, it soon relapsed toward the common vocabulary of black festivity: it became a competition in showy grandeur of costume, centered above all in the outsized headpiece with its waving ostrich plumes. Belisario says that its final, most showy version consisted of parading from place to place at night, accompanied by fife and drum and illuminated by candles "fixed on a large square frame of wood, supported by men . . . the enclosure acting as a protection to him against the pressure of the crowd from without."[6] Here is once again the resplendent king-figure or "chief," conducted by music, moving through the admiring crowd, stopping now and then to strike a grandiloquent pose.

Just as there developed a double version of the Indian in New

Orleans, one side emphasizing sovereign splendor and the other aggressive prowess, as expressed in the respective costumes of the Chief and the Wildman and in the respective performances of parading and challenging, so in Jamaica there had developed a century earlier in relation to the Christmas holidays the same duplicity in the figures of the respectively savage and "aristocratic" (i.e., Koo-Koo boy) John Canoes.[7] The semiotic split also occurred in Trinidad when sometime in the earlier twentieth century the Fancy Indians differentiated their "bands" from those of the Wild Indians.

This split is not specific to either African or Afro-Caribbean culture. It occurs among European wildman groups as well. That is why I have included a fourth drawing for comparison with the Mardi Gras Indians, one from the 1970s in Bulgaria (plate 33). This figure, documented with the name "kuker" for the past one hundred years in south Slavic Europe,[8] is one of the vast number of wildman *personae* recorded since the Middle Ages in all parts of Europe as maskers who usually appear at one of those two festive moments which have also dominated Caribbean and Gulf Coast celebrations: Christmas–New Year and Carnival.[9] I have chosen this particular version of the kuker because it is relatively accessible to view[10] and because some details of this costume are specifically comparable to those of the Mardi Gras Indians and the other Afro-Caribbean figures studied in the previous chapter. The parallels between East European kukers generally and the Mardi Gras Indians show how similar cultural phenomena may develop in vastly different societies between which there can be no question of contact. At the same time the differences of Mardi Gras Indians and of Afro-Caribbean festive practices generally from those of European wildman festivities emerge more clearly.

Pàdarevo's *kuker* possesses no grand, over-spreading headpiece. The face, however, is covered, and partly built up above the head by a feathered mask. Such bird-men, especially common in northeast Bulgaria, often possessed in the early twentieth century horns extending up from the mask, and in some cases these horns were in turn supplemented by eagle's feathers.[11] Since the 1930s the kuker's headpieces have grown spectacularly, in ways very similar to those that led to the extraordinary arch above a Mardi Gras Indian's head. Some headpieces rise a meter and a half over the head and are a meter in width, filling their latticework frame with colored paper, feathers, ribbons, and fresh flowers.[12] In comparison to the latter, the Padarevo kuker's mask is, as it were, pushed down upon the face,

33. "Kuker" from Padarevo, Bulgaria,
mid-20th Century (drawing by Toan Le)

concentrating its naturalistic power there. The red (paprika) pepper used as a nose gives the face both a dapper and absurdly comic appearance. The kuker's blouse and vest are festooned with ribbons, little mirrors, and feathers. The aim, like that of the Mardi Gras Indians, is to give a gay appearance by means of bright colors and glinting glass; but there are no signs here of representational elements—pictures of birds, cowboys, horses, Indians—or of crowded geometrical designs of glittering stones. The upper torso, like the lower torso, is covered in the peasant's holiday-white clothes: kuker masquerades are a rural, not urban, custom.

Covering the trousers of the Padarevo kuker around the hips is an elegant, skirt-like overgarment decorated with the same kind of ribbons as those on the vest. But there are also little bells. In the case of other kukers, these waist-stitched bells are anything but little. Some kukers' belts are crowded all around the body with huge cowbells, ten to fifteen of them, with the bell-jar having in some cases a five- or six-inch diameter, so that the whole group of bells may weigh 150 pounds or more. The men carrying these bells are of large girth, sturdy peasant folk who not only carry the bells but leap with them to make them ring during the dance that is part of their performance.[13] The kukers carry sometimes a sort of hoe which is sharpened to a point on the side opposite to the broad hoeing edge. During the dance they link these "kliunks", as they are called, to help support each other and remain in unison as they leap and kick. At other times, at least in the old days, the kliunks were used as weapons and were lethal enough to kill.[14]

One version of the kuker, then, is costumed as a supernatural creature, a man monstrously transformed and fused with several animals, performing dances and other ritual gestures which were concerned with the renewal of fertility for the New Year.[15] Another version of the kuker—found typically in southern Bulgaria, toward the boundary with Greece—was costumed in the late nineteenth and early twentieth centuries in a more socially pretentious way, like that adopted by Koo-Koo boys in Jamaica. In Nikola, Bulgaria, for example, the headdress was a white turban; the face, bedaubed with flour, was festooned with a white moustache and a beard which reached to the waist. This kuker wore a suit of white with many medals attached to the vest: he was called "the czar." He was pulled about in a two-wheeled cart in which he sat covered with a white linen blanket. Belying his generally dignified appearance, he carried a phallus-shaped piece of wood, painted red on the end, with which he pricked men by preference. This pseudo-king, after being wheeled around and after indulging in phallic games (he also possessed a whip, or a baton with a knotted end or a dripping rag on the end, with which he laid about, trying to hit or smear others with mud), jumped from the cart and led his troupe in plowing and sowing a symbolic field in the marketplace.[16]

"Savage" versions of the kuker masquerade moved in groups of seven to fifteen men, similarly costumed, from one house to the next. They would rush into each village farmstead's garden areas, jump up on trees, trample through the soon-to-be resown vegetable beds, and point their kliunks (or in other cases wooden swords) at the trees and beds in symbolic gestures of phallic refertilization. Their dancing, with its noisy leaping, was supposed to stimulate the earth to put forth its powers and make the new year's crops grow as high as the leaps. They might rush into the house and steal food, and their phallic vigor also might be directed toward the women-folk, swept up for a moment in a wild twirling dance. These moves have little counterpart in the rituals of Mardi Gras Indians. But they are not entirely foreign to Louisiana: they are very similar to the masquerades, conducted in rural Louisiana by the Cajun farmers, called "courir le mardi gras."[17]

The "aristocratic" versions of the kuker masquerade had a more narrative side to them, which might, depending on village tradition, be expanded into skits with plots similar to the mumming play on which the Koo-Koo boys drew in Jamaica. But here too the basic motif was the renewal of fertility. Although the "czar" was costumed in a comically grand manner, the band of ten to fifteen young men accompanying him at Nikola bore signs of the "savage" version of the kuker, wearing sheepskins over head and shoulders and the red pepper for a nose. They concluded their theater with its plowing and sowing climax—as the savage kuker also usually did—by a quete for gifts in money or kind for their performance, and at the end of the day they all repaired to the czar's house to drink and banquet.

European wildman costuming, whether turned toward natural or social disguise, is in continuity with local conditions of politics and economics. Some understanding of the conditions of life in the European peasant village is essential to make sense of the costuming's semiotics.[18] Afro-Caribbean forms of wildman costuming, including that of the black Indians of New Orleans, are, it seems, more urban in their origin. The urban situation, with its complexities of social and economic opportunities—and their lack—lends itself less easily to direct ritual statements of economic and political desire. Is this why the Afro-Caribbean wildman masquerades seem more fantastical? Being an Indian carries no direct economic implications and has few topically political overtones.

A second difference between the European and the Orleanian black wildman is the low-tuning of heterosexual byplay among the Indians. For the kukers the renewal of nature is like the phallic aggressiveness of men toward women. Metaphors of costume and performance make continual reference to this.[19] For the New Orleans tribes "masking Indian" is more a matter of male bonding and male rivalry. Again the urban setting, as opposed to the rural agricultural one, with its age-old metaphors about fertile mother earth, has much to do with this difference.

The reliance on bright colors, feathers, and glinting mirrors and stones is, on the other hand, a striking similarity between kukers and Mardi Gras Indians, superimposed as it is in both cases on the fantasy of disguising oneself as a half-human, half-animal force of nature. Both wildman types also place chief emphasis on the head and its attached decoration to carry the main symbolic message. The extraordinary height and spectacularly colored and waving form is not simply an attention-getter, like an outsized figure on a float. The headpiece is grand for a double reason. It is for the Mardi Gras Indian partly a crown, signifying the sovereign power of a tribal leader or, less grandly, the prowess of a tribal hero (one recalls the waving ostrich plumes and umbrellas carried above the heads of the Ashanti war captains and chiefs). And it is a revelation of the phantasmic change of a human into something that is more than human, into a being of fur and feathers, into a peacock in the case of the leader of the White Cloud Hunters, into some unknown bird-form in the case of the kuker of Padarevo—or rather, considered collectively, as these figures always present themselves, into a bewildering miasma of shimmering, vaguely naturalistic forms. The costumes of the black Indians suggest social and natural power at the same time; no division exists between the two, in contrast to what seems to have been the case with the old costuming of savage John Canoe and civilized Koo-Koo boys.

The way the costume of the Mardi Gras Indians encloses and blots out the natural articulation of the human body is unmatched in any other Carnival wildman figure I know. The costume's density and intricacy obliterate more than transform the human.[20] This quality is common enough in both serious and merry celebrations of nonliterate cultures outside European traditions. It struck Edward Curtis as particularly characteristic of the rituals of the Kwakiutl and other Northwest Coast Indians; his photographs of the birdbeak-masked players in these rituals, however theatrically rearranged for purposes of the photograph, convey unerringly the ritual aim of eradicating the human dimension and of entering into a supernatural realm by fusing natural elements in *un*natural, uncanny ways.[21]

The easiest way to measure the importance of this quality is to contrast it to the costumes of white Mardi Gras Indians—like those, for example, in the Iris parade of 1987, which displayed several dozen young maidens nicely spaced down the avenue, no two costumes alike (plate 34). Or should we say that they *are* alike in their studiously insignificant way of varying the standard elements of colored glass, sequins, eagle feathers, and ostrich plumes?[22] Below the bravely waving headpiece is plenty of soft, loose hair to sweetly frame a girl's healthy young American face, and at the other extremity a pair of cushiony sneakers to take the jolts out of a long trek down the parade route. The true sign and symbol of this "mask" is the majorette-like figure-fitted tunic, long strands of fringe swaying around the hips, spangles all over the tunic, and a bored costume-maker's half-hearted attempt at some kind of plant motif in light-colored fabric along the breast line and along a line where hips join the loins. In spite of its mediocrity and evident mass-produced fabrication the costume loudly proclaims that it is for a leggy American girl and that such a girl on parade ought to look sexy. The girl's girlness gives this masquerade whatever quality it has; the costume directs attention to the expressiveness, the personality of its wearer—which at the moment of this photograph was neutral. Nothing wild about this Indian. And certainly nothing the least supernatural. The headdress sits on top of a familiar set of signs as an allusion to something or other calculated to add a fillip to the pleasing sight. One can practically hear what the folks are saying: "Oh yeh, you know, those black guys who're always maskin' around here with big kinda feathered Indian tops. That must be it. I'll betcha them feathers cost a lot. But hey, ain't she smooth?"[23]

Comparison of the black Indians with the Koo-Koo boy and the kukers brings out one more difference, the tendency of European and European-influenced forms of the wildman to move toward narrativity, making a little story out of the Carnival roles. No narrative tendency is observable among the black Indians:

34. Indian Parader in Krewe of Iris, New Orleans, 1987 (photo, Norman Magden)

everything is dance and song, visual shimmer and verbal vaunting. In the case of the Bulgarian kukers or the English mummers the impetus to tell a story results in part from the connection of village communities to a general power structure yet their remoteness from it. The general power structure was for both English and Bulgarian mummers steeply hierarchical, with a king, court, and ministers as its personifications. Carnival plays burlesqued the pretensions of this hierarchy by imitating it in comic fashion. But what fun would it be, what release of frustrations might it serve, to burlesque city, state, or national "representatives of the people," if you are a black resident of a Southern metropolis's poorest quarters? Such people's subordination was and is so woven into the fabric of everyday institutions that its source is everywhere and nowhere: this hierarchy can have no personification. The best way to play with it is to fantasize something else entirely.

Discussion of the Mardi Gras Indian way of using the wildman figure may conclude with several general points suggested by comparison with the European, African, and Caribbean figures. First of all it is obvious that the Orleanians' large feathered headdress, iconographically central to their costume, is not merely an Indian motif. Its context in New Orleans is Carnivalesque and Caribbean as well as American. From the point of view of Carnival semiotics, the feathered headdress is celebratory and naturalistic, like that of the "savage" kuker. From the point of view of black Caribbean semiotics, derived from both African and colonial experience, it represents aristocratic splendor and sovereign power. From the point of view of American popular culture, it bespeaks belligerence and unconquerable pride.

To enlarge upon this first point, we can see now that the comparisons of related figures show why the Indianness of the Indians is not their most important feature. Far more important both in understanding what the Indians mean to say and how they say it is the Afro-American festive pattern first outlined in chapter 2, to which we attributed three aspects (ceremonial authority, aesthetic-artistic demonstration of ability or prowess, communal closeness and responsiveness) and four roles (hierarchical figures, stewards, heroes, choruses).[24] With respect to performance the closest parallel to the Mardi Gras Indians' arrangement of this pattern is found neither in Trinidad among the Wild or Fancy Indians nor among Jamaican John Canoes and European kukers. It is native to Haiti, where it may date from the colonial period before 1789. Critical investigation of Carnival festivities in Haiti is, however, recent, and no firm dates have been established between the dance descriptions of Moreau de St. Mery for the end of the eighteenth century, descriptions which do not relate to Carnival, and the beginnings of folkloric investigation in the 1930s.

Katharine Dunham, the well-known Afro-American dancer who has her own New York–based dance company, wrote a study of Haitian dances after fieldwork in that country in 1936–37. The Mardi-Gras "bands" of dancers that she saw did not wear Indian costumes, but they were organized and they behaved in ways very parallel to those of New Orleans black Indians. The chorus element of the bands might be very large, sometimes numbering four or five hundred when they paraded down the Grande Rue in Port-au-Prince. The bands grouped themselves about a "major-domo" or "king." He wore "short trousers, shoes and stockings, a jacket heavily encrusted with beads, mirrors, and brilliants, and a huge headdress of paper flowers, mirrors and ostrich plumes." He was called a major-domo, perhaps, because he "leads the mardi-gras band, baton in hand." Thus, as in the New Orleans and Jamaican bands but not the nineteenth-century Cuban groups in the cabildos, the heroic and hierarchic roles were combined: the chief/king not only presided but performed. When he performed in Haiti, however, it was determined in the 1930s by a steward of a surprisingly transitory kind: "The stopping points and general direction of the march are directed by a self-appointed guide, usually with a whistle and a *bâton*. When he tires of his job, he passes it on to a neighbor." Even the chief/king role was less powerful than in New Orleans. Although they were "professional, often the same ones leading bands year after year in the undisputed privilege of best dancers," nevertheless their authority was "negligible": "It is as heterogeneous a gathering as one could imagine, with no head authority, a minimum of restrictions (anything goes here!) no stability (one joins or leaves the carnival band at will, today behind one 'major,' tonight behind his rival), loose organization, no set behavior patterns. . . ."[25]

Like the Mardi Gras Indian chief, however, the essential role of the major or king is to "out-dance any other king whom the band chances to meet in its wanderings in town and country."[26] Like New Orleans' "second line," the crowd standing by "may stop to watch the dance of competition, cheering the more agile and ridiculing the loser, or they may go into a frenzy of dancing alone or with random partners. They may join in the drinks which the losing band must buy, or they may continue dancing,

Grotesques        227

perhaps oblivious to the fact that there has been a break in the march."[27]

The most noticeable difference in Haiti's festive pattern is thus the ephemeral character of the steward role. At New Orleans, spy boy and flag boy share this role, and they share, too, in the demonstration of dancing prowess when there is a challenge from another tribe. In Haiti everything in the 1930s was concentrated in the "major" or "king" figure in a way reminiscent of Beauvallet's Havana monarch of 1856 or Flint's Orleanian "king of the wake" in the 1840s. By the 1950s in Port-au-Prince Carnival groups called *bandes-mascarons* ("masked bands") had developed a more complex organization which was closer to that of the black New Orleans Indians: they were led by a flag man who carried a sign called a banner or flag ("Bannière") and by another marching alongside the king with a basket to collect coins from the crowd after the dance exhibitions (the quete). By the 1950s there were two, three, or four kings in the band. A "special chorus" surrounded a king when he danced to the rhythm of a drum. "They lift their feet with elegance, supporting themselves occasionally on sticks [*bâtons*]. They turn, twirling themselves and making their shoulders tremble."[28]

Even the 1950s form of Carnival group-dancing in Haiti differs sharply from that of the black Indians. "Some costumes of our Carnival kings recall those of Indian dancers," Professor Honorat writes without further explanation in speaking of the 1950s version.[29] There is no general modeling of the competitive dancing around an Indian masquerade; costumes seem rather to be modifications of white colonial elegance, like that of the Koo-Koo boy.[30] In Haiti the violent side of Carnival dancing was attributed to groups with a different name, "meringue bands" who had no kings and who rarely stopped to dance as they moved rapidly from street to street accompanied by three or four musicians performing a rapid meringue beat. When two meringue bands felt themselves strong enough to confront each other, the struggle left people wounded and sometimes dead.[31]

The violent mode of Haitian black dancing was entirely separate from the aestheticized mode, but the violent mode was just as murderous as those wildman forms studied elsewhere. Was this because the meringue bands stemmed from crowded, criminally connected sections of the city, as the Mardi Gras Indians did? "I'm talking about men who'd kill you with their fists," said Tuddy Montana of the Yellow Pocahontas in a 1982 interview, speaking of the old violent period. "Stone killers. Today people run to the Indians. During them days, people would run away from the Indians."

Violence and beauty, wildness and aesthetic prowess are intertwined in the Mardi Gras Indians in ways which in the rest of the Caribbean seem to have been separate. The closest parallel here is to the behavior and evolution of the East European kukers who, like the Orleanians, have under political and social pressure dropped their violent side today. The intertwined functions in the Orleanian tribes may explain the role-splitting and role-combinations. Like the chief, flag boy and spy boy are both ceremonious and heroic figures. Conversely, the wildman role allows a display of violence untrammeled by the pressures of either ceremony or dancing prowess.

There is little information on the wild man in the early days of the tribe. Montana, however, related in his interview some details about one such figure which, if representative, throws a flood of light upon dynamics within the group. "Wild Man Rock was a cat who lived out by a junk heap, way down Elysian Fields [Avenue] where people dumped their garbage. . . . And let me tell you: he was *wild*. You never saw him so much until Carnival came. Then he'd come bargin' out with a ring in his nose, carryin' bones and a spear, whoopin' and carryin' on, used to throw that spear and scare all hell out of people."[32] This wild man, a kinetic, emotive intensification of the general sign beneath which all the black Indians moved, resorted to specifically African semes to make his meaning clear: not bow and arrow but spear, not scalp but bones, not war-paint but nose-ring. While the chief's role was practical, his wildman alter ego acted symbolically, "whoopin' and carryin' on."

In the general rush to create the finest show for the tourist's camera, the wildman role among present-day tribes has come to be relatively neglected. But there still exists an unspoken balance and also tension between this role and that of the chief, between the archaic origins of wildness, represented in the wildman's retention of furskins and ox-horns, and the aestheticized improvement of wildness, represented in the chief's finery. The two roles signify the difference between excessive and proper power, or perhaps simply between a more specific and a more generalized representation of that power; after all, the wildman remains a member of the tribe, and represents something of its essential nature.

This principle of tension yet balance in roles and symbols is the same as the one most strongly communicated in performance: the rhythmic quality, which in the case of Mardi Gras Indians refers to a group-created quality. The practices are the place to recognize this most intensely, because the group functions within a more enclosed space, where people respond more to each other and less to the open-ended surroundings of a parade. I have scarcely entered into the analysis of particular songs with their apparently senseless, purely phatic refrains (Handa Wanda, Too-way Pack-a-way, etc.). But it is clear that such lines are more than percussive punctuations or onomatopoeic expressiveness. Through much repetition their syntactic meaning has been sheared away and their ritual meaning ornamented and enriched. Their meaning, at whatever point in this continuing process of augmentation and diminution they are heard, is a shifting, adjustable part of an oral-rhythmic text woven by the interplay of bodies, tambourines and voices moving in polyrhythms which are so complex that they baffle the ear—but not the body.

The chief, or any other Indian taking his improvisatory turn, calls out a pattern not just with the voice but with a thump of the feet, a gesture of hands, a thrust of the head; and the response from the surrounding players is similarly performed with the whole of the body and its extension, the tambourine. What is practiced from week to week and month to month is not any particular phrase, no artful sequence of steps, no technique for pounding the tambourine, but simply the integration of call with response in ever more intricate polyrhythmic closeness. What is practiced is the power of uniformly felt action, the participation in a collective creation of something more than words or music or even sound, something, I repeat, too intricate for the ear alone to decipher. The body's nerves seize upon it and translate it into that series of torso bobs and weaves, knees going left and right, hands snapping in time, elbows and shoulders doing the buck-and-wing and everything else. Each body is a medley of parts and sounds and both are moving in a dozen counterdirections, while all these directions, all these sounds, all the bodies in a group are held together by the force of an elliptically moving, commonly felt axis, which allows them to function flexibly, giving and taking in turn. This *rhythm* is where meaning inheres: the rhythm *in*-volves, you twirl into and out of the action, by turns leading and being led, thrusting along the crest of the wave, carried along in the lee of it. Unless you move—*all* of you—with this engulfing rhythm, you're not part of it at all.[33]

The Mardi Gras Indian creation of this rhythm is a marvel, but it is almost commonplace within Afro-American culture generally, merely a variant of the rhythmic genius which expresses itself in jazz, in break-dancing, in the unbelievable ballets exhibited in all kinds of sport competitions, in Gospel singing and Gospel preaching.[34] The genius is always that of the group, even when it seems most personal. Individual performances, individual challenges are variants on an action first felt in and through the group. The group nurtures the individual who, now here and again there, launches a new call, contrives a new cross-rhythm, stimulates a new initiative. Dancing, singing, chanting develop along a continuum; they are not separate performance modes, let alone different categories of artistic talent, as tends to be assumed in Western European elite-cultural tradition. Is this because these (to Europeans) eminently respectable artistic modes are in Afro-American culture developed in continuity with what we see as much less respectable and also much more exalted artistry: with boasting, with "slanging each other," with marketplace taunts and churchly ecstasy, with oaths and promises, curses and trance?[35]

Corresponding to this group-created, communally nurtured flow is the nonlinear, nondirected general quality of performance in the streets as in the tavern. What a difference from the white Carnival societies' linear thinking and linear performances: you go straight down the street, escorted by police and marching bands, you throw your beads and trinkets into a sea of anonymous faces, you arrive at the ball and participate in the Grand March and the tableaux, the captain blows the whistle and the ball is over, you go home. In letter-centered culture you obey the letter of the prescribed program: it whistles inside your skull.[36]

Perhaps the most unsettling moment for me of the visit to the White Cloud Hunters on mardi gras, 1987, was that early-morning arrival at the house which was supposed to be the tribe's gathering-place. There I found—nobody, for ten, twenty, fifty minutes. My inner whistles were blowing loudly. But when I later realized that my attempts to be inconspicuous in the street had prevented earlier awareness of my expected arrival, and realized that all the people in this neighborhood, all the players in Charles's gang, had known for hours about the difficulty with the peacock costume and the delay in starting, the knowledge allowed me to turn off the whistles and the clock in my head and to enter into the manner of this other culture. A black Indian parade does not start at a time and place marked or markable on somebody's city map. It begins at a house, or rather at a dozen houses where the gang assembles its symbols with a flexibility which allows for some kid stumbling on the stairs, no cereal in the cupboard, a car which breaks down, a peacock falling. The tribe moves through a neighborhood among people who know more or less about all that, where information is being passed through many small channels, where coordination grows as the time flows.

Zulu wildmen, like the black Indian version of these figures, celebrated Carnival in flexible, nonlinear ways until recently.

> When King Zulu's parade begins there is a long day ahead. Like the white Mardi Gras monarchs, he has certain places to stop and certain streets through which he must pass, but as a whole his route is much more haphazard. . . . Time means nothing, for the Zulus parade all day long.
> Most of the stops are at bars. In 1947 the first pause, however, was a grandstand about three blocks from the starting point, where a large crowd of subjects waited, and where His Majesty was toasted again and again. From there the parade swung neatly across the street and paused before a bar. Here bartenders brought drinks for all. . . .
> The queen and her maids awaited their mates on a balcony in front of the Geddes and Moss undertaking parlors. Here there was a long pause, with an exchange of speeches and the presentation to His Majesty of the keys to Zululand in New Orleans. The king toasted the queen and the queen toasted the king. . . . After the toasts of the rulers, the dukes and the maids also toasted each other, and then the dukes passed bottles around to the warriors on the floats, and a special one to the Big Shot of Africa. . . .[37]

Today the Zulu parade is a major parade, the first on mardi gras morning to march down the white man's route along St. Charles Avenue to Canal Street. The barstops have been eliminated. The Zulu Social Aid and Pleasure Club has become chic, integrated, and not really very wild.

Perhaps this was foreseeable. The Zulus' aim diverged from that of the Indians from the beginning. The Mardi Gras Indians developed Carnival freedom toward *ritual* independence of the white society by which they were dominated every day but this one, devoted to pure fantasy. They developed confrontational rituals which, for all their merriment, had a very serious side and expressed in aggressive as well as artistic ways the cohesiveness of neighbors. The Zulus on the other hand aimed at satire, both of themselves—that is, of blacks in their situation—and no less of the whites who lorded it over them. Their symbols were accordingly more double-edged than those of the Indians. The Carnival roles as well as the symbols of the Zulus have also been less intricately developed. Their Carnival activity is simply an annual parade and ball, not a ritually ongoing connection.[38]

"Early in 1909 a group of laborers who had organized a club

named 'The Tramps' went to the Pythian Temple Theater [owned by the black Knights of Pythias] to see a musical comedy by the Smart Set. A skit portraying a Zulu tribe had as its title, 'There Never Was and Never Will Be a King Like Me.'" Such is the version of the Zulus' foundation consecrated in the programs of the Zulu Club which are given to members at their Carnival ball.[39] The Tramps changed their name to Zulu and appeared with one William Story as king on mardi gras, 1909. He wore a lard-can crown, carried a banana-stalk scepter, and paraded on foot with his friends, "clad in ragged trousers." These and other details about the early days seem to be the orally collected memories of early members. Some years later, it is said, the king wore "a white starched shirt, an Italian bread neck-tie, and an onion for a stickpin."[40] According to another equally undocumented source, the king once wore a silver foil suit made from the inner linings of cigarette packages, at another time a rabbit-skin costume, and on a third occasion a suit sewn of different flags.[41]

If these reports are even approximately accurate, they indicate that early costuming reflected the group's earlier name, the Tramps, more than the Zulus. The trademarks of the Club's parades, black-sooted bodies bare of everything but a grass skirt, are not certainly documented until 1923, when King Zulu's horse-drawn wagon was photographed (plate 35). The king is shown just right of center, standing solemnly at attention with a scepter in his right hand and a crown on his head. Queen Zulu, if she is present at all on the float, can be faintly seen standing behind two little Zulu princes wearing crowns, to the king's left. Identifying this person as the queen is in fact an inference: the photograph is not explained in the pamphlet in which it appears. A Zulu queen was first chosen in 1923; it was a man masking as a woman. The transvestite practice continued for ten years. Plate 36, showing king and queen in 1931, designates the queen more clearly by means of a long gown and low-cut bodice.

To the king's right is a person gesturing toward the king with the rod of a royal official. Is this the Grand Marshal? In 1964 an unidentified personage who shared the king's float looked a little like this figure of 1923, wearing "a tentlike yellow costume and a top hat" and standing at the head of the float "like a burlesque figurehead, with one hand resting on a lion and the other on [a] zebra."[42] In 1941 a photograph of the king, another role-figure called the "Big Shot," and the Grand Marshal, shows the

35. King Zulu and retinue on float, New Orleans, 1923 (photo, Norman Magden, from pamphlet, "Zulu Social Aid and Pleasure Club Presents 1939 King Zulu," courtesy of New Orleans Public Library)

Grand Marshal wearing a derby and a light-colored silken cape.[43]

The customs and symbols of Zulu merriment took shape gradually.[44] As with the Mardi Gras Indians, the Club was very much a male affair; women did not invade its activities so easily as they did those of the white societies. The transvestite queens of 1923–32 must have seemed an even more shocking ridicule of the *grandes dames* of New Orleans elite society than did King Zulu's unspoken spoof of Rex (note in the 1931 photograph the immensely long trains held by little-boy Zulu "pages" or princes; whether they wore crowns like their predecessors in 1923 is not clear).

Although spare and makeshift, the thrust of the satire is unmistakable. To the white societies' ultracivilized royal robes and mythological surroundings the Zulus oppose the wildman symbols of naked bodies and swatches of tall jungle grass in 1923. In the 1931 photograph human wildness has been intensified, and made more comic, by the white greasepaint around eyes and mouth. If the 1923 photograph is accurate, then the additional convention of representing these savages by means of jet-black skin only emerged sometime between 1923 and 1931. Henceforth black greasepaint and long underwear, dyed black, were costume necessities.

We have seen this "black varnish" before; it was used from the mid-nineteenth century in Caribbean Carnivals as the mark of a "primitive negro," one recently arrived from Africa. Already this early the whites'—and many blacks'—skin-color prejudices were being ridiculed in Afro-American Carnivals.[45] In the case of the Zulus the connection was probably made by means of the reference to the word Zulu. Danny Barker, the jazz musician born in New Orleans about 1910, speaks of the racial slurs he encountered as a teenage street musician there: "As we smiled and entertained the drunks, both men and women reared back and yelled this epithet, 'Dem coons sho' can play.' And if it wasn't that it was niggers, darkies, Zulus, piccaninnies, Africans, monkeys, gorillas. . . ."[46]

The Zulus make perfectly conscious, grotesque use of the white man's racial clichés. Sambo makeup, used by whites in the "minstrel shows" which were a main component of American

36. King Zulu and retinue, New Orleans, 1931 (photo, Norman Magden, from pamphlet, "Zulu Social Aid and Pleasure Club Presents 1939 King Zulu," courtesy of New Orleans Public Library)

Grotesques          235

popular entertainment down to the Second World War, is combined with clever inversions of white Carnival's royal ceremonies.[47] The combination was cathartic, and was recognized as such in the 1960s by at least some black radicals. Robert De Coy, speaking with the tones of a prophet, referred to the Zulus as a symbol of the black man's capacity to escape from the see-saw of white-controlled social aspiration and black inability to beat the system: "I have given you a Day. A Carnival celebration, the Mardi Gras, which Niggers may now claim as their own. For this is the day in which we are all free to mask in the blackface make-up of the King Zulu, whereby we parody that which we actually are."[48]

The Zulu masquerade is, from De Coy's point of view, *doubly* ambivalent. It cuts against black people's internalized image of themselves as too low but also too high, too savage and too noble.[49] At the same time it plays with the whites' aristocratic image of themselves as royal and with their idea of blacks as primitive.[50] Because of this double-cutting ambivalence, Zulu symbols are hard to co-opt by any social group, high or low, black or white. The more predictable the rest of the parades have become, the more the Zulu parade has stood out in zany contrast.

The four-part role system of black festivities is usually observable in Zulu parades. At the side of sovereignty is the steward in the form of a Grand Marshal. Sometimes he is doubled by a Captain, but the Zulu's captain resembles a white captain only in name. He is ummasked, rides no horse, and represents no behind-the-scene authority. In 1964 the Captain, "resplendent in a green silk costume and a plumed hat . . . jitterbugged with the King and Queen" from the Poydras Street Wharf to the floats, where they were joined by the Grand Marshal, "who had on tails over black tights and was wearing a pink sash."[51] The heroic role is played by Witch Doctor and/or the Big Shot of Africa. Warriors on and alongside the floats and second-liners along the parade route provide plenty of communal amplification.[52]

The Witch Doctor, like the Wild Man among Mardi Gras Indians, represented the most savage version of the Zulu troupe, displaying large ox-horns on a fur headpiece and wearing a grass skirt, a leopard-skin tunic, and another tattered skin as a cloak in an undated photograph from the 1940s or 1950s (plate 4). This primitivism especially drew the ire of respectable black organizations and middle-class blacks in the 1960s, and it does not seem to be enacted any more, at least officially.[53] But we photographed an unnamed wildman with the traditional symbols on a float in the 1987 parade (plate 37), wearing ox-horns and a leopard-skin jacket trimmed with black fur, leaning from the float, to gesture—to cast a spell?—with a huge bone in each extended hand.

37. Witch Doctor, Zulu parade float, New Orleans, 1987 (photo, Norman Magden)

The Big Shot of Africa, the king's other antagonist and alter ego, sometimes wears ox-horns and fur skins, too.[54] But the Big Shot represents less Africa's shamanic lore than its wealth. "Those coconuts of his are not coconuts—they're from his diamond mine in Africa," a Zulu member explained to the journalist Calvin Trillin in 1964. "He comes over and brings gold to you poor fellows here."[55] The Big Shot's role is to pretend superiority to the King. The King benevolently smiles and waves to his subjects, but the Big Shot merely responds to yells and whoops with a cool nod. "He spoke to almost no one," wrote a reporter of his behavior in the 1947 parade; he sat with crossed legs, "flashing jewelry and elegant cigar, letting all spectators know that he was superior to them all, a real big shot."[56]

If Paul Johnson was to be believed in 1964, when he claimed to be "the original Big Shot," the role was probably added in the later 1920s (Johnson was King Zulu in 1930). Its signature was already the display of power as a matter of money. "They try to imitate him but they don't come up to him," a fellow member said of Johnson in 1964. "He spent some *money.*"[57] The Big Shot of 1964, Milton Bienamee, wore large diamond rings on both hands, a leopard-skin cape with large imitation diamonds sewn on it, gold earrings, and a large pendant. He carried a large, sequined coconut and a gold cane, and smoked a huge cigar. This Big Shot was the black man's version of the All-American dream of making it as a capitalist. The bank president's cigar was, so to speak, his scepter.

Is there some kind of pendulum-swing between the wild and the civilized sides of Carnival's grotesque maskers, developing contrasts between the Mardi Gras Indians' Big Chief and their Wild Man, between the Zulus' Witch Doctor and their Big Shot? As one side grows in prestige, must the other diminish? In the 1980s, as far as the Zulus are concerned, the pendulum seems to have swung away from both Witch Doctor and Big Shot back toward the King, who is considerably more civilized in appearance. But this is a function of a general change in the character of the organization, a change which began as a result of the bitter struggles in the 1960s. The NAACP, CORE, the main Christian churches, and many other organizations put pressure on the Zulus to abandon their parodic pleasures as undignified. They nearly succeeded. But it was clear to those city officials concerned with tourism that this would eliminate a very popular

38. King Zulu and page on float, New Orleans, 1987 (photo, Norman Magden)

attraction. They pressured the Zulus to keep up the old-style parades. Although membership dropped to as low as twenty members in 1964 and the parade consisted of only four floats that year, sufficient old-timers were wedded to the traditional customs to survive the pressures from outside.[58] They did not survive the pressure from inside. Black middle-class and even some upper-class people joined the organization. By 1976 the king was a doctor.[59] By the 1980s the coronation ball was held at the Rivergate Convention Center, like those of important white societies. The Queen's gown was imported from France and her maids' court included many of the most prestigious black debutantes in the city.[60] The president in his introduction to 1980's Coronation Ball program emphasized his efforts to put the Club on a new footing by introducing "sound fiscal policies while cautiously implementing cost effectiveness in an effort to safeguard investments and liabilities."[61] Among other consequences of these new responsible policies was the discontinuation in 1987 of the gifts of Zulu gilded coconuts to people on the streets, due to damage suits brought by people who claimed to have been hit by the decorated fruits even though the organization's members had been cautioned to hand them out, not throw them.

Although the king (plate 38) in his richly embroidered tunic, with matching gloves, scepter, and feathered crown, shows scarcely an inch of unbecoming nakedness, there is a little black and white greasepaint on his face, and a few wisps of the grass skirt peak out from beneath the tunic. Nose-rings, gold earrings, and other such uncouth articles have disappeared.[62] The most convincing remaining reference to Africa, perhaps, is the plastic leopard on the front of the float.

The old spirit of grotesque play has not been completely wrung out of the Zulus, of course. Here in plate 39 is a rider on one of the handsome new floats in 1987 holding up a large sign with the one word no one ever needs to say—or could be heard to say—amid the roar of the throwing game along St. Charles Avenue: Louder![63]

In 1974 one of the Mardi Gras Indian tribes, the Wild Magnolias, released a record together with the rhythm-and-blues singer "Willie Tee" Turbinton. As a follow-up, Turbinton persuaded a half dozen members of the tribe to go on the road with the band, in costume. They not only played major cities in the south and east but Carnegie Hall in New York, and after that went briefly to Paris, meeting with great success everywhere. In 1976 the re-

39. Zulu float-rider, New Orleans, 1987 (photo, Norman Magden)

cently founded (1972) Wild Tchoupitoulas joined forces with the
Neville Brothers, four fine rhythm-and-blues performers whose
uncle was the Tchoupitoulas' chief. More successfully than that
of the Wild Magnolias with Turbinton, their record retained the
contrast between Indian chants by the tribal group and the Neville Brothers' songs, inspired by the chants but introducing
Afro-Cuban rhythms and the close quartet harmonies which
have made them the best-known local group in popular music.[64]

Some Indian tribes, or individuals from them, might be found
for a brief time in the wake of the Rex parade or other major
parades outside their neighborhood from the 1950s onward. But

this was exceptional and unplanned. The contracts and tours with musical groups in the 1970s were planned, and they brought not only city-wide but national renown, something hitherto unknown. In 1976 and 1979 important documentary films about the tribes were made.[65] Image-seekers began following the Indians, and conversely the Indians began to seek their image, appearing in the main streets more often and following major parades. The wild, it would appear, is being domesticated in this case as in the case of the Zulus, although for reasons less of social respectability than of the media's (and the tourist's) search for novelty.[66]

Perhaps it is only possible over the long term for the figure of the wildman to appear in Carnival in domestic clothes, like the bear-man who accompanied Rex's fat ox in 1873 (plate 17), or the gorilla in bow-tie and sequin jacket who turned up in 1987 (plate 40). The wild is always being changed into the grotesque.

With one exception, it seems. From the 1930s until at least the 1960s there was another tribe which regularly moved through the black neighborhoods, striking as much terror into the hearts of children as the Indians used to do: "the Skeletons," George Reinecke called them, reminiscing about his childhood in a mixed black Creole-white neighborhood in the 1930s;[67] "Skelykins," a woman living in the much poorer Eighth Ward said, speaking of the 1960s: "They'd dye union suits black, paint white bones on 'em, and make paper mashey skulls. . . . That's all we knew 'bout Mardi Gras, jus' Zulus, Indians, Baby Dolls, an' Skelykins."[68]

The tradition is old, and once again Caribbean-wide and European-connected. In 1848 Charles Day saw in Port of Spain, Trinidad, not only the black-varnished "primitives" referred to earlier but a "personation of Death, having what was understood to be a skeleton painted on a coal-black shape, [who] stalked about with part of a horse's vertebra attached to him and a horse's thigh bone in his hand. . . ."[69] What makes this mask so terrifying is its connection with diabolism, very strong in any cultural tradition based on reverence for nature's powers, as black African faiths nearly always are. I have quoted in a note Lafcadio Hearn's magnificent description of a Carnival dance by a red-clad devil and his boyish followers in Martinique in 1888, a Carnival celebrated in the most macabre manner in the midst of a small-pox epidemic in a provincial town. The devil wore a

40. Street masker, "wildman," New Orleans, 1987 (photo, Norman Magden)

white horsehair wig "to make him look weird and old"; he and the boys chanted for hours, as they danced through the death-stricken streets: "The Devil and the zombies sleep anywhere and everywhere!"[70]

African beliefs about the unquiet spirits of the dead and the necessity for those still living to properly bury and remember deceased family members gave rise to religious practices which resisted Christianity more than any other part of African heritage.[71] One reason for this, of course, is that the dead live on in some sense for Christians, too, and so ideological combats on this issue have always been confused, lending themselves to syncretic compromise. But why did such beliefs concerning the continuing "life" of the dead come to the surface in Carnival rather than at other times? Because Carnival, we may well remember, falls near a turning of the year, the March kalends, the spring equinox, which among many European ethnicities, and even among the ancient Romans until late in Republican times, was as important as the January kalends and winter solstice.[72] A variety of ceremonies concerned with "carrying out death," housecleaning and purifying the household, and ceremoniously renewing the fields, seem to have been transferred from pagan religious calendars to the date of Carnival in Europe's rural areas, where they were found by mid-nineteenth-century ethnographers.[73] The ceremony of burying an effigy of Carnival, or of burning or drowning such a puppet on the evening of mardi gras, also carries overtones of the idea of an old year's ending.[74]

Given this double sanction, African and European, for thinking about death at the time of Carnival, is it any surprise to see skeletons along the Gulf Coast at Mardi Gras rather than—in accordance with the more usual American folklore—at Halloween? Is it any surprise that Folly chases Death, and Death chases Folly, around a broken Corinthian column of Mobile's most well-known Carnival float?[75] Is it not altogether in accordance with the character of Africanized Christianity for black Orleanian Carnival revelers of the past generation to visit the tombs of family members on the day after Mardi Gras, Ash Wednesday, to light candles on the graves, signifying prayers to the ancestors and the saints for peace and prosperity, and to deposit little written messages to the dead through slots in the grave monuments?[76]

Until the 1970s the climax of the Zulus' parade took place at

41. Street Masker, "death"(?), French Quarter, New Orleans, 1987 (photo, Norman Magden)

the Geddes and Moss Funeral Home. There the queen and her court and guests sat in a grandstand and toasted—and were toasted by—their comic king, exactly as Rex's queen was greeted at the Boston Club. But why in the world did they choose the home of death for the happy celebration of Zulu's monarchy? Of course it is true that the Geddes and Moss home contributed handsomely to the Zulu Club, like many other businesses—above all bars—in the black community, and each of them was in the old days entitled to a halt and salutation along the way. Nevertheless, the funeral home held this special place among the stops. Here was where the day's festivities reached their culmination, with dancing in the streets and music-making carried on as long as energies and liquor allowed. To engage in such springtime high jinks at the altar of death is nearly unthinkable for a white Westerner.[77] For such black folk as the Zulus, unburdened by up-and-down, high-and-low metaphysics which separate life from death and the sacred from the profane, celebrating Carnival at such a place is as natural and appropriate as the honoring of a deceased neighbor with both funeral dirges and joyous jazz.[78] After all, the Zulu Social Aid and Pleasure Club served in part as an insurance scheme to aid sick members and the families of deceased members; the combination of life-giving and death-aiding functions is expressed in its very name.

For the rest of us, dispossessed of this remarkable sense of pleasure's entwining with pain, death lurks as a menace which on this holiday out of all holidays ought to be dismissed. In vain. As my photographer friend and I rounded a street corner near the cathedral on mardi gras in 1987, our way was suddenly barred by a stout staff. Before us stood a preternaturally tall man, handsomely dressed in a rhinestone-studded, satin cassock and a long, brilliantly colored sash thrown over one shoulder, caught up on the arm just above the elegant glove to which jewels were also attached (plate 42): death stared at us, empty-eyed, from a face turned into that of a bird, a wild bird, feathers sweeping up from the forehead like tongues of fire. But it was also a man's face whose nose and cheekbones seemed to have been eaten away and replaced by little rows of beads hanging horridly before a vacant maw where mouth and chin once were (plate 41).

It may be that this masker did not intend to represent death, a death slightly ecclesiastical, slightly diabolical in its bejewelled,

42. Street Masker, "death"(?), French Quarter, New Orleans, 1987 (photo, Norman Magden)

purple-cassock overtones. I did not ask. What was significant was not the identity but the aura of the masquerade. Anyway, the aura was, like everything else at New Orleans, double. Chinless he might be, but he still apparently needed the liquid in a paper cup from some fast-food vendor (plate 42).

New Orleans' Carnival offers space for the imagination to take flight, the imagination of both performers and spectators. One of the characteristic directions of this flight is the crossing of the wild with the ominous. Today this crossing is found, it seems, more often in individual figures than in groups. It is not a frequent thing, but it recurs, ever and again. An inertial factor in Carnival behavior was encountered earlier in the form of the regular appearance of four roles among black festive performers: is this another example of such a structural pattern? Does the very exuberance of Carnival carry us around the street corner to rumination about life's opposite?

Is this why the "dukes" seem to stare from corpse-like masks which contrast strangely with the comic-strip expressiveness of their floats (plate 51)? Is this what fascinates us, Medusa-like, in an exquisitely constructed confection of ribbons and bells framing a blank, frozen beauty (frontispiece)?[79]

The Zulus, in fact, were never wild, nor did they intend to be. Like the *boeuf gras* bear-man, like the black man accompanying the bear-man, like death in a feathered, beaded face, they intended to be grotesque by means of being wild.[80]

The Mardi Gras Indians, on the other hand, living like the Zulus in conditions which could properly be called those of a wilderness in every respect except that the conditions have been humanly imposed, sought to express their wildness rather than to make fun out of it. In spite of themselves they have now been assimilated to the grotesque by the white spectators who in increasing numbers flock to see them. Their marginal, messy, nonlinear space has, in an age of instant information-retrieval and ever more novelty-seeking media, become an indispensable adjunct to the space of the main streets with its straight lines and inexorable routines. The black Indians appear to people from this linearly developed spectator world as the same kind of exotics as Totila the barbarian or Comus the god, a happy distraction, a pleasant variation on more well-known floats, part of the "cast" of that great show, Carnival.[81]

The cultural matrix shifted enough, nationally and locally, in the 1960s and early 1970s, to give one or two Indian groups a chance to develop a persona beyond their neighborhood and even beyond Carnival; it shifted enough to open a spectator's window where one could peek in, fascinated, at these strange creatures. But the social matrix did not change. The situation is the same now as before the housing projects, before the end of legal segregation, before the election of black mayors, before the gentrification of the French Quarter and a limited end to white flight to the suburbs.[82] Is there a mechanism in industrial society beyond the reach of reform which perversely preserves this kind of wilderness in our cities? Does "clean" Carnival (which is today both black and white) perhaps *require* this peepshow into what must seem to it a sordid otherness, as white Carnival certainly did require it in Lyle Saxon's youth?[83] Should we, the tourists from elsewhere, amateur or professional as we may be, even wish for anything to change, since it is certain that if the social fabric in black New Orleans changes in fundamental ways, that will mean the end of nonliterate culture, the end of black-Indian style, the end of this kind of neighborly, personally created Carnival?

# CHAPTER
# 9

## A Great American Spectacular

During the civic-minded era (about 1850 to 1900) business and professional elites in New Orleans and Mobile found that through their orderly leadership they could manage the pursuit of pleasure in Carnival just as successfully as they managed the pursuit of profit. During the succeeding national era, however, the destiny of Carnival has been shaped as much by people and institutions outside the city as within it. In the 1880s and 1890s political, economic, and cultural trends conspired to encourage perception of this dependence of the two cities on the outside world. The restoration of white supremacy after the period of Reconstruction brought no return of prosperity; this solution to the defeated South's problems turned out to be a way of avoiding them. Meanwhile the nation outside the South was growing and prospering; the cultural attitudes embodied in the slogans of the "Gay Nineties" and the "Gilded Age" express a loosening of the Protestant work ethic, a willingness and even eagerness to grant a place to leisured enjoyment. New Orleans took advantage of this conjuncture of local politico-economic stagnation with the national willingness to invest some of its wealth in leisure by advertising itself as Romantic New Orleans, the City that Care Forgot. The city of Mobile, less agile, or perhaps too small to develop a national reputation, continued to hold on to its local habits of festivity.

The late nineteenth-century move to develop tourism was not democratic in thrust. It was based on the attractiveness for Northerners of a rather imaginary Southern, Creole-French way of life which placed high value on chivalrous conviviality and devoted itself wholeheartedly to it, even if only for a few days each year. New Orleans' Carnival offered an America that was publicly committed to equality its secret dream of aristocratic inequality. The attractiveness of the Carnival-society parades was their quality of slightly recondite illusion. The Carnival societies—and there were still only four of them in New Orleans and four in Mobile that regularly paraded at the beginning of the twentieth century—sought in their parade themes a blend of the esoteric with the platitudinous, a blend that would delight the crowd with its mixture of the mysterious, the learned, and the commonplace.

National inclinations with regard to cultural activity thus rhymed with the local desire to look to the past and maintain the status quo in social terms. This does not mean that no concessions were made to the spirit of the new century—to America's growing fascination with scientific progress, for example. In 1910 the wonders revealed by the biologist's microscope and the geologist's digging tools were treated more positively than in the days of satires on Darwin's evolution. A patina of science was added to the much cherished Greco-Roman references and the Romantic era's affection for things medieval. The parade of Momus, led by that demigod seated on a sinuous sea dragon, displayed the wonders of nature in the insect world, a world including mythic hobgoblins at one extreme and fossil pterodactyls at another. There were "wasps, butterflies, humming birds, dragon flies, night moths, mosquitoes, bumble bees, will of the wisps, the winged nautilus, katydids, devil horses, doves, and hobgoblins." Rex's parade was led by a magnificent rendition of a griffin, "a grisly creature flying through the air and bearing on its back an armed man . . . about to attack the Moslem Knights who had come to its lair in search of the treasures [and "winsome maidens"] heaped in the rear of the car." Floats followed showing Scylla and Charybdis, the Chimera, the Minotaur, the Sphinx, and then unexpectedly, the Midgard serpent of Nordic myth, followed by another Greek evocation, Neptune and his sea horses, and then by the "ogre" of medieval mythology. The Greek strain reappeared: centaurs came forward, followed by the Roc, one of the characters from the Arabian Nights; then came Greek Cerberus, and so on. Comus's parade was more symbolically coherent, although no less fantastic, representing the history of Mohammed in twenty installments, his wives, his followers, his paradise, and his visions in the desert. The parade of Proteus pictured fifteen floats superintended by Father Time: the twelve zodiacal constellations, the wandering comets, the sun itself.[1]

What has changed since 1910 is less the grandiose symbolic storehouse than the technical means of producing it. I refer to two qualities with the word "grandiose," the first of which, ambivalence, is common to most Carnival celebrations; the second, semantic inflation, especially distinguishes the national era. Carnival symbols are nearly always both silly and serious. The Carnival king is a crowned fool; he provokes admiration and laughter. The Carnival king is not merely grand, but grandiose;

43. Bacchusaurus, float in Bacchus parade, New Orleans, 1987 (photo, Norman Magden)

the line between self-glory and satire is crossed back and forth all along a parade's route, and indeed all through the long process of selecting costumes and constructing floats. Modern technology has encouraged the development of the second aspect of Mardi Gras's grandioseness, the inflation of symbols through better advertising, bigger floats, larger grandstands, longer parade routes.

The easiest date to point to in the latter process is 1969, when the Krewe of Bacchus was founded. The krewe was organized by tourist entrepreneurs rather than by locally oriented businessmen; a float-builder and a restaurateur were the prime movers. They constructed floats towering two stories high. One of their floats depicts a Walt-Disney-like dinosaur, crowned with grapes and bowing its head benignly, labeled "Bacchusaurus" (see plate 43).[2] The symbol might have been used by Momus in its 1910 parade, but probably not the dimensions, and certainly not the glossily brilliant plastic materials and the cartoon absurdity of the animal's name and facial features. The idea of using large, caricatural features which can be seen from afar in a large crowd is no innovation. It was understood by those who drew the sketches for New Orleans' Carnival floats from the beginning of the twentieth century, as we have seen from the mask of Comus surrounded by grape clusters in 1906 (plate 10). At Nice the principle was put into practice by 1905 in an early triumph of engineering that created a gigantic dragon remarkably similar to Bacchusaurus in dimensions and cartoon exaggeration (plate 44).[3] But Comus's float and the dragon at Nice were accompanied by supplementary symbols and maskers which, although they emphasized the gigantic scale of the main vehicle of significance, nevertheless cluttered its visual effect. Bacchusaurus is all of a piece, simplistically oversized and plastic-slick in every detail. No hint of realism is allowed: Bacchusaurus is a machine suggesting an animal, and the suggestion is all that is desired. Small may be beautiful, but big is powerful.

Instead of a tableau ball after the parade, the Krewe of Bacchus offers a supper dance at the huge Rivergate Convention Center, to which anyone can come by paying admission. The "king"—that is, the man riding in the first float as a personification of the god of wine—is not a local man but a national celebrity: Danny Kaye in 1969, Phil Harris, Bob Hope, Glen Camp-

44. "Lou Babau," carnival float, Nice, 1905 (photo, Norman Magden, from Annie Sidro, *Le Carnaval de Nice*)

bell, Henry Winkler ("the Fonz") on other occasions. The god's identity is disclosed in a full-page advertisement in the chief local paper, inviting "the people of New Orleans and their guests to participate with . . . Bacchus."[4] After the success of Bacchus another group, Endymion, became a "Super Krewe" in imitation. Its floats rival those of Bacchus in inflated size, and its eleven hundred members hold the largest of all supper dances in the Louisiana Superdome. The parade is not in these cases a public facade behind which elite groups bow and curtsey to each other. The dance is a direct extension of the street scene, a reminiscence of the old Creole habit from the 1840s of dancing from the parade outside directly into the Opera House and onto the stage, there to participate in the galopade at the end of Auber's *Gustave*. In this new technical era, however, it is not people who dance into the stage setting of the krewe's ballroom, but floats. At Endymion's and Bacchus's balls the colossi from the parade are hauled into the arena prepared for dining and dancing, as if to inspire the scene with their frozen smiles[5] (see plate 45).

These changes illustrate the fact that Mardi Gras in the national era has made special efforts to accommodate the tourist. The efforts are not new, but like the caricatural floats they are done more effectively. Rex from its beginning in 1872 until as late as the 1920s tried to accommodate at least "reputable" outsiders at its ball, and in a history of New Orleans published in 1922 it was still cited as representing the "popular" side of Carnival, in contrast to the krewes of Comus, Proteus, Momus and some nonparading societies.[6] The krewe of Hermes, "founded [1937] by businessmen seeking to promote Carnival as a tourist attraction" during the difficult years of the Depression era, similarly made tickets available to out-of-towners for its balls and tableaux.[7] But the leaders of Bacchus have not merely offered their services and astutely suited their symbols to people with no knowledge of New Orleans. They have actively assisted the New Orleans Tourist Convention Commission in attracting people to Mardi Gras, paying, for example, for 12,500 color postcards to be mailed by the commission all over the nation as advertisement for the 1987 Carnival.[8]

Today, it seems, one must do more than accommodate tourists from everywhere else who already want to see New Orleans. One must actively recruit tourists by showing that New Orleans is like everywhere else, only a little gayer about it all. In 1976, to

45. Bacchus, float in Bacchus parade, New Orleans, 1987 (photo, Norman Magden)

celebrate the American bicentennial, Bacchus announced its parade theme as "The Spirit of '76." After floats entitled the "Spirit of Exploration," "Spirit of Liberty," "Spirit of Expansion," "Spirit of Completion," "Spirit of Brotherhood," and nearly last, but there anyway—dear old Bacchusaurus, came the very last float, the "God Bless America Spirit." The official parade poster is a pastiche of the famous painting commemorating the American Revolution called the "Spirit of '76" which shows a wounded fifer and drummer struggling up a knoll with a flagbearer in the middle. In the poster Bacchus himself, a vaguely Roman-looking fellow wearing a beard and leather sandals and wreathed about the temples with grapes, marches between fifer and drummer, beating a drum of his own.[9]

Television, it was announced in late February 1987, would fully cover the "Endymion Extravaganza" at the Superdome. The spirit of gaiety is now wafted to millions who have never seen a parade or had access to Carnival societies.[10] Here, too, Endymion imitated Bacchus, the elder superkrewe, whose Superdome extravaganza in 1978 was paradigmatic in its shattering of traditions and its mixture of everything together with everything.

Bacchus had already replaced the idea of Carnival-society tableaux with "headliner" entertainment at its balls. Now in 1978, since complaints were loud about the long wait which ball-goers had to endure while the parade wound through the streets, Bacchus admitted ticket-holders—some 30,000 of them—into the Superdome at 3:30 P.M. while club members mounted their floats. Then during the parade the party began:

> As the floats departed, marching bands entered the arena. . . . The party was only now beginning . . . with six hours of entertainment to follow. The show, billed as the greatest in the history of Mardi Gras, included appearances by local groups Wild Tchoupitoulas and the Neville Brothers [note well!], along with Wolfman Jack, the Shirelles, Elvin Bishop, Levon Helm, Dr. John, Paul Butterfield, Booker T. and the MGs, and others.[11]

When the floats finally arrived at the Rivergate Convention Center, the ball proper began and the entertainment at the Superdome ended. Something for everyone, everywhere, all the time.

Bacchus and Endymion and a good number of other societies that imitate them in lesser degree have not merely replaced a pseudo-king with a "real" all-American star. They have changed the ambiance. The pseudo-king projects and is supported by a set of symbols designed to remove the spectator from the present. The star projects and is supported by a glittering intensification of what passes for the real present, with its mind-boggling possibilities—the "Spirit of Expansion," indeed. The Bacchus version of Mardi Gras transports Disneyland to New Orleans in more than its cartoon-like floats. Disneyland is child-like in its representation of reality as a stage upon which anything can happen, anything can be seen because you're not old enough, critical enough, caring enough to look to see how it works. Disneyland is dream-realization with a minimum of effort, and so is Bacchus's Carnival: a maximum of show for a minimum of personal participation. You don't even have to put any paint on your face. Just let your eyeballs roam and your feet stroll. It's all there for you to walk around in—just like on TV, but more real, see?[12]

In the course of the twentieth century Carnival has acquired a more generalized function than it ever had during the civic era: It has been advertised and developed in ways which make it part of an all-American mode of festive life. Much of what is placed on view at Gulf Coast Carnivals is also paraded at half-time in hundreds of football stadiums, exhibited at summertime folk-festival revivals, played in the streets at Halloween, and sung and danced at New Year's Eve parties. And vice-versa: a Mardi Gras float from Mobile appeared in the Rose Bowl Parade at Pasadena on New Year's Day, 1989, with real live revelers from the home town on it. As Jack Ludwig has written, American festivals today are nationally franchised.[13] From one point of view this draws attention to the fact that only in the twentieth century has a national commercial base existed which is capable of attracting tourists from everywhere and handling them smoothly. The airlines, hotels, restaurant chains, highway connections, and police coordination which pull people into New Orleans also draw local residents elsewhere. What was once a peculiarly Gulf Coast way of life is in the late twentieth century less distinctive. Americans there look, think, and act much the same as Americans do elsewhere, and they want the same things in their parades.

Although the parades of 1910, with their hobgoblins, griffins, and Mohammed, had little to do with the place of celebration, their mythological way of fabricating an escape from everyday life was part of the centuries-old tradition of Carnival. But what can one say about the masks adopted by Louis Diemert, who between 1920 and 1950 regularly won the costume contest in Mobile by impersonating "a Jewish pedlar, an Italian hurdy-gurdy man, a Scotch golfer, Old Black Joe, an old witch, Haile Selassie, Scarlet O'Hara, Abe Lincoln, Neville Chamberlain, Adolf Hitler, and Santa Claus"?[14] With the possible exceptions of the Jewish pedlar and the Italian hurdy-gurdy man and the certain exception of Old Black Joe, the most salient characteristic of these masquerades is that they have scarcely any relation either to the occasion or the place of celebration. Bacchus's parade in 1982 concerned "American Heroes and Heroines": Jim Thorpe, Mark Twain, Andrew Jackson, Pecos Bill, Amelia Earheart, George Washington, and so on, down through Casey Jones, Louis Armstrong, and even including that great "American" Christopher Columbus. Like Diemert's costumes, the superkrewe's choices substitute the symbolically real for the typically mythical. They state that the dreams of those who come to Carnival today are no longer articulated in terms of Euro-Caribbean-American traditions, but instead are anchored in national ideologies.[15]

In the nineteenth and early twentieth centuries the man selected to play Rex was usually a banker or lawyer of power and status in the local community. In the late twentieth century locally important men are simultaneously important nationally and even internationally; their power is diffuse and their interests are difficult to categorize in local, civic-minded terms.[16] The indirect controls which national and international forces exercise over local life are expressed not only in the masks impersonating historically existing characters but in those portraying comic-strip characters, Mickey Mouse and Superwoman, on the floats and in the streets. Like President Eisenhower or President Reagan such comic-strip people are symbolically real: our politicians and our comic-strip heroes and heroines deal with our world better than we can hope to do because this world is beyond the grasp of lives lived locally, where most of us do still pass our time. These figures do not need to represent the way historical events actually came to pass or the way life is really managed in the present. They need only inject a simulacrum of meaning into local life by making what is far off and grandly looming seem, if only for a moment, startlingly understandable and available to us here and now.[17]

Twentieth-century Carnival completes an evolution begun in the European Renaissance. Mardi Gras is no longer an expression of religious beliefs. The festival has lost its metaphysical dimension. In the Middle Ages the occasion, part of larger cycles in the seasonal and religious calendars, expressed humanity's ambiguous character, caught between the claims of the body and the soul, between the natural and the supernatural, between the need for participation in nature's springtime resummoning of productive energies and that of participating in the Church's chastening discipline of the spirit. In modern times Carnival juxtaposes society's work-a-day routines, with their tedium and mechanistically imposed hierarchies of organizational efficiency, to their leisurely opposite, the dream-time of abundance and indifferent equality. As this change has taken hold, Carnival has become an occasion for fantasies rather than rituals.

Rituals embellish, entwine, and sacralize daily life; fantasies are the evasion of it. The old coordinates which guided merrymakers in the construction of their masks are fading away. Carnival no longer calls for mythic celebration, for the coordination of heaven and earth. The sense of a reality stretching from the very high and heavenly to the low, demonic, bowel-like interior of the earth has so disintegrated that a masker's coordination of earthly with supernal realities is scarcely any longer even interesting. Masking is a profane, earthly affair of infinite variety, but it is always conducted along the same, human-centered, horizontally visible plane.[18]

Although the new symbols of twentieth-century Mardi Gras seem hyper-American, therefore, this very nationalism is international. It is its secular rather than national bent that is significant in terms of the history of festive behavior.

Has Gulf Coast Carnival then become what Jack Ludwig calls a "great American spectacular" made up of "interchangeable parts": marching bands, pompom girls, fast food, beer and a variety of competitions to enliven the spectacles?[19] Not exactly. For one thing, Mardi Gras fills a certain slot in the emergent national configuration of what to do on vacation, the slot of gay Southern abandon. But the feelings clustering around this identification are as often as not belied: On the Gulf Coast the weather is warm in contrast to nearly anywhere else in February and March (but it frequently rains, and does so coldly); everyone is happy, and behaves with pagan abandon during Carnival, in contrast to their reserved WASPish behavior elsewhere (but the police are always at hand, and if they go on strike, as in 1979, there is no Carnival); and people mix in openhearted, freewheeling sociability, in contrast to the business-and-family-controlled contacts which they otherwise pursue (but most activities are organized by clubs for their own—usually exclusively local—members).

For another thing the victory of the "lateral" over the "vertical" principle, defining Carnival as the display of human differences rather than as a theater of divine-human clash and monstrous combination, implies a broadening of participation in Carnival, and a corresponding increase in diverse kinds of action. We have already commented on the peculiar manner in which the Carnival-society idea was democratized, by encouraging ever more organizations to form, each with its own restrictions, each soon ranked as part of a cultural pecking order dwindling away from the glory of Comus.[20] After Rex's invention in the 1870s of a civic-minded elitism, and the initiation of women's Carnival societies in the 1890s, the next major organizational idea to broaden participation came in the 1920s and 1930s. From the 1880s onward informal groups, ethnic organizations, and fraternal orders had occasionally trailed along in wagons or on foot in the wake of the Rex parade. By the 1930s, with the widespread use of motor vehicles, people were decorating their cars and trucks in the same way as floats, and driving about the city. They were in principle barred from driving along designated parade routes, however. In late 1934 Chris Valley, a member of Elks Club Lodge 30 in New Orleans, was able to convince city officials to give the lodge a permit to drive a number of trucks filled with merrymakers from the lodge down Rex's route in 1935 after Rex had passed. The idea proved immensely popular. By 1981 there were 181 trucks in the Elks' parade, with an average of forty people per truck. Although the decorations and the masquerades were in some cases rudimentary, in others they were extremely elaborate, a tendency encouraged by giving trophies for the best-decorated trucks.[21]

The popularity of the idea proved so unwieldy that the Elks Krewe of Orleanians, Chris Valley's organization, was finally restricted to 150 trucks, for another group of Elks, called the Crescent City Elks, had joined their vehicles to the end of the Orleanians' parade; the two truck parades now comprise nearly 300 vehicles and 12,000 costumed riders.[22] Meanwhile, in 1924, what seems to have been the first neighborhood club in a middle-class section of town developed a regular parade, the Seventh District Carnival Club, which has now become the Krewe of Carrollton. As in the case of the Elks' trucks, what was new was not the mode or location of the masquerade but its organization on a regular basis with a regular route along which to provide a spectacle.[23] Schools have traditionally allowed stu-

46. Masker on a balcony, French Quarter, New Orleans, 1987 (photo, Norman Magden)

dents to develop projects having to do with the traditions of Mardi Gras as the festival approaches, and some children's parading krewes have been formed, especially in the suburbs.[24] Since World War II, in fact, krewes and parades have bloomed in many outlying districts, perhaps in part due to white flight. Between 1950 and 1980 white population in the city proper declined by one-third.[25] The great white middle class dominates Carnival, at least in its most visible, parading form, and it has spread that form throughout the sprawling metropolitan area of New Orleans.[26] Dominance of middle-class white residents and concentration on public parades is equally strong in Mobile, and the schools and children participate, if anything, even more fully than in New Orleans. But there is less regional development. Nearly all the area's Mardi Gras parades take place along the same streets in downtown Mobile.

The blending of national trends with local traditions to issue in more diverse kinds of action could not be better illustrated than by the new modes of sexual display. Prostitutes are no longer the center of attraction on this unbuttoned occasion. There are too many other sources of sensuous excitement for the prurient.

New Orleans' most famous competition in the 1970s became the masquerade contest sponsored by the gay community in New Orleans, held on a street corner in the French Quarter on mardi gras afternoon. Up and down the adjoining streets parties on the Spanish-style ironwork second-story balconies go on all day with transvestite males displaying superbly feathered inventions (plate 46). Homosexual men and women came to New Orleans in increasing numbers in the 1960s, finding it easier there than in most cities to pursue their own lives and styles. Nine Carnival societies have been formed by gay people since 1960 and have become well known for their risqué elegance.[27] The informal tolerance habitually granted the gay community and the fascination directed toward them on mardi gras, however, are not just demographic effects. They also reflect shifts in the meaning of sexuality, private and public. Open display of a semi-nude male body, revealing its capacity for sexual ambivalence, attractiveness, and beauty, has become possible because of the decline of patriarchal roles for men. The pendulum of sexual fashion has swung heavily in the opposite direction from the rigid, family-centered roles for men and women which I discussed with reference to women's queenly roles in the Carnival societies. Because the family has been weakened by a variety of factors in its old role as the nearly exclusive locus of emotional and sexual life, it is not merely women's roles and men's which have changed; the very meaning of sexual difference, of erotic beauty and seductiveness, has become an open—and in Carnival-time a gaily fashionable—question.

Erosion of the old sense and function of sexuality is generally reflected in the mass media in elegant, aesthetic ways, by reducing male and female bodies to surface-sharp and surface-smooth terms. The emphasis is on sex-as-vision: this version of sexual difference, veiling and unveiling well-shaped muscles and glands, can be broadcast, replicated, and commercialized. Sex can be as public as you please, as long as it is capable of being publicized. Even portrayal of the modes of intimacy—touch, smell, and the enfolding of bodies—is limited today less by prudery than by the criterion of what can glitter for the camera's mercantile eye. The compatibility between this marketable sexuality and the deeper trend toward variable rather than family-bound modes of intimacy has opened up the cultural space that gay people have used in Mardi Gras. The general resonance of their innovation is illustrated by the fact that several of their winning costumes are part of the permanent Mardi Gras display, along with those of Rex and Rex's queens, in New Orleans' Cabildo Museum.

It is not only a question of gays using this festival, but also of the festival using them. The fascination with which transvestites are regarded as they parade on streets and preen on French-Quarter balconies is a good example of Carnival as inversion. Men masking as elegant women is a lurking fantasy for the male who, denying all androgyny, prides himself on his machismo. During Carnival today this tempting vision can be pursued, and even acted out without reprisal. Masking as women has been and still is a favorite masquerade of "straight" males.[28]

But the exhibitionist role which quadroon balls played in frontier society and which prostitutes played in romantic New Orleans is not only represented today by the gay costume contest and the gay society balls. The new, open sexuality is still available in a practical sense only in mediated, voyeurist, commercialized forms from day to day, so people's rising expectations extend themselves in all directions during Carnival's licensed omission from routine. What is this naked cowboy after (plate 47)? Is his video camera for use or only one of his props? Since national-era Carnival is preeminently spectacle, the best costumes frequently seem to include, intentionally or not, an ele-

47–48. Street maskers, French Quarter, New Orleans, 1987 (photo, Norman Magden)

ment of reversed representation.

Along comes a masker in a costume laying out the female body for the middle-class male eye in an astute combination of dainty ready-to-wait-on-you symbols (lacey cap, collar, and

apron in starched white) with aggressive femme-fatale clichés
(black leotard, fishnet stockings, high-heeled boots) (plate 48).
Then you raise your eyes to the face and, as in the case of the
purple-cassocked bird-man, you are plunged for a moment into

the abyss of the diabolically naturalistic. The costume becomes a variant on the old phantasm of the beautiful witch. . . . But no, that's wrong, too. Look at her camera. All she's out to do is to take pictures of everybody else.[29]

Other folks figure that a krewe necklace, G-string, and some glitterdust are enough for today's stroll (plate 49). This is spring-time sex, the sex associated with loose women (the female's ac-cented nudity, the male's sloppy lack of anything resembling a costume, except for some plastic beads), sex which is seductive and titillating. It is not reproductive sex, heavy and grand with autumnal fruit. Women are here to be gawked at, tasted, tossed aside; they are here to be taken in excess, like Carnival food. Not many genitals, lots of mammaries. Sex is gay in every way in Mardi Gras. It revolves around male bonding.

Sexual revolution or not, positivization or not of male bodies, most of the skin parts being exposed in today's Carnivals are female. The sexual-sensuous ethic orienting most people's fan-tasies is available for a few dollars any day of the year on Bour-bon Street. It's not much different during Carnival, just more pervasive. For the college-age sector of Mardi-Gras participants in particular, the motto of the Krewe of Tucks sums it up: "booze, beer, bourbon, and broads" (members are mostly white students, male —and female! —from Tulane, Loyola, St. Mary's Dominican, Newcomb).[30]

The national era nationalizes differences, so that what is ad-missible anywhere has a democratic right and a commercial ten-dency to turn up in the form of at least momentary novelty on the streets or in the parades. I was struck by the inventiveness of the street maskers at New Orleans who used everyday utility and amusement items like kitchen gloves and dime-store toys to transform themselves into creatures of a third kind, neither ani-mate nor inanimate but both at once. The "Junkfood Junkies" used the same principle, that of enlargement, as the Krewe of Bacchus did in its "Bacchusaurus." But in the former case an everyday feature of modern American life, the production and consumption of food in impersonal assembly-line fashion, was personified and humanized by the jumping, jiving pop-bottle and hamburger people. In the latter case the capacities of mod-ern technology remained just that: technical and inhuman, and spectacular only in size and shiny slickness. If in modern mass culture everything must become a cliché for it to be recogniz-able, then turning the cliché into carnivalesque, ambivalent form demands something other than a change of dimensions and the simplification of surface features. A yellow rubber glove on a

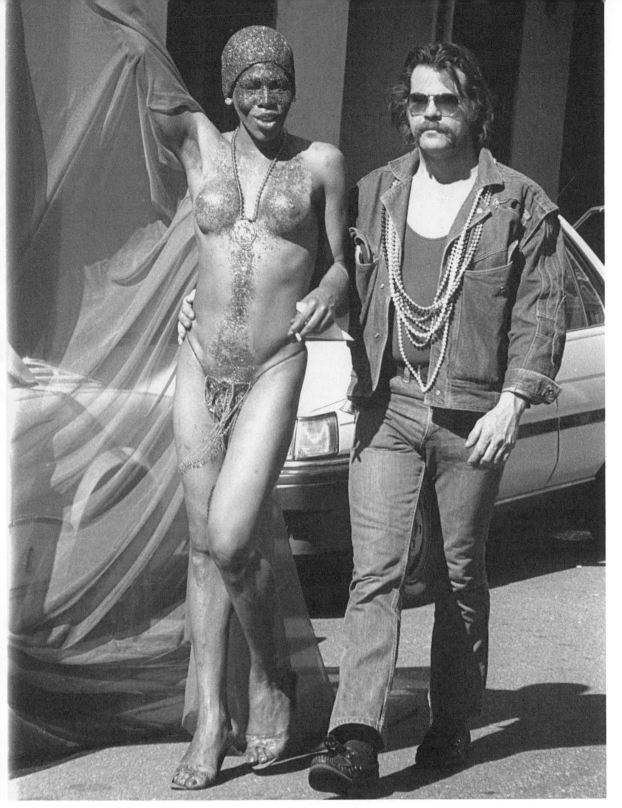

49. Street masker, French Quarter, New Orleans, 1987 (photo, Norman Magden)

masker's foot changes everything but its shape and size. Its ordinary meaning is shattered, and its new possibilities hop away in all directions. Such gadget costuming has little to do with inversion or satire of everyday life. It draws upon the pragmatic-inventive bent of America's technological preoccupations in a simple, lighthearted way.[31] The sexiest male in 1987 was a totally "naked" robot man (plate 50: note the tennis-ball testicles). This masker allows just enough humanity to peek out at face and knees to make his impersonation of a set of coil springs doing a dance step thoroughly delightful rather than a reference to some ominous mechanical future.

With respect to these twentieth-century developments Mobile has followed rather than led. Just as the Alabama city was not large enough to allow for the development of countercultural phenomena like the Mardi Gras Indians and the Zulus, so its socioeconomic fabric has not proved to be elastic enough to take initiatory rather than imitative steps in adapting Carnival to twentieth-century America's nationalized festive culture. Mobile moved rather lamely in the wake of national homogenization; it did not take creative part in the process like its old rival New Orleans. The manner of its homespun adaptation resembles that of thousands of other middle-class, middle-level cities in America.

"Le Krewe de Bienville," named for the French-Canadian explorer and early governor of the Louisiana colony, was founded in 1962 to promote tourism by allowing outsiders to buy tickets to a ball imitating the tableaux and ballroom formalism of the old Carnival societies. Rex and later Hermes in New Orleans had been offering tickets to outsiders with the same touristic purposes for many decades before this. The Bienville idea was never combined with the grandiose, in the specifically techno-comic sense of that word which was developed by Bacchus after 1969.

Mobile has never lacked popular elements in its Mardi Gras celebration, from the time of the Cowbellions to that of Joe Cain's Chief Slackabamorinico and Dave Levi's Comic Cowboys. With the exception of the Comic Cowboys, however, popular parody and the grotesque have recurrently died out in Mobile. These qualities have not in the long run been able to withstand the chilling effects of elite society's stiffness, a quality prized in

50. Street masker, French Quarter, New Orleans, 1987 (photo, Norman Magden)

Mobile but looked at askance in New Orleans. In terms of the way it celebrates, as Caldwell Delaney concluded in his celebratory history of Mobile, "Mobile retains its standing as the most formal of American cities."[32] By "formal" Delaney means, with respect to Carnival, not merely commitment to austerely conventional clothing at Mardi Gras balls, but highly routinized protocol in the selection of those who will lead the dance at these affairs, close scrutiny of respectability in the selection of the king, queen, and court reigning over the city, and careful all-city supervision of Mardi Gras activities generally, to see that things don't get out of hand.

One of the great democratizing moves in Mobile's Mardi Gras came in the 1930s when a Grand Public Masked Ball was instituted on the Municipal Wharf at the foot of Dauphin Street at the city's center. The only requirement for admission was a mask. At one of these balls, it is said, 26,000 people attended. The king and queen of Mobile's white Carnival at first visited these affairs, but after the "mystic societies" removed their balls from the downtown hotels to the Armory at Fort Whiting, somewhat further away, royalty ceased to attend because it was too difficult to move from the wharf to Fort Whiting. "It was [thought to be] better for Felix to cease visiting the public ball than for him to stop attending those of the mystics." Eventually interest in the ball "died out." It was briefly revived between 1949 and 1952.[33]

In 1968, partly in response to the clamoring youth of the "hippie generation" and partly due to the efforts of the journalist Julian Rayford, Joe Cain Day was revived in Mobile.[34] It quickly became the lodestone of the disorderly in the opinion of the Carnival elders, the dignified leaders of societies whose parades had dominated Carnival for so many decades. In fact, the disheveled, helter-skelter quality of Joe Cain parades was partly due to the stiffness of the Carnival societies. Mobile did not develop and still does not have something resembling New Orleans' spectacular "superkrewes" to answer popular demand for something safe yet spectacular. So the Joe Cain procession, advertised as the "people's parade" because anyone in a mask was at first free to join in, gradually became "unmanageable," as a staff reporter for the chief local newspaper put it. To "manage" the parade, the groups participating in it were after 1983 limited by city ordinance to thirty-four, and each group was required to apply for a parade permit, indicating the content of their parade. Even the most grotesque among the groups which have marched in the procession, like the "Mistic Order of the Moonpie," have gradually surrendered to propriety. In 1988 "the Moonpies are saluting the XV Olympic Winter Games in Calgary, Canada, because the games begin Saturday [three days before mardi gras, one day before the Joe Cain Parade]. The float will represent all events and have a seven-foot mock-torch on the front and a ski lift on the back."[35]

The spirit of Mobile Carnival has remained much the same from the mid-nineteenth to the late twentieth century, homespun and a trifle silly, rigidly committed to order and tradition in principle, but a little strange in the event.[36] Julian Rayford quotes an anonymous letter to King Felix, the annually selected white king of Mobile's Carnival, written during the Prohibition era:

> I would like to suggest that throughout the whole of Mardi Gras you remain on a somewhat even keel. . . . It might be rather embarassing to be known in later years as 'The King Who Fell Off the Float.' However I don't imagine you need these few words of fatherly advice as no doubt by this time, the whole family has delivered many orations upon this subject.
> Seriously, though, I would go at it to have the very best time I could without spending too much money and yet without being cheap about it. I suggest to you that you purchase two different grades of fermented beverages, one for yourself and intimate friends, and one for the many hangers-on who will attach themselves to you. I suggest to you that you use any reliable Negro except Willie for the dispensing of same. That boy, Marion, and his brother, from the Country Club, did very good work for me.[37]

*Plus ça change, plus c'est la même chose.* As Rayford (who is writing in 1962) comments: "To the King's Valet, every King—well, almost every King —is a hero. Gainie Peter Coleman has been valet to Felix III for thirty years. A Negro, he is stout and peaceful and happy."[38]

Closeness of the races, distance of their mental images of each other. "There are still many [colored people in Mobile] who will not go near a Mardi Gras parade," wrote Caldwell Delaney in 1948, "insisting that the masquers are 'Ku-Kluxers.'"[39]

Like the development of Carnival in twentieth-century Mobile, upper- and middle-class black celebration of the occasion in both Mobile and New Orleans is largely an imitation of white upper-class conventions. The first Carnival societies were founded in the same year, 1894: the Order of Doves in Mobile held a ball that year and selected a lady to "lead" it.[40] The Illinois Club in New Orleans (since 1927 the Original Illinois Club) held its first ball the following year. The man who organized the Illinois Club had lived in Chicago (hence the name), and ran a dancing school. He introduced a special twist to the ballroom parades which has survived, and which in some manner allows a tinge of the Afro-American's rhythmic culture to enter an otherwise stuffy ceremonial scene, replete with king, queen, and maids in the Orleanian style. It is called the "Chicago Glide" and is a circle dance during which the costumed members of the society, paired with the debutantes and maids, move counterclockwise in a sequence of slow bows, curtseys, and dignified swings around their partners.[41]

Mobile's blacks founded a Zulu Club in 1938, the "Knights of May Zulu Club," A. S. May, founder, "featuring the rhythm of the members beating on buckets and tubs" in their first parade that year during "the first Colored Mystic Parade in Mobile." The organization continued to parade until 1952. Over the years their floats included, besides those of the king and queen, "Flying Alligator of the Jungle," "Monster of the Jungle," "The Proud Horse," "Stairway to the Stars," and "The Wild Man and the Dragon."[42] It is curious to learn that in 1947 the black association of Carnival societies in Mobile stated that the Zulu parade in New Orleans was "a burlesque of which we colored people in Mobile are truly ashamed." Perhaps the pressure of these middle-class and upper-class clubs was the reason why the Knights of May Zulu Club in Mobile did not parade in 1947. But in New Orleans the Zulu king was quoted in the papers as saying "Nuts to those people from Mobile."[43] Did continued pressure finally force the Mobile Zulus to disband in 1952?

The first "Colored King of Mardi Gras" was elected by the Colored Carnival Association of Mobile in 1939. Since 1940 he has been called "King Elexis."[44] Parades and coronation balls for the black king and queen are supplemented by the convention of the Carnival king's reign over the black part of the city, which has necessitated creating a "Mayor of Colored Mobile." On the Sunday before mardi gras at the black Elks Club Elexis receives the key to the city from the outgoing "Mayor," after which the new "Mayor" takes over. Besides all this, black junior and senior high schools choose in January a Teen-Age Queen and maids to rule during Carnival.[45]

The gradual replacement of civic-oriented by nationally syndicated features of festivity was inevitable. Even in their nineteenth-century heyday, American cities were built up as transportation way-stations and terminals in a vast national and international web of commercial exchange conceived in a capitalist manner. However much they temporarily serve to concentrate business and social energies, the city's thrust is always otherward, insofar as its destiny is determined by business elites. The sucking-in is a function of the giving-out. Moreover, because the national-international web must be managed, all parts of it are increasingly arranged in hierarchical order, an order which changes in response to shifts in the centers of finance (large banks, and the Washington political controls over them), in raw materials (offshore oil in the case of New Orleans since the 1950s), and in labor supply (cheap, unorganized immigrant labor, like slave labor, has dwindled in the twentieth century for the Gulf Coast). What is at one level a point of attraction for the surrounding territory (the Mississippi Valley for New Orleans and its river's transport facilities, the Tombigbee River Basin for Mobile with its fine port) is at other levels in the hierarchy itself part of a territory being drawn in and ordered in accordance with socioeconomic energies elsewhere. In a twentieth century during which the nation's founding ideologies of growth and progress have scarcely been questioned, let alone challenged, it has become more and more clear that the only appropriate place to hold a Carnival is right where the blacks have continued to spread their mardi gras picnics: under the big interstate highway along Claiborne Avenue, a concrete monument to this country's tendency to direct people's chief energies elsewhere, outward, onward, always on the run.[46]

Becoming a Great American Spectacular is as much a matter of psychology as of economics. Carnival has changed because the tourists keep pouring in and because Gulf Coast people keep looking out. The South is no longer romantic, in New Orleans it is scarcely even Southern any more. People have changed inwardly, linking themselves to a national consumer-belt of cultural understanding fed on a daily basis by the average five hours of television to which every man, woman and child in America, it is calculated, is now exposed. People in Mobile and New Orleans already want to give what the tourists come to see. The psychological side of the suction-and-expulsion pump is probably more important than the economic one.

Nevertheless, Carnival remains Carnival: it is not by any means a hotdog-and-beer-fest with a Southern name. Why? In Mobile's case the occasion remains special because of the place's sluggish, small-city conservatism, the weight of too many years and too little social change. In the case of New Orleans it is because the city is too big, too corrupt, and hence too variable in its social milieus to be able to unite around any public program. New Orleans' Zulus were saved from destruction in the 1960s because blacks couldn't pull together. Ernest Morial, who went on to become mayor in the late 1970s, was then president of the New Orleans National Association for the Advancement of Colored People. Interviewed in 1964 about the Zulus' offensive symbols, he said "This [black] community has never really been able to get together. I can't do any more than suggest the possibility of a blackout [of the Zulus' and other black Carnival clubs' activities, in order to pursue serious civil rights goals], because I don't have that kind of branch support. . . . People love those dances. Also, there's a lot of confusion."[47]

Beyond any and all such differences, however, the two cities share a reason for the continued special festive character of Carnival: the clannishness of the Carnival societies—and their private character. The two other grandest Carnival traditions of the New World are currently at a point of crisis. In Rio de Janeiro as in Port of Spain, Trinidad, the government, in concert with the tourist industry, has stepped into the organization of Carnival so massively—in both cases, great numbers of high-cash prizes are offered for many different categories of dancing and costuming—that participation has become industrialized. It is so expensive, so time-consuming, and so exhausting to be a winner that none but professionals enjoy taking part any more. The danger is that concentration on a grand "national" festival, supervised by government, will shrivel the roots not only of local, informal participation but of spectator interest in an ever more ordered and hence predictable show. The bubble, blown bigger and bigger, may burst.[48]

Is it possible that the elitism and privatism of Gulf Coast Carnival's anchorage in the parade-and-ball societies is what conserves its enthusiastically public, open-ended viability?

# Cultural Codes

Not all members of socioeconomic elites share elite culture; nonelites, too, do not automatically adopt popular cultural values. Those coke-sippers whom one sees in tulle and tails in Mobile's streets on mardi gras may be postmen or state senators.[1] The semiotic codes which people express in their choices of food, dress, gesture, and language are not simple reflections of their social class, least of all in Carnival. During this festival, after all, excess is the norm. More nonelite elitists and more elite populists run around expressing their proclivities on this occasion than on any other.

Cultural values are of course connected with rational and rationalized class interests, but they also represent shared enthusiasms. Carnival generates enthusiasms because it nurses people's illusions. Carnival's essence is the masquerade, because masking stimulates expression of the self's multiplicity; the "inverse" side of the self, suppressed by everyday social arrangements, is only part of this multiplicity.[2]

Our subject in this chapter is less the excess beyond or the multiplicity of normalized selfhood than the coherences which may be discovered between the mask and the person behind it, the relation between individual choice and social identity. There are four general codes displayed in Gulf Coast Carnival: elite, popular, neighborly, and official. Any of them may be used with others, producing the cross-cutting combinations just mentioned. Neighborly culture is based on communicative exchanges typical of restricted, closely knit neighborhoods in city, town, or village; it is related to the orally centered, nonliterate culture defined earlier and is often termed "folk" culture.[3] The code used by the groups who preside over Carnival—police, bureaucrats, city, state, and national dignitaries—will be called official.

The fondest dream of elites is stability. Life, ideally arranged, offers an ever-returning sequence of the same elements: recirculation of family alliances, recapitulation of the bids for political and economic power which have proved successful. For those gathered in the older and more prestigious Carnival societies,

Mardi Gras floats and masks should emphasize the remotely mythological in elegant and beautiful—that is, in smoothly undisturbing, decorative—ways. The affection of the top krewes for learned and recondite themes which require considerable education to decipher is therefore not simply an arrogant show or an attempt to bolster the idea of Mardi Gras's Creole and European origins. This affection stems also from the setting of mythological themes in a never-never land beyond the reach of time. Mythological themes refer to a seemingly unchanging and inaccessible past, a time-space so distant that no convictions, no deeply held beliefs, no ideological difficulties need beset the viewer.[4] Elite Mardi Gras is coded in terms of fantasy because it needs little social reassurance. It is a flight beyond rather than a flight from the everyday world. Its cultural messages emphasize the traditional: innovation should be only grudgingly and slowly admitted.

This world of the "best people" is so self-assured that even its most ludicrous gestures, performed in the name of tradition, acquire the luster of prestige. We have noted the parade of the surviving Cowbellions in their cow-head masks in 1889.[5] Equally interesting to imagine in its effect is this report of the 1940 ball of the Atlanteans, commonly reported to be an even more exclusive "old-line" society than Comus:

> In 1940 the golden anniversary was elaborately celebrated by a reproduction of the introductory tableau of Atlantis in 1891. It was whispered about that the only living original member, who was Poseidon at the first ball, was persuaded to don royal robes and reign with Gifford Glenny, the granddaughter of his first queen, who was honored together with a distinguished assemblage of other former queens.[6]

For those hoping to join such elites as these, on the other hand, Mardi Gras' floats and masks should express not remote fantasies but historicizing myths, which serve to reassure aspiring gentlemen and ladies that careers in America are ever open to talent; this is the myth of heroism. Rex is its most obvious embodiment, seated on a gilded throne in Renaissance finery, served by a gallant page clothed in the same jewelled splendor (plate 2). Rex wears his crown without further disguise. No face-paint, no body-altering paraphernalia obscures his easy grandeur. Rex and the Rex krewe are images of popularizing elitism. Although the krewe is extremely difficult of access, it is still possible for a successful man without the right family pedigree to aspire to membership, and it is possible for the extremely successful man, having become very well-known locally, to dream of sitting open-faced for all to see upon the throne.

Bacchus's king, a figure as famous nationally as Rex is locally, is an image of elitizing populism. He too is presented without a face-mask in order to make explicit the myth of heroism. Bacchus's rulers are ordinary men who have become great by virtue of their popular, representative qualities rather than like Rex by virtue of their exceptional qualities. They have achieved grandeur through the power of the media rather than through political or economic prowess. Their power lies in their ability to project grandly what is familiar; they arrive at the throne, having been "a part of America's living rooms and dens for years."[7] Their apotheosis in Carnival comes to them unexpectedly, as something deserved, perhaps, but almost unbelievable to such nice, common guys.

Both hybrid forms, elitizing populism and popularizing elitism, serve the goal of reassuring nonelites in an America whose unusual opportunities for rapid social ascent make people both avid and nervous (can I make it? can I really, really do it? of course you can!). Unlike purely elite and purely neighborly modes of Carnival, these forms efface the line between reality and dream, everyday life and festive escapism. They offer fabulously unreal images which ask to be taken as possibilities for any one of us, if we will only try.

Elitizing but popular Carnival societies like Bacchus, the other superkrewe, Endymion, and many of the suburban organizations in both Mobile and New Orleans, are open clubs, in which membership can be obtained for a fee and committee procedures and personnel are more or less well known. Elite and popularizing elite societies like Comus and Rex, the Order of Myths and the Infant Mystics, on the other hand, inculcate their hierarchic values by means of a system of open, half-closed, and fully closed participation. The spectators enjoying Carnival in the open space of their parades are supposed to interpret the doubloons, beads, and other trinkets thrown to them as the prelude to the half-closed space of the balls, where New Orleans' and Mobile's top debutantes parade in a luxuriantly brilliant atmosphere as witnesses to the aesthetic dividends accompanying well-controlled hierarchy. The costume balls are staging systems which simultaneously register the relative prestige of certain families and their solidarity vis-à-vis the others; debutantes circulate from one ball to the next as queens, maids-of-honor, and attendants in turn. Behind this half-closed space, to which access is possible on invitation from a member of the Carnival society, lies the completely closed space of the society's meetings during the year, where competition takes place about who will manage next year's parade and ball.

Because of the support that official culture has for more than a century given to the elite and elitizing system of the Carnival societies, there is a schism between the image of Gulf Coast Mardi Gras and its form. Its image is that of errant, untrammeled gaiety. Its form is that of a show staged by competing private societies, to which access is difficult and whose customs are arcane. While some sight of wildmen or grotesques seems to be indispensable to a sense of participation, in practice most people do most of their looking at parades. For the rest, they read the papers and Arthur Hardy's *Mardi Gras Guide*, which is mostly devoted to cataloguing the parades. The complacency of the media in doing the will of the ongoing Carnival societies—and this unfortunately includes not only newspapers and guides but nearly all the books ever written about Gulf Coast Carnivals—nearly insures the fact that most Mardi Gras revelers become more adept at reading costumes and behavior for their social coding than for their naturalistic fantasy.[8] Within days of arrival at New Orleans the tourist knows which are the "old-line," aristocratic krewes staging parades, which parades are the most spectacular and which are most generous in the trinkets they throw, when and where Rex will acknowledge his queen, when and how Comus will pass by and also pledge the queen, and so on. After a few years of steady Carnival-going, after the masked personnel on horseback and on the floats become familiar, the reveler acquires friends on the floats, learns where to stand for which parade in order to see and be seen, and eventually, no doubt, joins a krewe.

The mechanism generating concentration on what quickly show themselves to be repetitive parades, balls, and society meetings can be simply described. As indicated in chapter 5, it consists in Mobile of relating Mardi Gras to the formal introduction into local society of "young ladies of rank." In 1952 the Mobile Carnival Association proposed creation of an annual Camellia Ball on Thanksgiving evening as an alternative to individual coming-out parties for these women. This was, at the time, "a growing national trend" which spared families the cost of planning and executing separate balls by presenting all the girls of the season at the same affair.[9] Nevertheless, between the Camellia Ball and Mardi Gras a seemingly endless sequence of teas, cocktail parties, and buffets still take place which circulate the young women and their escorts and so eventuate in the selection of queen and maids, king and knights, to reign over Mobile's Carnival.

Pedigree, therefore, predominates. In 1982 King Felix III,[10] a twenty-five-year-old employee in his family's sugar refining firm, had a grandfather who was king in 1930, a grandmother who was a lady-in-waiting in 1925, and two brothers who were members of previous courts. Felix began his climb as a page in the 1967 court and as a knight on the 1970 one. His court included eighteen knights and twelve pages, all having backgrounds similar to his. Knights enter the court as escorts of the debutantes who accompany the carnival queen. The king and the queen are selected by the Carnival Association from sealed bids by families of pretenders to the offices, bids that reportedly include donations. On the Saturday before mardi gras, the king crowns the queen before a huge crowd in the Municipal Auditorium.

The twenty-three-year-old queen's father was king in 1957; her mother was a maid in the court of 1954. She had earlier received the honor of presiding as queen over the children's mardi gras ball and had been the leading lady or queen at several Carnival society balls. Her brothers, uncles, and aunts have also figured in past carnival courts. Thus, as one of my Mobile informants put it, "The persons who participate in this game from beginning to end perpetuate in the name of fun and celebration a closed society." Most often they belong to the same college fraternities and sororities at the University of Alabama, the same social and country clubs, and occupy themselves with the same businesses and political groups, marrying among themselves and settling in their native city.

The situation in New Orleans is more complex both because it is less centralized and because the Carnival-society system serves more diverse interests. Unlike the situation at Mobile, where there is only one generally recognized white king and queen of Carnival, each "krewe" at New Orleans has its king and queen (or "god" and "goddess"),[11] which qualifies Rex's claim to be king of all the city. Moreover, instead of serving singlemindedly the interest of social recirculation of the elite by always choosing young debutantes as first ladies at the balls, some Orleanian organizations dedicate themselves to enjoying the fruits of power. The societies called the Atlanteans and the Mystic Club are two of these. They have never given parades, and yet are among the most exclusive of all Carnival clubs. The Mystic Club was specifically formed in 1923 to honor "matronly consorts," married women instead of debutantes.[12] Nevertheless, at its apex the system is much the same, circulating the season's most important debutantes and most eligible young men among the top krewes.[13] "In 1973 the Queen of Rex was also an attendant to the Queen of the Elves of Oberon (Old Line); the Queen of the Krewe of Mystery and the Queen of the High Priests of Mithras (Old Line) were attendants at the court of the Queen of Rex; the Queen of the High Priests of Mithras had in her court the debutante who was also the Queen of Proteus—etc., etc."[14]

The most coveted public positions are those of Rex and Rex's queen and Comus and Comus's queen. Among these the "younger" and more publicly oriented Rex society yields to Comus in ways that symbolize both an elite conviction and a broader political one. We have noticed that at midnight on mardi gras Rex and his people join Comus's ball, not vice versa: politics (Rex is the "King" of New Orleans) bows to the superior social power of aristocracy in the form of the oldest and most venerable emblem of Carnival, Comus and his krewe. But this elite proof of superiority is at the same time evidence that power in America is not located in any kind of visible apparatus, political, bureaucratic, or otherwise. Comus remains masked even at his own ball.[15] His identity is known only to the insiders in his own organization. Power is a private thing. Public position is merely its approximate indication.[16]

Appropriately enough, therefore, there is no absolute order among New Orleans krewes. Part of the spirit of Carnival is the game of comparing parades and balls of the most prominent societies in order to decide whether their social reputation has been raised or lowered by the performance. Since there are krewes for all social classes, representing all possible social interests, this game is for everyone. Its impetus for the nonelite is the dream of social mobility, the essential dream for the middle classes.

Obsessive concern with the "best" Carnival societies is in fact a middle-class more than upper-class concern. Unlike upper and lower classes, the grand American middle class seldom justifies its interests and activities for their own sake: they are justified, rather, because they lead upward or avoid downward social movement. The quintessential newspaper articles for middle-class consumption are those with titles like: "Who's Who on the Boston Club Balcony" and "Unmasking New Orleans' Queen for a Day."[17]

The inclusive exclusiveness of the "krewes" rhymes with the hieratic democracy of American life generally—anybody can run for president and anybody can vote, but how one gets elected is another story. The number of Carnival clubs is neither limited nor exclusive, but the internal structure of most of them is authoritarian, run by a small group of insiders and old boys. Americans *believe* in open politics, but they *know* that the political process is controlled secretly. That is why the secrecy of the societies is obligatory: it is delicious to be able to peek and guess at the social ties being forged behind the raucous parades and the balls reported in local newspapers. Democracy stimulates hieratic feeling. The order of prestige among carnival clubs fosters not complacency or attempts to undo the system but scrambling competition, year in and year out. It is competition based less on conquest or defeat than on the maintenance of facades. Each club vies with the next to have the biggest floats and the most impressive throwaway trinkets; within each club individuals work out their power plays, sharpening leadership talents for business or political arenas as they prepare elections to the courts of the queen, select tableau-ball themes, and construct the floats.

These power plays cannot be described in detail. The secrecy of the more elite societies is effective. No one has ever reported in detail the means by which a man became president or chairman of a krewe (or mystic society in Mobile), acquired the pivotal power that goes with being captain of the parade (or leader of the ball in Mobile), and maneuvered his candidates for queen, maids, knights, pages, and so on, into acceptance by the other men of power in his society. It seems unlikely that this will ever be historicized in detail. And perhaps there is no need to do so, since the general means—wealth and will—are known.[18] The following story, for example, is no doubt true in its general outline, even in the absence of precise names:

> A captain of one large krewe was rich, influential, and determined to be Rex. He notified the Boston Club of his willingness, but he received no cooperation. It was essential to belong to the club, and he was not a member and had never been invited to become a member. Angered, he formed another krewe, elected himself captain of that, then made himself king of both his krewes in the same year. The result, however, was frustration, for his identity as king of the two balls over which he presided could not be revealed even to the members of the Boston Club, and most of them never knew it at all. At last, years later, he managed to become a Boston Club member, and then, through sheer will power and persistence, he had the satisfaction of seeing his daughter selected as Queen of the Carnival.[19]

American Carnival places social power on parade, allowing people to see what they have always suspected, that social status is not an open system. The vision is delicious not because it turns the democratic surface upside down, but because it plays on the difference between the hidden and the revealed. This play does not stop with simple vision. Mardi Gras's elite dimension is not simply spectacle; it is a *performance* of the tension between surface and deep reality created by adherence to elitist codes in a democratic polity.

The performance occurs in the throwing game. For the majority of those who line the sidewalks to catch beads and the tin money called doubloons one would suppose that these "throws" which the "dukes" cast from on high represent what they seem to be: free gifts from the elite to the people. And yet the clamorous, rhythmically swelling roar which goes up when a float pulls past a dense crowd of revelers has little to do with greed or need. It expresses none of the querulous beggar's appeal for a handout. Twenty-four hours afterwards no one will have any use for the gaudy trash being feverishly accumulated. At most points along the parade routes people seem to be already decorated with a dozen necklaces and to have in hand an assortment of doubloons. There is competition among the "dukes" on the float to throw to the prettiest festooned lady out there, to the most avid kid skittering out perilously between cops and tractor in a daredevil appeal. The chant and the trash are purely formal elements. The roar is one of playing the game, of being caught together in a shared imagination of largesse, of riches cast from on high by these masked demigods to the happy people of "Cockayne," that mythical Carnival land where everything exists in plenty (see plate 51).[20]

"Big Lou" Canizzaro, owner of a wholesale packaged food company, became a Mardi Gras fanatic after he became a father. Soon he was carrying stepladders from place to place along parade routes so that his kids could climb above others' heads and get a chance to grab the bead necklaces as they came flying off the float. He joined a carnival club, and the day came when he rode a float as a duke for the first time. "The noise got louder and louder. . . . Just to see all those doggone people. You're flabbergasted. . . . If I had to ever give up anything, this is the last thing I'd give up."[21]

The geometric form of the throwing game, its *static* structure

51. "Dukes" about to throw, Rex parade, New Orleans, 1987 (photo, Norman Magden)

which is based on high-low difference, is derived from the dream of a land in which an infinite supply of everyday needs is freely furnished. In late medieval and Renaissance times when the overwhelming majority of people were poverty-constricted peasants and artisans, this dream became associated with the Carnival moment of indulgence in pancakes, sausages, and limitless leisure, just before Lent. In twentieth-century urbanized, consumerist America the dream refers not to food but to costume jewelry and money. The narrative unfolding of the throwing game, its *dynamic* structure, possesses historical resonance, too. Its European origins are found partly in the quetes and partly in the throwing of confetti or ashes and in smearing with soot, vainly denounced by authorities from the fifteenth century onward.[22]

Quetes for sausages presupposed an inflexible social hierarchy. Unlike Big Lou, the young male maskers who moved from household to household during the old European version of the throwing game could not convert their position into that of a person dispensing carnivalesque plenty. Big Lou's position either as duke or as commoner is also ambivalent because of the nature of what is traded between high and low. Beads and doubloons, and even the junk-food Moon-pies at Mobile, cannot be consumed in the sense that pancakes and sausages can. The trinkets exchanged in the Gulf Coast throwing game can only be shown off, and then disposed of without recycling. But pancakes and sausages were not mere trinkets in the days when people dreamed of the Land of Cockayne. They were not tossed aside. The food acquired in their rounds by the young men was consumed during the evening in joyous banqueting. After eating and resting, the young men paraded and performed again the following day. In a tic-tac-toe of reciprocities, production of plenty through the quete was arranged separately from its consumption and both of these were separated from the subsequent recycling of the householders' bounty in the form of parades, skits, and chases staged for the general communal pleasure on the morrow.

Insofar as the throwing game is an exhibition of largesse it is, properly speaking, an inversion of these quetes, for it is the dukes who are the givers, not the spectators. This kind of performance was already noticed in the sixteenth century, when a "fool on a donkey" in Kiel, Germany, was described among the maskers in a Carnival parade. The fool held two sacks from which he drew nuts to "throw among the people."[23] In the 1840s maskers in carriages tossed sugarcoated almonds (*dragées*) and bonbons in New Orleans. Santa Claus, a figure in the Mother Goose parade of the Twelfth Night Revelers in 1871, pitched "gifts" to the crowds, and Rex's knights started throwing peanuts and candy in 1881 [24] As in the case of queting, such largesse presumes a steep social hierarchy, and it has more meaning the more that there is real need on other days of the year.

The other part of the throwing game's ancestry has little to do with social differences. The throws of the dukes in modern Carnival are permutations of the flour pellets flung by boys in nineteenth-century New Orleans, just as those pellets in turn were permutations of eighteenth-century plaster confetti.[25] They are permutations of the wild kuker's ritual of touching fruit trees, garden beds, and women, rendering them fruitful, permutations of the phallic mud-smearing comically performed by the "civilized" kuker, the pseudo-czar with his long "scepter." They are permutations of the running and chasing which made anyone and everyone rich with the vigor of wild nature.[26] The fertilizing gestures, or rather the rough reciprocities between man and woman which are symbolized by the presence of women along the parade route, ready and willing to have things thrown at or upon them by males, remain embryonically present. A girl need only flash her breasts by opening a bodice or lifting up a T-shirt, and beads will be flung by the dozens. If this happens—as it does, over and over—it is because of the roar, because of the intoxication created by the high-low situation played out in a narrow, pressed-together time-space. People are surely unaware of any relation between fertility in springtime and these aggressive sexual gestures. Everyone grabs and tumbles, screams and giggles, shoves and gouges: catching *that* bead *now* means everything—and then it is gone, the float is passing on. The alchemy of Carnival transforms the national ideology of success-through-accumulation into something gay and absurd. People are rarely hurt seriously; the parades remain benign family affairs, for all their fever and raw action: everybody has disguised himself or herself more or less, and everyone believes in the trash game only as long as the disguises stay on.

One of the most important side effects of the combination of traditions which has made the throwing game central to Gulf Coast Carnival is the reinforcement of this festival's official anti-commercialism in two cities whose very existence depends on trade. The advertising vans which followed in the rear of Rex's parade in the first years after it was organized were banned after 1890. In Mobile too all trace of advertising was eventually prohibited. With the exception of the balls and "extravaganzas" of the two superkrewes, Endymion and Bacchus, no tickets are sold and no parades are subsidized in a formalized, regular way by public agencies or private businesses.

This anticommercialism allows consumerism to flourish the more. Conspicuous consumption is the soul of the event. The throwing game is a capitalist sport. You assume and you also "consume" as many masks as possible during this feverish festival, by walking around, seeing as much as you can, and above all by catching as much as you can. The fellow and girl with the biggest piles of beads around their necks have accumulated the most capital, they are the cynosure of all eyes, their accumulation immediately pays rich dividends in kisses and glances (and little by little the removal of the beads).

Mardi-Gras time is a period during which people decide—and it *does* require a conscious effort—that making money has nothing to do with having fun. "It's a good feeling to just get up there and throw it away for free." That is an enormous inversion of an American's everyday assumption. "You know there's no telephones up there on the float."[27] The reversal of values is so enormous that to bring it about requires some support from nearby mythologies—like that proverb, all that glitters is not gold, which justifies the bead-worship, and that fairytale of the good prince and the deserving pauper, which explains both one's generosity (if you're a "duke") and one's avidity (if you're a "commoner") as incomparable virtues.

"Duke" and "commoner" are symbiotic. The position above is exciting because the position below is too, and vice versa. The appeal of Carnival to Big Lou Canizzaro was as strong when he was catching beads with his children as it is now when he throws them. Merging with the crowd, competing with it, winning the beads together with others: It is delicious to be totally dependent on aristocratic power, to feverishly and frankly worship the grandeur of somebody else's accumulation. This perhaps infantile need is nevertheless also an overt recognition of the unequal distribution of power in American society, a recognition scarcely permitted in everyday life.

"We are all the same": the people perform the same gesture, they form a ritual chorus for royalty. "All the doggone people": the duke imagines himself below as he throws from above. Total assimilation. For Big Lou Canizzaro Mardi Gras provides not escape from but contact with the meaning of everyday experience: A "mass" society is one organized to produce massively, and consume massively. "Big" Lou (he weighs well over two hundred pounds) is Everyman. We are all Big Lous on Mardi Gras Day, simultaneously bigger than and less than any "one" individual, any American Hero, because we are part of the mass, possessing nothing to distinguish us from anyone else, either as consumers or as producers. The problem for people thinking along popular-culture lines is how to find escapist thrills without making much effort to change, without dropping one's commonplace identity and becoming part of some elite. The solution found in the throwing game is to become part of the crowd. It is the roar and the din in a suddenly crowded, constricting space, it is the simultaneous reaching of hands which merges "you" and "me" into an all-powerful egalitarian totality, reducing this duke or the next, all those Great People above, into instruments of Us (plate 52).

The dynamics of the game, then, rely as much upon the desire to exhibit utter dependency as upon the urge to stand above the crowd as a hero. The throwing game reveals the two sides to people's commonplace feelings about power in a mass society, those associated with becoming a great individual, someone independent of social needs and supports, and those associated with becoming an absolute nonentity, an anonymous, irresponsible particle carried along in the massive flow of social change. This hero/mass codification of social differences shows how easily the popular-culture code may take on

52. Carnival crowd, nighttime parade, New Orleans, 1987 (photo, Norman Magden)

53–54. Captain emeritus, in the throwing game, Krewe of Iris, New Orleans, 1987 (photos, Norman Magden)

an elitizing tone. The throwing game's ambivalent structure, elite or popular according to the players' conception of themselves, lends itself to shifting movements.

Comus, Momus, Rex, and other elite actors in the old-line parades participate as members of groups, not as individuals who merge with or distinguish themselves from the mass. They smile and nod to each other in concerted action. To the strictly elitist mind the crowds are there as an accessory chorus; the great moment for members of the old-line societies occurs when they pass the reviewing stands at Gallier (formerly City) Hall and on Canal Street at the site of the Boston Club: group acknowledges group; one elite bows to others; elite acknowledges officials, officials acknowledge elites. How is it, then, that these grand figures strive so mightily for places on the floats? There

is a popularizing aspect to the elite cultural code expressed here, a desire for acknowledgment from the crowd, a secret participation in its plebian tastes. Even a captain emeritus, however serene, may find herself irresistibly intrigued by nothing more than three or four fingers, smartly flung up as in plates 53 and 54. (Part of the game consists in allowing the person to whom a duke or captain or other aristocracy points have the first go at catching the bauble when it comes flying—unless you are a rank blackguard and no gentleman, sir!)

Elite and popular codes mesh in the throwing game, and if Big Lou is any indication, they also mesh in each individual. People participate in the game because of the ambivalence it allows to both of the players. "The real Mardi Gras is a series of private parties and the parades are just for tradition and to share with the public," drawls Rex's captain. Nonsense. From the beginning of Gulf Coast Carnival to the present day, elites have found it as indispensable to recognize and, ambivalently, to identify with crowds as the latter have found that they need kings, and need to strive to be like them.[28]

The sounds which make up the throwing game, however engulfing, do not create a sensuous continuum like that which Mardi Gras Indians weave. It is more of a sense-deafening surrounding of one's organism than a gradual enfolding in organic ebbs and flows. The roar of the voices, including one's own, seems to come from outside, like the boom-boom and tackity-tack of the marching bands which precede and follow the floats, like the steady hum of the tractors which pull them. There is certainly a rhythm involved, and the rhythm makes the thrill of it, makes it imperative to scream and catch right now, at the cataclysmic moment of deafened enclosure, as the beads come glittering, flying, floating, on the air. The float passes. You assess what you've got and you estimate your luck, compared to that of your neighbors, and you've hardly got time because here they come again. Part of the power of the throwing game is that it moves so fast, and that it happens again so repetitively. Gratification and frustration turn out to be twins. And you already know that both of them will recur, and that the recurrence too will turn out to be ephemeral, displaced by the roar of the crowd down the street: the next float approaches!

Bubble of beer, rattle of beads, scraping of doubloons one on the other. Mechanical sounds, sounds which can be stopped and started again anywhere, anytime. Sounds which in Carnival-time will certainly come again. There's the next float, and the next parade, and tomorrow night, and next year. This ephemeral, repeated quality, fleeting, fragile, inconsequent . . .

When I put on a mask and walk down the street, I initiate a dialogue. Here am I: who are you? I ask you to look at me and to perceive the game I'm playing between who I never am and who I might be, behind the mask. And because I am asking you to play this game with me, I am suggesting that you play it with me, too. I grant, I even prefer that you become explicitly on this day of masquerades what all of us implicitly are—persons mysterious and multiple.

When I put on a mask and get up on a float, I initiate a spectacle. I pressure the people whom I see to participate in my exaltation, not in my escapism. Look at me in awe, not in expectation, with receptivity not with whimsy. Who are you? That doesn't concern me. I ask for your attention: I'll give you anything, everything for your *eyes*. Neither your body nor your soul concern me.

Street masking moves others to join in. A spectacle pressures the onlooker toward nonmasking, toward passivity, toward abandonment of the onlooker's body to its ideal form, at once grotesque and grand, upon the float, the rostrum, the TV or cinema screen. The image upon the screen, the rostrum, the float has taken over the onlooker's body: the *spectacle* enacts it.

So that is why one has this dishevelled, scatterbrained feeling after the parade is over. Carnival-as-spectacle is a head trip. Everyone is leaving, without a word, without a rendezvous. Everyone has left, scuttling through the streets like the empty popcorn boxes and coke cups drifting in the gutters.[29]

The most unusual book ever written about Gulf Coast Carnival was published in 1953 by an Italian taxi driver from New Orleans named Tom di Palma. "I dedicate 'Turning the Lights on New Orleans' to you, my Sightseeing Customers . . . who since 1910 have been putting up with my bad English and made for me a fair living." Di Palma in his Foreword recounts how he showed his book to a friend who then asked "'Who keeps the Carnival Spirit up and Growing?' . . . 'That's easy—why its the little people like *the John Does, the George Spevlings,* you and I,' I answered. 'Well,' he came back at me . . . 'you did not give us any credit and glory; you bla, bla, bla about the big shots; you mention their names, but what about ours?'"[30]

Di Palma's book as a whole, like this excerpt, exemplifies to perfection the popular way of understanding Carnival. The answer which he made to his friend represents di Palma's conviction; his friend's criticism represents di Palma's performance. Most of the book gives lists of krewe names, krewe themes, and names of kings and queens. The lists are leavened by an ordinary man's awe ("Get an earful of the names of the most important balls" he writes at the beginning of an alphabetical list extending from Achaeans to Zulu), a sensible man's bemusement ("you can be a jackass [on Mardi Gras], an angel, a goat . . . or even a tiger, even if during all your life you have been frightened out of your wits by a mouse—for all of this is in fun"), and a small man's need to empathize with the great. His explanation of the meaning of Carnival queenship reveals the popular roots of that institution's success as no analytic approach possibly could.

> Years ago I often had the pleasure of driving about town a little girl of an aristocratic New Orleans family, her sister and her mother. For some reason or other, I always had the idea that some day this little girl, when grown, would become Queen of Carnival [i.e., Rex's queen]. Possibly it was because she had red hair and my first flame, when I was wearing knee pants, was a carrot-top. . . . This flower of an old family tree . . . did become Queen of Rex in 1933 . . . I saw her that Mardi Gras night. . . . She was truly queenly if you know what I mean.
>
> In my lifetime I have known two real Queens. . . . They were Queen Margherite of Savoie, wife of King Umberto I, and Queen Elena of Savoie, wife of Victor Emmanuele II. In time of war and disaster they both gave generously of their time to work of mercy. Like

them this Carnival Queen . . . has given generously of her time to charitable efforts. Like real Queens this little red-haired, freckle faced girl whom I had visioned a potential queen . . . reached the height of my secret ambition for her and reigned Queen for a day.[31]

Di Palma's heroine-worship has none of the elitizing overtones of Big Lou Canizzaro's love of Carnival. He idolizes at a distance. He measures the queen's authenticity against "real Queens," and the "real queens'" authenticity by their "work of mercy," their concern for ordinary people like taxi-drivers. Yes, the Mardi Gras institution of pseudo-kings and pseudo-queens has deep historical roots and possesses powerful social-structural reasons for being. But it also derives its strength from the need of commonplace people—as nearly all of us are most of the time—to believe in real queens, persons who in a democratic and egalitarian century may still serve as paradigms of behavior and desire.

Such are the elitizing and nonelitizing reactions of the great many who go to see Carnival-as-spectacle. But how do nonelites *plan* Carnival for their fellows? The general rule is to mix everything with everything, as the superkrewes do. Endymion's 1987 parade theme was suitably vague: "I'd Rather Be . . ." it was called, which allowed different floats, as Hardy's *Mardi Gras Guide* explained, to depict "various fun-filled activities such as ballooning, fishing, skiing, golf at Pebble Beach, and visits to exotic lands—Carnival in Rio, sailing the Nile, a trip to the Taj Mahal, at the Oktoberfest [in Munich], visiting the Louvre, etc."[32] The definition of everything in the popular-culture code has two parts: Whatever is included must be already known and immediately recognizable, so that its interest lies not in its intrinsic quality but in its unexpected adjacency to other things already known (peanut butter next to jelly, kiwi fruit in ice cream). And whatever is included must be sensorially high-pitched or large in scale; it must be big or it must glitter, preferably both. The superkrewes are as good illustrations of this second quality as they are of the first. Endymion has eleven hundred members; they threw two million doubloons in 1987.[33] Of Bacchus's overpowering "Extravaganza" we have already spoken.

The tendency in the twentieth century to widen Carnival's appeal by expanding middle-class participation in Carnival societies and adjusting what is put on parade to national more than regional tastes has meant the increasing dominance of popular-culture coding both in street masking and at the parades and balls. There is more and more of the same. That which has already been tried and found to be popular, in Carnival or out, will be tried and tried again; all the floats and all the masks look alike, mirroring each other. Poverty of imagination spreads like a miasma. More than a dozen other krewes have adopted Bacchus's idea of leading the parade with a guest celebrity.[34] Movies have become "an all-time popular theme" because, as one newspaper man commented, using the unmistakeable language of symbolic realism to explain the cinema theme of a 1987 krewe, "flicks cover just about anything."[35]

The most popular of all themes in the some sixteen hundred New Orleans carnival-society parades since 1857 (most of them occurring since World War II) is "children's stories and fairy tales," according to Arthur Hardy's *Mardi Gras Guide* for 1987. This category, then, far outstripped the categories of "mythology" and "history" and was even more popular—but only slightly—than "U.S. and World Geography" (that is, the evocation of familiar otherness like the Rocky Mountains, the Louvre, and the Oktoberfest).[36] Recycling the familiar, it would seem, is best achieved by regression to the fantasy world of childhood.

The favorite way of expressing popular-culture values in Carnival is parading, in Elks Club trucks if not in krewes, on side streets or in one's own neighborhood if not along the central streets. Next to parading on floats, and antedating it as a popular Carnival activity, is parading around on foot with a band. The Jefferson City Buzzards, founded in 1890, are the most venerable of New Orleans' famed Carnival marching clubs, although Pete Fountain's Half-Fast Walking Club is probably better known today.[37] The marching clubs partly initiate and partly burlesque the New Orleans tradition of brass bands and jazz bands.[38]

> At daybreak [on mardi gras, the Jefferson City] Buzzards wearing bright costumes and carrying poles of colorful [paper] flowers meet at Tchoupitoulas Street and Audubon Park in the uptown section of the city. The first order of the day is the ritual of fortification, whereby all members partake of their favorite alcoholic beverage to chase the chill of the morning air. . . . The next task is to line up in total disarray behind the purple and gilt banner that proudly proclaims that these are the antics— dancing, prancing, strutting, and every once in a while marching—of the proud and famous Jefferson City Buzzards. The band sets a jazzy pace with the syncopated rhythm of the snare drum and the sweet high notes of the trumpet. . . . Along the first block every girl is given a flower and a kiss, plus an array of proudly displayed Buzzard dance steps.

> The first stop of the day is made at the bar on the corner. According to the Buzzard creed, it would be un-Buzzardlike, discourteous and unthinkable to pass up a barroom on Mardi Gras.[39]

In other words part of the popular-culture code for Carnival is to get soused. That too is a tradition as old as the holiday, one hardly needs to add.[40]

Official-culture support for Carnival, the backing of city officials and even of church groups and welfare organizations, is complementary to elite-culture enthusiasm. How could it be otherwise, since high officials are very frequently also part of the city's social elite? "Officially" Carnival is an "unofficial" activity, a private affair, but it is as clear to the city's politicians as it is to most citizens that Mardi Gras is an unbelievably good commercial investment. The city, it was calculated in 1977, spent $963,000 for the sanitation, advertising, police and other security services involved in Carnival. For that outlay it received fifty million dollars in tourist business alone, ten percent of the estimated total annual tourist trade in New Orleans.[41]

Nevertheless it is considered just as bad manners today to mix politics with Carnival as it is to overtly commercialize it, and this is surely testimony to the strong influence of elite over official norms. The elite's desire for remoteness from social strife has helped, along with the American ideology which supposes that the least government is the best government, to keep most political references out of parades.[42] The promotions of the city's tourist bureau, the overseeing of parades by a mayoral assistant, erection of stands and decorations, the typing of Rex's proclamations of his reign in the public relations office at City Hall, are not matters of public interest, from either the elite or official point of view.[43] They are simply evidence of the inseparability of orderly care from elegance and courtliness.

The silent partnership between elites and officials was, when Rex began, more of a matter of public record. His first public communication asked for cooperation from the police to "organize the disorderly." Addressing himself to the mayor, the pseudo-king wrote (his "letter" was published in the *Republican* on February 1, 1872):

> His Majesty . . . believing that both the peace and prosperity of the city could be better secured by organizing the wandering maskers on Mardi Gras into a procession . . . respectfully requests . . . the cooperation of the police in enforcing his "self-assumed" authority.[44]

The mayor responded immediately in a note to the chief of police which ordered full "assistance and protection." The note was published along with Rex's letter, an astute move which advertised the coming event and reassured the propertied. During the 1870s and 1880s Rex's parades had a strongly military flavor. The procession escorting Rex on the occasion of his arrival from his imaginary realm in 1880 included "the Household troops, the 13th Infantry Band, followed by that splendid corps of United States troops, the 13th Infantry. Then came that fine body, the German Regiment, Sphorer's Band, and two old favorites, the Louisiana Field Artillery, then the splendid Creole Bataillion, the Orleans Artillery, followed by that spirited Regiment, the Second Infantry," and so on: thus runs the encomium of James Waldo in his 1882 book designed to advertise Mardi Gras to the rest of the country.[45]

King Felix of Mobile has long affected the same military ambiance. Already in 1898 "the [United States] government did honor to the [then styled] mystic emperor by sending a naval vessel to carry him to his royal city and the crew of the vessel took part in the imperial entry. . . . Felix II . . . arrived in imperial state, amid the firing of cannon and the music of the imperial band. . . ." In the 1950s Mobile's white king and knights boarded "the Royal Yacht, usually a Coast Guard cutter, for a run down the [Mobile] Bay . . . and back to . . . Government Street. There the King mounts his throne float with his escorts from the Navy and the Air Force."[46] From the 1950s to the present Rex's parade has been led by Texas A. & M. University's one-hundred-man Ross Volunteers drill team, setting the tone of snappy military orderliness with its "pure precision."[47]

Carnival groups in some present-day southwestern German towns, like their predecessors in various European locales since the fifteenth century, take over town government with comic violence, carrying the mayor bodily from his chambers and hoisting a Carnival flag over city hall. Nothing could be further from the custom along the Gulf Coast, where the official-culture rather than popular-culture code rules in ceremonies denoting the transfer of political authority to pseudo-kings.[48] At Rex's first appearance in 1872 he was presented at City Hall (now Gallier Hall) with the keys to the city by the mayor himself. The mayor of Mobile in the late nineteenth and earlier twentieth centuries similarly presented the key to the city to the Carnival king at Bienville Square. More recently something more of fantasy and popular sentimentality has entered in: the child king and queen

55. Boeuf Gras, Rex parade, New Orleans, 1987 (photo, Norman Magden)

of Mobile, after their "reign" in the Floral Parade, give the key to Felix.[49] When Rex's parade passes Gallier Hall on mardi gras the mayor toasts Rex and Rex toasts the mayor. As with Thomas di Palma's sense of queenliness, there seems to be an effort to make real politics and fairytale politics mix rather than develop in contrast.

The codes of officials are determined by those from whom they derive their power, but who exactly holds that power is often so hard to determine that official values tend to be straddling ones. Ernest Morial was the titular leader of black people in New Orleans in 1964, as president of the local NAACP which officially wished to eliminate the Zulu parade. In an interview that year he said: "I don't have any real quarrel with Zulu myself. Sure I would like to have no Zulu parade and see the Negro community integrated into the regular parades—allowed in the Krewe of Orleanians, the line of trucks that follows the Rex parade, for instance. But that might not happen until a long time from now. . . . Sure it's undignified, but so are a lot of things that Negroes do all year long. This is only one day. And the Zulus themselves just love it."[50] For people with official-cultural values in a democratic polity, anything is all right if it has the support of a constituency and does not threaten seriously the feelings of other constituencies.

What middle-class people require of their officials, in Carnival as outside of it, is security. In response to this police regulations have become complex in the extreme as Carnival has grown. Their spirit was already in evidence in these regulations proclaimed by the Mobile chief of police in 1908.

> With the influx of visitors to our city during the visit of His Majesty Felix, there will, without a doubt, come amongst us many disreputable characters, foot-pads, sneak thieves and other classes of criminals.
>
> While there will be ample police protection given the entire city, and special officers in citizens' clothes will be stationed in all the residence portions of the city, still citizens are requested to co-operate with the department in preventing crime and disorder.
>
> Citizens coming down town to see the parades should see that their homes are securely locked and not carry any valuables or money that would be convenient for pickpockets. . . .
>
> The Masking Ordinance will be strictly enforced by the Police Department, also the Ordinance in regard to the throwing of rubber balls, confetti, or substance of any kind, character or description at any person on Mardi Gras day or night.
>
> Feather dusters, canes and whips will not be tolerated. . . . In the interest of the good of our law-abiding citizens it is essential that decency and order be maintained. . . . Vulgarity of any character, anything bordering on indecency, intoxication, or profanity will not be permitted; also the blocking up of streets by carts, wagons or other vehicles on streets on which the parade passes will not be permitted during the time of the parade. . . .[51]

"Immediate arrest" for vulgarity of any description is the Mobile police chief's recipe for Carnival happiness. This sort of thinking, together with the ever-present pressure to create an American spectacular, explains what has happened to the *boeuf gras* in the twentieth century. In 1901 Rex decided to discontinue parading the animal. It was, they declared, "not in harmony with the beautiful displays which are produced in this era." A hairy boast in the central city, leaving behind him smelly residues—hardly beautiful! But the *boeuf gras* represents a traditional element of Carnival and to both the elite and official mind maintaining tradition is part of maintaining order. So in 1959 the *boeuf gras* reappeared in the old shape it had before 1901, except that now it was made of plastic.[52]

It is not merely that the animal is now all white and squeaky clean. The butchers are too, (see plate 55). In fact they aren't butchers anymore, they're chefs. That is made extra-clear by a chef molded in plastic on the float behind the ox and by the chefs' hats worn by the dukes riding on either side of the animal. After all, it's not nice to kill. Meat in plastic—who's ever seen it otherwise? The Fat Ox, moreover has lost his fat. He is noble and grand, clean and pure, and so are his friends the chefs. This bull is no longer full of * * * * or vulgarity of any other description.

Official-culture concern with orderliness thus rejoins the elite-culture desire for images of static beauty, and both are quite compatible with the popular-culture tendency to look for an easy time and hence to prefer occasions which are safe and smooth. Official-culture control of Carnival, as it increases, renders everything all right, to the point where the essence of the old festival, its explosive ambivalence, seems entirely leached away. Today in New Orleans Carnival is all right even with most Protestant churches, which one hundred years ago found not just Carnival but nearly everything going on in "the city of the great valley" absolutely satanic. In 1973 "numerous churches announced . . . prelenten . . . sermons on themes such as 'Christ and Joy'; or 'Frolic begins in the Heart,' or 'Man does not live by bread alone.' "[53]

The spirit of official culture, like the other codes, lives in each of us; no institution and no institution's leaders incarnate it half so well as our own feelings, when the right psychic buttons are pushed. If this spirit eventually reduces Carnival to a pablum of predictable images, it will not be due to the bias of the official-culture code toward consonance as such, nor even its inclination to totally surround, contain, and define allowable social behavior. It will rather be the comfortable lie underpinning this bias and inclination, which is that the social body has no ultimately conflicting aspects to it, and hence that social doctrines, whether they be inspired by elitism, populism, neighborliness, or official-ese, really don't matter in the long run. It will be the refusal to recognize that there is always something radically wrong with social relations and that therefore a healthy body politic requires not only ceremonials and celebrations but occasions when it can let it all hang out.

Hey, look out! Here come the pigs! (plate 56).

Elites look for recognition from others in Carnival; officials are satisfied with conciliation. The populace massed along the sidewalks seeks power, a fantastic, impossible power which in such festive moments can be articulated, symbolized, and expressed

56. New Orleans police, nighttime parade control, New Orleans, 1987 (photo, Norman Magden)

with impunity. The fourth type of culture found in Gulf Coast Carnival is more modest in intention. Unlike elite modes, the neighborly modes of communication used by groups like the Mardi Gras Indians seek local rather than generally recognized prestige; unlike popular modes, they are concerned with local reputation rather than general, abstract, ideal images of power.

> Now de prettiest little thing that I ever seen
> Mardi-Gras Indians down in New Orleans
> Sewed all night and he sewed all day
> Mardi Gras morning went all the way.

The Wild Tchoupitoulas begin their boasting song by locating themselves and stating their claim to fame.[54] Sewing together their flamboyant costumes over weeks and months, Indians signify the importance and integrity of this communally engendered, locally oriented culture long before they appear on the streets. They advertise the authenticity of their mode of life to each other. The mores peculiar to their neighborhood are refreshed and refurbished at this moment of exemplary public display. This is the significance of the "second line"; the noncostumed dancers picked up along the parade route amplify the movement of the Indians. The community is swept into the rhythm of the performance.

In the Indians' costumes commonplace materials like buttons and beads are mixed with exotic things like ostrich plumes to reinvigorate everyday reality. It is not important for these groups to appear in the central streets. The Indians mark with their rituals the bounds and bonds of neighborhood. They were and are formed not to take advantage of big-city centralization as the Carnival societies have been, but in order to isolate themselves from the big parades' lacquered acceptance of black inferiority, in which they have participated only as torch-bearing or music-making servants.

The wildman masking practiced by Mardi Gras Indians is based on the kind of communication and serves much the same ritual purposes as those of European villagers whose culture, like theirs, has traditionally been orally centered and slow to change. The males who gather in each other's houses to sew their costumes or in taverns to practice their songs come together in a twentieth-century urban version of the medieval confraternities, the "joyous societies" headed by lords of misrule or the smaller, less formal groups of unmarried youths to which we have referred.

For the Mardi Gras Indians, Carnival masking does not involve impersonating great individuals—the hero/mass dichotomy of popular culture; or grand myths—the traditions preserved by elites; or social peace—the conciliatory security symbolized by self-satirizing police officers. It is rather devoted to dramatizing social closeness and enclosure. This mode of celebration, we should remember, has been as much imposed as chosen, a fact which illustrates again the "ecological" principle that barriers, when they are not too high, encourage cultural creativity. When barriers are too low, cultural expression is diluted. The truck parades which follow the Rex floats on mardi gras morning are also expressions of neighborly ties, but their symbolism and their parade behavior too often imitate those of others. Their codes of representation hover on the edge of the commonplace, sometimes with exemplary zest and sometimes with exemplary platitude.

The difficulty with enclosed, self-protective neighborhood celebrations is their political vindictiveness. Neighborliness is most easily built up through enmity and divisiveness, through cultivating a sense of "turf."[55] Insofar as this reached murderous proportions in the old days, the Mardi Gras Indians' activities clashed with the other cultural codes of Gulf Coast Carnival and were suppressed. Is this why there are fewer and fewer tribes? Or is it simply that the nationally franchised society is taking its toll here too, leaving black ghettos too open to outside penetration, criticism, and renown?

The Introduction to this book suggested that there are two Carnivals in both Mobile and New Orleans, above all because of the seemingly ineradicable heritage of racial repression and segregation. In later chapters and especially in chapter 5, the idea was substantiated that the white-black Carnival line converted itself in white people's minds into the difference between "high" and "low" behavior, into the distance between the grandeurs of Canal Street before the Boston Club and the lewdness of balls along Basin Street. Hence, we also suggested, Mardi Gras is mentally as well as physically double.[56]

We have now complicated this picture by suggesting that what people look for in Carnival is coded in four divergent ways, ways which are related to but not identical with social class differences. What is the relationship between the cultural codes and the split between first and second Carnivals?

The neighborly culture code developed because barriers between parts of the cities were high. They were highest between black and white, but this was by no means the only distinction.

Working-class neighborhoods, immigrant neighborhoods, suburbs each had their particular forms of cohesion. Few of these particularities except those isolating certain black areas, however, have survived into the late twentieth century. We have mentioned the tendency of truck parades to repeat each other. The marching clubs, too, seem to have lost most of their neighborhood roots. The Jefferson City Buzzards survive because they have become a city-wide curiosity, not because they represent something special about a now-vanished locale called Jefferson City.[57] In the smaller city of Mobile the concern with orderliness and—no less important—the desire to be seen and heard by as many people as possible has produced a kind of obsessive pressing together into one giant central-city parade, the Joe Cain Parade, of all the separate and separatist impulses inspiring people at Mardi Gras.

The values embodied in elite, popular, and official coding of Carnival behavior have developed in close and reciprocal, although not always harmonious, interaction. They have been the magnets pulling attention away from neighborly activities toward creation of all-city extravaganzas in the central business district: here is where Carnival can be most popular, but also where it must be well controlled and finally most elite in its way of ordering things. The first Carnival has been created in consonance with America's and Western society's pursuit of perfection as a summation of power: power over people, power over nature, power over machines. The vision of such power liberates great energies, provoking in the field of festival endlessly new ideas for bigger, better amusements, attractions, and spectacles, just as it brings endlessly new technologies, opportunities, and employments to light in the work-a-day world. The second Carnival has developed in accordance with no such searching, Promethean goal. Its symbols are community-bounded in significance, however complex and far-flung their origins may be, as they certainly are in the case both of the Mardi Gras Indians and the Zulus. They draw on and produce limited energies and manage by modest means, working out of and back into an ever-recycled set of fantasies based on local circumstances.

It would seem that the days of the second Carnival are numbered, insofar as it is created and preserved by the limited visions of the neighborly-culture code. The visions of the Zulus and Mardi Gras Indians are no longer bounded by their immediate environment. Black people in Mobile, although they have been kept in their separate place, have tended to recreate in their Carnival a mirror-image of that which sails along Government

Street. Like the many elite black Carnival societies in New Orleans, black organizers of Mardi Gras in Mobile seem to see Carnival as a place to play with visions of unlimited social mobility and elite privilege no less than do whites.[58]

Such a prediction of the second Carnival's disappearance is, nevertheless, as far as New Orleans is concerned, almost certainly wrong for the foreseeable future, because this second Carnival is now taking shape in a new place even as its old locales disappear: the French Quarter.

Until the 1950s the grand parades of the krewes trundled their way through the Quarter's narrow streets as they always had. Then the march of technology, the press of tourists, and the fears of officials forced them to abandon the area.[59] The Quarter had from the early part of the century been abandoned by the last wealthy Creoles. It was increasingly dilapidated. Yet it was too valuable as a year-round tourist item simply to be bulldozed and replaced by modern skyscrapers and wide boulevards.[60] So the place gradually has become a refuge during Mardi Gras from all the conventions of Big City Carnival. Because of its narrow, inwardly turned, human scale, it is not only all right, it is almost necessary here to be someone else, to play out the dialogues of street-masking. With all the iron balconies, the horsedrawn cabs, and the commerce devoted to servicing persons who have come here for leisurely purposes, it is easy enough to feel outside the everyday world at any time of the year. During the last days of Carnival this romantic otherness takes the particular shape of a garish, sensuous costume.

The Quarter's exoticism flourishes because of Canal Street's conventionality. One supports the other, borrows from, satirizes, needs the other. As the parade-spectacles drain away people's impetus to mask, these same persons begin to count more and more on the Quarter to bring Carnival back to them, even if it's only to look at Mardi Gras's other face. "The parades are ending Uptown. The tourists are moving in, and they don't mask. They are dressed sensibly—for shopping in Duluth [this was 1986, a cold Mardi Gras] —and carrying cameras to photograph the crazies. They line up in front of each costumed reveler and wave him to a halt. Snap, snap, go the cameras."[61] To the merry-makers in the Quarter these unmasked people "look odd and vaguely menacing, reminders of car pools, income taxes and the rest of the year. Today, and today only, I have a lot more in common with the cheese and tomato sandwich approaching from the distance."[62]

Putting on a mask pries open the rule-ridden personality with its relentless impulses toward uniformity and anonymity in the name of efficiency. The human diversity normally reserved for the sacrosanct privacy of the home pops out and struts along the street. Bizarre and eccentric behavior alienates others in the everyday frame of things because it distracts them from their goals. It has no utility; it impedes achievement. But in Carnival's framework of never-never time-space every strangeness becomes a marvel. This loosened framework presents for social inspection the intimacies we spend the rest of our lives scarcely daring to gaze upon, even in our own mirror.

How is this related to the neighborly-culture code? Psychogeographically. Few enough of the cheese-and-tomato sandwiches wandering around the Quarter actually live here. "Brother, brother, brother, brother": there is little of that.[63] Masking here is hyper-individualistic, not communal. The power of the Quarter to pry open the personality depends on its geographical location, adjacent to the central city, and its psychic location, in the id. You already know when you go there what will happen, and why you want it to happen. The Quarter is small, but unlike other neighborhoods it possesses a large emanating power. It is not hidden away, like those of the black Indian tribes. Its individualizing scale and ethos casts its spell over Mardi Gras in New Orleans entirely.[64]

The policemen in plate 56 are not street maskers from the Quarter. They were photographed at the beginning of one of the krewe parades in 1987 as they went about the business of clearing the center of the street so the floats could pass. How could this happen? I had seen police garlanded with beads and tossing around doubloons, but this kind of assumption of popular-culture cartooning?—Never.

It was the Quarter. It must be because of the Quarter, the atmosphere emanating from over there, where you encounter every thinkable kind of animal by the tens of dozens, and every kind of animal-human. On this day they are all funny and loveable, as loveable and laughable as Miss Piggy and the cops.

The Carnival-society idea of Mardi Gras is by far its most socially involving aspect for both society members and spectators. Yet the development of the societies in the twentieth century, the ever-increasing number of non-elite organizations and the pursuit of ever more popular spectacles, has brought out a contradiction implicitly there from the beginning. Carnival societies simply organize the anti-organizational urge which expresses itself in the tactics of masquerade: turn reality upside down, extend reality beyond its reasonable bounds toward the infinity of fantasy; turn the personality inside out, extend selfhood in the direction of dream.

At first one gets the impression that whatever happens in this celebration takes place in and around and after the parades. But isn't it the other way around? Whatever happens in the parades and at the balls afterward is the imitation—cosmeticized, immobilized, spectacularized—of what goes on in the streets. That is the way the Quarter exercises its mesmerizing power.

# Carnival's American Style

The four codes, neighborly, popular, elite, and official, are known and shared psychologically by everyone, even though they are given form and social power by different fractions of the community. Imaginative sharing of the total repertoire of Carnival fun is no less important for the success of Gulf Coast Carnival than the social support from different classes and the nationwide support which is insured for Mardi Gras by decking it out as a Great American Spectacular. But how does this imaginative solidarity arise? Even if one shares others' values in some part of the psyche, one's reaction to their expression is likely to be repugnance and denial of them, especially if they threaten one's social interests and identity. Why then do people tolerate each other's foibles so gaily on this holiday? The social peace which reigns in Carnival is puzzling. Sexual and racial loves and hates, taboo the rest of the year, are lavishly displayed. In fact Carnival is peaceful *because* it is explosive.

The meaning of this paradox can be illustrated by showing where it is less than true, in Mobile as opposed to New Orleans. We have noted that Carnival is culturally less varied at Mobile; its social, ethnic, and historical frontiers have been fewer. Southern white Anglo-Protestant power, less contested here than at New Orleans, has in turn allowed less chance for buffering contrasts to emerge among the elements of the social system. Tensions are therefore less openly expressed, particularly between blacks and whites.

Whites do burlesque other whites, however. The Comic Cowboys are one perennial instance, and since 1968 many satirical groups have joined in the Joe Cain parade, sometimes exhibiting a shockingly scatological bent. In 1982 a truck marked "The Order of the Mystic Moonpies" joined the parade down Government Street, carrying a masker in top hat and cape with a sign identifying him as Reverend Moon. Who was the "butt" of this satire, the sectarian religious group led by Moon, the well-dressed members of Carnival societies, or the makers of the inexpensive cream-cakes called "moon-pies" which are thrown to the crowds in Mobile? The masker stood on high, graciously doffing his elegant hat to left and to right, and gesturing with his hands to solicit attention. All this, however, was not designed so that he might encourage Korean Christianity or throw cakes like the dukes, but so that his subsequent action would not be missed, as he stooped over now and again, lifting his black cape to expose bare buttocks and suggest with these two "half-moons" the source of his grandeur.

No one protested this display; the police led the parade calmly on amid cheering and jeering throngs.[1] But when on the next morning the black version of Mobile's pseudo-monarch, King Elexis, stepped off a "royal yacht" at the foot of Government Street to begin his parade, the white police force clustered heavily around him and his group of black notables. There was little need. King Elexis is no King Zulu; he, his queen, and his court of dukes were without masks and were properly attired in tails and tulle. No white satire—or black. If there had been, it would have been to little effect. The only whites at the disembarkation were the police and me. The police escort literally whizzed the motorcade of six cars down the main street past a sparse crowd. Most black people did not come to the central streets and most whites stayed away.

For Carnival to be successful in liberating people from their everyday selves it seems to require two disparate qualities, sharp edges and an atmosphere of play. When these two unexpectedly conjoin, differences can be flaunted and evacuated, reduced to their true status as arbitrary fabrications for the good not of society but of some social fraction. In this comically plosive sense the low needs representation of the high in Carnival, and vice versa. The parade needs the informal skit, the confrontational costuming, and vice versa. In 1987 at New Orleans Norman Magden and I turn a corner near the French Quarter. There is a mini-Zulu tribe: four blacks with drums and spears followed by three whites decked out in black-face, grass skirts, furs, nose-rings, face-paint, and what-have-you (plate 57). They trot along the street together. Where else in America is that both physically possible and symbolically resonant in the 1980s? Apparently not in Mobile, even in Carnival.

By 1969 the Zulus achieved what Ernest Morial said five years earlier would probably take a very long time. They abandoned their route through mostly black neighborhoods and followed approximately the same sequence of streets as Rex on Mardi Gras morning. They have tractor-drawn floats and throw bead necklaces. What do their grass skirts and "nigger Sambo" face paint signify today? It may be true that the Zulus' gaily ambiva-

57. Wildman troupe, near French Quarter, New Orleans, 1987 (photo,
Norman Magden)

lent play with their own and the white man's stereotypical images of black people is being flattened into a patented symbol
which no longer carries much shock value. But in terms of the
larger history of Carnival's American style, the Zulus' bridging
of the gap between the first and second Carnivals is an extraordinary event, as epochal in its way as the black-and-white satire
of the Zulus' satire by street maskers near the Quarter.

The Zulus have not only been "integrated" into the white
man's Carnival in the streets; they have also included whites in
their membership. However, we do not yet see blacks and
whites openly riding on the same floats in their parades, much
less on those of any other society, including Rex, which by 1987
reputedly had some blacks among its members.[2] And the Zulus

are still the only black Carnival society parading along New Orleans' traditional white-only routes in the central city. The school desegregation crisis in New Orleans which in so many ways deepened racial and racist convictions among whites and blacks, is but one generation past.[3]

Carnival in America, people say, could only exist in a richly mixed culture like that of New Orleans. Aside from the fact that this does not account for its equal rootedness in the less richly mixed culture of Mobile, such a statement has no analytic value because it disregards the dozens of American melting-pots without such a festival. The differences of Mobile and New Orleans from other places may be stated metaphorically, I have suggested, as a set of barriers. These barriers are highest in the area of race, but even there it is well to observe the exactness of the metaphor. Barriers are not walls; they are moveable and they are crossable; the more they are shoved about and built up and pulled down, the more people get the idea of their temporary quality. This is what I mean by the difference between New Orleans and Mobile, and also what I mean by the peace-making explosions of Carnival. In New Orleans barriers are more visibly displayed than they are in Mobile, where blacks and whites seem to have tacitly agreed not to see each other in Carnival and where behind-the-scenes pressure ended promptly such things as the half-moon displays on Joe Cain Day, although nothing was done openly at the time. In New Orleans the defiance of taboos is acted out, not so much with the intention of making them disappear but so that they can be experienced from another, from any number of other angles. Barriers of many kinds are displayed in Carnival, sometimes upside down, sometimes sideways, and sometimes just as they are everyday, only more vividly so.

This is not to say that every Carnival reveler experiences the event as one of violation and trespass. There are as many psychological mechanisms barring recognition of the ambivalences involved in worshiping a duke, imitating an Indian, or burlesquing an African chief as there are mechanisms which generate the ambivalences. Zulus traditionally included enough side-shuffling disguises to allow whites to imagine that parodies of themselves weren't there.

One path to the definition of Carnival's American style is that of sociopsychological analysis, coupled with an attempt to discern the pattern of the festival's coded values, as has been done here and in the preceding chapter. Another path consists in discovering the pattern of Mardi Gras' historical development.

Our conclusions about this development break with received opinion. Gulf Coast Carnival is neither a colonial nor a French inheritance. Until the 1840s Mardi Gras was one occasion among many during the convivial winter season. Christmas and the Twelve Days were just as important as Carnival, and indeed Carnival's third enduring element, the permanently organized parading society, first developed around Christmas, not Carnival. (Street masking and society balls had preceded the invention of such parading societies in 1831.) The sense of Carnival as part of a larger festive period has in fact been preserved down to the present. Elite white society in Mobile, we recall, inaugurates "Mardi Gras" at Thanksgiving with the Camellia Ball, elite white society in New Orleans with the Twelfth Night Revelers' ball on January 6. The less-than-elite Phunny Phorty Phellows, a late nineteenth-century group devoted to satire which has been revived in recent years, holds a "streetcar parade" on January 6.[4]

The period previous to the l840s had two main phases that affected the character of Mardi Gras when it later emerged as the winter season's supreme festivity. First came a phase of colonialization of the European festive repertory by groups which, whatever the subordination of one to the other, were not sharply segregated: white masters and mistresses, and black slaves and freed persons. From about 1810 this colonial set of practices, French and Spanish, African and Caribbean, began to melt together with newer elements of Anglo-American custom in the two port cities.

Linguists maintain that foreign language acquisition begins with the learning of vocabulary. After this "surface" of the foreign tongue is imitated, sentence patterning is gradually added; deep syntactic grasp comes slowly. When large groups of people with different languages confront each other over time a third stage may follow and supersede the task of accommodation to a foreign tongue. So much of the syntax and vocabulary of the subordinate group may be welded into the dominant language that a dialect develops which with the passing of time may become a language in its own right. Something like this happened to winter festivity in New Orleans and Mobile. Until the 1840s ethnic groups and social classes borrowed each other's rituals in haphazard manner: they imitated each other's vocabularies and sentences. By the 1840s and 1850s the words and syntax particular to Creole winter festivities had been so absorbed by the politically and demographically dominant Anglo-Americans that it was reformed into a new dialect which only slightly differed in accent in the two cities. America's "first Carnival" emerged, a festivity available to elites and to would-be elites, as long as they were white.

Since the 1840s Carnival has developed in two stages, civic and national, the second of which has not yet ended. In the light of the analysis of cultural codes in chapter 10 we can see that during both stages tension between elite and popular ideas of the holiday directed events. Unlike the situation shown by the history of Carnival in many other countries, official-culture directives and neighborly, folk-culture elements were at no point predominant. In general the elitizing tendency led in inventiveness during the civic phase while the popularizing tendency has gained increasing power in the national period after 1900.

Carnival's American style emerged clearly and, it seems, indelibly, due to events and circumstances peculiar to American history, Southern history, and indeed to the history of these two Southern cities in particular. The regal imagery which in the twentieth century has turned out to be as populist in character as it is elite, was developed not simply from European customs of Carnival kings but in extenuation of the Confederate cause, that of a white aristocracy which defends itself and its prerogatives over others with the sword. The imagery of grandeur, whether regal or mythological in tone, has served the function of socioeconomic escapism—an old and appropriate function for Carnival!—as the South regionally and these two cities in particular turned inward to retain connection with their prewar period of greatness.[5]

Because of this strong politico-military marking of Carnival, the Carnivalesque—all that is grossly irreverent, excessive, and inversive—could during the civic phase exist only by hiding away from Carnival's white elite form or by showing itself in express contradiction to that form, as seems to have been the reason for tolerating the Ball of the Two Well-Known Gentlemen (along with the surreptitious complicity of a good number of the elite). The Carnivalesque could not be acknowledged as an extension or complement to white elite activities, as is the street masking in the French Quarter today. When Carnivalesque activities defied the principles upon which white elite Carnival was based, those activities were suppressed. Thus during the civic phase the late eighteenth- and early nineteenth-century tradition of African festive dancing at and near New Orleans was broken. However, by the 1880s at the latest, a new "dialect" took form which synthesized African, Caribbean, and American cultural strains around the popular Carnival masquerade of the Indian. It developed in the poorer, black neighborhoods without much relation to the white elite and popular forms. Here, along with the black versions of the elite Carnival societies which were founded in Mobile and New Orleans in the 1890s, were the beginnings of the separate organization of Carnival for blacks. It was a fortunate misfortune which led to inventions scarcely possible if the blacks had continued in the less segregated but more marginal position which they had occupied in Carnival up to the end of the nineteenth century.

Meanwhile the despised or ignored miscellany of street maskers were beginning to develop a new kind of accommodation to the world beyond the Gulf Coast, no longer European but American in orientation, no longer aristocratic but popular in taste. Comic-strip maskers began to appear by 1900,[5] trucks and cars carried the sameness of white-middle-class taste for glitter and noise out and around and through every part of the city; the desire for easy-to-obtain spectacle was finally integrated with the economic advantages of mass tourism in the superkrewes of the 1960s. This was the first subphase of the national era of Mardi Gras. It developed in consonance with the evolution of American culture generally. Mardi Gras became part of the national systemization of leisure-time; a trip to New Orleans in late winter for the Carnival might follow upon winter skiing in Colorado or sunning in Florida and would precede summer vacation in the Adirondacks or Wisconsin.

Out of this came rather more unexpectedly a second set of innovations, begun in the 1960s and, as with the initiatives of the first part of the national era, almost entirely centered around New Orleans' first Carnival: Its pure white color began to disappear. So did its patriarchally supervised sexism. The Zulus preceded Rex's parade through the streets.[6] The black Indians were discovered by the media. At Bacchus's balls the national-celebrity "king" made a point of sharing the spotlight with black coeds.[7] The balls of the gay krewes, male and female, became the measure of brilliant, risqué fashion. And in the French Quarter the exposure—bodily, that is—of every conventionality, high or low, black or white, male or female, found a sanctuary. Carnival and the Carnivalesque were reunited. The festival showed a renewed capacity to assimilate, stimulate, and assuage people's most diverse aspirations, not only their acknowledged social ones but their nearly unacknowledged and asocial desires.

The more closely this line of evolution is studied, the less predetermined it seems. So many special circumstances intervene at each stage that its richness appears a matter of chance. Its richness can never be entirely explained, dependent as it is not only on the motion of groups and the policy of governments but on the often momentary inventions of individuals. But just as subjective understanding does not determine public meaning, so indeterminacy of stylistic origin does not put in question Gulf Coast Carnival's general pattern. The partly repetitive, partly innovative pattern offers us more than a picture of how Mardi Gras came to be what it is today. It also gives some idea of the general reasons for festive creativity or stagnation.

Carnival stimulates the expression of multiple social roles and social aspirations rather than simply the inversion of their everyday forms. But different Carnivals express multiplicity in different degree and at different times. There is a reciprocal relation between social multiplicity and cultural ambivalence. If social possibilities are few because ethnic differences in a population are minimal and the politico-economic situation is frozen by caste or blocked by international circumstances, then people's sense of their desires will be straitened. Their ambivalence about their lives will be less expressed, and the reach of desire toward total pleasure will be less embracing. Carnival as a machine for stimulating desire and augmenting the imagination will be less powerful, and Carnival fun will more often take that inversive character so readily attributed to it by the folklorists, anthropologists, and historians who have come to the study of this festivity from the background of "cold," slow-moving, nearly static tribal societies. In such societies rituals do indeed frequently play the role of casting light on everyday relations by looking at them upside down.

Carnivals in many European rural communities between 1500 and the present day also seem to have approximated this inversive model. But Carnivals in European cities, Carnivals in the eighteenth- and nineteenth-century Caribbean area, and Carnivals along the Gulf Coast have reflected this paradigm only sporadically. The ethnic and social situation in these areas has just as often been "hot," fast-moving, dynamic. Two moments of heated festive change in Mobile, for example, when social multiplicity and hence cultural ambivalence were at a maximum, were the 1830s and 1860s. The city grew between 1830 and 1840 from 3,000 to more than 12,000 persons. New Orleans was not yet an overwhelming regional presence; Mobilians were pushed toward cultural novelty, toward new and unheard-of ideas, by their immigrants and their mixed agricultural and sea-trading,

Anglo-American and Franco-Spanish colonial roots. If Krafft and his friends had not invented the Cowbellions in 1831, someone else would have created something just as richly redolent of this frontier. . . The 1860s were to whites a horror in Mobile. But economic and political regression somehow produced cultural innovation: Chief Slackabamorinico is only one example of the fascinating caprices of Mobile Carnivals during the late 1860s and 1870s. The enemy of culture in Mobile has been less depression and catastrophe than stasis.

If this barrier theory of cultural change can be generalized, then one may expect another cool-off period in New Orleans after the rapid developments of the last two decades. In looking toward it one might even praise what is so often pilloried, the conservative attachment of the oldest Carnival societies to what Dr. Russell of the black Mobile carnival association called the "classical side" of Carnival.[8] The mistaken idea of these societies and many of those who imitate them—that is, that Mardi Gras stems from some general pre-Christian idea of festival which was taken over by Europeans, who in turn passed it on to their colonies—has in fact been an incentive to Carnival's preservation as an interesting mascarade. In spite of the drive to mix and dilute every thinkable symbol in order to appeal as widely as possible, Gulf Coast masking has remained attached to a wide repertory of pre-Christian myths, legends, and historical events, and to the imagination of specifically European courtly forms of ceremony.

In fact from the international and comparative point of view the situation in 1980 is nearly the reverse of what it was in 1900: old-line krewes in New Orleans and old-line mystic societies in Mobile look like Mardi Gras's most unique American feature, as all the world rushes toward the production of indiscriminately eclectic spectacles. Carnival along the Gulf Coast may prolong its life into the twenty-first century not because life is gayer or more lax there, but because its connection to elite society is stronger and that elite society is more straitlaced.[9]

The overall historical pattern of Gulf Coast Carnival's development shows, besides its unregenerate elitism, several other characteristics giving it a special style. They are characteristics which in some ways extend and in others qualify the point just made about Mardi Gras' bright future. However arrogant and indifferent their stance, the elites who celebrate Carnival orient themselves to the populace no less than the populace orients itself to the elites. In America hybrid elitizing and popularizing forms of imagery and performance predominate over pure statements of high or low orientation. Even the Twelfth Night Revelers and the Atlanteans, even the Strikers and the Order of Dragons, who give only private balls, do not simply ignore the people as royal and aristocratic revelers did in Europe for centuries. They like to see their affairs reported in the papers.[10]

Again, Gulf Coast Carnival is chivalric in its notion of ideal human relations, from the Buzzards' paper flowers for girls to the mysterious captains on horseback leading the krewes. As Mark Twain put it in *Life on the Mississippi*, "Take away the romantic mysteries, the kings and knights, and big sounding titles, and Mardi Gras would die, down there in the South. The very feature that keeps it alive in the South—girly-girly romance—would kill it in the North or in London. *Puck* and *Punch* [London satirical magazines] and the press universal, would fall upon it and make merciless fun of it, and its first exhibition would also be its last."[11]

These American Carnivals devote nearly equal efforts to abolishing history and recapturing it. In this nation the past disappears too quickly, but also not quickly enough. People come from everywhere to become Americans; it is felt that they should assimilate as quickly as possible. Yet it is also felt that, just because life and occupations and people's connections change so constantly, one should hold on to "the American heritage." American heroes and heroines not only provided Bacchus's theme in 1982; there are parades like it every year.[12]

Finally, because of the double religious heritage of Mardi Gras, as Protestant as it was Catholic in its early enthusiasms, the devil has retained his place in the festival. In 1981 Comus's ball invitation, one of the most beautiful in the society's history, depicted the cloven-hoofed demon seated on his throne in a hall of fuming ice.[13] The devil is an occasional escort of the superbly decorated nude women who turn up in the Quarter.[14] The idea of sin as weakness of the flesh lives on in the twentieth century and therefore Carnival as fleshly indulgence cannot shake itself loose from its Christian origin, even if the relation of the festivity to Lent has been forgotten. The wild and the deathlike, on the other hand, although they too recur, tend to lose their ominous character and become sweetened in America. Significantly enough there is no celebration of the death of Carnival in New Orleans and Mobile, while this for many centuries has been and still is a frequent theme in European Carnivals.[15] After Rex waves his scepter at midnight on mardi gras in New Orleans to end the festival officially, the private party continues. At Mobile on the Order of Myths' emblem-float Folly chases Death but not vice versa. Americans believe in the happy ending, or rather in no ending at all.

The more ceremonious a Carnival is, the more it will have a simply inversionary relation to everyday reality. The more Carnivalesque it is, the more it will be complexly transgressive. Ceremonious Carnivals are dedicated to reassurance: reality has only two sides, the practical and the fantastic, and the expression of the fantastic demonstrates the wisdom of the practical. Social relations and their cultural expression can be totalized. Carnivalesque Carnivals, on the other hand, are totalizing, not totalized. The double-edged qualities of life, hidden and revealed, practical and fantastic, workaday and festive, are played with to such bewildering degree that they engender an impetus which is something like a baby's erratic eagerness in seeking the nipple. The "carnivalesque spirit," to use Bakhtin's phrase, understands Fat Tuesday's fatness as excess, and not simply as exception. It celebrates an infantile, early springtime dream of ever-renewed, ever-varied transgression and fulfillment.

Limits and the illimitable: is it not between these two visions that most European and American Carnivals at court and in villages, at monasteries and in towns, have oscillated since their beginnings in the Middle Ages? Which of the two visions dominated at a particular time and place has depended, as at New Orleans and Mobile, on local circumstances of social support, politico-economic opportunities for development, and the inertial power of the festival's previous history in that locale.

The difference in the two visions is that one reacts to a barrier by approaching and testing it, the other by moving away. Ceremonious Carnivals encourage a sense of distance from barriers, so that they appear to be vague or not even there. The hardness and inflexibility of workaday exchanges between people are smothered in billowy clouds of wishful sentiment. In this sense ceremonious Carnivals actually celebrate limits surreptitiously: the more the real sociocultural barriers can be kept hidden by emphasizing an illimitably fantastic perfection on mardi gras, the more solid the barriers will appear on Ash Wednesday. Carnivalesque Carnivals, on the other hand, challenge and taunt the limits accepted in everyday life; they play on and about the barriers, testing their hardness, vaulting them, and occasionally tearing them down. They may hurt psychically and maim physically. They are always, in some way or another, grotesque.

The two extremes of ceremony and the Carnivalesque are antagonistic; they are also complementary. Side streets build up the uncoordinated energies that funnel into the unified roar of main street, and vice versa. In the cultural behavior of individuals, too, both modes are present because of the complementary character of mental and physical participation in Carnival. If the racial, sexual, economic barriers in a community are represented as hazy walls or low and flimsy barriers during Carnival—as in the transvestism of street maskers and the willing largesse of the float dukes—then one can wager that the organizers of the representation imagine them and then indeed act as if they are pretty high, hard walls the rest of the year. If they are represented as hard walls and indelible differences during the festival—like the boastful supremacies of the black Indian tribes and the imperturbable grandeur of the pseudo-kings—then one may guess that they look to the organizers as if they are unstable in actuality, in need of shoring up, refurbishment, and everyday attention.

Studying Gulf Coast Carnival explains much more than a once-a-year occasion in a southern marshland between continent and sea. Because Carnival is a performance which holds a *distorting* mirror up to society, it unsettles everything. It affords a moment for reflection about our daily lives, but that reflection is untrustworthy, or at least ambivalent in its means. The more ceremonious, grand, and admirable the image in the mirror appears, the more liable it is to look excessive and silly—that is, Carnivalesque—on Ash Wednesday. But this, as we have just observed, is because Carnival allows us not simply to express our repressed selves but to construct our ideals. Carnival's symbolic codes are active constructions as well as passive reflections of people's day-to-day ways of dealing with reality.

Some people use the codes to construct ceremoniously, others to construct grotesquely. But since the constructions are only part of Carnival, and tend to change their significance afterwards, what indeed do these dreams mean? Maybe the best thing to do, you know, even if—just a minute, let me check, I think, yes, it seems so—even though it's now Ash Wednesday, is to laugh about it.

# Afterword

The first Carnival, and the second. The ceremonious, and the grotesque.

One Carnival asks us, as tourists and spectators, as men and women of high fancy, to play the mirror game. As duke and queen and nobody, as the mirroring surface which allows us to assume any kind of role, we look at Carnival as an object. No longer the hard, impenetrable, "real" object of yesteryear; we are too sophisticated for that. Carnival is a construct, its mirroring capacities depend upon its dimensions, its placement, its relation to sources of light. Carnival is a technique, on the float, on the ballroom floor, in the news pages, in the society pages, in the pages of books, in glossy prints. Carnival is an object, ours is to play its game, to objectify.

The other Carnival does not ask. It bumps into "you," jars this you-ness of you, upsets it. You may lose your-self. You may join unthinkingly in the fun. The second Carnival bumps you into your self-otherness, throws you into a crowd of subject-objects, jars you loose from your tranquility as an object and a maker-reflector of objects. No more poses. No more naked cowboys holding videos, watching chambermaids taking snapshots there. A subject-object self-other not exactly anywhere, just go with the flow. No way to tell you how. Maybe sew all year with your friends on a costume. Maybe just get up early on mardi gras and start bumping around.

History, sociology, and personal participation do not corroborate each other. Their variable results set inquiry at odds.[1] Carnival's meanings are not simply social-functional ploys, historical residues, or psychic projections, imaginative constructions, neurotic releases. These meanings clash, and so do people's reasons for going downtown, going south, going over to the city to see the maskers and the parades. The reasons clash; they encounter obstacles and engender argument. They encourage other meanings—as the next book about Carnival will surely show.

# Appendix

## Schema of Semes Used in Chapters 6 and 7

The following is the schema which was used to classify materials concerning Mardi Gras Indians and their analogues for comparative analysis.

I.  Costume Semes
1.  Order of being as indicated by general gestalt.
    Toward animals? Toward human differences of class, ethnicity, race, office? Toward the superhuman (spirits, gods)?
2.  Body parts.
    Face: how decorated? covered? deformed? ( = d, c, d)
    Upper body: how d, c, d? (e.g., hunchback: Punch)
    Mid-Section: how d, c, d? (esp. stomach, anus, genitalia)
    Limbs, Hands, Feet: how d, c, d? (esp. knees, wrists, elbows, ankles)
3.  Body extensions.
    Head covering? Hair arrangement?
    Bodily extensions (tails, horns)?
    Materials held above or before body (umbrellas, canopies, fans, flags)?
    Insignia, labels on body (crown, names, symbols)?
4.  Part/whole analysis.
    a.  Primary body-part or body-extension emphasis:
        What orientation in space, and vis-à-vis others, does this primary emphasis give the figure? Is the costume oriented upward, downward, or laterally (correlation with 1), backwards or frontwards? Do the costume's features wrap the body closely or loosely? Are there significant apertures?
    b.  No primary emphasis: same series of questions as in (a), plus this: is the nonprimary emphasis done in order

evenly to distribute costume effects or in order to introduce contradictory relations among the effects?

5. Materials.

| | | |
|---|---|---|
| beads | mirrors | sequins |
| eagle feathers | ostrich feathers | ribbons |
| skins | furs | textiles |
| tassels | animal tails | leather |
| felt | shells | |
| jewels and | | |
| glittering | | |
| stones | | |

6. Order of significance as deduced from preceding items and their context.

Toward sacred or profane?

Toward classical (finished; self-contained) or grotesque (unfinished, broken open, distorted)?

II. Performative Semes

1. Preparation.

Prepare roles ("practices")? How are organizational decisions made?

Prepare costumes (sewing sessions)?

Time sequence and periodicity of preparation

2. Timing of performance.

Before, during, after mardi gras?

Day or night?

Duration?

3. Spacing.

Inside or outside?

Relation of festive route to homes or businesses of participants?

Spacing between different masking roles?

4. Festive organization regulating performance.

Second-liners? Nonparticipant spectators?

Other functions of festive organization (e.g., charity to sick, dead)?

5. Normative sequence of festive action.

Is there a typical *stance* of the role players?

Queting?

Toward narrative or toward dancing?

6. Semi-normative disruptions of sequence.

Challenges (fight, boast, dance)

Pauses for drinks and conversation in taverns

7. Roles.

| | |
|---|---|
| Pseudo-King | master of ceremonies figures |
| pseudo-wild/medicine man | (shaman) (spy boy, flagboy)? |
| pseudo-queen | musicians? |

8. Primary emphasis in sequence (cf. 5, 6, 7)? No primary emphasis, or two foci? (See I.4.b.)
9. Traditional performative elements honored or discarded easily? (Is this a function of amount of competition?—see 6.)

# Notes

Introduction

1. See, e.g., Peter Burke, *Popular Culture in Early Modern Europe* (New York, 1978), 190: "Carnival was, in short, a time of institutionalized disorder, a set of rituals of reversal." He cites Gluckman's work as a useful paradigm for the explanation of Carnival's "license in ritual," ibid., 201. Burke is speaking of the period from 1400 to 1800 in Europe, the time when most of the elements of Gulf Coast Carnival can first be documented. Emmanuel Le Roy Ladurie, in his *Le Carnaval de Romans* (Paris, 1979), 338–39, refers to Edmund Leach's *Rethinking Anthropology* (London, 1961), 132–36: "Pour Leach. . . le temps des sociétés traditionelles et festives est *pendulaire*. . . . Le temps s'écoule normalement pendant l'année puis repart brièvement en sens inverse pendant la durée festive, pour reprendre son écoulement normale au cours de l'année (ou de la saison) qui va suivre. . . .L'analyse de l'anthropologue anglais s'applique bien au Carnaval de Romans, et à travers lui, à d'autres carnavals européens. . . ." Both Burke and Le Roy Ladurie use other models besides that of role reversal and inversion in analyzing European Carnival; they do not reduce the idea of Carnival just to its socially inversive content. And in fact the quite subtle analysis of Leach on which Le Roy Ladurie draws does not cite Carnival as a rite of "role reversal" but rather as one of "masquerade," that is, as a ritual which exaggerates everyday behavior rather than inverting it. Max Gluckman, "Rituals of Rebellion in South-East Africa," in his *Order and Rebellion in Tribal Africa* (New York, 1963), 110-36, bases his analysis of inversive rites on James Frazer's references to "temporary kings" in Fraser's *The Golden Bough.* Gluckman, 127, does not refer explicitly to Carnival, but he developod in a classic manner the social logic of role reversal and inversion which commentators on Carnival have so frequently found useful: "The acceptance of the established order as right and good, and even sacred, seems to allow unbridled excess, very rituals of rebellion, for the order itself keeps this rebellion within bounds. Hence to act the conflicts, whether directly or by inversion or in other symbolical form, emphasizes the social cohesion within which the conflicts exist." It should be noted that Gluckman's analysis was open-ended; he concluded his essay (136) by posing questions, not dogmas: "Why is the reversal of roles so important a mechanism in this process? How does the ritual itself keep within bounds the rebellious sentiments which it arouses?"

2. Da Matta, "Carnival, Informality, and Magic," in Edward Bruner, ed., *Text, Play, and Story* (Washington, D.C., 1984), 236. Mikhail Bakhtin, *Rabelais and His Times* (Moscow, 1965; trans. Cambridge, Mass., 1968), introduction and chap. 5. In spite of its semiotic similarity, I am not suggesting that debasement plays exactly the same social-functional roles as exaltation, of course.

3. Victor Turner, "Dewey, Dilthey, and Drama," in E. Bruner and V. Turner, eds., *The Anthropology of Experience,* (Urbana, Illinois, 1986), 42. Turner does not limit tribal ritual practices strictly to bodily exaltation. I have omitted from his list two items: "architectural forms (temples, amphitheaters). . . [and] the enacting of mythic and heroic plots drawn from oral traditions. . . ."

## Chapter 1

1. Performances of the Lupercalia are last mentioned in the late fifth century by Pope Gelasius. Other ancient pagan festivals thought to be direct forerunners of Carnival are last documented even earlier. As indicated in the text, Carnival means etymologically to take away meat. The root *carnem-valere* alternates with *carnem-levare* and *carnem-tollere* in tenth-, eleventh-, and twelfth-century sources. See Paul Aebischer, "Les dénominations du Carnaval d'après les chartes italiennes du Moyen Age," in *Mélanges de philologie romane offerts à M. Karl Michaelsson* (Gothenburg, 1952), 1–11.

2. There is no reliable general study of Carnival, although there are many excellent detailed studies. The Tübingen University Group for the Study of Carnival has provided one of the richest recent examinations of city and village carnivals, analysing hundreds of locales, past and present, in the three collectively edited volumes entitled *Fasnacht* (Tübingen, 1964), *Masken Zwischen Spiel und Ernst* (Tübingen, 1967) , and *Narrenfreiheit. Beiträge zur Fasnachtforschung* (Tübingen, 1980). The volumes have no editors indicated. Two attractive picture-book studies with reliable brief texts are: Annie Sidro and Pierre Falicon, eds., *Carnavals à travers les Ages du Monde,* (Nice, 1984), and Françoise Giroux, ed., *Carnavals et Fêtes d'Hiver,* (Paris, 1984). See Louis Duchesne, ed., *Liber pontificalis,* II (Paris, 1889), 172–73, for the twelfth-century text, written by Canon Benedict of St. Peter's Cathedral in Rome.

3. The assault on the folkloric explanation of Carnival has been led by German scholars. This is perhaps natural, since the Germans, led by Jacob Grimm, were especially adept and especially careless in developing the notion. Pride of place in demonstrating the mistaken interpretations of source materials and in reconstructing the ideology supporting those interpretations must be given to Hans Moser. See esp. "Der Folklorismus als Forschungsproblem der Volkskunde" (first published in 1964) in the collection of his articles, *Volksbräuche im geschichtlichen Wandel* (Munich, 1985).

4. See Barry Ancelet, "Courir du Mardi Gras," *Attakapas Gazette* 15, no. 2 (Summer 1980), Harry Oster, "Country Mardi Gras," in Richard Dorson, ed., *Buying the Wind* (Chicago, 1964), 274–81, and William Rushton, *The Cajuns* (New York, 1979), 243–48. A longer version of Oster's article, including more Mardi Gras songs and comparison of the songs to the New Year's custom of La Guignolée is in H. Oster and R. Reed, "Country Mardi Gras in Louisiana," *Louisiana Folklore Miscellany,* 1, no. 4 (January 1960), 1–17. Nicholas Spitzer's "Zydeco and Mardi Gras: Creole Identity and Performance Genres in Rural French Louisiana" (typescript; copyright by N. Spitzer, 1986) shows with ethnographic precision that "black Creoles," living in the southern Louisiana area west of New Orleans which was settled by the Acadians, developed an interesting variant of the white Cajun *courir* at an unspecifiable date. The black Creole *courir* continues to flourish in the smaller towns

and villages of that area in close proximity to the Cajun form. (I would like to thank Professor Roger Abrahams, University of Pennsylvania, for securing a copy of this manuscript for me. In 1986 Mr. Spitzer became a folklorist for the Office of Folklife Programs, Smithsonian Institution, Washington, D.C.)

5. There is an annually edited pamphlet which publishes the names and routes of Carnival parades in New Orleans: Arthur Hardy, *Mardi Gras Guide 1987* (New Orleans, 1987), 3, lists fifty-two parading societies, of which twenty-seven have Greek, Roman, or Egyptian names. (I do not count the societies named Rex, Sparta, Octavia, Caesar, Centurions, and Gladiators, which have historical rather than mythological referents.) Mobile does not possess a similar annual guide. Bennett Wayne Dean, *Mardi Gras, Mobile's Illogical Whoopdedo* (Mobile, 1971), provides a list of Mobile Carnival societies since 1830 at the end of his book. The list shows rarer resort to mythology for names.

6. The best general book on the semantics and ideology of Renaissance Carnivals is Bakhtin's *Rabelais and His World.* Bakhtin refers to the parallels between Carnival's fat puppet and the heroes of Cervantes, Shakespeare, and Rabelais. He does not develop the parallel to Rabelais' *Quaresmeprenant,* however, and his idea of the political and social import of Carnival ideology is questionable, as I have indicated in *Rabelais's Carnival: Text, Context, Metatext* (Berkeley, 1990).

7. This Renaissance notion is developed with special force in Dietrich Gresemund's *Podalirii Germani cum Catone Certomio de furore germanico diebus genialibus Carnisprivii dialogus* (Mainz, 1495), reprinted in Joel Lefebvre, *Les fols et la folie* (Paris, 1967), 391–401.

8. The customary violation is probably due to the fact that the Roman Church changed the date of the beginning of Lent in the eighth century. Before this time Lent began on Quadragesima Sunday, the Sunday following Ash Wednesday. Even after the Roman Church began to urge observance of the earlier date to begin fasting, Ash Wednesday was not generally seen in Western churches as the proper beginning of Lent until the twelfth century, and in some places it never succeeded in displacing earlier custom.

9. See Alain Faure, *Paris Carême-prenant* (Paris, 1978) , 47–54, on elite balls and 25 and 128 on *boeuf gras* at Paris in the nineteenth century.

10. Ibid., 63, 96–97, 66–68.

11. Henry Rightor's collectively written *Standard History of New Orleans* (Chicago, 1900) includes the chapter "The Carnival of New Orleans" by Rightor himself and also an important further section about Carnival in "The Amusements of New Orleans" by B. R. Forman. See the books by Delaney, Higginbotham, and Reynolds in the Bibliography concerning Mobile's history, as well as the books by Dean, DeLeon, and Rayford, entirely devoted to Mobile's Carnival.

12. The New Orleans figures were cited by James McLain in "Behind the Mask: the Future of Mardi Gras," taped round-table discussion at New Orleans Public library, May 31, 1977, on deposit at the New Orleans Public library. The six-million-dollar total was suggested by an article in the *Azalea City News and Review,* Mobile, Alabama, for February 26, 1981, p. 4. Dean, *Mardi Gras,* 168, cites the figure for the Mobile Carnival societies. Munro Edmondson, "Carnival in New Orleans," *Caribbean Quarterly,* 4 (1956), 240, gives the estimate of fifty-percent participation.

13. Only those truck organizations associated with the Elks Krewe of Orleanians and the Krewe of Crescent City are allowed to parade along the St. Charles Avenue route after the Rex parade. (The word "krewe," a synonym for "Carnival society," is explained on p. 117.) But all over the city and its suburbs there are trucks, moving both along prearranged routes as well as haphazardly, which reflect neighborhood involvement in Carnival. Andrew Hardy, *Mardi Gras Guide,* 61, estimates the truck maskers in 1987 at 14,000.

14. Joan Martin, "Life among Black Creoles in the Early 1900's," taped lecture, New Orleans Public Library, October 9, 1980, on deposit at the New Orleans Public library: Martin's grandmother told her that their way of celebrating mardi gras in the early twentieth century was to give private masked balls. "Later on [in the 1930s?] Claiborne Avenue got to be the place where the family was taken and there had to be a picnic. It was especially a big family affair."

15. Dean, *Mardi Gras,* 196.

16. Jay Higginbotham, *Mobile, City by the Bay* (Mobile, 1968), 193, 198.

17. The tradition of holding open house for friends, if you live in one of these grand homes, is old. Margaret Lecorgne has described its importance to "uptown" white people in the l930s and its pleasantness for upperclass children of that era in Lecorgne and Elsie Martinez, *Uptown/ Downtown, Growing Up in New Orleans* (Lafayette, La., 1986), 156–58.

## Chapter 2

1. Charles Gayarré's monumental four-volume *History of Louisiana* (New York, 1854–66), although politically rather than socially focused, contains some details about social life under Vaudreuil in volume 2. Volume 2, p. 28, gives the population figures quoted in the preceding paragraph. Lyle Saxon, *Old Louisiana* (New York, 1929), 77–84, recounts the life and death of Bébé in amusing style; he does not indicate his sources and is not always reliable in other regards, as we will see. Guy Frégault's scholarly but politically focused biography of Vaudreuil, *Le Grand Marquis, Pierre de Rigaud de Vaudreuil et la Louisiane* (Montreal and Paris, 1952), devotes only a half-dozen pages to sociocultural affairs in Vaudreuil's time and does not mention Bébé. Neither Bébé nor any of the festive occasions later celebrated (Christmas, Carnival, Twelfth Night, etc.) are indicated in Bill Barron, *The Vaudreuil Papers, A Calendar and Index of the Personal and Private Records of Pierre de Rigaud de Vaudreuil* (New Orleans, 1975).

2. The document of 1781 is discussed on pp. 25–26.

3. Jay Higginbotham, *Old Mobile* (Mobile, 1977) , 108. Higginbotham cites a manuscript source for his information, but does not quote it directly.

4. See Caldwell Delaney, *Remember Mobile* (Mobile, 1948), 34–35 and 41–42, for the epidemic and the eventual change of the site of the Mobile River settlement. Bernard Reynolds, *Sketches of Mobile from 1814 to the Present Time* (Mobile, 1868), 6, gives the population in 1704 as consisting of 180 soldiers, 11 Indian slaves, and 27 "families."

5. Julian Rayford, *Chasin' a Devil Round a Stump* (Mobile, 1962), 25. Nicholas L'Anglois was a soldier at Fort Louis de la Louisiane. Higginbotham, *Old Mobile,* 218 and 422, cites contemporary documents to this effect.

6. A convenient chronological summary of the history of New Or-

leans is Martin Siegel, *New Orleans, a Chronological and Documentary History* (Dobbs Ferry, New York, 1975). Gayarre's *History*, vol. 1, treats these eighteenth-century events in detail.

7. Gayarré, *History*, 2: 28, and 3: 170, gives the Mobile figures. Virginia Dominguez, *White by Definition: Social Classification in Creole Louisiana* (New Brunswick, New Jersey, 1986), 116–17, gives a table of populations of New Orleans, for the most part every ten years, which distinguishes black and white and slave and free between 1721 and 1970.

8. William Bartram, *Travels in North and South Carolina* (New Haven, 1958; first published 1791), 256.

9. Liliane Crété, *Daily Life in Louisiana, 1815–30* (Baton Rouge, 1978), 76.

10. Dominguez, *White by Definition*, 101–2.

11. These and the preceding figures are from Dominguez, *White by Definition*, 116. Rightor, *Standard History*, includes an interesting chapter on the development of sugar-cane exploitation near New Orleans: "The Origin and Evolution of the Sugar Industry of Louisiana" by W. C. Stubbs.

12. Berquin-Duvallon, *Vue de la colonie espagnole du Mississippi* (Paris, 1803), 34, 284.

13. Dominguez, *White by Definition*, 116.

14. The French "Black Code" of 1724 is reprinted in Siegel, *New Orleans*, 63–65. See Dominguez, *White by Definition*, 24–25, on Spanish leniency.

15. When in 1824 Mobile's elite subsidized the construction of the first theater in the city, it was arranged, like those already built in New Orleans, so that the "colored population" might occupy only the upper tier. But this upper tier, writes the manager of the first theatrical troupe in that city, was "subdivided so as to accomodate a certain class of them known as 'quadroons,' who, having a portion of white blood in their veins, would not condescend to mix with those that had purely negro blood, and whom they looked upon as an inferior class." Noah Ludlow, *Dramatic Life as I Found It* (St. Louis, 1880; reprint, Bronx, New York, 1966), 265. The emotional dynamics of this twisted situation for both whites and free blacks are skillfully portrayed in Ann Rice's novel, *The Feast of All Saints* (New York, 1979), set in New Orleans during the 1840s. On quadroons see also n. 21 below.

16. Perry Young, *The Mistick Krewe: Chronicles of Comus and His Kin* (New Orleans, 1931), 32, quotes the *Louisiana Gazette* of March, 1824 (Young does not give a precise date or page number).

17. The reference to 1805 occurs in a memoir written in 1840 by the lawyer and judge Thomas Nicholls concerning his arrival at New Orleans in January 1805, at the age of seventeen. This passage of the memoir is published in Saxon, *Old Louisiana*, 109: "The eternal jabbering of French in the street was a sealed book to us. Drums beat occasionally at the corners of the streets, suspended for a moment to allow the worthy little drummer to inform the public that on such and such a night there would be a Grand Ball at the *Salle de Condé*, or make announcement of a ball of another sort, for colored ladies and white gentlemen. Such were our visions of New Orleans in 1805."

18. I quote Young's paraphrase of the Cabildo document in *Mistick Krewe*, 17.

19. Young, *Mistick Krewe*, 18n., here quotes directly from Cabildo documents. According to Henry Kmen, *Music in New Orleans: The Formative Years 1791–1841* (Baton Rouge, 1966), 53, slave attendance at free-black balls continued until 1862 and the end of slavery; in 1834 fifty of seventy-five blacks arrested at a free-black ball were slaves.

20. Quoted in Albert Fossier, *New Orleans of the Glamour Period 1800–1840* (New Orleans, 1957), 359.

21. Quadroons were young women who were supposed to have not more than one-fourth African "blood." They were schooled by parents and friends in dancing and polite conversation with a view to acquiring the favor of rich white men, unmarried or married, who would set them up as mistresses. While the quadroon balls were on the surface a place of interracial contact in which white males did honor to black women, their motivating fantasies exploited sexual slavery similar to that exercised elsewhere by the plantation master. Quadroon balls were also held at other times than Carnival. Henry Kmen, *Music in New Orleans*, 42ff., gives a good description of them, documenting their licensed existence from November 1805 (Tessier's ballroom). Within a few years a half dozen ballrooms offered quadroon balls every day of the week and gradations of price had been introduced, as well as the subscription-ball device, so as to make some of them very distinguished affairs (ibid., 47, 51). There is a superb description of the elegant dress of the quadroons in the early 1800s in Thomas Ashe, *Travels in America* (London, 1808), reprinted in Etolia Basso, ed., *The World from Jackson Square* (New York, 1948), 89–90.

22. Fossier, *New Orleans*, 359.

23. Ibid., 362–63.

24. Siegel, *New Orleans*, 5.

25. Crété, *Daily Life*, 219–20.

26. Rightor, *Standard History*, 466. Young, *Mistick Krewe*, 30, gives the date as 1816, not 1813.

27. Many travelers spoke of the commercialism of the city. By the 1840s it became custom to contrast Creole "laziness" or "love of leisure" with Anglo-American bustle. See Abraham O. Hall's *The Manhattan in New Orleans* (New York, 1851), 23, speaking of his visit in the mid-1840s: "'Work, work, work,' is the unceasing cry. . . Except among the Creoles—the aborigines of the place—a man of leisure is a wonder."

28. Benjamin Latrobe, *The Diary and Miscellaneous Papers* (New Haven, 1984), 183.

29. As explained in chapter 3, Mobile's destiny, too, was to serve as a commercial center, an entry-and-exit point for a vast agricultural productivity. Mobile bloomed only in the 1830s. In the first year of that decade the city counted only 3,194 souls (Reynolds, *Sketches*, 22).

30. Latrobe, *Diary*, 182–83.

31. Claiborne's letter is reprinted in Siegel, *New Orleans*. Claiborne wrote on January 31, 1804. Mardi gras was February 14.

32. Quoted in Lynn Thorndike, *University Records and Life in the Middle Ages* (New York, 1944), 345.

33. See Roy Strong, *Splendor at Court: Renaissance Spectacle and Illusion* (London, 1973).

34. Quoted in Young, *Mistick Krewe*, 34.

35. Fredrika Bremer, *Homes of the New World: Impressions of America* (New York, 1853), 2:319.

36. Franklin Knight, *The Caribbean: Genesis of a Fragmented Nationalism* (New York, 1978), 65. Knight makes many of the points alluded to in my text, as for example: "However long the elite remained physically *in situ*, they were psychologically transients, with a myopic confusion of social order and productive efficiency. The most enduring and sometimes the most interesting features of the society were created by the lower classes, who were often told what they could not do but rarely what they ought to do."

37. Charles Summersell, *Mobile, History of a Seaport Town* (Tuscaloosa, Alabama, 1949), 3–30, reconstructs the early history of Mobile after it became American territory, and cites these population statistics.

38. See J. G. Stedman, *Narrative of a Five Years' Expedition Against the Revolted Negroes of Surinam* (1796) reprinted in Roger Abrahams and John Szwed, eds., *After Africa: Extracts from British Travel Accounts and Journals* (New Haven, 1983), 285. The same practice of dancing through the weekend is reported for Jamaica in the 1820s by H. T. De la Beche, *Notes on the Present Conditions of the Negroes in Jamaica*, reprinted in Abrahams and Szwed, *After Africa*, 302.

39. Kmen, *Music*, 226, refers to the 1786 law. In his article, "The Roots of Jazz and the Dance in Place Congo: A Reappraisal," *Yearbook for Inter-American Musical Research* 8 (1972), 9, Kmen quotes the ordinance of 1817. Dena Epstein, *Sinful Tunes and Spirituals* (Urbana, Ill., 1977), 93, quotes the ordinance of 1808.

40. Epstein, *Sinful Tunes*, 84. I, not the anonymous traveller, identify the dates he gives as falling midway in Catholic Lent (mid-Lent Sunday, the fourth Sunday in Lent, was the occasion of a revival of Carnival in many European locales).

41. Kmen, *Music*, 227.

42. Latrobe's religious background was certainly not Catholic. He makes no entry in his diary on mardi gras—an omission also testifying to the relative unimportance of the day itself in 1819, since his diary is so fulsome and so interested in cultural matters. On Ash Wednesday he sets down a number of general remarks about slavery, never mentioning the religious significance of the day.

43. Benjamin Latrobe, *Journals*, ed. E. Carter, J. Van Horne, and Lee Formwalt (New Haven, 1980), 3:203. Emphasis Latrobe's.

44. "The allowed amusements of Sunday have, it seems, perpetuated here, those of Africa among its inhabitants. I have never seen anything more brutally savage, and at the same time dull and stupid than this whole exhibition." Latrobe, *Journal*, 204. The quotations in the following paragraph are all from this same page of Latrobe's journal.

45. Kmen, "Roots," 10.

46. That is, people classified as white, part-white, or fully African.

47. Georges Joyaux, "Forest's Voyage aux Etats-Unis de l'Amerique en 1831," *Louisiana History Quarterly* 39 (1956), 468.

48. Timothy Flint, *Recollections of the Last Ten Years . . . in the Valley of the Mississippi* (Boston, 1826) , 140. Emphasis added. Flint introduces his remarks in a gently philosophic manner: "I have often contrasted the savages, in all these respects, with the negroes, and it has seemed to me that they were the two extremes of human nature brought together. . . . To the Indian, stern, silent, moody, ruminating existence seems a burden. To the negro, remove only pain and hunger, it is naturally a state of enjoyment. As soon as his burdens are laid down, or his

toils for a moment suspended, he sings, he seizes his fiddle, he dances. When their days are passed in continued and severe toil, their nights,— for like the cats and owls they are nocturnal animals,—are passed in wandering about from plantation to plantation, in visiting, feasting, and conversation" (139–40).

49. Ibid., 140. Nothing in Flint's book indicates that he knew anything about the black governors and kings in New England states where on festive occasions a remotely similar figure appeared, as discussed on pp. 43–45.

50. A good account of the New Orleans institution of "jazz funerals" is in Danny Barker and Jack Buerkle, *Bourbon Street Black* (Oxford and New York, 1973), 187–97.

51. See F. Flugel, "A Voyage Down the Mississippi in 1817," *Louisiana Historical Quarterly* 7 (1924), 432. Flugel presents an edition of the diary of J. G. Fluegel in this article.

52. Quoted in Epstein, *Sinful Tunes*, 95. The reference to the women's rich silk, gauze, etc., dresses matches Thomas Ashe's comments on the elegant and brightly gleaming quadroon costumes (see n. 21 above). What is seen as "oriental" was instead an adaptation of African taste.

53. Pierre Laussat, *Mémoires sur ma Vie, à Mon Fils* (Pau, 1831), 394– 95. This book is extremely rare. There is a copy in the Tulane University Library's Special Collections. The French original may be of interest to those doing research on Afro-American culture: "Hier, mercredi des cendres, j'ai visité, en compagnie de MM. Perpigna et Henri, un de ces *bamboulas de rivière,* où les negres sont dans l'usage d'aller faire leurs adieux au carnaval.

"Le *bamboula* de cette année avait lieu à la *rivière des Pères,* audessus du *canal du moulin à sucre de l'habitation Thoumazeau.* Les deux rives sont hautes et escarpèes. Le ruisseau y forme plusieurs anses et plusieurs îles. Des foules de negres et negresses y étaient éparpillées par groupes. Les uns dansant des *bamboulas,* les autres des *contredanses,* et d'autres se régalaient autour de nappes couverts de gros mets et de sausses noires.

"D'aigres flageolets et un bruissement sourd, mêlés d'éclats de rire et d'éclats de voix, animaient la scène et l'annonçaient de loin.

"Il y avait nombre de curieux, dont une trentaine à cheval, repandus parmi les sentiers et les rochers."

54. Médéric Moreau de Saint-Méry, *Description topographique, physique . . . et historique de la partie française de l'isle Saint-Domingue* (Philadelphia and Paris, 1797), 1:44–45.

55. George W. Cable, "The Dance in Place Congo," *Century Magazine,* 31 (1886), 523–24.

56. Henry Kmen, "Roots," 13–14, summarizes a memoir published in the New Orleans *Daily Picayune,* October 12, 1879, about Congo Square dancing "sixty years ago"—that is, in 1819—along the lines which Cable embellished in his magazine piece. To this description may be added an account published after Cable's article which gives still another eyewitness view of Congo Square, in this case dating from the 1830s, Henry Castellanos' *New Orleans as it Was* (New Orleans, 1895; reprint New Orleans, 1978), 157–60. Castellanos emphasizes the multiple uses of the spot. It was the place of public executions, balloon ascensions, "the chosen ground for popular exhibitions" and above all of circus performance, so much so that it was also called Circus Square. As

for the black dancing, "White people, from motives of curiosity or fun, invariably attended these innocent pastimes," but on the other hand *"nègres 'Mericains* were not invited. There was no affinity between them." The French-Creole/American split among blacks, which was in evidence elsewhere, apparently also pervaded this spot.

57. Lafcadio Hearn, "The Scenes of Cable's Romances," *Century Magazine*, 27 (1883–84), 45. Hearn and Cable were close at this time, although they later fell out. Hearn wrote about this same backyard bamboula on two other occasions, as Kmen shows in "Roots," 12–13. With reference to Hearn's use of the word "convulsive" and Cable's reference to "frenzy," one should note that some nineteenth-century black dancing in New Orleans, especially in locales concealed from the public, almost certainly was concerned to produce trance-states, insofar as it was related to vodun ("voodoo") rituals whose presence there is well authenticated. See further, n. 29, chap. 6.

58. Quoted by Thomas M. Fiehrer, "The African Presence in Colonial Louisiana: An Essay on the Continuity of Caribbean Culture," in *Louisiana's Black Heritage*, ed. Robert Macdonald, John Kemp, Edward Haas (New Orleans, 1979), 25–26, from C. M. Chambon, *In and Around the Old St. Louis Cathedral of New Orleans* (New Orleans, 1908).

59. Joyaux, "Forest's Voyage," 469. My translation is an adaptation of the looser French translation of the Creole words, in Hélène Allain, *Souvenirs d'Amérique et de France* (Paris, 1883), 167 (where Allain erroneously attributes the song to a Haitian composer in about the year 1840). The French jargon term in Haiti for a mulatto slightly darker than a quadroon was *griffe* (masculine) or *griffonne* (feminine), according to Moreau de Saint-Méry, *Description*, 1:72.

60. Epstein, *Sinful Tunes*, 94, mentions the connection between Rousseau's song and the 1811 publication, but does not know about Forest's reference to it or the republication in the 1850s.

61. Lyle Saxon, Edward Dreyer, and Robert Tallant, *Gumbo Ya-Ya, A Collection of Louisiana Folk Tales* (Boston, 1945), 240–41.

62. Jean-Baptiste Labat, *Nouveau Voyage aux Isles de l'Amérique* (The Hague, 1724), 2:154–58.

63. See Moreau de Saint-Méry, *Description topographique*, 1:45. Emmanuel Paul, *Panorama du folklore haitien* (Port-au-Prince, 1962) , 56–64, explains the difference between Labat's account and Moreau's by pointing out that Labat visited Haiti after passing much time in the Windward Islands. Therefore when he saw the hip-twisting dance in Haiti he assumed that it was called the same thing there as it was further south in the Caribbean. This may be true. On the other hand nearly a century separates Labat's observations from Moreau's, ample time for evolution in the dance postures or for shifting of the names of dances to occur. The calinda was also mentioned by Antoine Le Page du Pratz in his *History of Louisiana* (London, 1763), 387, as part of blacks' plantation festivities in Louisiana in the 1730s. Le Page du Pratz came to Louisiana in 1718. He was a planter there sixteen years. He published his *History of Louisiana* in Paris in 1758, and it was translated into English in 1763. He mentions "Calinda or the dance"—thus seeming to employ it as a generic term for all forms of the blacks' Sunday dancing—as a mischievous practice to be discouraged among slaves. Carl Brasseaux, "The Administration of Slave Regulations in French Louisiana, 1724–1766,"

*Louisiana History* 21 (1980), 144–45, provides further references (non-descriptive ones) to the *calinda* in Louisiana in 1751, 1755, and 1764.

64. Peter Marsden, *An Account of the Island of Jamaica* (Newcastle, 1788), in Abrahams and Szwed, *After Africa*, 230.

65. Kmen, *Music*, 26–28, recounts several amusing stories about the intense attachment of the French and the non-French to their respective versions of the quadrille; this attachment is what so puzzled Governor Claiborne in 1804 when he wrote to James Madison (see p. 28).

66. A. C. Carmichael, *Domestic Manners and Social Conditions of the West Indies* (London, 1833), quoted in Abrahams and Szwed, *After Africa*, 256.

67. Laussat, *Mémoires*, 394.

68. Abrahams and Szwed, *After Africa*, 249–50. Several other writers commented on this "saturnalian equality" and parodic daring at Christmas celebrations on the islands of Jamaica, Saint Vincent, and Barbados in the first half of the nineteenth century. See ibid., 256, 257, 315.

69. Dr. J. G. Wurdemann, *Notes on Cuba* (Boston, 1844), 113–14.

70. Ibid., 83–84.

71. Roger Bastide, *African Civilizations in the New World* (London, 1971), 7–10.

72. Ibid., 182. There are obvious difficulties with this. Which slaves in the New World came via Europe, and how and why would they gain ascendancy over newly arrived Africans, so as to impose their Afro-European custom? Bastide's authority on this point is Fernando Ortiz, "Los cabildos afro-cubanos," *Revista bimestre cubana* 16, no. 1 (1921), 5–39. Ortiz quotes a chronicle written in the 1470s in Seville, Spain, to show that blacks were permitted to hold dances and festivals in Seville, perhaps as early as 1390. However, Ortiz's first evidence of black societies called cabildos in Spain dates from 1601, and is cited from a secondary source. His first evidence of black societies in the New World is from the "eighteenth century" in Peru, again from a secondary source. The latter claims that public processions of black cabildos were led by an elected queen, luxuriously dressed, accompanied by her court, male musicians, and women carrying candles. Ortiz does quote firsthand a Cuban edict of 1792 regulating the days and hours when "cabildos negros" were permitted to hold dances, and holding their "capataces" (captains) responsible for violations. One must conclude that African imitation in Spain or Portugal of white regal customs as the basis for their New World festive behavior has not yet been well substantiated.

73. Bastide, in ibid., makes reference to Brazil and Peru. Black royalty in the Virgin Islands is described in the 1860s by Thurlow Weed, *Letters from Europe and the West Indies* (Albany, 1866), in Abrahams and Szwed, *After Africa*, 381.

74. The fullest as well as one of the earliest documentations of what is called in present-day scholarship "Negro Election Day" occurs in an anonymous account of Rhode Island customs published by Orville Platt in his "Negro Governors," *Papers of the New Haven Colony Historical Society* 6 (1900), 323–24. Platt quotes:

> At this time (1756) there were in Newport over 1300 negroes settled inhabitants, principally slaves, besides many more, the slaves of such as had a temporary residence only. . . . Their election took place some time in June, and every negro who had a pig and sty at this time was allowed to vote. . . . They

. . . went through the ceremony of escorting the Governor [whom they had elected the previous year?] to the place appointed, which in fair weather was frequently under a large spreading tree. . . .

There is incoherence in the text at this point, for the anonymous author now says that "each *freeman* put in his ballot" whereas in a previous paragraph he notes that the election day was accorded by the "masters, who foresaw that a sort of police managed wholly by the *slaves* would be more effectual in keeping them within the bounds. . . ." The anonymous text continues:

The election declared, a general shout announced that the struggle was over—and here, contrary to the masters' practice, the vanquished and victors united in innocent and amusing fun and frolic—every voice upon its highest key, in all the various languages of Africa, mixed with broken and ludicrous English, filled the air, accompanied with the music of the fiddle, tambourine, the banjo, drum, etc. The whole body moved in the train of the Governor-elect, to his master's house, where, on their arrival a treat was given by the gentlemen newly elected, which ended the ceremonials of the day.

Whether before or after the libation at the master's house (the time is unclear), the author states in a previous paragraph that "they amused themselves with personal rencounters etc., such as cudgelling, jumping, wrestling, playing at the various games, and on the musical instruments of their native country; besides dancing, fiddling, and drinking."

Besides these festive activities the governors supervised the discipline of black people who were deemed to have violated local mores. Platt provides a number of instances of this. Thus Wurdemann's observation of the policing function of the tribal kings in Cuba was correct and was repeated elsewhere.

Platt's point of view is local and antiquarian. Joseph Reidy's "'Negro Election Day' and Black Community life in New England, 1750–1860," *Marxist Perspectives* 1, no. 3 (Fall 1978) , 102–17, emphasizes the political and social significance of these festivities for the evolution of Afro-American life in the United States, while Aimes, "African Institutions in America," *Journal of American Folklore* 18 (1905), 15–25, views the same instances from an international and anthropological point of view.

75. James Eights, "Pinkster Festivities in Albany Sixty Years Ago," *Collections on the History of Albany* (Albany, 1867), in Abrahams and Szwed, *After Africa*, 381. The black celebration was forbidden by city ordinance in 1811. Shane White, "Pinkster: Afro-Dutch Syncretization in New York City and the Hudson Valley," *Journal of American Folklore* 102 (1988–89), 68, cites an anonymous description of the same events as Eights describes which was written much closer to their performance (White cites their reprint in a newspaper of 1803, but does not establish the date of their original publication, presumably only a few years before 1803). This description provides several details about the dress of the musicians ("decorated with feathers and cow tails," ibid., 69) and movements of the dancers (males and females performed "most lewd and indecent gesticulation, at the crisis of which the parties meet and embrace in a kind of amorous Indian hug") which parallel those of the descriptions of Afro-American festive behavior at New Orleans which we have already or will later consider. White, 71–73, skillfully shows the Albany blacks' amalgamation of Dutch, Anglo-American, Indian, and

African elements into a unique festive whole, and plausibly hypothesizes that this synthesis took place only toward the end of the eighteenth century. The New York state legislature passed a law in 1799 providing for the gradual abolition of slavery, which helps authenticate the date of this festivity.

76. Aimes, "African Institutions," 16–19.

77. Fredrika Bremer, *Homes*, 2: 379. Eva Meyerowitz, *The Sacred State of the Akan* (London, 1951), gives a ceremonially oriented account of a state in West Africa in which the queen mother is the supreme political authority. See n. 72 above for an eighteenth-century Peruvian cabildo headed by a queen. Bremer does not mention the "captains" of the Cuban cabildos in the edict of 1792, which are referred to again in edicts of 1835 and 1842 (Ortiz, "Los Cabildos," 20–21); perhaps the captains were the same as those Bremer called kings.

78. Bremer, *Homes*, 2: 380–81.

79. Wurdemann, *Notes*, 83–84.

80. Abrahams and Szwed refer to the West African *susu* institution in *After Africa*, 8–9, and indicate the sociological literature. Daniel Crowley briefly describes its working in Florida, the Bahamas, and Trinidad in "American Credit Institutions of Yoruba Type," *Man* 53 (1953), 80.

81. Leon Beauvallet, *Rachel and the New World: A Trip to the United States and Cuba* (New York, 1856), 364.

82. One of the earliest European reports concerning an Afro-American festive dancer concurs exactly with Bremer's interpretation. Edward Long, *History of Jamaica* (London, 1774), 2: 424, describes the black dancing which he observed while resident in Jamaica over a long period from the mid-eighteenth century: "Their tunes for dancing are usually brisk. . . . The female dancer is all languishing, and easy in her motions; the man, all action, fire, and gesture; his whole person is variously turned and writhed every moment, and his limbs agitated with such lively exertions, as serve to display before his partner the vigor and elasticity of his muscles."

83. Frederick Cassidy, *Jamaica Talk: Three Hundred Years of the English Language in Jamaica* (London, 1961), 256–59, reviews a variety of interpretations of "John Canoe," before seeming to conclude, on linguistic grounds (without actually saying so), in favor of an interpretation which derives them from words in the African Ewe language meaning "sorcerer-man or witch-doctor" (259).

84. Anonymous article, "Characteristic Traits of the Creolian and African Negroes in this Island. . . ," in *The Columbia Magazine; or Monthly Miscellany* (Kingston, Jamaica) for 1797, as reprinted in Abrahams and Szwed, *After Africa*, 233.

85. Long, *History of Jamaica*, 2: 424.

86. French *quête* means, literally, "quest"; the Halloween custom of "trick or treat" is a form of quete. The French word has been internationalized by folklorists. See also n. 37, chap. 6.

87. "Characteristic Traits," 233.

88. Ibid. The author contrasts these stewards with John Canoe's accompaniment in his "former unpolished state." Then his attendants were "a great number of negroes, beating old canisters, or pieces of metal, singing "ay, ay, John Canoe. . . ."

89. Michael Scott, *Tom Cringle's Log* (Edinburgh and London, 1881; but

first published as a magazine serial, 1829–33), 109; also reprinted in Abrahams and Szwed, *After Africa*, 237.

90. "Characteristic Traits," 234.

91. Long, *History of Jamaica*, 2: 425.

92. "Characteristic Traits," 234.

93. Matthew Lewis, *Journal of a West Indian Proprietor* (London, 1834), 56.

94. M. Scott, *Tom Cringle's Log*, 108–9.

95. James Phillippo, a Baptist minister in Jamaica from 1822 to 1842, contrasted city and country "public holidays": "On such occasions each of the African tribes upon the different estates formed itself into a distinct party, composed of men, women, and children. Each party had its King or Queen, who was distinguished by a mask of the most hideous appearance, and attired from head to foot in gaudy harlequin-like apparel. They paraded or gambolled in their respective neighborhoods, dancing. . . ." James Phillippo, *Jamaica, Its Past and Present State* (London, 1843), 242. What Phillippo reported as "hideous" and "harlequin-like" was probably commonplace African festive apparel. Phillippo's account of the town processions of John Canoe is copied from Long, and it is unclear whether he was an eyewitness. In any case, kings and queens are absent from Long's account. They are also absent from the town celebrations described by Matthew Lewis, *Journal*, 50–58 and 73–75. Lewis points out a certain competition in grotesqueness among the John Canoes in town, which would have had less meaning in small-town or rural situations where tribal affiliations were still strong: "A little wag of a negro boy whipped . . . up [a portion of another John Canoe's costume], clapped it upon his head, and performed the part of an impromptu Mr. John-Canoe with so much fun and grotesqueness that he fairly beat the original performers out of the pit, and carried off all the applause of the spectators, and a couple of my dollars." Lewis shows that these performances were less articulated by Afro-American rituals than by commercial considerations: "The John Canoes are fitted out at the expense of the rich negroes, who afterwards share the money collected from the spectators during their performance. . . ."(75).

96. They may have come to North Carolina via the Bahama Islands, where there was a John Canoe as early as 1701, according to Ira De A. Reid, "The John Canoe Festival," *Phylon* 3 (1942), 353. Reid does not footnote this or other materials in this article on the North Carolina tradition, but he does provide a bibliography and a cursory list of archives in which he worked. John Canoe troupes are numerous today at Nassau and other towns in the Bahamas during the Christmas season, where the old festival has been adapted to modern tourism. "With the thumping of goatskin drums, the jangling of herd bells, the clarion of horns, whistles and other noisemakers . . . , Junkanoo [sic] is launched early in the morning of Dec. 26. Some revelers are "scrappin'—riotous folk garbed in scraps of cloth and paper. Others seriously compete for prizes . . . with costumes that represent months of work with crepe paper, wire, glue and extreme skill. Singly or in groups, participants cavort, dance and strut through streets. . . ." Activities culminate in a second parade in the wee hours of New Year's Day. "Though archivists trace these revels to the 1700s, the word *junkanoo* first appears in the 1950s. Before then, the celebrations were tied to the season, and starred

Johnny Canoe—a famous folk hero among West African slaves in the Bahamas. . . . Whether he ever existed . . . is moot." Dianne N. Lawes, *Fisher Annotated Travel Guides: Bahamas 1984* (New York, 1984), 4.

97. Dougald MacMillan, "John Kuners," *Journal of American Folklore* 39 (1926), 54.

98. On the variations in East Coast black people's autonomy and assimilation of white culture, see Ira Berlin, "Time, Space, and the Evolution of Afro-American Society," *American Historical Review* 85 (1980), 44–78, and Berlin's book, *Slaves without Masters* (New York, 1974).

99. See further on John Canoe in chapter 6 below.

100. Beauvallet, *Rachel*, 364–65. The word "holes" may be a misprint for "halls"; written by hand, the two words would appear very similar.

101. Could this be an evocation of a leopard, frequently used as a symbol of African royal power? Bremer, *Homes*, 2: 382, seated between the two youthful queens of the Cabildo de Gangas at Havana, saw this: "On the wall opposite to us was a large and well-painted leopard, probably the symbol of the nation."

102. These are probably the "Moko Jumbie" dancers, definitely of African derivation, who have a long history in the Caribbean. They were noted in the 1790s in Trinidad (Errol Hill, *Trinidad Carnival* [Austin, Texas, 1972], 12), where they might still be observed in the 1950s. D. Crowley, "The Traditional Masques of Carnival," *Caribbean Quarterly* 4 (1955–56), 208, provides a sketch of them in the 1950s. They were also observed at Saint Vincent in the 1840s and in British Guyana in the 1890s (Abrahams and Szwed, *After Africa*, 315, 327).

103. Xavier Marmier, *Lettres sur L'Amérique* (Paris, 1851), 2: 40–42.

104. The Trinidad maskers and their parallels to Gulf Coast figures are discussed in chapters 6 and 7.

105. There are helpful chapters on the latter kinds of Afro-American rituals in Abrahams and Szwed, *After Africa*.

106. James Creecy arrived in New Orleans in October 1834, and stayed about two months. He seems to have returned to the city in early 1835 and to have seen the Carnival. His account of his travels was not published until after his death. For the quotations here, see his *Scenes in the South* (Philadelphia, 1860), 21–23.

107. See Hill, *Trinidad Carnival*, and Monica Rector, "The code and message of carnival: 'Escolas-de-Samba,'" in *Carnival*, ed. Thomas Sebeok (Berlin and New York, 1984).

Chapter 3

1. See Liliane Crété, *Daily Life*, 266, for brief reference to Epiphany celebrations in the early nineteenth century. Fossier, *New Orleans*, 462, associates the same customs with New Year's Day in the New Orleans of this period.

2. Charles Baskerville, "Dramatic Aspects of Medieval Folk Festivals in England," *Studies in Philology* 17 (1920), 36, refers to thirteenth-, fourteenth-, and sixteenth-century documentation of the *Rex Fabae* in England, France, and Scotland. See further A. A. Bernardy, "Il 'rey de la Faba,'" *Studi medievali*, n.s., 3 (1928), 522, for an instance in Aragon in 1480.

3. During James I's reign Twelfth Night (January 6) was the most common date chosen for elaborate Christmas entertainment at court. Ben Jonson wrote nine masques for presentation before the king on that

date, as compared with only three for presentation on or about Shrove Tuesday and only six for presentation at any other time during the winter festive season (December–March). One of Jonson's masques was called "Christmas His Masque." Presented sometime during the twelve days of Christmas, 1616–17, it included in its allegorical cast a character described thus: "Baby Cake. Dressed like a boy, in a fine long coat, big-gin, bit, muckender, and a little dagger; his usher bearing a great cake with a bean and a peas [sic]." In Jonson's time the pea was hidden in a second piece of cake; the person receiving it was "queen": this part of the custom is not documented at New Orleans.

In today's "king's cake" at New Orleans the cake contains no bean but instead a tiny plastic male baby doll. Is this the Christ-child, recognized as king by the three magi, is it Baby New Year, as seems to be symbolized by "Baby Cake" in Jonson's masque, or is it both? See Ben Jonson, *The Complete Masques*, ed. Stephen Orgel (New Haven, 1969)

4. Young, *Mistick Krewe*, 16–17. The only document which Young offers to support his idea and dating of the *bals du roi* is a poem published in a New Orleans newspaper in 1828 about them, which furthermore does not refer to this method of selection.

5. Twelfth Night is documented from the fifteenth century in some European locales as the beginning of the Carnival season. The pseudo-monarch chosen to reign over that day was often dubbed a "lord of misrule" and was in some cases the leader of a "joyous society" (*société joyeuse*) dedicated to organizing Carnival fun during the ensuing period. See Emmanuel Le Roy Ladurie, *Le Carnaval de Romans* (Paris, 1979), 294–304, for such societies in southern France between the fourteenth and seventeenth centuries, and more generally Natalie Davis, "The Reasons of Misrule: Youth Groups and Charivaris in Sixteenth-Century France," *Past and Present* 50 (February 1971), 41–75.

6. James Alexander, *Transatlantic Sketches* (London, 1833), 237.

7. See Christian Schultz, Jr., *Travels on an Inland Voyage Through the [United] States* . . . , II (New York, 1810), 60–61: "February 1, 1808. . . . They have, however, a very pretty practice of introducing their balls at the commencement of the carnival [presumably the festive season following Twelfth Night]. . . . Two or three ladies make arrangements with their male friends for the first ball, during which two or more elegant bouquets are presented by the ladies to as many gentlemen; this piece of ceremony raises the select number to the rank of kings. . . . The gentlemen then each make choice of a favorite lady, to whom with great politeness they present their bouquets: this mark of distinction likewise raises the favored ladies to the rank of queens. . . . This ceremony having passed, it becomes the duty of the royal parties to give the next ball. . . ."

8. The system is described in detail later in this book.

9. Dominguez, *White by Definition*, 116–17.

10. As ibid. shows at length, the term "Creole" before 1840 referred to blacks and whites born in Louisiana without distinction of nationality or race. After 1840 the term was gradually redefined by whites to exclude descendants of people with any fraction of African blood. Many blacks then developed the term "Creole" to refer to descendants of persons with any element of French or Spanish ancestry and/or persons manumitted from slavery before the Civil War.

11. Ibid., 127. See also 112–19 and 130–32.

12. The phrase is Richard Wade's in his *Slavery in the Cities: The South 1820–1860* (New York, 1964), 245.

13. Kaye De Metz, "Theatrical Dancing in Nineteenth-Century New Orleans," *Louisiana History* 21 (1980): 35–37.

14. Kmen, "The Roots of Jazz," 13–14, skillfully proves that Congo Sguare dancing ended in the 1840s, against those who have claimed that the dancing continued as late as the 1880s or 1890s.

15. By "conjuncture" I mean a set of evolving circumstances which have combined to create a characteristic situation of relatively short duration, from one to a dozen years. The three sets of circumstances mentioned here, demographic, political, and sociocultural, changed at different rates of speed over time, but they knotted together in the 1830s to create a particular situation, a combined set of circumstances which stimulated the disparate Carnival impulses and activities to coalesce and take lasting form.

16. Young, *Mistick Krewe*, 31.

17. Ibid., 40. Kmen, *Music in New Orleans*, 34, cites an amusing regulation of 1834 which shows the lengths to which controlling racial contravention pushed the city fathers: "ladies who may wish to go out of the ballroom, to unmask themselves, as well as such as will remain under mask, will apply for a countermask to the doorkeeper, so as to be identified by the manager, whose duty shall be to recognize masks."

18. Creecy, *Scenes*, 43–44. Was Creecy an eyewitness of this array? It should be remembered that Creecy wrote his *Scenes from the South* an undetermined number of years after his visit to New Orleans in 1834–35 (see chap. 2, n. 106). Did he add elements to this list of masks from others' later reports? One suspects this because there is no other report for seventeen years with such a panoply of exotic street costumes. See P. Young, *Mistick Krewe*, 54, for his summary indication of the grand variety of street maskers in 1852.

19. Ibid., 44–45. Giorgio Vasari describes a "Triumph of Death" float in a Florentine Carnival parade (ca. 1510) as frightening as Creecy's (see Vasari's "Life of Piero di Cosimo" in his *Lives of the Artists* [London: Everyman Library edition, 1963], 2:178–79). I have discussed similar Nuremberg examples in my "Presentation and Representation: Carnival at Nuremburg 1450–1550," *Representations*, no. 13 (Winter 1986): 5ff..

20. The first step in creation of the legend about young Creole gentlemen returned from Paris has been traced by Young, *Mistick Krewe*, 43n., to an unsigned news story in the mardi gras issue of the *New Orleans Times* in 1870; the date of their return is given there as 1835. In 1873 the *Times* added the statement quoted in the text, with its implication that street parading was imitated from Paris, this time offering the date 1837. Young points out an internal contradiction in this story, since it equates 1837 with John Davis's opening of the Orleans Ballroom, which took place in 1817. In 1885 the *Times*' statements were picked up in James Coleman's *Historical Sketchbook and Guide to New Orleans* (New York, 1885), 210, and the date changed to 1827. In that form it has been repeated in "hundreds of publications," according to Young.

21. Arthur La Cour, *New Orleans Masquerade* (New Orleans, 1957), 12, gives the following description of the *Picayune*'s account of the street parade in 1837: "The Daily Picayune mentioned the parade of boisterous 'Cowbellions' . . . . The costumes were described as outlandish and grotesque and the parade as noisy, followed by urchins, vagrants

and onlookers of other sorts." The parade was accorded no notice in the French-language press.

22. The similarity of the wording of this sentence to the fabrication in the *Times* of 1873 makes one wonder if the *Times* reporter had happened upon the *Picayune* account of 1838. The *Times* wrote in 1873: "It was in 1837. . .that a number of young Creole gentlemen organized the first grand street procession of masqueraders in New Orleans" (Young, *Mistick Krewe*, 43n.)

23. Young, *Mistick Krewe*, 42.

24. La Cour, *New Orleans Masquerade*, 12–13, not only prints the *Commercial Bulletin's* review but also portions of a review in the French-language *La Créole;* now the French press began to report events in the street.

25. Young, *Mistick Krewe*, 45.

26. In ibid., 43.

27. Louis Tasistro, *Random Shots and Southern Breezes* (New York, 1842), 2: 47 and 50.

28. Young, *Mistick Krewe*, 49. On the throwing of ashes, etc., in fifteenth-century Nuremberg, see Kinser, "Presentation," 3.

29. Kinser, "Presentation," 50n.

30. See Coleman, *Historical Sketchbook*, p. 211, on the shillelaghs. The Coleman volume was collectively written, and the section on Mardi Gras does not bear any special author's name. Was the *author* perhaps Irish, and the boys non-Irish, carrying clubs with no particular name? Whoever wrote pages 210 and 211 was an eyewitness of these street celebrations in the late 1830s and early 1840s. The anonymous writer introduces his account of these years, speaking of Carnival in 1839, with the words: "We very well remember . . . that long and brilliant cavalcade . . ." (ibid., 210).

31. Young, *Mistick Krewe*, 51, quotes Pickett's rare pamphlet, *Eight Days in New Orleans in February, 1847*.

32. Young, 53; new balls at Histrionic Hall in Nayades Street (the early name of St. Charles Avenue, according to Young) and at Empire Hall in Lafayette.

33. Faure, *Paris Carême-prenant*, 46, who cites sources from 1656 and 1727.

34. Ibid., 46–47, cites the Parisian occasions. Tobias Smollett, *Travels Through France and Italy, 1763–65*, ed. F. Felsenstein (Oxford, 1979), 155, describes Carnival subscription balls at Nice in 1763, which, to judge from Smollett's report, were somewhat less select than the corresponding New Orleans affairs.

35. Tasistro, 2: 51.

36. Faure, *Paris Carême-prenant*, 47.

37. Ibid., 47n., cites this practice as occurring "during the Restoration" at Paris (1815–30). But Auber's opera was composed in 1833. At the Paris Opera, as at the Orleans Theater in New Orleans, the parquet was raised to the stage level at the conclusion of the performance, it seems, so that the theater became a ballroom.

38. We have seen Satan in the 1835 parade described by Creecy; he appeared again in 1847 according to Pickett's *Eight Days* (cited in Young, *Mystick Krewe*, 51). The rooster is remembered in the reminiscences of the 1839 parade in Coleman, *Historical Sketchbook*, 210 (see n. 137). "We very well remember the appearance of this long and brilliant cavalcade

as it passed up St. Charles Street near Lafayette Square, one of the most conspicuous figures being an immense chicken cock, six feet high, who rode in a vehicle and whose stentorian crow as he flapped his big wings elicited cheers of admiration and applause from the crowds on the sidewalks."

39. Among the most famed Renaissance examples of elaborate floats in Carnival parades of masked figures were those of Nuremberg. See Kinser, "Presentation," 1–6. Faure, *Paris Carême-prenant*, 62–65, on the other hand, emphasizes that Carnival practice in nineteenth-century Paris was highly individualistic and antagonistic to organization.

40. See Sean Wilentz, "Artisan Republican Festivals," in Michael Frisch and Daniel Walkowitz, eds., *Working Class America* (Urbana, Ill., 1983), and Mona Ozouf, *La fête révolutionnaire 1789–99* (Paris, 1976).

41. See Faure, *Paris Carême-prenant*, 50–51, 62–65, for the Paris precedents, Tasistro, *Random Shots*, 2: 48–49, for an enthusiastic account of the masking organization known as the Bedouins in the parade of 1841, and Fossier, *New Orleans*, 456, for the remarks of Karl Postl, a German visitor to a Carnival ball at New Orleans in 1826: "Some young merchants and some planters took it into their heads to assume the character of poor paddies . . . The Creole demoiselles when addressed by their lovers had not a word to say except: 'Oh we know that you are no paddies! Oh, you are not an Irishman—you are rich Y.'"

42. Laussat, *Memoires*, 394.

43. Faure, *Paris Carême-prenant*, 64. Faure's illustrations 1–7 are helpful in establishing the atmosphere of street and ball masking in Paris Carnivals, 1800–1850.

44. Laussat, *Memoires*, 394.

45. Louis-Sébastien Mercier, *Le Tableau de Paris*, ed. J. Kaplow (Paris, 1982), 299.

46. Fossier, *New Orleans*, 459.

47. Mid-Lent developed rich symbolic and ritualistic overtones during medieval and Renaissance times. These have retained customary power in some areas, notably in Italy. See Lidia Beduschi, "La vecchia di Mezza-Quaresima," *La ricerca folclorica*, no. 7 (1981), 37–46. On the New Orleans custom in the twentieth century, see "Saint Joseph's Day," in Saxon, Dreyer, and Tallant, *Gumbo Ya-Ya*, 93–106. Kmen, *Music in New Orleans*, 30, concludes that Saint Joseph's Day balls were mainly celebrated by lower-class residents.

48. Kmen, *Music in New Orleans*, 8.

49. In 1853 de-Catholicization of Carnival was recognized publicly. The following attack on the supposed decadence of recent Mardi Gras celebrations, published in the *Daily Crescent*, combines this theme with that of Creole-American enmity:

> In the early days of our city, when it was peopled by a Catholic community who understood and could appreciate the observance of the day, Mardi Gras was a season of striking and memorable peculiarities. Then people of elevated rank took part in the processions, long lines of carriages, filled with gaily dressed masquers, troops of revelers, decked in costumes representing every nationality and filing through the streets in glittering throngs, gave to the thoroughfares a gala day brilliancy [sic] . . . But now the aspect of things has changed. Our population is not what it was. The old regime is no more.

It has fallen into the list of forgotten things, and the sway over
manners has passed to the swine-eating Saxon.

Similar views were expressed in the *Bee* and the *Daily Delta* of 1856. See
P. Young, *Mistick Krewe*, 56–58.

50. I have mislaid the precise date, page number, and secondary
source in which this quotation appeared, hastily copied down while I
was working in New Orleans libraries in 1982.

51. Quoted by P. Young, *Mistick Krewe*, 31–33: I have translated some
few words left in French by Young.

52. Quoted in ibid., 44.

53. Saxon, *Old Louisiana*, 125–27, gives both these examples. Saxon's
own writing in this book, in *Gumbo Ya-Ya*, and in *Fabulous New Orleans*
(New York, 1928), exemplifies the cultural quality described here. Saxon
does not give the month or day of the carnivalesque transvestite act of
the tight-rope dancer.

## Chapter 4

1. There are no detailed histories of nineteenth-century Mobile comparable to those by Fossier, Gayarré, Rightor, and others for New Orleans. Amiable general guidance to this era of Mobile is to be found in
Delaney, Reynolds (see n. 2 below), and Summersell, *Mobile*. The Mobile and Ohio Railroad, connecting Mobile to a point near the Ohio
River in Kentucky, was constructed between 1847 and the outbreak of
the Civil War. See Delaney, *Remember Mobile*, 151–52.

2. Delaney, *Remember Mobile*, 137, 147. Bernard Reynolds, *Sketches of
Mobile from 1814 to the Present Time*, 6, cites Mobile's winter population
in 1830.

3. See Reynolds, *Sketches*, 22, and Summersell, *Mobile*, 1–33, 39.

4. Delaney, *Remember Mobile*, 151.

5. Even the old French Fort Condé (1717) was pulled down in 1821;
on its site the first theater was constructed in 1824–25 (see chap. 2, n.
15). Of course a strong Catholic presence remained. The diocese of Mobile stretched from the Atlantic to the Mississippi through the old Spanish possessions. The engravings in Delaney's book illustrate the public
and private buildings and styles mentioned here.

Although Mobile's demographic take-off occurs only after 1830, the
*élan* preparing it is observable from the mid–1820s. Noah Ludlow, the
manager of a number of theatrical companies operating in the Mississippi River valley and particularly at Mobile, reports on the atmosphere
at Mobile during the winter of 1824–25, when the local residents built
the new theater and engaged Ludlow's company: "The winter of 1824–
5 was a very joyous one with Mobilians; business was prosperous;
people were liberal with their money, and generally disposed to enjoy
themselves. There were many delightful parties given, and much sociability prevailed generally." It seems significant that Ludlow mentions
no Carnival celebration. Instead he continues: "One of the festive occasions of the season was a grand banquet, given early in March, in honor
of the inauguration of John Quincy Adams as president of the United
States." At the end of the theatrical season in May, 1825, Ludlow reports, "three or four ladies of the company had sent to them from their
friends neat little complimentary presents of jewelry; and for myself I
was the recipient of a handsome cane mounted with gold and ivory."

See Ludlow, *Dramatic Life*, 264–65. Obviously Mobile during the winter season was the glittering residence of many prosperous planters from the surrounding areas; it was already much more than a little country town, in spite of its permanent population of less than 3,000.

6. Six accounts of the incident are mentioned by the two most detailed chronicles of the occasion, Bennett Wayne Dean's *Mardi Gras, Mobile's Illogical Whoopdedo* (Mobile, 1973), 14–17, and Julian Rayford's *Chasin' the Devil Round a Stump* (Mobile, 1962), 36–44. Four of the accounts are anonymous and uncertain in origin; they are excessively precise about a few particulars and vague about more general parameters. Another is by Louis de Vendel Chaudron, *Mobile Mystics and the Story of the Mardi Gras Societies* (Mobile, 1912), 3–4, written apparently from secondhand accounts eighty years after the event. The sixth is by one Charles Kennerly, and was written in 1870, by which time Krafft and the society he supposedly founded were famous. Kennerly knew Krafft and his associates: "I am asked, as one of the original turnout to give my recollection of the initiatory facts. I am very positive from its connection with other facts of my personal history . . . that the date was 1831. . . . I was not a member of the Christmas frolic . . . but I have given the facts as I learned them at the time, and as they have been in my memory ever since" (Rayford, *Chasin'*, 39 and 41). Although one cannot be certain of any man's forty-year-old recollections, they are the best we have and I have accordingly followed Kennerly's account, given at length in Rayford. The quotations in the text here and in following paragraphs are to be found in ibid., 39–44. The account of the Cowbellions in P. Young, *Mystick Krewe*, 64–65, is thirdhand and unreliable.

7. See, e.g., the custom as reported in Alice Earle, *Colonial Days in Old New York* (New York, 1912), 185–88.

8. See Rayford, *Chasin'*, 42, citing Kennerly: "Making our way through the crowd, which in proportion to population [ca. 3,200] was quite as dense as it is nowadays [1870: ca. 40,000]. . . ."

9. See n. 86, chap. 2, on quetes and queting. Waldemar Liungman, *Traditionswanderungen von dem Euphrat bis zum Rhein*, part 2 (Helsinki, 1938), 794–98, gives an account of the Alpine custom and also refers to the cognate furry figure of the Bulgarian *kukeri*, whose costume (illustrated in Liungman and also here, plate 33) usually includes cowbells and sometimes a kind of hoe, called the "kliunk." In German areas agricultural implements are less often used but cowbells are regularly part of the costume. Celebration here varies between Christmas, New Year's, and Carnival (ibid., 923ff.), but a belsnicle/*Pelznickel* would normally appear during the Twelve Days, and would bring some small gifts. The historical development of this particular wildman figure has not yet been worked out. See, e.g., the difficulty in separating mid-nineteenth-century *Pelz-nickel* from *Pelz-Märtle* (Saint-Martin-in-furs) in southwest German Christmas customs, as explained by Wilhelm Kutter, "Pelzmärtle und Christkindle in oberen Enztal und verwandte Gestalten," in *Ländliche Kulturformen in deutschen Sudwesten: Festschrift für Heiner Heimberger* (Stuttgart, 1971), 203–9. For the American use of cowbells, usually by German immigrants, see Richard Baumann, "Belsnickling in a Nova Scotia Island Community," *Western Folklore* 31 (1972): 234, and more generally on American belsnickling, Alfred Shoemaker, *Christmas in Pennsylvania* (Kutztown, Pa., 1959), 21 and 73–85.

10. Rayford, *Chasin'*, 44.

11. Susan Davis, *Parades and Power: Street Theater in Nineteenth-Century Philadelphia* (Philadelphia, 1986), 105.

12. Quoted in Shoemaker, *Christmas*, 77.

13. Rayford, *Chasin'*, 59, quotes the poem and other information from "the Mobile *Item*, printed in 1901," which allegedly quoted a document "from the Diard collection" about events in "the early 1850s."

14. The spirit of Mobile's citizens in 1831 was abrasively summarized by the Englishman Thomas Hamilton thus (in ibid., 47): "Mobile is a place of trade—nothing else. . . . The wealth of the Mobile merchants must accumulate rapidly, for they certainly do not dissipate it in expenditure. . . . Of amusement of any kind I heard nothing." The opinion is, of course, as partial as that of Noah Ludlow in 1825, quoted in n. 5 above. It is hard to imagine life in the still very small cotton town, swarming with avid merchants, as affording much time or place for that pleasurable leisure which was becoming the distinctive tone of New Orleans.

15. Dean, *Mardi Gras*, 18. The moral denunciation implicit in using "heathen" to modify gods and goddesses was presumably expressed with the same gay ambivalence as the New Orleans Carnival society of Comus exercised in their parade of 1857, entitled, "The *Demon* Actors in Milton's Paradise Lost" (emphasis added).

16. Ibid.

17. Ibid., 20–40, 219–21, 249–50, offers some particulars about these two societies.

18. The quotation is from the same document of 1901 as that quoted in n. 13 above, in Rayford, *Chasin'*, 59. The owl and torch presumably refer to the society's night-owl activities. Rayford, 48, says that in the early years they were often called "the Midnight Revelers."

19. Ibid., 58 (as so often, no document is quoted).

20. Bremer, *Homes*, 2: 219-20.

21. Mark Heywood [Joseph T. Wiswall], *Mr. Christopher Katydid*, 2 vols. (London, 1864), 2, 180–88.

22. See pp. 122–24 below.

23. Delaney, *Remember Mobile*, 157, makes this identification and quotes Wiswall extensively. The Strikers' emblem includes a ram rampant. See Dean, *Mardi Gras*, 249.

24. Wiswall, *Mr. Christopher Katydid*, 2: 182.

25. Richard Froning describes the social and festive functions of the Limpurg Society and those of a similar society, the Ladarum Society, in his "Die Familie Rorbach," *Archiv für Frankfurter Geschichte und Kunst*, 3d series, 2 (1888): 148–50 and 170–73.

26. On shooting in the New Year, see Esther Singleton, *Dutch New York* (New York, 1927), 301–9, and Charles D. Welch, Jr., "'Common Nuisances:' The Evolution of the Philadelphia Drummers Parade," *Keystone Folklore Quarterly* 8 (1963): 95–106.

27. In addition to the sources cited in the preceding note, see Susan Davis, *Parades and Power*, and G.M. Story, "Mummers in Newfoundland History," in Herbert Halpert and G. M. Story, eds., *Christmas Mumming in Newfoundland* (Toronto, 1969), 168–75. The history of festive custom along the eastern seaboard is obviously rich in documents. Nothing has been done to coordinate the scattered work of local historians.

28. La Cour, *New Orleans Masquerade*, 12, refers to the *Daily Picayune* report of the Mardi Gras parade in 1837, which mentioned the boister-

ous, masked Cowbellions. The same paper announced the return of the Cowbellions in 1838 on the day of mardi gras, but its report of the parade on the following day did not mention them. See Young, *Mistick Krewe*, 42.

29. Among the most famous examples of this today are the "Gilles" Carnival maskers from Binche, Belgium.

30. Young, *Mistick Krewe*, 55.

31. Ibid. Young believes that this was the second ball, following a first one by the New Orleans Cowbellions in 1852. But the newspaper quotation which he gives does not support the point. Zuma Young Salaun, *Mardi Gras Facts and Fancies* (New Orleans, 1983), [5] (pages are unnumbered in this short brochure) states without documentation that the Cowbellions held six balls in New Orleans between Christmas eve and mardi gras in 1853–54.

32. Young, *Mistick Krewe*, 45–48.

33. The names of the first nineteen members of Comus are listed in the anonymously written pamphlet history of the "krewe": *One Hundred Years of Comus* (n.d., n.p.), 6–7. A note on the verso of the title page states that it is a "reprint of a brochure issued in 1947 with emendations, additions and a rearrangement of the material as well as the list of queens and maids brought up to date." The list ends with 1955. The parade subject for 1956 is announced but not the name of queen and maids. Hence the pamphlet must have been published in early 1956 at New Orleans. Names of members of the Bedouins, etc., have not been recovered; their Creole background is my deduction.

34. See also n. 15 above, concerning the Cowbellions' parade, "Heathen Gods and Goddesses."

35. The Cowbellions seem to have teased members of the Comus society about this for many years. The costumes for Comus's first parade were borrowed from Mobile, as their informal history, *One Hundred Years*, 8, admits.

36. The reaction of Creole newspapers, however, was not very favorable, as Young, *Mystick Krewe*, 62, points out.

37. *One Hundred Years*, 7 (the Constitution), and 5.

38. Quoted by C. Goreau in his article "Mardi Gras," in Hodding Carter, ed., *The Past as Prelude: New Orleans 1718–1968* (New Orleans, 1968), 349. See in general on the difficult mid-century years, Robert Reinders, *The End of an Era: New Orleans 1850–1860* (New Orleans, 1964).

39. S. Davis, *Parades and Power*, 26–30, and 110–11, emphasizes that festive violence was specific to the maturation of a polarized class structure in Philadelphia in which chaotic economic growth, producing increased social strains, resulted in upper-class complaints about the evils of working-class social life exhibiting such violence.

40. Lewis Mumford, *The City in History* (New York, 1961), 457.

41. Carnival and/or the *idée fixe* of New Orleans as an oasis of Creole high culture are traditionally invoked by civic reformers and historians as alibis responsible for upper-class failure to address New Orleans' civic problems seriously. See the severe criticism of social relations of Joseph Tregle, "Early New Orleans Society: A Reappraisal," *Journal of Southern History* 18 (1952): 20–36. One of the best general treatments of the way in which the burgeoning industrial-capitalist system typically overtaxed cities' resources and led to avoidance rather than analysis of social problems, 1800–1850, is Louis Chevalier, *Classes laborieuses et*

*classes dangereuses à Paris pendant la première moitié du XIX^e siècle* (Paris, 1958).

42. Already by 1848 Americans were participating in the most prestigious Creole Mardi Gras balls in large numbers, as for example that at the St. Louis Hotel, according to a reporter that year. Conversely Creole couples came more and more often to the balls at the St. Charles Hotel in the Anglo-American section of town. See Reinders, *End of an Era*, 157–58.

43. The engraving is reproduced in ibid., 156.

44. Quoted in ibid., 157.

45. Young, *Mistick Krewe*, 71.

46. Quoted from the *Daily Crescent*, in *One Hundred Years*, 10.

47. It will be remembered that Wiswall reports the same five-part sequence (tableau/march/ball/whistle/banquet) for the Cowbellions in his novel published in 1864. Did Wiswall, who was a Mobilian (according to Delaney, *Remember Mobile*, 157), report observations made only in Mobile, or did he conflate the Cowbellion celebration with those of Comus which had begun in 1857? Rayford, *Chasin'*, 52, asserts that one of the six founders of Comus from Mobile was a Cowbellion. Perhaps the whole five-part sequence was already routine among Cowbellions in the 1830s or 1840s.

48. Alexis de Tocqueville, *Democracy in America* (Oxford, England: World Classics edition [abridged], 1946), 388–90 ("Public Associations").

49. *One Hundred Years*, 8.

50. See Reinders, *End of an Era*, 159, for this quotation from an article about the Boston Club in the New Orleans newspaper, *True Delta*, for May 10, 1857.

51. La Cour, *New Orleans Masquerade*, 23.

52. Mystification is as fascinating as royalty to citizens of democratic polities. In 1878 the Gulf Coast formula of a private masked ball and public parade, planned by a secret, elite society, was inaugurated in St. Louis on the same pseudo-mystic basis by Charles and Alonzo Slayback, recent emigrants from New Orleans (see chap. 5, n. 77). The name chosen for ball and parade (it survives today) was "the Veiled Prophet," a reference to the semihistorical hero of Thomas Moore's mid-Victorian Romantic poem of Persian adventure, "Lalla Rookh." The rhetoric of mystery continues to be a vital part of New Orleans Mardi Gras organizations. Two of the most prestigious Carnival societies (offering only balls, not parades) are the krewes of "Mystery" and the "Mystic Club" (see Laborde and Osborne, *Mardi Gras*, 90, 92).

53. *One Hundred Years*, 24.

54. I have alluded to this "triumph of Death" in n. 19 of chap. 3. See Vasari, *Lives of the Artists*, 2: 178–79.

55. Giuseppe Pitré, *Usi e costumi, credenze e pregiudizi del popolo siciliano* (Palermo, 1889), 1: 8n.

56. *Carnivaliana* (Paris, n.d.; advertisement inside cover dates it as 1811), 34. Translation mine. The verses are part of a long four-page poem signed by "M. Désaugiers." The reference to Comus places priority on his older function as the god of feasting, as he prepares his cooking furnace. See n. 118 below.

57. One such reverse image was to be made to ride backwards on an ass. There are many instances and many variants of this recorded from

the fourteenth century onwards. See the excellent collection of papers from a conference on charivari customs, *Le Charivari*, Jacques Le Goff and Jean-Claude Schmitt, eds., *Le Charivari* (Paris, The Hague, New York, 1981).

58. Gerald Capers, *Occupied City: New Orleans under the Federals 1862–65* (Lexington, Ky., 1965), covers this period from every point of view, economic, social, ethnic, and cultural, as well as political and military. In a concluding chapter he surveys events down to April 1877. See also John Blassingame, *Black New Orleans 1860–1880* (Chicago, 1973) from which the quotation from the *Bulletin* is taken (173).

59. There is a reproduction of Joe Cain in Chickasaw costume in Dean, *Mardi Gras*, 41.

60. Ibid., gives the names from which I deduce their Irish extraction. I emphasize the Irishness of the participants not only because it perhaps indicates the nature of the friendship tie among the participants and not only because the Irish, coming to the Gulf Coast as laborers, had long been noted for antagonism to the rival laboring blacks, but also because any Irishman, even if no longer a practicing Catholic (Cain died a Methodist), was probably aware of the meaning of Fat Tuesday before Catholic Lent.

61. Ibid.

62. See Claudie Marcel-Dubois, "Fêtes villageoises et vacarmes cérémoniels, ou une musique et son contraire," in *Les Fêtes de la Renaissance*, ed. Jean Jacquot (Paris, 1975), esp. 608–9.

63. Of course some parading continued on or near New Year's Eve. The Cowbellions paraded until 1881 at the old season. See also Dean, *Mardi Gras*, 43. The same kind of historical reduction to the dimensions of a heroic symbol has gone on with the shift from New Year's Eve to Mardi Gras as with Krafft's connection to the Cowbellions. Julian Rayford, a Mobile journalist, was especially active in this respect, instigating removal of Cain's body from its original burial place outside Mobile to the Old Church Street Cemetery in a public procession on Mardi Gras Sunday in 1967. Dean, *Mardi Gras*, 42, describes the occasion and Rayford, *Chasin'*, 65–74, develops the heroizing, inseparable from the still active resentment at northern interference. Did the civil rights movement of the 1960s have something to do with Cain's renewed popularity? Here is Rayford's concluding peroration, p. 73: "Joe Cain, sitting there in his charcoal wagon, in that year of doom for his Southland, when he and all his region had been defeated and were being ground under by Reconstruction. . . . It was . . . a delicious bit of symbolism. . . . It meant a whole people could still look up—look up in pride—and still keep going on. The faith of Joe Cain changed the old Boeuf Gras to our modern Mardi Gras. . . ." I have commented, pp. 38–39, on Rayford's supposition, without documents, that Mobile celebrated mardi gras each year from 1711 by parading a fat ox. Rayford, *Chasin'*, 73–74, also reproduces Cain's obituary in a local newspaper which asserts that Cain was a founder of the "T.D.S." (see p. 129), and that this society ceased to meet after his death.

64. Young, *Mistick Krewe*, 125.

65. Ibid., 126. The illustration appears in Edward King, "Old and New Louisiana," *Scribner's Monthly* 7 (November, 1873–April, 1874): 1–32.

66. Young, *Mistick Krewe*, 125. Darwin was sent notice of the parade. He was not, Young reports, amused (126).

67. Ibid., 85, 92.

68. The 1873 parade of the Twelfth Night Revelers was, like that of Comus in 1873, patently racist and highly political. It was called "The World of Audubon," and alluded to the members of the Louisiana state legislature, predominantly black at the time, as crows, bats, and buzzards. See ibid., 107–10.

69. Ibid., 141–49, gives a very full description of this parade. Young was an ardent Southerner and patriotic Orleanian, whose segregationist feeling is expressed at many points in his book lionizing the white Carnival societies.

70. Arthur Hardy, *Mardi Gras Guide*, 47.

71. There were a variety of other anti-Reconstruction, antiblack, and pro-Confederate expressions in the Carnival parades of the 1870s and 1880s, and no doubt even more informal expressions. In 1877 Comus's parade was entitled "The Aryan Race." In 1882 its parade of the world's religions included a group of wildly gesticulating black men, dancing before a huge wooden statue near a tree from which hang grinning skulls, to represent "Africa. Fetish Worship" (see the reproduction in La Cour, *Mardi Gras*, 20). In 1884 the "first Court" of queens and maids at a Comus ball honored the daughter of Jefferson Davis and several Confederate generals and in 1893 Winnie Davis, another daughter of the president of the Confederacy, was named queen of Comus's ball.

72. Edward King, "Old and New Louisiana," *Scribners Monthly* 7: 142 (this part 2 of King's article was published in December 1873).

73. Whether from policy or statesmanship, the solidly antiblack feeling of whites after the war was not at first solidly anti-Northern. Comus's parade of 1866 was conciliatory. Called "The Past, Present, and Future," it counseled peace and compromise as a way of burying the bitternesses produced by the conflict. Similarly in 1877 Rex's parade ("The Military Progress of the World") included as float 22 "United States and Confederate States. A camp scene, but one of amnesty. Yankee lads and Johnny Reb intermingling peacefully." This float is reproduced in J. Curtis Waldo, *History of the Carnival at New Orleans from 1857 to 1882* (New Orleans, 1882), 13 (no black troops are shown, of course).

74. Young, *Mistick Krewe*, 95–106, offers an ample account of Rex's foundation. La Cour, *New Orleans Masquerade*, 42–43, reprints words and music of the theme song, except for the verses concerning the grand duke, which I take from Laborde and Osborne, *Mardi Gras*, 56. The grand duke is not mentioned in the sheet music published at the time, but Robert Tallant, *Mardi Gras* (Garden City, 1948), 136, asserts (without a footnote identifying his source) that "some of the people in the street began to sing it, adding a parody," that is, the verses referring to Alexis and an impromptu kind of rodeo.

75. This development is obscure. Carnival as a royal fat man personifying the festival existed in literature by the thirteenth century, but he paraded in the streets only from the early sixteenth century. See Martine Grinberg and Samuel Kinser, "Les Combats de Carnaval et de Carême, Trajets d'une Métaphore," *Annales: Economies, Sociétés, Civilisations* 38 (1983): 165–98.

76. It is curious that *One Hundred Years* includes no quotations from newspapers or other sources about the appearance of Comus in the early years of the society. Even the report about the first parade of 1857, 87–9, although it says that Comus led the parade, does not quote anyone to that effect and the news reports omit him while enumerating the devils in some detail. Young, *Mistick Krewe*, 60, quotes an earlier version of *One Hundred Years*, it would seem, without a footnote identifying this source and in such a manner as to seem to quote a contemporary source citing Comus's presence. It would make more historical sense if Comus was not impersonated during the early years of the society. The club's paradigm, the Cowbellions, singled out no personification and the early idea of participation seems to have been strongly collegiate. In 1862 the fictive Comus signed a proclamation suspending his festival until the end of the Civil War (ibid., 21). In 1866 all members of Comus's tableaux carried goblets, the insignia of their idea of Comus, as will be seen later in this chapter. The year 1882, it seems, was the first one when a Comus in person met a Rex in person. There was, on the other hand, a Lord of Misrule who "reigned" at the balls of the Twelfth Night Revelers from 1870 onward.

77. See, e.g., the poems and accompanying ceremonies hailing Cologne's first Carnival monarch in modern times, the "Held Karneval" of 1823, reproduced in Joseph Klersch, *Die Kölnische Fastnacht* (Cologne, 1961), 86–88. Although "Held Karneval" means "Hero Carnival," not "King Carnival," the words of the songs sung in 1823 greet him as a monarch restored to his "old throne" after a long interval. Klersch, 18, provides a drawing of Held Carneval in 1824 with crown, scepter, and ermine cloak. The proclamation by the leader of the Bedouins in 1841 of the route which his parade would follow through New Orleans was not, on the other hand, a proclamation of Carnival sovereignty.

78. Young, *Mistick Krewe*, 99–101.

79. See ibid, 81–82, and Huber, *Mardi Gras, A Pictorial History*, 26, on the gate-crashing.

80. Waldo, *History of the Carnival*, 16.

81. Ibid., 15, 16, 28. The Oxonians were a spoof: the Ancient Order of Ox Onians, dressed as cowboys "representing the meat industry," acted as an escort to a *boeuf gras*, according to Young, *Mistick Krewe*, 114.

82. Waldo, *History of the Carnival*, 22. In view of the seething resentment of Federal "tyranny" at the time, the reference was presumably to Totila's resistance to Emperor Justinian. There is a minor historical mystery here. Following Leonard Huber, *Mardi Gras*, 38, we have reproduced in plate 8 the engraving of Rex included in King's 1873 article (see n. 72 above) as if it were the "Totila" of 1874. Waldo, *History of the Carnival*, 16-18, does not provide any description of the 1873 Rex: was he indeed also supposed to look like Totila? Huber, *Mardi Gras*, 17, includes a photograph of the Rex of 1874 which to present-day eyes makes him appear more like Santa Claus than Totila.

83. See Young, *Mistick Krewe*, 114, for these elements of the 1873 parade. The London Lord Mayor's parade, which dates from the fourteenth century, was apparently familiar to Carnival organizers in both Gulf Coast cities. The Order of Myths in Mobile adopted that spectacle as a part of their parade in 1884. See the reproduction of this incident in the anonymously written *Highlights of 75 Years in Mobile* (Mobile, 1940), 8.

84. King, "Old and New," 26.

85. Some reasons for this are explored in chapter 5. See pp. 127–28 and nn. 25–26.

86. La Cour, *New Orleans Masquerade*, 51–52.

87. Ibid., 52.

88. Ibid., 53.

89. The questions of priority and/or imitation have not been investigated. Dean, *Mardi Gras*, 58, and Rayford, *Chasin'*, 134–35, make brief reference to the Mobile foundation. Thomas DeLeon, one of the founders of the Carnival Association which organized the reign of Emperor Felix, curiously makes no reference to the earliest beginnings of Carnival monarchy in his brief book, *Our Creole Carnivals* (Mobile, 1890).

90. In fact, New Orleans' Rex sometimes also wavered between imperial and royal imagery.

91. DeLeon, *Our Creole Carnivals*, 21–22. Felix and the Carnival Association sponsoring his parade had a checkered history in the nineteenth century. Names and a few anecdotes are recorded concerning the rulers between 1872 and 1885. There is then a hiatus of seven years until a second Carnival Association, also associated with the enthusiasm of Thomas DeLeon, was formed in 1893. A brief account of the 1893 revival of the parade was published in *Highlights*, 42–43. A list of those rulers known in 1971 is to be found in Dean, *Mardi Gras*, 295–96.

92. Momus, formed in 1872 for the mardi gras parade, shifted its celebrations to New Year's Eve for 1872, 1873, 1874, and 1875. In 1876 it returned to parading on the Thursday before mardi gras. Involved here was the desire to distinguish itself from the other elite societies by celebrating and attracting attention on a different date.

93. Rayford, *Chasin'*, 12.

94. The title-page of Rayford's book reproduces this emblem. The society, founded in 1867, first celebrated on mardi gras, 1868, which is the reason for the dating on the emblem.

95. Dean, *Mardi Gras*, 45. Dean assigns no date to this occurrence and offers no document. Since Cain was presumably also leading the Lost Cause Minstrels in 1867 and afterwards, the story seems doubtful.

96. Ibid., 59.

97. Ibid., 54.

98. I have not pursued the origins of this unlikely idea. It comes from an undocumented and undated manuscript by one Frank Diard, a Mobile collector of Carnival lore in the early twentieth century who wrote, according to Rayford, *Chasin'*, 26: "The Spanish Mystic Society was instituted by the Spanish population on January 6, 1793. The great Don Miguel Eslava and the men folks of his wife's family . . . were early members. This society . . . dressed in phantom costumes of pure white . . . and pushed a car along the streets bearing a statue of the Virgin Mary. They danced and made merry . . . ," etc.

99. The quoted words are Dean's, *Mardi Gras*, 55. They do not represent, perhaps, the interpretation of the society, which still parades today. The emblems of H.S.S. and I.M. are illustrated, 53. The Spanish title, *infante*, was given to all the sons of the Spanish king except the crown prince.

100. *Mobile Daily Register*, February 6, 1874. This illustration and text are reproduced in Dean, *Mardi Gras*, 42, although the date is not given. The text is dated February 7, 1874 in Rayford, *Chasin'*, 68–69. The image

was repeated on several occasions in the *Register.* On February 14, ibid., p. 7, the image was accompanied by quite a different text.

101. In 1872 the Minstrels daringly satirized Duke Alexis on the very occasion of his New Orleans visit, that which saw the birth of Rex. In Slackabamorinico's decree that year he announced: "His Imperial Highness, the Grand Duke Alexis, will edify his spectators with his unique performance on the single-wheel velocipede. He performs this stupendous feat on his head, propelling the machine with his teeth." Rayford, *Chasin'*, 110.

102. Samuel Eichold, *Without Malice, The 100th Anniversary of the Comic Cowboys, 1884–1984* (Mobile, n.d. [1984?]), 16–17.

103. Ibid., 25–26.

104. Ibid., 30.

105. Ibid., 38, 42.

106. Some people, writes Rayford, *Chasin'*, 28, do not consider the early years of the Comic Cowboys as constituting a regular Carnival society because they were "almost entirely Dave Levi." "As long as he could talk up a few bucks to get his floats ready, he could always be sure of enough comic maskers to roll with his parade."

107. Young, *Mistick Krewe*, 152.

108. Ibid., 156–58.

109. Ibid., 159.

110. See, e.g., the *Mobile Times-Register,* March 8, 1987, sec. 1, p. 1. See also n. 52 above.

111. *One Hundred Years,* 7.

112. See "Crew," *Oxford English Dictionary* (Oxford, England, 1975), and n. 119 below.

113. The anti–Laudian political overtones to the masque, which need not concern us, are excellently analyzed by Leah Marcus, *The Politics of Mirth* (Chicago, 1986), 169–212.

114. Milton, "Comus," lines 63–65, in *The Poems of John Milton,* ed. James H. Hanford (New York, 1936), 79.

115. While Rex presides over his ball with a scepter in hand, Comus opens his ball cup in hand. See the photo of this moment in Huber, *Mardi Gras,* 76.

116. Milton, "Comus," 79 (lines 68–77).

117. Ibid., 76.

118. *One Hundred Years,* 8. See Young, *Mistick Krewe,* 60–61, for an extended listing of the characters enacted in the tableaux of 1857. Comus, a minor Greek divinity mentioned by ancient mythographers like Philostratus, is generally depicted in ancient times as presiding over luxurious, drunken, and sometimes lascivious feasts. This meaning, in contrast to Milton's more sinister development of the figure, could have been shaped to the krewe's eventually "refined" purposes well enough, as could also the secondary associations of the deity with song and dance. But in the 1850s Milton's darker Protestant vision of the god presumably provoked more recognition, if not understanding, by the Anglo-American founders of Comus.

119. "Mistick" has existed in the past as a variant spelling of "mystic," according to the *Oxford English Dictionary* (no dates or examples given), but "krewe" seems to be an invention: no entry for it exists in the *OED,* and the altered spelling is entirely dissonant with the word's etymology.

120. *One Hundred Years*, 11.

121. Ibid., 9.

122. "Comus edition," *Carnival Bulletin*, February 27, 1906 (a copy is conserved in the New Orleans Public Library).

## Chapter 5

1. See chap. 2, p. 24 and n. 16.

2. P. Young, *Mistick Krewe*, 91–94. There were two versions of the 1871 occasion, according to Young. One claims that the person who really received the bean did *not* reveal her good fortune and hence there was no queen. The other names the queen (Emma Butler); I have followed this account in my text.

3. *One Hundred Years*, 17.

4. Young, *Mistick Krewe*, 115–16.

5. Ibid., 151. Before the dance begins there is a grand march of krewe members with their partners to further display the select ladies, a custom recalling the *bals de bouquet* (see pp. 000–00).

6. Ibid., 162–63 and 166–67.

7. The Boston Club (named for a card game, not the city) became associated with membership in the Rex organization, as the Pickwick Club had been associated with Comus.

8. Dean, *Mardi Gras*, 84.

9. See the interview by T. L. Brannon in the *Azalea City News and Review* (Mobile, Alabama) for February 8, 1981, pp. 2–3.

10. Unlike the situation in the krewe-society balls of New Orleans, the most important male at Mobile's mystic-society balls, usually an older man, is simply called leader of the ball. In Mobile there have traditionally been only two kings of Carnival, one black and one white. However, the leading lady at the many balls is often—not always—called queen.

11. The call-out system, isolating a chosen few, and the fact that most invited guests are seated above the dance-floor, where they can see but not dance, insure this effect. Carnival-society balls at New Orleans follow the same format as those in Mobile, including the balls of the female-organized krewes to be discussed in the next pages of this chapter. A circumstantial account of such a krewe's ball in New Orleans, paralleling and augmenting mine about Mobile's customs, is given in William H. Davis, *Aiming for the Jugular in New Orleans* (Port Washington, New York, 1976), 83–86.

12. Edward Tinker, *Creole City* (New York, 1953), 334–35. By the 1940s, as indicated in Tinker's account, the Boston and Pickwick Clubs were located side by side on Canal Street; the viewing stands were thus located as prominently as possible so as to be viewed, no less than to view.

13. Dean, *Mardi Gras*, 227. This was the group's only manifestation, according to Dean. Dean here as elsewhere in his list of "mystic krewes" mixes what may have been thought of by the participants as a one-time occasion with organizations intending permanence.

14. La Cour, *New Orleans Masquerade*, 199–200. A similar usage was instituted in 1911 in Mobile. The Spinsters, the oldest women's Carnival organization surviving in that city today, gave their first ball after proclaiming on Valentine's Day the person whom they had selected as Bachelor of the Year. See Dean, *Mardi Gras*, 97–98.

15. La Cour, *New Orleans Masquerade*, 113. Iris disappeared in 1929 but was later renewed and began parading in 1959.

16. The first queen of Rex was a married woman, an exception to what subsequently became the rule for that organization. (The first Rex was a Jew, Lewis R. Solomon, a similar exception.) The krewe of Pandora was in 1948 the first to permit wedded pairs (La Cour, *New Orleans Masquerade*, 164). The innovation was followed in Mobile in 1951 by the Etruscans (Dean, *Mardi Gras*, 119). La Cour and Errol Laborde and Mitchell Osborne, *Mardi Gras*, offer the best collections of photographs of the costumes of the kings and queens. In the late nineteenth century the costumes had medieval Germanic features, as if borrowed from a Wagnerian opera company. In 1873 Rex appeared in chain armor and helmet as Totila, last king of the Ostrogoths (d. 552). (See plate 8.) But the medieval or Renaissance symbolic framework for royalty should be seen as only vaguely historical. It can also be seen as a reference to contemporary British royalty, whose official costumes, still rather familiar to mass audiences, remain strongly archaizing, especially for women.

17. As with earlier women's societies, the identity of Venus's king was revealed; the queen's was not. The second parading krewe was Iris. See Laborde and Osborne, *Mardi Gras*, 98 and 103. Three other nonparading women's societies were formed in the 1930s and six in the 1940s.

18. This innovation seems to have been made by Amor (ibid., 96). In 1987 the queen and king of Iris, both without face masks, were seated side by side on the back of a convertible at the head of Iris's parade.

19. The embodiment of overeating in fatman figures has been part of the utopian significance of Carnival since at least the sixteenth century. See Laborde and Osborne, *Mardi Gras*, 36, 158, for present-day photos of the figure in New Orleans' Carnival.

20. Eichold, *Comic Cowboys*, 116; see the photograph of Loris in his role on 118.

21. The placard is cited in the story on the Comic Cowboys in the *Azalea City News and Review* for February 26, 1981.

22. In 1850 there were only 57 free black males for every 100 free black females. In 1860 there were 78 black slave males for every 100 black slave females in Orleans parish. See John Blassingame, *Black New Orleans 1860–1880* (Chicago, 1973) 14 and 8. But later in the century "the sex ratio in the white population . . . reversed itself, with white women outnumbering white men by 1870 . . . " (ibid., 202).

23. The system of quadroon mistresses was also a matter of economics for the whites. Frederick Olmstead explained this in *A Journey in the Seaboard Slave States* (New York, 1856), as republished in part in Basso, ed., *The World from Jackson Square*, 168–69: "Unmarried men, who come to New Orleans to carry on business, [find] that it is much cheaper than living at hotels and boarding-houses. As no young man ordinarily thinks of marrying, until he has made a fortune to support the extravagant style of housekeeping and gratify the expensive tastes of young women, as fashion is now educating them, many are obliged to make up their minds never to marry." So, as a young man explained to Olmstead, his quadroon mistress "did the marketing, and performed all the ordinary duties of housekeeping herself; she took care of his clothes, and in every way was economical and saving in her habits—it being her

interest . . . to make him as much comfort and as little expense as possible, that he might be the more strongly attached to her."

24. James Alexander, *Transatlantic Sketches* (London, 1833), 233.

25. The reference is both to the subject of Comus's first parade, the Satanic kingdom in Milton's *Paradise Lost*, and to the literary origin of "Comus and his crew" (see pp. 115–16). Parading as the devil has been a constant among street maskers, too (cf. chap. 3, n. 38).

26. For an excellent close-up photo of Comus's benignly silly mask-type, see Laborde and Osborne, *Mardi Gras*, 101. In European Carnivals the type is often found juxtaposed to masks with grimacing features of wildmen, devils, or witches. Wilhelm Kutter, *Schwäbisch-Alemanische Fasnacht* (Salzburg, 1976), includes a broad array of photographs and descriptions of the so-called "smooth" (i.e., insipidly happy) and "ugly" grimacing masking pairs which have for several centuries been used in southwest Germany. See also Charles Camberoque and Daniel Fabre, *La Fête en Languedoc* (Toulouse, 1979), on the smooth-faced maskers at Limoux, a small town in southwest France. The oldest extant German wooden Carnival mask, carved, very probably, in the late seventeenth century, happens to be of the smooth-faced type. This type was also used by the aristocratic *Schembart* runners in Nuremberg's fifteenth-century city parades on mardi gras.

27. Young, *Mistick Krewe*, 78, 92, 163.

28. Al Rose, *Storyville* (Tuscaloosa, 1974), 22. Storyville acquired this, its unofficial name, from that of the alderman who sponsored the carefully worded city council bill banning prostitution throughout the city *except* in this infamous district. Storyville was legally recognized from January 1, 1898, to the fall of 1917. The second well-known gentleman was a man named Frank Lamothe. Rose cites December 31, 1883, and not mardi gras in 1882, as the date of the first ball of the two well-known gentlemen.

29. Henry Rightor, chapter 25, "The Carnival of New Orleans," in his *Standard History of New Orleans* (Chicago, 1900), 632.

30. Rose, *Storyville*, 62.

31. Ibid., 63–64. One must caution the reader that Rose does not document this story with quotations from newspapers or other sources.

32. Peter Burke, "Le carnaval de Venise, Esquisse pour une histoire de longue durée," in P. Aries and J. Margolin, eds., *Les jeux à la Renaissance* (Paris, 1982), 58, refers to W. Thomas's *History of Italy* for the story of Venetian prostitutes in the 1520s. Burke, 59, also cites a case in 1663 of Venetian prostitutes going masked to the public balls. Joseph von Hübner, *La vie à Rome au temps de Sixte Quint*, (Paris, 1870), 2:107–8, mentions the prostitute who scandalously paraded in Monsignor Volta's carriage in 1588. An analogous scandal was reported by the *Bee* in New Orleans on Ash Wednesday, 1854: "painted Jezebels exhibited themselves in public carriages." See Robert Tallant, *Mardi Gras* (New York, 1948), 106.

33. See Martine Boiteux, "Les Juifs dans le Carnaval de la Rome Moderne (XVe–XVIIIe Siècles)," *Mélanges de l'Ecole Française de Rome*, (1976), 762–63, Paul Achard, "Les chefs des Plaisirs," *Annuaire de Vaucluse* 20 (1869): 44, and especially Richard Trexler, "Correre la Terra; Collective Insults in the Late Middle Ages," *Mélanges de l'Ecole française de Rome* 96 (1984): 845–902.

34. The custom is explained and early sources such as Thomas Overbury's *Characters* (London, 1614) and Thomas Dekker's *The Honest
Whore*, part 2 (London, 1605) are cited in John Brand's *Observations on
Popular Antiquities* (London, 1853), 1:88. Brand's handbook of folkways,
revised and reedited many times, is particularly complete in the third
edition of 1853.

35. The subject is explored in the next chapter.

36. Alan Lomax, *Mr. Jelly Roll* (Berkeley, 1950), 49.

37. See Rose, *Storyville*, chap 3.

38. Cribs were rudimentary one-story wooden structures lining the
streets of Storyville behind the brick and stone mansions on Basin
Street. Often less than twelve feet square, they were just large enough
to accommodate prostitute, customer, and bed. In the black section of
"the District," as its residents called it (instead of using "Storyville," the
accusatory bourgeois term), a woman might rent a crib for as little as
twenty cents a night in 1899 (ibid., 173). "Crib" in the sense of a small,
hovel-like dwelling was used by Shakespeare (1597) and "crib" in the
sense of a child's small bed occurs in English, it seems, in 1649 for the
first time. See *Oxford English Dictionary*, "crib." Did the name of the
place suggest the costume of the Baby Dolls, or vice versa, or are the
two unrelated?

39. Lyle Saxon, Edward Dreyer, and Robert Tallant, eds., *Gumbo Ya-
Ya* (Boston, 1945), 14, 8–9, 15. The date of this report, "Mardi Gras Day
of 1940," is specified on p. 3.

40. Hill mentions Louis Armstrong and his Hot Five (mid-1920s) and
the Zulus and their first balls (ca. 1916–20), as if they were contemporary with the Baby Dolls in 1912. Robert Tallant, who may be the un-
mentioned author of the section on the Baby Dolls in *Gumbo Ya-Ya*,
dates the foundation of the Zulus in 1910 (Tallant, *Mardi Gras*, 236), and
so does the author of this chapter (*Gumbo Ya-Ya*, 3), which makes Hill's
story plausible. But few others claim that the Zulus existed that early.
Whether or not Tallant was the author of this account, he did not do the
interviewing: Robert McKinney, a black man, is given credit for collecting "most of the materials in the chapter entitled 'Kings, Baby Dolls,
Zulus, and Queens,'" (ibid., vii).

41. Saxon, et al., *Gumbo*, 15.

42. See plate 13, p. 000 below.

43. The complex Caribbean and African origins of the Mardi Gras Indians are discussed in chapter 6.

44. Lafcadio Hearn, *Two Years in the French West Indies* (New York,
1890), 210.

45. Hill, *Trinidad Carnival*, 108. "Jamet" is jargon for French "dia-
mètre," designating persons below the diameter of respectability: underworld characters. We do not possess a description like Hearn's for
the late nineteenth-century Baby Doll in Trinidad. According to Hill, in
the early twentieth century her costume was "that of a gaily dressed
doll: bonnet tied under the chin, a frilled dress reaching to her knees,
colored cotton stockings, and strap shoes. . . . She carried a small doll
that stood for her illegitimate child, stopped male passers-by, and in a
falsetto voice accused them of being the father" (ibid.). The description
corresponds in some details to the costume seen in a photograph of
New Orleans' Baby Dolls from about 1940 (plate 12). The Trinidad Baby
Doll developed her *persona* as a burlesque mother into semidramatic

skits, according to Hill. This may reflect European influences, where Carnival games involving illegitimate motherhood are also played. The New Orleans paraders do not carry a doll representing a child: they *are* that child in short skirts reaching to mid-thigh, too young in costume to be capable of the showy sexuality they display. They do not engage in a burlesquing skit about paternity with male passersby, but instead move through the streets as a group, singing and strutting. Daniel Crowley, "The Traditional Masques of Carnival," *Caribbean Quarterly*, no. 4 (1955–56): 209, includes a sketch of the Baby Doll costume described by Hill.

46. The high point of Baby Doll parading seems to have been reached in the late 1930s or 1940s. Saxon et al., *Gumbo Ya-Ya*, 26, and Tallant, *Mardi Gras*, 239–41, refer to two other groups of women maskers who, competing with the Baby Dolls from the 1930s through the 1950s, danced through the black sections of the city on Mardi Gras: the Gold Diggers and the Zigaboos.

47. See in general Joy Jackson, *New Orleans in the Gilded Age 1880–1900* (Baton Rouge, 1969) and especially 287–91 on Hearn. Edward Tinker, *Creole City* (New York, 1953), has an excellent chapter on Cable, 208–22. The Englishman George Sala in his book *America Revisited* (London, 1883), 295–96, offers an illustration of the late nineteenth-century image of Romantic New Orleans:

> I had not been many hours in the Crescent City before I fled from bustling St. Charles and pushing Carondelet streets, and plunged headlong and haphazard into "La Bonne Vieille France." Of course, ere long, I lost my way; and then I ventured to ask a passing gentleman, in a broad-brimmed hat and with a sandy "goatee," in what part of the city I might be. He replied, in a strong Northern accent, that he guessed I was on Charters-street. This did not sound very Gallic, and I felt slightly discouraged. Proceeding a few paces forward, I again plucked up heart of grace, and addressed another gentleman. . . . He wore an embroidered velvet calotte, and a short blue linen blouse by way of vest; and he was sitting on a cane-bottom chair on the side-walk, attentively perfecting the heel of a lady's pink satin boot, and whistling melodiously the while an air from "Giroflé-Girofla." "Mais, Monsieur," he made answer to my inquiry, "vous êtes en pleine Rue de Chartres." I was overjoyed.

48. Edwin Rozwenc, *The Making of American Society* (Boston, 1973) 2:147.

49. Young, *Mistick Krewe*, 159.

50. See chap. 4, n. 79.

51. Waldo, *History*, 25–26.

52. Before the advent of electricity, the flickering gas lamps of the city were supplemented for the nighttime parades by black men carrying torches alongside the floats. The flambeaux (torch) runners who flank the parades of Comus, Proteus, and Momus today—three of the oldest societies—are still invariably black (just as these societies' members are still invariably white). Elite black Carnival societies are discussed later in this volume.

53. Waldo, *History*, 17, giving a description of Rex's parade in 1873.

54. See, e.g., the summary of the mid-century situation in Gerald Capers, *Occupied City*, 15–16. There is virtual consensus on this point by historians of nineteenth-century New Orleans. Young, *Mistick Krewe*,

153–54, ardently but anecdotally defends Comus from the charge of lack of civic spirit by pointing to krewe members' generous donation of time, money, and personal effort in 1879 during the yellow-fever epidemic.

55. B. J. Forman, in Rightor, *Standard History,* 463.

56. See Coleman, *Historical Sketchbook,* 220, for the quotation. Ducal decorations and ball favors—dazzling, although by no means the really expensive items—are preserved in tray upon tray at the New Orleans Public Library. Some are in Huber, *Mardi Gras,* 28–29. The efficacy of dangling wealth before the fascinated eyes of tourists was clear to Waldo, *History,* who sprinkles his account of the parades with statements like "The entire affair was quite up to the standard originally reached by this mystical association and proved at least one thing—that they were gentlemen of unlimited means and the most distinguished taste."

57. This is not a book on the social history of New Orleans. But it is not possible to omit all notice of the as yet unexplored disaster which took place for free blacks in the 1840s, a disaster which forecast the general repression of black people in New Orleans at the end of the nineteenth century: there was an enormous decline in the numbers of free blacks between 1840 and 1850, from 19,222 to 9,961. The slave population declined too, but not so precipitately: from 23,448 to 18,068. While black New Orleans constituted 40 to 60 percent of the population, 1760–1840, it suddenly declined to 24 percent in 1850 and still further to 14.3 percent in 1860! This demographic collapse is not commented upon by Blassingame, *Black New Orleans,* or by Dominguez, *White* (from whom I take these figures, 116–17). Some of it may be due to the redrawing of city and parish boundaries. But H. E. Sterkx, *The Free Negro in Ante-Bellum Louisiana* (Canbury, New Jersey, 1972), 154–55, points to a great decline of free blacks in rural Louisiana after 1840 also, and attributes it, without analyses or statistics, to a high death rate and emigration to Haiti (the latter is discussed briefly on p. 302: less than 300 persons emigrated). Robert Reinders, "The Free Negro in the New Orleans Economy, 1850–60," *Louisiana History* 6 (1965): 273–85, similarly notices the New Orleans phenomenon but does not try to explain it; his article generalizes about the 10,000 free blacks left in the 1850s.

58. The association was played upon by "reformers" like Philip Werlien of the Progressive Union who in 1910 declared with reference to Storyville: "The filthy hovels in which the negro and French women live are distasteful to the women who conduct their houses in better style. . . . The negro woman must be stamped out of the district . . ." (Rose, *Storyville,* 64). Such clichés were not simply pejoratives used by moralists; they were part of the very identity of the area, lending themselves to the special kind of illusion characteristic of lives lived marginally. Friends, says Jelly Roll Morton, "took me to the *French*man's on the corner of Villere and Bienville, which was at that time the most famous nightspot after everything was closed. . . . All the girls that could get out of their houses was there. The millionaires would come to listen to their favorite pianists. There weren't any discrimination of any kind. . . . They all mingled together just as they wished to and everyone was just like one big happy family" (Lomax, *Mr. Jelly Roll,* 42; emphasis added). For Morton as for Werlien a house—even a brothel—should be conducted in the kind of "style" that would make it seem a home.

59. The little boy is depicted as old enough to read signs in black bars, while still small enough to ride comfortably and happily on a black man's shoulders; he is also described as uninterested in and unknowing of the sexual side of what he sees. Lyle Saxon, *Fabulous New Orleans* (New York, 1928), 32, 25, 44.

60. See p. 37 on Cable's account of Congo Square. The periodical publication of the story is in vol. 116 (May–October, 1928): 680–90, and 117 (November, 1928–April, 1929): 85–94, of *The Century Magazine*. I suppose the story was first sketched in 1925 because Saxon refers to Comus's parade theme of 1900 at one point ("Legends of the Golden Age": *Fabulous New Orleans*, 59) and he says that he is writing about his first visit to New Orleans "25 years ago" (ibid., 6).

61. Saxon, *Fabulous New Orleans*, 19.

62. Ibid., 33.

63. Rightor, *Standard History*, 631. The characterization had become a cliché by the 1880s, if not much earlier. See the German traveler Emil Deckert's brief comment on Mardi Gras in 1886: "People of New Orleans are filled with cheerfulness . . . [as is evident in Carnival]. It rivals similar events in Rome and Naples. Here we saw again, above all else, colored people acting very unruly and wild." Frederick Trautman, "New Orleans, the Mississippi, and the Delta through a German's Eyes: the travels of Emil Deckert, 1885–1886," *Louisiana History* 25 (1984): 88.

64. Particularly interesting among the descriptions of subsidiary parades is that of the Jefferson City Buzzards (still active today) as dressed something like the later Baby Dolls (Saxon, *Fabulous New Orleans*, 35–36). This masking type is further considered later in this book. There are some surprising discrepancies in the description of the Rex and Comus parades. Rex, who always went unmasked in the parade, looks like Comus: "His face was covered with a simpering wax mask, benign and jovial" (ibid., 37); the Comus ball is led by "King and Queen" (ibid., 66–67), although of course there has never been a "King" of the Comus krewe.

65. Ibid., 31.

66. See p. 66 above.

67. Saxon, *Fabulous New Orleans*, 52–53.

68. Ibid., 52.

69. See the description of how social dances in Haiti, especially those during Carnival, provoke "the development of artistic values through the exhibition of skill." Katharine Dunham, *The Dances of Haiti* (New York, 1937), 47.

70. Saxon, *Fabulous New Orleans*, 47–50.

71. I am not saying that black peoples' balls were not violent or hypersexed at this time, or that the violence and sex were not attractive. But whether it was representative of black behavior or desire, as Saxon allows his readers to believe, is quite another matter. Danny Barker, a black jazz musician, provides more contextualized memoirs of the eruptive violence in the ballrooms which he experienced as a boy growing up in New Orleans at the beginning of the twentieth century. See Barker, *A Life in Jazz* (London, 1986), 11–19. Dunham, *Dances of Haiti*, 41–48, puts the seasonal dancing of Carnival, with its sexual exhibitionism and rivalries, still more richly in context, in this case in a black Caribbean nation long independent.

72. Eichold, *Without Malice*, 76. Eichold explains, ii, that he has simply used the files of the *Mobile Register* for his descriptions.

73. Rightor, *Standard History*, 629.

74. De Leon, *Our Creole Carnival*, 29–33.

75. Ibid., 13.

76. Ibid., 12–13. See Young, *Mistick Krewe*, 177–90, for a circumstantial account of the Ogden, Utah, occasion. B. W. Dean has published an article on the brief rise and fall of Mardi Gras in Birmingham, Alabama, between 1896 and 1900. The first three celebrations (1896–1898), organized by the local Commercial Club, were greeted with enthusiasm; Birmingham's pseudo-monarch was named Rex Vulcan, King of Iron, and reigned with a queen. But in 1899 Mardi Gras fell on a day when the temperature went to 30 below zero, so the event was postponed until May. When in 1900 the weather was again dismayingly cold, the Commercial Club discontinued its sponsorship. See Dean, "Jack Frost brought early end to Birmingham's carnival [sic]," *Azalea City News and Review* (Mobile), January 11, 1989, pp. 1 and 3B.

77. The Veiled Prophet Parade and Ball were invented by two newcomers to St. Louis from New Orleans, Charles Slayback, a grain merchant, and his brother Alonzo. They made the parade part of the October fair: their purpose was avowedly to attract commerce. The Slaybacks formed a committee of prominent businessmen, a "mysterious brotherhood," just as the Carnival-society organizers in their native New Orleans had done (see chap. 4, n. 52). Their nighttime parades of mythological floats resembled those of Comus. In 1969 the parades were switched to daytime and in 1981 to the Fourth of July.

## Chapter 6

1. Louis Duchesne, ed., *Liber pontificalis* (Paris, 1889), 2: 172–73, includes the text written about 1140 by Canon Benedict of St. Peter's Cathedral, Rome, concerning Carnival games in that city. William Fitzstephen's "Vita Sancti Thomae" (ca. 1190; published 1877), 9, has a passage describing Carnival practices in London during Fitzstephen's childhood; see James C. Robertson, ed., Public Record Office, *Rerum Britannicorum Medii Aevi Scriptores*, vol. 67, pt. 3 (London, 1877), 9. Chapter 3 of my book, *The Birth of Gargantua, Festive Culture in Renaissance Europe* (forthcoming), surveys the thirteenth- and fourteenth-century sources.

2. A fine photograph of the captain of Rex is in Laborde and Osborne, *Mardi Gras*, 68. Like much else having elite symbolic value, the captain's ominous anonymity has been in recent years both imitated by noncaptains and abandoned by other captains, so that it has lost some of its force. In Mobile, the place of the organizer of the mystic society's parades and balls is often marked by the parade marshal, a figure like the captain on horseback but not necessarily masked.

3. Linnaeus's system of differences is explained in John Burke, "The Wild Man's Pedigree: Scientific Method and Racial Anthropology," in *The Wild Man Within*, ed. Edward Dudley and Maximilian Novak (Pittsburgh, 1972), 266–67.

4. See in addition to the articles in Dudley and Novak, *The Wild Man Within*, Winthrop Jordan, *White over Black*, and Robert Berkhofer, Jr., *The White Man's Indian* (New York, 1978).

5. "At or near:" It is probably no accident that the artist who drew plate 13, the scene of street masking at New Orleans in 1873, placed a

white man playing an instrument and another white man in a clown costume with a white woman in a sexy, close-fitting outfit most evidently in the center, while showing an Indian and a group of black people to either side.

6. See pp. 99–100.

7. See, e.g., plate 4 to my article "Presentation and Representation," showing a wildman as he was represented in the Nuremberg, Germany, Carnival of 1518. The legends surrounding wildmen in medieval and Renaissance times are well treated in Richard Bernheimer, *The Wild Man in the Middle Ages* (Cambridge, Mass., 1952).

8. I commented in an earlier chapter on the fading Catholic sense of the festival. See Young, *Mistick Krewe,* 104, and R. Tallant, *Mardi Gras,* 162, on the distribution of meat. The idea was not original. It was, for example, done in medieval and Renaissance times at Venice. See Peter Burke, "Le carnaval de Venise," 57–58. The ritual at New Orleans meant a lot of meat for the king, queen, and their court. Waldo, *History of the Carnival,* 55, says that the Fat Ox in 1880 weighed a scarcely believable four thousand pounds. (Prize steers today weigh between 1,000 and 1,400 pounds; a cattleman of my acquaintance, however, states that he once took a class in farm management in which a steer weighing 3,700 pounds was reported.)

9. La Cour, *New Orleans Masquerade,* 17, reproduces an illustration from *Frank Leslie's Popular Monthly* of Comus's parade in 1867, which shows at the right the *boeuf gras* with a garland around its neck in the traditional manner. According to Young, *Mistick Krewe,* in the caption to plate II, facing p. 15, the *boeuf gras* in this parade was actually made of papier-mâché and was supposed to represent a huge *plate* of roast beef, although the head and horns were retained. The theme of Comus's parade was "The Triumph of Epicurus." Young, 52, cites a French newspaper in New Orleans, *La Chronique,* which in 1849 referred without further specification to the good old days "où la procession du boeuf-gras envelloppait [sic] toute la ville dans ses interminables replis."

10. Laborde and Osborne, *Mardi Gras,* 35, show an illustration of the Paris *boeuf gras* "about 1820," already accompanied by two wildmen with the same (un)clothing, headdress, beard, and club shown in 1852; a single cupid, aiming his bow, rides the ox. There is no Roman helmet, nor is there any in Gustave Doré's 1856 engraving, which otherwise includes the same elements (there are, however, no cupids in Doré), reproduced in Orloff, *Carnival,* 39.

11. Faure, *Paris Carême-prenant,* 128–29.

12. A Parisian broadside of 1843, reproduced in Samuel Glotz, ed., *Le Masque dans la tradition européenne* (Binche, Belgium, 1975), 172, showing two butchers leading the ox, and a drawing of the 1861 Parisian *boeuf gras* from *Frank Leslie's Illustrated Newspaper,* reproduced in La Cour, *New Orleans Masquerade,* 6, show that the idea of butchers with slaughtering instruments conducting the animal also had its precedents.

13. After riding on horseback in 1872, 1873, and 1874, Rex from 1875 until the 1880s sat in a carriage. By 1885 he had assumed a high throne on a float (see the illustration of that year's parade, reproduced from *Harper's Weekly,* in Laborde and Osborne, *Mardi Gras,* 149).

14. The Carnival Bulletin in question, preserved in the New Orleans Public Library, like other bulletins from the 1880s and 1890s, includes artists' renditions of all the floats in the parade in color, and also pro-

vides brief explanations of the floats' themes. The other bulletins show the Comus, Proteus, and Momus parades in the same way and are also preserved at the New Orleans Public Library. The tradition of these bulletins seems to have ended in 1940, just before World War II.

15. Dean, *Mardi Gras*, 220. Purebred heifers were first imported from the island of Jersey to Alabama via the port of Mobile in December 1882. The occasion was commemorated by an impromptu procession through the city. Can this recent occurrence have inspired the Cowbellions? See First National Bank of Mobile, *Highlights*, 29–30.

16. Dean, *Mardi Gras*, 220.

17. Note that in the account by Michael Scott quoted on p. 50 above, the butchers carry knives and wear aprons.

18. I have considered in some detail the many versions of the wild-man in medieval and Renaissance Carnivals in *The Birth of Gargantua*, chapter 4. On the legendary bear/wildman relationship and the idea of the "master of animals," see Lutz Röhrich, *Sage und Märchen* (Freiburg, 1976), 147–95. On the bear-man in present-day southern French Carnivals see Daniel Fabre, "Le monde du Carnaval," *Annales E.S.C.* 31 (1976), 389–406.

19. At New Orleans, Indian costuming in Carnival, apparently by whites, is found in 1838 (Young, *Mistick Krewe*, 42), 1839 (La Cour, *New Orleans Masquerade*, 13), 1846 (Young, 51), 1852 (Young, 54), 1855 (Young, 57), 1857 (Young, 59), 1873 (plate 13, this book; see also plate 7, Darwin ball of 1873: feathered headdress in central background), 1877 (Waldo, *History of the Carnival*, 29: one of Rex's floats), and so on. At Mobile they led the parade in 1866 and 1867 (Chief Slackabamorinico). Indian masking was just as commonplace in other American festive traditions. Charles Welch, "Oh, Dem Golden Slippers," *Journal of American Folklore* 79 (1966): 531, writes that a legend maintains that no Philadelphia Mummers Day Parade (January 1) ever went "up the street" without Indians.

20. Choctaws and Chickasaws sold goods in the marketplaces of Mobile and New Orleans in the second half of the nineteenth century.

21. The most famous use of Indian disguise in American history is that of the patriots who dumped British tea into Boston harbor in December 1773. Alfred Young shows in his book *In the Streets of Boston* (forthcoming), chapter 14, that this masking as Indians was not at all an isolated way of protesting politically. It was preceded and followed during the American revolutionary period both by other masquerades and by many references to the "Indians" in newspapers and pamphlet literature. The double quality of Indians as impossibly "savage" and nevertheless nobly unconquerable was fully recognized by their most redoubtable foes, the white colonists. Young also shows how this image and use of the Indian remained active among the popular classes in political protests all through the nineteenth century.

22. Today, however, when white men mask as Indians, the masquerade usually carries only a movie-wild-Indian resonance. As the famed Pete Fountain, leader of the Half-Fast Walking Club during New Orleans' Mardi Gras, explained in an interview in 1982, "For years we used to salute the Italians . . . the French, the Chinamen—saluted all the nationalities, and then we ran out. . . . Like next year we might be possibly Hawaiians, but we're not saluting anybody now. This time we're just being the Indians." As everybody knows, the Indians—un-

like the Hawaiians?—are not and never have been a nation; how could you "salute" them? "We got some Indians out of Baton Rouge making the headdresses. Our group has all chiefs—no Indians." *Arcade* (New Orleans weekly news magazine), February 16, 1982, p. 8. The role of walking clubs in Carnival is discussed in chapter 10.

23. Daniel Crowley points out that Indians are also the most popular masquerade in the four largest Brazilian Carnivals, in his "Spettacolo e participazione nel Carnevale, uno studio comparato," *La ricerca folclorica*, no. 6 (1982): 85.

24. Rightor, *Standard History*, 631. This testimony has not previously been noticed by students of the Mardi Gras Indians.

25. The chant, performed in 1938 by Jelly Roll Morton on tapes conserved in the Library of Congress, is transcribed and edited in Alan Lomax, *Mr. Jelly Roll* (Berkeley, 1950), 280. Morton, born in 1886, recorded his memoirs orally in 1938 and described the Indians' behavior at the same time as he performed the song (ibid., 14–15); see further on the song's date in note 62 below. The song's refrain, which is transcribed in Lomax as "T'ouwais, bas q'ouwais, ou tendais" that is, as a Creole phrase (which neither Morton nor Lomax risks translating), recurs as a "nonsense" phrase one generation later in a song sung by the Red, White, and Blue Tribe in 1940 ("Tu-way-pa-ka-way": Saxon, Dreyer, Tallant, *Gumbo Ya-Ya*, 20), and again a generation after that in a song sung and recorded by the Wild Tchoupitoulas tribe (*The Wild Tchoupitoulas*, ILPS 9360, Island Records, 1976, "Golden Crown"); where it is transcribed on the record jacket as "Tu way pok-y way." Jason Berry, Jonathan Foose, Tad Jones, *Up from the Cradle of Jazz: New Orleans Music Since World War II* (Athens, Georgia, 1986), 218–19, suggest that the second part of the refrain, "ou tendais" (lost in the 1940 and 1970s versions) meant "entendez" or "attendez" "you understand [don't you?]" or "listen, you!" (the authors here change "*ou* tendais" to "*on* tendais," a questionable change): The first part might mean, they say, "Tu[n']avais pas [de] couilles," "you've got no balls." They also cite looser ideas of its meaning by the Indians and by a former Tulane University student who was interested in the Indians' songs, Finn Wilhelmsen (see n. 54 below). But these are all conjectures. The phrase's meaning was presumably already lost when Morton recalled it in 1938, thirty or forty years after he says that he heard it. Its adoption into an environment of English words in the 1940s and 1970s is a good proof of the continuity of oral tradition, but also of its elisions.

26. Joan Martin gave a lecture on October 2, 1980, at the New Orleans Public Library, "The Black Indians Don't Sing Your Mardi Gras," which states the subcultural thesis at its most extreme (conserved on tape cassette at the Library). Another strong advocate of this view is Maurice Martinez, "Two Islands: The Black Indians of Haiti and New Orleans," *Arts Quarterly* (New Orleans), 1, no. 7: 17-18. See also chap. 8, n. 66, for reference to a film by Martinez.

27. Berry, Foose, Jones, *Up from the Cradle*, 210–11. Berry is a journalist writing regularly on black culture, jazz, Mardi Gras, and related topics at New Orleans. In a Prologue Berry explains his collaboration with Foose and Jones, whose research talents were indispensable to the book.

28. Ibid., 211.

29. See chap. 2, p. 37. Hearn arrived in New Orleans from Cincinnati

at an undetermined date in 1877, early enough for him to catch yellow fever several months later during the hot summer. In November 1883, he published in *Century Magazine* the first of three accounts of what seems to have been a single opportunity to see this black dancing. The location of the bamboula which Hearn saw is given by Herbert Asbury, *The French Quarter: An Informal History of the New Orleans Underworld* (New York, 1936), 252, presumably on the basis of information published by Hearn in his account of the occasion in the *New York World* in the "middle 1880s." Asbury does not give a precise date for Hearn's apparently anonymous description in the *World*. It is H. Kmen, "Roots of Jazz," 12–13, who establishes the *World* writer as Hearn. Neither Asbury nor Kmen quote in full Hearn's third account of the same occasion, which is part of a letter to the musicologist H. E. Krehbiel. The letter calls the dance not a bamboula but "the Congo:" "There are no harmonies—only a furious contretemps [crossrhythm?]. As for the dance—in which the women do not take their feet off the ground—it is as lascivious as is possible. The men dance very differently, like savages, leaping in the air." This does not sound like the performance of men and women "old or beyond middle age." See the complete letter in Elizabeth Biskind Wetmore, *The Life and Letters of Lafcadio Hearn* (Boston, 1906), 1: 336.

30. Berry, Foose, Jones, *Up from the Cradle*, 212.

31. Saxon, *Fabulous New Orleans*, 31.

32. Rightor, *Standard History*, 631, found the performances "in the vicinities of the Saint Bernard and Tremé markets, in Frenchman Street and elsewhere in . . . the Old [French] Quarter." However, this Creole location may be due to Rightor's bias toward prizing the old and therefore Creole elements in Mardi Gras, and may be due also to the location of Kirsch's house, whose testimony we happen to have. Some of the people interviewed by Berry, Foose, Jones, *Up from the Cradle*, 210–13, claim that the Yellow Pocahontas were founded in 1896 in the Garden District and then went "downtown" (i.e., into the Creole section), while the Creole Wild West Tribe crossed Canal Street in the other direction, moving "uptown." If the tribes were as mobile as this, their relation to the black racial split between "Creole" (light-skinned) and "African" (dark-skinned) people must have been either very complicated or nonexistent. The sense of color among nonwhites was presumably higher, the more people felt that they had something to defend socially; that is, it was middle-class and upper-class more than lower-class. "Even now," wrote Calvin Trillin in 1964, "downtown Negroes occasionally refer to their opposite numbers living above Canal Street as 'American Negroes'. . . . Stories are still told . . . of Negro clubs that would admit nobody who was unable to show a blue vein in his arm, and of 'paperbag parties,' which included no guests whose skin was darker than a paper bag." Trillin, "The Zulus," *The New Yorker*, June 20, 1964, 68.

33. As Berry, Foose, Jones, *Up from the Cradle*, 212–13, point out, the white man's Indian influenced the name of the reportedly first black "tribe," the "Creole Wild West Tribe." There is a tantalizing parallel between this name and a particular entertainment which Paul Longpre, one of the black Indians interviewed by the authors of *Up from the Cradle*, says passed through New Orleans on an unspecified date in the late nineteenth century: the Hagenback Wallace Creole Wild West Show

(ibid.). It would be worthwhile trying to discover the exact date of this show and its Indian components.

34. Lomax, *Mr. Jelly Roll*, 15. Berry, Foose, Jones, *Up from the Cradle*, 212–14, give more detailed accounts of feuds and killings.

35. Berry, Foose, Jones, *Up from the Cradle*, 214. Any reduction of the fighting to uptown-downtown differences is too simple. Joan Martin, "Mardi Gras Indians, Past and Present," *Louisiana Miscellany* 3 (1973): 51, points out that two tribes from the same area often fought. What was perhaps most important was the gang-like sense of "turf." Morton in Lomax, *Mr. Jelly Roll*, 12, says, speakng not of the black Indians but of parades around the year 1900 generally, "You see, whenever a parade would get to another district the enemy would be waiting at the dividing line. If the parade crossed that line, it meant a fight, a terrible fight."

36. Transcribed by Berry, Foose, Jones, *Up from the Cradle*, 222, from a record made by the Wild Magnolias in 1970. See n. 25 for a similar phrase documented over seventy or eighty years.

37. The ritual of the quete (see chap. 2, n. 86) has accompanied rural masquerades and many city mumming performances since the Middle Ages. Herbert Halpert, "A Typology of Mumming," in Halpert and G. M. Story, eds., *Christmas Mumming in Newfoundland* (Toronto, 1969), 36–38, gives a convenient résumé of the place of the quete in traditional masking practices.

38. Jason Berry, "Goodby Chief Pete," *Gambit* (New Orleans), November 14, 1981, p. 21.

39. Laborde and Osborne, *Mardi Gras*, 130–32, quoting Franklin Davis, spy boy for the Yellow Pocahontas Tribe.

40. Joan Martin, "Mardi Gras Indians, Past and Present." This article is based on undated interviews with former chiefs of the tribes.

41. See n. 35. The words are from a song called "Meet the Boys on the Battlefront" by the Wild Tchoupitoulas tribe, recorded on *The Wild Tchoupitoulas* (see n. 25).

42. Claude Lévi-Strauss, *The Savage Mind* (Chicago, 1966; originally Paris, 1962), 16–37.

43. Associated with the principle of playful creation is an idea which seems even stranger, indeed perverted to the white, literate mind, that work is private and play is public. There are many ramifications of this idea, explored with insight by Roger Abrahams in his collection of articles, *The Man-of-Words in the West Indies: Performance and the Emergence of Creole Culture* (Baltimore, 1983). More generally and loosely stated, what the idea means is that play in this culture is more important to social definition than work. One must add, as Abrahams emphasizes, 51, that this idea in black Creole culture is very sex-typed in its expression. Women, in charge of the home, have control over and responsibility for work; men, whose spheres of control and responsibility lie beyond the home, develop these qualities in sportive play and competition. If play is what gives a man social definition and prestige, then it is less surprising that a man may spend up to $3,000, a quarter of a year's earnings or more, for his costume. Abrahams' book is helpful at many points and in many ways in understanding black Carnival activities in New Orleans; he devotes attention in many of the articles in *Man-of-Words* to specific features of Carnival performance and Christmas-season performances in Trinidad, St. Kitts, Tobago, and St. Vincent.

44. Michael Ventura, *Shadow Dancing in the U.S.A.* (Los Angeles,

1985), 156, quotes Lewis; Lewis's theme is eloquently pursued throughout Ventura's book.

45. Bakhtin, *Rabelais and His World*, devotes chapter 6 to "Images of the Material Bodily Lower Stratum."

46. Berry, Foose, Jones, *Up from the Cradle*, 222. A record eventually developed out of the meeting of Turbington with the Wild Magnolias. See pp. 241–42.

47. For this culture such inner entities explain the nature of human creation even when the "inside" is inspired by a force—like God or innate ideas—from "beyond" the world.

48. Berry, Foose, Jones, *Up from the Cradle*, 222.

49. An extraordinary description of religious trancing in New Orleans' "African [Methodist] Church" in the 1850s is given by Fredrika Bremer, *Homes of the New World*, 2: 234–38. The interrelations of black Christian singing and dancing, *vodun* ("voodoo"), and "rock and roll" music are explored in Ventura's *Shadow Dancing*, particularly in the chapter "Hear that Long Snake Moan."

50. Photographs of these healers, their churches, and their ministrations are included in Smith's *Spirit World: Pattern in the Expressive Folk Culture of Afro-American New Orleans* (New Orleans, 1984), which was prepared as the catalog to an exhibition of Smith's photographs at the Louisiana State Museum, New Orleans, in 1983.

51. See Claude Jacobs, "Spirit Guides and Possession in the New Orleans Black Spiritual Churches," *Journal of American Folklore* 102 (1988–89), 45–67, which includes further photographs by Smith and bibliographic reference to other studies of the black spiritual churches. Leaf ("Leafy" in Jacobs's article) Anderson's spirit guides are discussed, 48–65.

52. Ibid., 60. Note on the altar the beadwork drapery with Indian motifs, probably taken from a Mardi Gras Indian's costume, as indicated, ibid., 54.

53. Smith, *Spirit World*, 89. Jacobs, "Spirit Guides," 55–56 and 65, develops the symbolic associations between Black Hawk, Saint Michael, Martin Luther King, and Jesus, to explain the way in which the nineteenth-century Indian warrior could play the double role of an exemplary sufferer (King; Jesus) *and* defender (Saint Michael), particularly of poor female heads of household, so prominent in these churches. Not mentioned by Jacobs or Smith, perhaps because it is so obvious, is that Black Hawk includes the word "black" in his name. Have no myths developed about an African ancestry or connection in Black Hawk's life? Even if none have, the word no doubt functions powerfully in making Black Hawk the most popular symbol, according to Jacobs, in black New Orleans Spiritual churches.

54. Berry, Foose, Jones, *Up from the Cradle*, 213. See also Finn Wilhelmsen, "Creativity in the Songs of the Mardi Gras Indians of New Orleans, Louisiana," *Louisiana Folklore Miscellany* 3 (1973): 56, on the way the roles are introduced with "Indian Red."

55. Martin, "Mardi Gras Indians," 53. I deduce the date in the 1960s and early 1970s from the date of her article, 1973, since she uses the word "today" with reference to this information about one of the people she interviewed at an unspecified date.

56. Last stanza of "Meet the Boys on the Battlefront": see n. 41 above.

57. For additional materials on the concept of subculture and a broader historical perspective on its Western occurrences, see the final section of my "Presentation and Representation": "A Question of Method," 30–33. As to the case in question here, the combination of repressions and opportunities for blacks attained an apparently stimulating summit between 1890 and 1915, when New Orleans' special sexual tradition (Storyville) was coupled with the elimination of blacks from civil and political life (the segregation system was enacted into law both at city and state levels, 1880–1910). Jazz and the Mardi Gras Indians developed many of their essential forms in relation to these barriers and crossing-points. The idea of jazz's formation in this conjuncture is suggested in Lomax, *Mr. Jelly Roll*, 79–80, and it is implicit throughout Berry, Foose, Jones, *Up from the Cradle*.

58. Officially black people numbered only 77,714 in 1900 New Orleans, but this was close to the high point of disfranchisement and segregation. Blacks had few reasons to report their actual numbers, and whites had many reasons not to record them. See Dominguez, *White by Definition*, 116–17, on the figures for 1900 and 1950, and U.S. Bureau of the Census, *State and Metropolitan Area Data Book* (Washington, D.C., 1982), 178–79, for the 1980 totals. My 1989 figures are informal estimates. Al Rose and Edmond Souchon, *New Orleans Jazz, a Family Album* (Baton Rouge, 1967), 3, give the figure for jazz professionals. I have calculated the figure of one thousand Mardi Gras Indians on the basis of all the sources available to me. Alison Miner Kaslow estimated a total of about three hundred Indians ten years ago in her lecture, "Coconuts, Indians, and Mambos: The Black Celebration of Carnival," May 10, 1977, New Orleans Public Library (preserved on tape cassette at the Library).

59. Danny Barker, *A Life in Jazz* (New York, 1986), 59, 61.

60. See n. 32 above. Creole racism and its relation to family traditions is sharply expressed by the jazz musician Paul Dominguez in an undated interview, presumably in the 1940s, with Alan Lomax, and is poignantly related by Lomax to the difficulties of Jelly Roll Morton's career (*Mr. Jelly Roll*, 80–90). Danny Barker, *A Life in Jazz*, 21–34, speaks of the intraracial tensions and their relation to family traditions as they affected school, jobs, and the beginnings of his musical education. See more generally the useful sociological analysis of the New Orleans black community in the first postwar years by Munro Edmonson and John Rohrer, *The Eighth Generation Grows Up* (New York, 1964).

61. Once again the barrier was used creatively to stimulate foundation of self-help associations or benevolent societies, with their deep African roots in informal association to pool resources in case of sickness and death (see chap. 2, n. 80). Barker, *A Life in Jazz*, 49, wrote in 1986 that "quite a few of the old societies are still active, especially amongst black folk. The black societies were mostly small operations, and today it is mostly owing to custom and tradition and personal love that they are in operation." From this stopgap vehicle came another New Orleans glory, the jazz funeral: "These old societies bear the names of . . . The Young Men Liberty, The Young Men Charity, The Young Men Perseverance, The Young Men Vidalia; and there are the old tombs of many other fraternal societies: Masons, Elks, Knights of Phythias [sic], Oddfellows. Years back they all buried their members

with brass band music. In the twenties just about every day a brother was buried in blazing glory. Currently, most jazz musicians are taken down for the last time in style. Jazz funerals and the social club parades keep the brass bands functioning . . ." (ibid.).

62. Cultural analysis, like sociological analysis, has with the exception of Michael Smith's and Shane White's work been occasional or informal. However, mention should also be made of the work of the musicologist Andrew Kaslow who will, one hopes, make available soon in printed form his broad knowledge of New Orleans' Carnival music, including that of the black Indians. See Kaslow's lecture in the series of public lectures given at the New Orleans Public Library in 1977: "From Waltz to Boogie: The Music of Mardi Gras" (May 24, 1977; available like the others on tape cassette at the Library). Kaslow's lecture included the excerpt from the Library of Congress tapes during which Jelly Roll Morton sang the song "Tu-way Pak-a-way," which Kaslow dates as about 1915 (see n. 25 above). The series of public lectures on Mardi Gras, entitled "Behind the Mask of Mardi Gras," is described with an outline of the contents of the tapes in a mimeographed booklet available at the Library entitled *Jambalaya*. This and a number of other lecture series, 1977–80, which are described in *Jambalaya* were funded by a grant from the National Endowment for the Humanities.

63. The place of the bar as a "second home" for many black people is described eloquently in Barker and Buerkle, *Bourbon Street Black*, 189–91, with particular relation to jazz funerals. See also the place of the bar in the case histories of black people that make up the second half of Edmonson and Rohrer, *The Eighth Generation*. These local materials should be understood in the context of the Creole-Caribbean culture of the "man of words": the bar no less than the street is the daily employed forum for sportive play and for the education of young males in the perquisites of manhood (see Abrahams, *Man-of-Words*, passim).

64. There are on the other hand several good documentations of the Indians' actual parading on mardi gras. Especially to be mentioned is a sequence in Les Blank's film, *Always for Pleasure* (see chap. 8, n. 65) and the filmstrip about the Indians, prepared with the collaboration of Michael Smith, on display in "Ripley's Believe it or Not" commercial museum in the French Quarter. I have not been able to view Maurice Martinez's highly regarded film, *Black Indians of New Orleans* (see chap. 8, n. 65).

65. See n. 25.

66. Smith, *Spirit World*, 91–93.

67. Ibid., 74–75.

68. According to Roger Abrahams, there are very few female protagonists in the festive performances of Afro-Caribbeans in the small towns on Nevis, St. Kitts, St. Vincent, and Tobago, islands in the Caribbean where he has done ethnographic work. Even in the larger towns women appear only in "highly formal" ceremonies (personal communication, October 1988).

69. I owe this phrase to Roger Abrahams, who says that every performance of Afro-Caribbeans with which he is acquainted leads late or soon to such a verbal contest (personal communication, October 1988).

70. Martin, "Mardi Gras Indians," 52.

71. Signifying: confusing and defying your rival or enemy with quick, polyvalent repartee. Signifying: any verbal unit, which always consists

of subunits with some significance and in turn is always related to other parallel and larger verbal sign-units.

72. Record, *The Wild Tchoupitoulas*: from "Hey Mama." The intricate cross-rhythms in this song as it is performed cannot possibly be rendered by means of linear listings of its words.

73. Ibid., from "Hey Hey." Of course the very idea of titles to these chanting songs is foreign to the oral tradition, as is also the idea of a unique author, even when it is true that a particular individual gives a certain shape to a song. Thus, for example, on the record cover of *The Wild Tchoupitoulas* it is misleading to print: "Indian Red by George Landry"; "Golden Crown by George Landry" (Landry was chief of the Wild Tchoupitoulas at the time the record was made).

74. *The Wild Tchoupitoulas:* from "Brother John by Cyril Neville." Berry, Foose, Jones, *Up from the Cradle,* 234–35, show with respect to this song how the elisions and transformations proper to oral culture changed an earlier song about a woman, Cora, who died in an Indian fight into this song about John "Scarface" Williams. At one point in the song Cora reemerges! "Well now Cora he died on the battlefield/Brother John is gone/And the rest of his gang, they won't bow, they won't kneel/ Brother John is gone." Names and gender interweave, as the needs of rhythm, feelings, and memory dictate. Along with Cora and John there may be a third famous Mardi Gras Indian evoked in this song, the one Indian nearly everyone remembers who has been involved with the tribes over the past fifty years: Brother Tillman (also called "Brother Timber"), a man of great violence, who "dressed all in white and carried a hatchet with a decorated blade in his hand and wore a .45 automatic in the apron of his suit." He allegedly killed five or six men, but nevertheless seems to have died in old age himself in 1949. See Martin, "Mardi Gras Indians," 52–53. Chanting "Brother brother brother brother" like an invocation of this battler who "never would bow and he never would kneel" would be appropriate and evoke many people's memories. On the other hand, "Brother" is a generic term and may not refer to Tillman at all. Brother Tillman led the White Eagles for many years but then also the Creole Wild West (see the conflicting stories and dates about when Tillman led these tribes, ibid., 52–53, and Berry, Foose, Jones, *Up from the Cradle,* 212–14). Saxon, Dreyer, Tallant, *Gumbo Ya-Ya,* 22–23, report a meeting and conversation in a bar during the 1940 Carnival with Brother Tillman when he was still Chief of the Creole Wild West, although afflicted by declining eyesight.

75. A completely objective social science is neither possible nor entirely desirable. Subjective interaction is indispensable to the development of social and more-than-social human understanding. But the subjectivity which should be accepted rather than fought as part of social-scientific research should subsequently be sifted and objectified as far as possible by identification of the biases, ideological and other, which have articulated the human interchange.

## Chapter 7

1. See the Appendix for the schema of categories used to classify the components which I will mainly consider. I do not propose these categories as internally consistent or exhaustive, nor do I borrow consistently from any of the many well articulated theories of semiotic units or semes. The virtue of the schema is pragmatic: it deals well with what

has been recorded about the half-dozen festive figures which I shall compare. In a monographic treatment the categories would have to be refined, and their ideological presuppositions explored.

2. Charles Day, *Five Years' Residence in the West Indies* (London, 1852), 1:314, republished in Abrahams and Szwed, eds., *After Africa*, 269.

3. Daniel Crowley, "Traditional Masks," 205–13, discusses these different forms of Indian masking by black Trinidadians. Crowley's informative article is ethnographic in orientation, recording many details of performances and costumes. Differences of time are less well indicated; it would seem that Crowley collected his materials in 1954–55; he often generalizes about "the last few years" or "recent times" (212–13). According to Crowley the Trinidadian Indian maskers, due to "the variety and fantasy of their costumes," set the tone of Carnival in the 1950s (205). Errol Hill's *Trinidad Carnival*, written in 1972, reports an ambiance which has already changed toward more spectacular, stagey forms. Between Crowley's work and Hill's, Trinidad's independence from Great Britain was finally achieved (1962).

4. This engraving is reproduced in Alexander Orloff, *Carnival, Myth and Cult* (Wörgl, Austria, 1981), 71, and also on the endpaper, inside back cover, of Hill, *Trinidad Carnival*. The Indian is shown just to the left of and behind the devil who dances front and center. The Indian has a feathered headdress and a seemingly white face mask, but his feet reveal him as a bare-footed black man.

5. Crowley, "Traditional Masks," 205–13. The Fancy Indians, Crowley says (211), originated from the Red Indians, with the "desire to 'improve' their masque," so that "each year the headpieces grew larger and more elaborate."

6. It seems obvious that the development of six kinds of Indian-masking bands in Trinidad is the result of these political and social factors of prestige. See James Stewart, "Patronage and Control in the Trinidad Carnival," in Edward Bruner and Victor Turner, eds., *The Anthropology of Experience* (Urbana, 1986), 289–315, for an analysis of the private and public interests producing this system of Carnival prestige.

7. The drawings were made from a photograph in Smith, *Spirit World*, 70, and from the drawing of a Fancy Indian chief in Crowley, "Traditional Masques," 208 (some use was also made of the photograph of a Fancy Indian in E. Hill, *Trinidad Carnival*, 17).

8. As recently as 1940 Mardi Gras Indians wore warpaint. See Saxon, et al., *Gumbo Ya-Ya*, 17 (Rightor in 1900 also mentioned warpaint). Conversely, the account published in 1945, like earlier sources, does *not* mention the chief's high headpiece; presumably it had not yet developed in anything like its present spectacular form. As mentioned in chap. 5, n. 40, the materials in the chapter about Mardi Gras Indians in *Gumbo Ya-Ya* are said to have been collected in 1940. It is plausible, but not documentarily confirmed, to suppose that the undated photo of two black Indians accompanying the chapter (facing p. 23) was taken at the same time, although they wear no warpaint. Publication of the book was presumably delayed by World War II.

9. See p. 212 below: Bowdich's description of war-captain dress in 1817.

10. See plates 18, 20, 21 in Eva Meyerowitz, *The Sacred State of the Akan* (London, 1951).

11. See the sketch of a "Wild Indian"'s costume in Crowley, "Traditional Masques," 208, which shows a bird sculpture on the masker's headdress.

12. See p. 50 above for the baby houses of the 1790s, and Matthew G. Lewis, *Journal of a West Indian Proprietor* (London, 1834), 51, for Lewis's view on January 1, 1816, of a John Canoe "in a striped doublet and bearing on his head a kind of pasteboard houseboat, filled with puppets, representing some sailors, others soldiers, others again slaves at work on a plantation, etc."

13. Judith Bettelheim, "Jamaican Jonkonnu and Related Caribbean Festivals," in Franklin Knight and Margaret Crahan, eds., *Africa and the Caribbean* (Baltimore, 1979), 98.

14. See, e.g., plates 16 (Gelede Cult, Yoruba) and 73 (Bangangte tribe) in William Bascom and Paul Gebauer, *Handbook of West African Art* (Milwaukee, 1953), or plates 38 (Gelede Cult, Yoruba) and 72 (Ibo) in Frank Willett, *African Art, An Introduction* (New York, 1971). Crowley, "Traditional Masques," 205, says that Red Indian masks sometimes included "a wire and paper effigy of a fish, a bird, or even an airplane." Smith, *Spirit World*, 75, shows a child's Mardi-Gras Indian headdress including a sculpture of a house in beadwork.

15. See the fine sequence of color photographs, Smith, *Spirit World*, 70–73, 78, 102. See also the color photographs in Laborde and Osborne, *Mardi Gras*, 134, 135.

16. My generalizations about Trinidad Indians are conjectural, based only on printed evidence.

17. There is a drawing of a batonyé with his stick and heart-shaped panel in E. Hill, *Trinidad Carnival*, on an unnumbered page facing page 12.

18. See chap. 5, n. 45.

19. This summary of stick fighting and its ambiance, like the concluding quotation, is from Andrew Pearse, "Carnival in Nineteenth-Century Trinidad," *Caribbean Quarterly* 4 (1955–56): 191–92. See also the discussion of stick fighting in E. Hill, *Trinidad Carnival*, 25–27, who found a reference for the year 1838 to a mock combat, perhaps a forerunner of the stick fighting.

20. Crowley, "Traditional Masques," 195. See the discussion of Pearse, "Carnival," 192–93. Crowley, 194, suggests an origin for the fighting in "English cudgels or quarter-staves." To substantiate this would require showing that the English sport was practiced in Trinidad or somewhere where these lower-class blacks could have seen it.

21. Judith Battelheim, "The Jonkonnu Festival, Its Relation to Caribbean and African Masquerades," *Jamaica Journal* 10 (1976): 22. Two pictures of the Wild Indian, as he appeared in 1975–76, are included in the article (23). It should be added that another relatively new character in present-day John Canoe troupes, the Warrior, also wears a foil-covered cardboard heart on his chest (22). A third article by Bettelheim (for the second, see n. 13 above) includes three more photos of present-day John Canoe troupes, but they are less particularized iconographically: "The Jonkonnu Festival in Jamaica," *Journal of Ethnic Studies* 13 (1985): 85–105.

22. In 1951 and 1952 the *Daily Gleaner*, a newspaper in Kingston, sponsored a "John Canoe" contest which attracted as many as fifty

groups from many parts of the island. It seems reasonable to suppose that at least some of these groups had continued to function, perhaps only sporadically, from their hey-day in the earlier nineteenth century (86).

23. Crowley, "Traditional Masques," 205–6.

24. Interview by the author with Maud Lyon, Curator of Costumes, Louisiana State Museum, March 1, 1987.

25. This was probably already true in 1900. Jelly Roll Morton's recollection of the Indians in 1938, referring to the late 1890s or early 1900s, shows the form of the practice which I observed in 1987, in which the chief initiated chanting and dancing. This form of *individual* prowess, rather than only group dancing, already existed (neither Rightor nor Kirsch point this out): "They wore paint and blankets and when they danced, one would get in the ring and throw his head back and downward, stooping over and bending his knees, making a rhythm with his heels and singing—T'ouwais, bas q'ouvais—and the tribe would answer—Ou tendais" (Lomax, *Mr. Jelly Roll*, 14).

26. See n. 79, chap. 8, for the white masks, probably made of wire, which according to Lafcadio Hearn, noticing apparently similar ones in Martinique in 1888, gave the face a ghostly appearance. Crowley, "Traditional Masques," 195, writes that batonyé wore bright shirts and trousers turned inside out, the belts to which were strung with ribbons and colored handkerchiefs.

27. The tradition of black Indian masking remains strongly characteristic of Haitian Carnival today, although stick fighting has disappeared. See the face paint and spectacular headdress of a black "Arawak Indian" in Port-au-Prince, Haiti, in the 1970s in Orloff, *Carnival*, plate 97.

28. That is, the Jamaican wild Indian figure just possibly developed as early as the 1880s, when the Orleanian Indians appeared, and when both wild Indians and batonyé existed in Trinidad, and seemingly also in Haiti. For an eloquent methodological plea in favor of parallel and autonomous rather than single-origin, diffusionist ideas of cultural change, see Colin Renfrew, *Before Civilization* (New York, 1979), particularly chapter 12. His field of inquiry and hence his demonstrations concern the prehistory of Europe. It seems probable that such an autonomous mode of development accounts in large part for the skits performed by black troupes of "cowboys" and "Indians" on Nevis, a Caribbean island far to the north of Trinidad, colonized in the 1620s by the British. R. Abrahams has suggested that the cowboy-and-Indian dialogues, music, and improvised melees which these groups perform at Christmas derive from two sources, the old St. George-and-the-Turk mumming plays common in Great Britain, and the "Street and Smith cowboy magazines of the 1930s." Abrahams, "'Pull Out Your Purse and Pay': A St. George Mumming from the British West Indies," *Folklore* 79 (1968), 196. At the same time Abrahams has also reported at least one other trait which associates these Nevis Indians with the behavior of Orleanian and Trinidadian troupes. "The Indians talk in a kind of extremely fast gibberish, with lines usually ending 'King George said I be an *Indian*,' or 'President Roosevelt make me an *Indian!*'" Abrahams, "The Cowboy in the British West Indies," in M. C. Boatwright, W. M. Hudson, and A. Maxwell, eds., *A Good Tale and a Bonnie Tune* (Dallas, 1964), 170.

29. Crowley, "Traditional Masques," 212.

30. Cf. the Wild Magnolias' wildman, photographed in Smith, *Spirit World*, plates 76 and 77, with plates 4 and 37 in this book: the Zulu Society's witch doctor.

31. The wildman's costume in Smith, *Spirit World*, 76, includes some ostrich plumes and much traditional "wild West" beadwork (e.g., a rearing horse as his chest plaque). Still another tantalizing connection between the Trinidadian batonyé and the Mardi Gras Indians crops up in this connection. The batonyé's hat "sometimes" had "cows' horns" (Crowley, "Traditional Masques," 195).

32. Bettelheim, "The Jonkonnu Festival," (1976), 22.

33. It is made more difficult by the divergence in interests between anthropologists and historians interested in Africa. African anthropological studies offer a rich array of studies of individual tribes which, however, pay scarcely any attention to historical evolution or to comparative cultural patterns across the vastly diverse continent. African historical work is above all concerned with questions of the political and economic development of present-day African nations. Art historians and music historians, on the other hand, have developed excellent comparative studies. Alan Lomax, "African-Afro-American Musical Style," in John Szwed and Norman Whitten, eds., *Afro-American Anthropology: Contemporary Perspectives* (New York, 1970), 181–201, analyzed musical styles from all parts of Africa in terms of thirty-seven "cantometric factors" (a more sophisticated, statistically developed version of the kind of costume-seme analysis formulated in this chapter), comparing their form in different African regions with Haitian song style. John Szwed, "Afro-American Musical Adaptation," in ibid., 219–27, sets forth in an exemplary manner the complexity of Afro-American adaptation of African musical style by analyzing the difference between Afro-American southern U.S. church-song and blues styles. J. H. Kwabena Nketia's *The Music of Africa* (New York, 1974), has been particularly helpful to me here in understanding the range of Mardi Gras Indian dance and song behavior. Works by the art historians William Bascom, Robert Farris Thompson, and Frank Willett were also illuminating in a number of ways.

34. Lomax, "African-Afro-American Musical Style," 194–95, presents a table and map indicating that the two areas, West Africa and southeast Africa, possess a similar "equatorial" song style in terms of his factorial analysis. The word "African" in my text should be taken to refer to the cultures of this twin area of sub-Saharan Africa, unless specified otherwise.

35. The royal New Year's ritual, described by Hilda Kuper in 1944, has become a *locus classicus* of anthropological interpretation, soliciting not only the very important revisionist interpretation by T. O. Beidelman from which I mainly take my commentary but also major commentaries by Max Gluckman and Victor Turner. See T. O. Beidelman, "Swazi Royal Ritual," *Africa* 36 (1966): 373–405, and 397 for the quotation in the text here.

36. Ibid., 377, 398.

37. Ibid., 377, 400.

38. See pp. 49–53.

39. Robert Dirks, "Slaves' Holiday," *Natural History* 84 (December 1975): 94, suggests that the John Canoe figures combine English mumming practices with African dance movements.

40. Enoch Widmann, "Hofer Chronik," in *Quellen zur Geschichte der Stadt Hof*, ed. Christian Meyer (Hof, 1894), 202–3.

41. I have pursued this question with respect to parallel phenomena in nearby Nuremberg for the same period in my "Presentation and Representation."

42. Beidelman, "Swazi Royal Ritual," 385.

43. Trillin, "The Zulus," 111. The spokesman, Alex Rapheal, was a key organizer of the parades in the early 1960s, and the oldest living member of the Zulus in 1980.

44. It is interesting that Rapheal did not "read" the Zulu king's intensification of blackness by means of grease-paint and black-dyed underwear (see below, p. 235), a blackness made the more visible by contrast with the white-grease-painted eyes and mouth. Extra blackness meant extra low status in New Orleans' Creole-oriented middle- and upper-class black community: this body painting was one of the black community's focuses of attack on the Zulus in the 1960s, the time when Rapheal made his comment. There are many examples in African tribal ceremonies of bodies blackened and whitened with ritual designs. As we will see, however, the specific reference of the Orleanians' Zulu grease-paint was parody of the white man's "Sambo" image, whatever may be its deeper origins.

45. Here are the eleven points: (1) headpiece and/or head extension; (2) face; (3) upper torso, shoulders; (4) mid-section (genitals, anus, stomach); (5) arms; (6) hands; (7) legs; (8) feet; (9) materials held above or before body; (10) materials held by body; (11) insignia/labels on body.

46. Alfred Ellis, *The Tshi-Speaking Peoples of the Gold Coast of West Africa* (London, 1887), 246, 251 (Ellis reprints Bowdich's description in full).

47. The ram's horns, curling backwards (ibid., 251), do not of course have the same effect as bovine horns, spreading outward. These parallels should not be seen as exactly coincident. In 1871 another European military man named Ramseyer witnessed another Ashanti procession in Kumasi, which included the following: "Our old friend the general wore a small round cap, ornamented by buffalo's horns and falcon's feathers . . ." (ibid., 269). This is a more relevant image, as far as these particular costume semes are concerned, which comes from the same powerful and prestigious tribal group.

48. Ellis, *The Tshi-Speaking Peoples*, 252.

49. Ibid., 246.

50. Ibid.

51. Ibid., 246–47.

52. Ibid., 249.

53. Ibid., 255–56. A caboceer is a war-captain.

54. Ibid., 245–46.

55. See further on this last quality the instances in chap. 8, n. 20.

56. As other researchers know who are interested in pursuing historicization of interethnic cultural phenomena at the oral, mass-cultural level, three problems constantly recur which in my case impeded research, sometimes for months and years, until some chance encounter yielded a clue or some expertise. First, the heterogeneity of languages (in the case of this study, the immense variety of relevant African languages, the variants in Creole language from island to island, even the variants in popular American dialects, relevant to such problems as the meaning of John Canoe, belsnickle, *bas ouvrais*, etc.). Second, the inad-

equacy of words to group, let alone convey to others the visual, gestural, musical effects of festive action. Third, the dispersion of archives and source materials (there is a persistent rumor that the French ministry of foreign affairs possesses somewhere in its colonial archives some instances of Mardi Gras Indian dancing, impossible as that seems to me!). Will the computer (making an immense dictionary-bank of language equivalents as available as world cross-listing of archival holdings, according to subject-matter), tape-recorder, and TV camera solve all this? Perhaps, but probably not. What could the computer or some other technical means do to discover the explanation of that old New Orleans cry, "Mardi Gras! Chickle-le-paw!" nearly always thought to be deformed French? George Reinecke, "Mardi-Gras, Chooka Lapai: A Probable Meaning," *Louisiana Folklore Miscellany* 3, no. 1 (April, 1970): 77–79, shows that it is probably "a forgotten Choctaw expression," meaning roughly "Mardi Gras! Raggedy-men!" or "vagrants," "vagabonds"—a reference to wild maskers, especially rural ones, as in the country form of Mardi Gras practiced in rural Louisiana (see pp. 00–00 above). Reinecke's solution, as he recounts it, was not found simply by hunting through Choctaw dictionaries (that was involved), but was rather provoked by another scholar's wrong (to Reinecke) construction of the phrase and the memory of a joke told by his father about an Indian in a New Orleans blacksmith shop!

Chapter 8
1. See pp. 50–52.
2. I. M. Belisario, *Sketches of Character in Illustration of the Habits, Occupations and Costume of the Negro Population in the Island of Jamaica* (Kingston, 1838: extremely rare), in Abrahams and Szwed, eds., *After Africa*, 259–60. Belisario explains Koo-Koo thus, (259 n.): "It appears that many years back, this *John-Canoe* performed in pantomimic actions *only*, consisting of supplications for food—as being demanded by his empty stomach. At each request, an attendant chorus repeated "Koo-Koo," this was intended in imitation of the rumbling sound of the bowels, when in a hungry state."
3. Alex Helm, *English Mummers' Plays* (Cambridge, 1981) is perhaps the most comprehensive recent account of these plays. Henry Glassie, *All Silver and No Brass: An Irish Christmas Mumming* (Bloomington, Indiana, 1975) provides a pleasantly informal account of the custom.
4. Abrahams and Szwed, eds., *After Africa*, 260.
5. Ibid., 261.
6. Ibid.
7. The two figural types still existed in the 1920s in rural Jamaica, as is shown by Martha Beckwith, *Christmas Mummings in Jamaica* (Poughkeepsie, New York, 1923), 8, and we have seen that they continue to exist today (Bettelheim, "The Jonkonnu Festival," 1985).
8. The meaning of the word "kuker" is scarcely less controversial than that of "John Canoe," again because it occurs on the boundary between two cultural areas, Greek and Slavic, and may thus reflect criss-crossing influences taking place over a long period. I will not discuss the controversy here but simply recommend the interpretation of Constantin Romaios (Konstantinos Rhomaios), *Cultes populaires de la Thrace* (Athens, 1949), 152, who affirms that *kukeros* is a Greek substantive referring to an old man hunched over with age; in the Pontus area, the word is

sometimes used as an adjective, "head-bowed." The relation of this old-man meaning of kuker to the fertile wildman figure described in our text can be shown, although the route is circuitous and will not detain us here. The most important ethnographic work on the kukers was done by Mikhail Arnaudov in early twentieth-century Bulgaria. See his "Kukeri i Rusalii" (written in Bulgarian), *Sbornik za Narodni Umotrozenija i Narodpis*, 34 (1920): 1–244. A brief resume of this work is available in Arnaudov's *Die bulgarische Festbräuche* (Leipzig, 1917).

9. There are hundreds of these festive wildmen recorded by nineteenth- and twentieth-century folklorists in all parts of Europe, from Alps to lowlands, from Greece and Bulgaria to the Shetland Islands, each differing in details of costuming and performance. Since figures like the belsnickle should be included in the group, many more variants of the European tradition can be noted in the New World as well. No synthetic treatment of this persona exists. The most embracing list of its forms is in Waldemar Liungman's *Traditionswanderungen*, but he misses many of the Western European forms in southern France, Spain, and the British Isles, and diligent research has uncovered many more such figures since Liungman wrote in 1937. Samuel Glotz's *Le Masque dans la tradition européenne* (Binche, 1975) is geographically very broad in its treatment of wildman figures and has the advantage of profuse illustration.

10. The drawing is based on the photograph of a costume made for museum display at Binche, Belgium, and reproduced, in Glotz, *Le Masque*, 125. See also ibid., 384, for further information on the kuker of Padarevo.

11. Arnaudov, *Die bulgarische Festbrauche*, 33.

12. Cf. the photograph in Glotz, *Le Masque*, 114, and the photographs of old museum figures of the kukers in the 1930s in Liungman, *Traditionswanderungen*, 794–95. Marina Tcherkezova, "Les Jeux Carnavalesques bulgares," in Glotz, *Le Masque*, 112–26, explains that the kukers in the 1920s and 1930s began substituting more and more bird plumes and feathers for the traditional animal furs, another fortuitous parallel to the Mardi Gras Indians, who, as far as we can tell, began adopting the ostentatious ostrich plumes in the 1930s or 1940s.

13. See Glotz, *Le Masque*, 119 and 122, for photographs of kukers with huge bells. The Mardi Gras Indians' physical prowess is similar. Smith, *Spirit World*, 97, says that a full-length costume weighing 100–150 pounds will be carried twenty or thirty miles through the city on mardi gras.

14. The kliunks and the way they are hooked together are shown in photographs in Liungman, *Traditionswanderungen*, 790–805, whose account of the kukers is the fullest in a non-Slavic language. Liungman translates many of Arnaudov's descriptions in the latter's "Kukeri" with accuracy, but of course not always with completeness.

15. As indicated in chapter 2, the New Year in many parts of Europe was considered to begin in March, not January, close to the time of Carnival-Lent, not Christmas-New Year.

16. Nikola's kuker game is summarized in Liungman, *Traditionswanderungen*, 792–93, from Arnaudov, "Kukeri," 9–14.

17. See pp. 5–6.

18. Until 1918, for example, the paradigmatically supreme figure of political power for Slavic Christians, including those under Turkish

rule, was the Russian czar. He was for peasants, and especially Bulgarian peasants in the Turkish Empire, supreme but also distant and unfamiliar, so that his meaning could be playfully treated.

19. This does not mean that phallic symbolism is totally absent. Smith, *Spirit World*, 78, caught a fine example of it in his photograph of the *ithyphallos* glowing in beaded splendor between the thighs of the chief of the Black Eagles in 1980.

20. See, e.g., ibid., 99, a photograph called "tribes meeting," in which two black Indians, facing each other only a foot apart in the midst of a boastful exchange, scarcely seem to possess human countenances, so heavily do their costumes press in and down upon cheeks and foreheads. There is scarcely the space for nostrils and lips to emerge. It is as if the costuming were intended to blot out any attempt of the personality to interfere with the spectacular effects achieved by material elements. The sense of material surfeit is like that experienced by Bowdich, gazing upon the Ashanti captains and their attendants: "Some wore necklaces reaching to the waist entirely of aggry beads; a band of gold and beads encircled the knee, from which several strings of the same depended; small circlets of gold, like guineas, rings, and casts of animals, were strung round their ankles; their sandals were of green, red, and delicate white leather; manillas, and rude lumps of rock gold, hung from their left wrists, which were so heavily laden as to be supported on the head of one of their handsomest boys." Ellis, *The Tshi-Speaking Peoples*, 250–51.

21. Edward S. Curtis, *The North American Indians*, 20 vols. (Seattle, 1907–30); vol. 10 treats the Kwakiutl. Curtis has been much criticized by anthropologists for his theatrical staging of these photographs. Indeed, the masks in question were used in a very stagey film by him. Extended reading of Franz Boas's carefully circumstantial ethnographies of Kwakiutl rituals, however, shows that Curtis seized important aspects of the spirit of these ceremonies and their costuming.

22. See p. 125, and chap. 5, n. 15, above on the Iris "krewe." Ostrich-plume headdresses are a commonplace Mardi Gras costume effect today and, it seems, they were already so in Paris *boeuf gras* parades from the 1820s (chap. 6, n. 10) through the 1850s (plate 16). The feathered headdress becomes specifically Indian, as is the case here, when worn in the Plains-Indian-chief war-bonnet fashion, "around their heads way down in the back," as Elise Kirsch said (see above, p. 163).

23. A word about the difference of the Iris Indian girls from the Mardi Gras Indian "Queens" who march alongside their "chiefs": Indian Queens wear short-skirted costumes and sometimes figure-fitting blouses. They rarely include elaborate beadwork designs or grand geometrical designs but their skirts, boots, gloves, and large headdresses are kept in the style of the tribe to which they belong and the man whom they accompany. Femininity is thus given more emphasis in the women's than is maleness in the men's costumes. But female sexuality remains subordinate to black Indian qualities, the group's norm. In contrast to this, the Indian quality of the Iris girls' costumes was simply added as the top layer to a non-Indian sign, that of the majorette.

24. See p. 47.

25. Dunham, *Dances of Haiti*, 34–35.

26. Ibid., 34. Dunham's book is valuable, although sociologically (no class distinctions) and historically (no dates) frustrating, because she

reports both town and country performances. Even urban-rural differences in performance are too often sheared away in generalizations about "Carnival dances" in contrast to sacred dances. Dunham's prime interests are formal and esthetic.

27. Ibid.

28. Michel Honorat, *Les danses folkloriques haitiennes* (Port au Prince, 1955), 122–23.

29. Ibid., 120.

30. Honorat, in ibid., 122, writes that in the western region of Haiti the kings of the "bandes-mascarons" wore "(1) le Candale qui recouvre la poitrine, l'abdomen et les genoux du roi; 2ᵉ la couronne placée sur la tête du roi s'appelle communément 'Bolivar'; 3ᵉ le Manteau avec 'retourne' est brodé et pailleté. Le retourne est une espèce de pèlerine qui est attachée au manteau. Mais il sert à recouvrir le dos tandis que le candale tombe par-devant; 4ᵉ culotte ou pantalon; 5ᵉ souliers de velours bleu et rouge."

31. Ibid., 121–22.

32. Berry, Foose, Jones, *Up from the Cradle*, 211.

33. The finest evocation of this rhythmic quality of black Carnival dancing and singing ever written occurs in Lafcadio Hearn's description of Carnival in 1888 in Martinique. Here is a brief excerpt from the ten-page description (Hearn, *Two Years*, 213–16):

> Night falls;—the maskers crowd to the ball-rooms to dance strange tropical measures that will become wilder and wilder as the hours pass. And through the black streets, the Devil makes his last Carnival-round.
>
> By the gleam of the old-fashioned oil lamps hung across the thoroughfares I can make out a few details of his costume. He is clad in red, wears a hideous blood-colored mask, and a cap of which the four sides are formed by four looking-glasses;—the whole head-dress being surmounted by a red lantern. . . . Down the street he comes, leaping nearly his own height,—chanting words without human signification,—and followed by some three hundred boys, who form the chorus to his chant—all clapping hands together and giving tongue with a simultaneity that testifies how strongly the sense of rhythm enters into the natural musical feeling of the African,—a feeling powerful enough to impose itself upon all Spanish-America, and there create the unmistakable characteristics of all that is called "creole music."
>
> —"Bimbolo!"
> —"Zimabolo!"
> —"Et bolo-po!"
>
> —sing the Devil and his chorus. His chant is cavernous, abysmal,—booms from his chest like the sound of a drum beaten in the bottom of a well. . . . *Ti manmaille-la, baill moin lavoix!* ("Give me voice, little folk,—give me voice.'") And all chant after him, in a chanting like the rushing of many waters, and with triple clapping of hands:—"*Ti manmaille-la, baill moin lavoix!*". . .
>
>                              . . .
>
> About midnight the return of the Devil and his following arouses me from sleep:—all are chanting a new refrain, "The Devil and the zombis sleep anywhere and everywhere!" *(Diabe épi zombi ka dòmi tout-pàtout.)* The voices of the boys are still clear, shrill, fresh,—clear as a chant of frogs;—they still clap

hands with a precision of rhythm that is simply wonderful,—
making each time a sound almost exactly like the bursting of a
heavy wave:—. . . .

. . .Then the chanting grows fainter in distance; the Devil's
immense basso becomes inaudible;—one only distinguishes at
regular intervals the *crescendo* of the burden,—a wild swelling
of many hundred boy-voices all rising together,—a retreating
storm of rhythmic song, wafted to the ear in gusts, in *rafales* of
contralto. . . .

34. Nketia, *The Music of Africa*, 55–56, emphasizes the necessity
among African musicians, if they are to become singers of repute, of
possessing a repertory of talents—somewhat like the Harlem Globe-
trotters—which includes dramatic, linguistic, and psychic no less than
musical qualities. The relative priority given to rhythmized bodily
movement functions almost to guarantee the inseparability of them all:
Nketia has further emphasized the African "aesthetic concept which
makes the qualities of sound related to movement its primary focus of
attention" (217). Thus, music is oriented toward bodily gesture more
than verbal elaboration, toward dance more than song. Words are reduced to what can be chanted and the chanting is developed rhythmically more than melodically, phatically more than lyrically.

35. Wilson Turbinton, the rhythm-and-blues singer and composer
(see chap. 6, pp. 172–73), grew up in the 1950s in a housing project in
the old black uptown area of New Orleans. As a teenager he watched
the Indians in that neighborhood: "They had some instruments made
out of bottle caps and [they would] nail 'em on sticks, and the sticks
would be so long they could actually beat rhythms on the ground, but
also get a thud from the earth. And I made a couple of those and would
use 'em. It was the kind of groove that you couldn't resist. The pulse
affected you. You find yourself patting your foot . . ." (Berry, Foose,
Jones, *Up from the Cradle*, 220).

36. I want to disavow any intention which readers might think is at
work here or elsewhere in this book, of setting up a dichotomy between
black and white cultures, inside or outside of Carnival. That is why I
have used "first" and "second" Carnivals as terms with changing content, sometimes meaning white vs. black, sometimes Canal Street vs.
the French Quarter (see chap. 10), sometimes meaning centralized and
organized vs. neighborly, private, unsupervised.

More generally I think that black Americans' culture is inextricably
interwoven not only with Caribbean culture, with its manifold ethnic
tones, but with white North Americans' culture. For all the usefulness
of such meditations as M. Ventura's on the relations of African religions
to particular elements of Gospel singing, of jazz and rock-and-roll, and
of some parts of Mardi Gras Indian performance (*Shadow Dancing*, esp.
chap. 6), I think his emphasis on particular persons (e.g., Buddy Bol-
den), particular religious practices (especially *vodun*) and particular
places (Storyville in the 1890s) is misleading. Naming a few famous
times and places leads to a confining specificity, and may induce passive hero-worship, mistaken fetishism, and the ethnic stereotyping
mentioned above. These faults are not exhibited as such in Ventura's
book, but a balancing emphasis on the broad contours of Afro-
American culture and a sense of the countless paths of oral-bodily communication within it and between it and Anglo-American cultures
would have helped. I am speaking of the kind of insight exhibited by

Ralph Ellison in an essay on Leroi Jones's *Blues People* (*Shadow and Act*, New York, 1964, 246–47): "[One cannot] fashion a theory of American Negro culture while ignoring the intricate network of connections which binds Negroes to the larger society. . . . Attempt to discuss jazz as a hermetic expression of Negro sensibility and immediately we must consider what the 'mainstream' of American music really is." Or again: "Slavery was a most vicious system . . . but it was *not* . . . a state of absolute repression. A slave was, to the extent that he was a musician . . . a man who realized himself. . . . For the art—the blues, the spiritual, the jazz, the dance—was what we had in place of freedom." That very artistry had and has its political consequences, and handicaps.

37. Tallant, *Mardi Gras*, 245.

38. The ball until recent years took place on mardi gras eve. Now it is held a week earlier.

39. Zulu Social Aid and Pleasure Club, *Official 1980 Program* (conserved at New Orleans Public Library), 11.

40. Ibid. No source is indicated for these stories, which may represent agreed-on oral tradition.

41. Myron Tassin and Gaspar Stall, *Mardi Gras and Bacchus: Something Old, Something New* (Gretna, Louisiana, 1984), 46.

42. Trillin, "The Zulus," 114. In the 1964 parade, however, another person was treated as Grand Marshal, not this man in a tentlike costume, as I mention later in the text.

43. Huber, *Mardi Gras*, 64.

44. The club's banner says the club was founded in May 1916 and incorporated in September 1916. Strangely enough, the Zulus celebrated their fiftieth anniversary after forty-eight years, in 1964. Asked about the discrepancy, a club officer said that the banner was a new one, and its maker had copied the dates wrongly. Trillin, "The Zulus," 41, 94. It is possible that although Carnival parading began in 1909, the social aid functions of the club only were formalized in 1916. But all this dating should perhaps be taken lightly.

45. Charles Day recounted one skit played by blacks in the 1848 Carnival as follows: "The primitives were negroes, as nearly naked as might be, bedaubed with a dark varnish. One of this gang [of ten to twenty persons] had a long chain and padlock attached to his leg, which chain the others pulled. . . . As the chained one was occasionally thrown down on the ground, and treated with a mock bastinadoing, it probably represented slavery—" (Abrahams and Szwed, *After Africa*, 268). Probably, too, it was an astute way of using Carnival to advertise inhumanity to fun-makers who would rather not know about it. Hearn, *Two Years*, 210, saw in the Martinique Carnival, 1888, a similar masker with "nothing but a cloth about his loins; his whole body and face being smeared with an atrocious mixture of soot and molasses. He is supposed to represent the original African ancestor." Molasses, a product of sugar cane, was nearly as hateful a symbol to blacks in the islands as chains, and here it is in a similar way turned aside, played with, and made ominous in a new direction. By the 1880s a character called the "molasses devil" (*jab molassi*) might lead the Carnival dance. See E. Hill, *Trinidad Carnival*, 24, for these connections and his inside back cover for the engraving, earlier referred to (chap. 7, n. 4), of a *jab molassi* dancing in the streets of Port of Spain in 1883.

46. Barker, *A Life*, 37. It is probable that the Zulus have never intended to satirize or even to refer to the actually existing important African tribe of Zulus in southeast Africa. The New Orleans paraders are as far removed from the African prototype as are Mardi Gras Indians from any actual Amerindian group.

47. The "royal barge" by which in 1917 King Zulu arrived in his Carnival kingdom of New Orleans at the end of the New Basin Canal in the black uptown area was a rowboat, in imitation of Rex's arrival by yacht at the foot of Canal Street on the Mississippi.

48. Robert de Coy, *The Nigger Bible* (Los Angeles, 1967), 106, 19.

49. This is the tendency expressed in the masquerade of the Mardi Gras Indians, as it is of anyone, white or black, adopting the ambivalent Indian mask. But perhaps one should remember that the Mardi Gras Indians adopt it in Carnival, which dethrones every pretension to serious meaning.

50. This kind of not always subtle daring, we recall from chapter 2, was a tradition with blacks from colonial days. It was their way to make use of the slavery barrier and the caste barrier; in fact today, as the caste barrier grows weaker, so this festively satiric way of parodying white stereotypes disappears. In the 1930s the Zulus even included a character called "Kingfish," at the time when Huey Long was governor. I have not located a description of this Zulu character and float.

51. Trillin, "The Zulus," 114–15. The New Basin Canal was paved over in the 1950s and the Zulus began meeting their king at a boat on the Mississippi. Note that the presence of the Grand Marshal in tights here implies that the man with the tentlike costume (n. 43) is either some other sort of steward or an entirely different character.

52. They also provide plenty of the usual satire of whites. In the big parades of the 1930s, said one old-timer in 1964, there were not only thirty or forty warriors with spears but thirty or forty "dukes" who rode mules, not horses: "the oldest and deadest mules they could find" (ibid., 74).

53. Alex Rapheal, manager of the Zulu parade in 1964, said: "It appears at this junction that I'll be doing away with the Witch Doctor. The Witch Doctor is causing some of the trouble, and he's outlived his usefulness anyway." But Rapheal was irrepressible. He continued: "I'm thinking of replacing him with a Voodoo Doctor." That idea was squelched. Trillin, "The Zulus," 62.

54. Huber, *Mardi Gras*, 64, top of page: a photograph from 1941 (Alonzo Butler was king in 1941; the *Official Program 1980*, 24, gives a complete list of kings).

55. Trillin, "The Zulus," 113.

56. Tallant, *Mardi Gras*, 247.

57. Trillin, "The Zulus," 107.

58. In addition to Trillin's report of the conflict down to the year 1964, in ibid., see Goreau, "Mardi Gras," in Hodding Carter, ed., *The Past as Prelude: New Orleans 1718–1968* (New Orleans, 1968), 368–69, for brief reference to the following years.

59. Leonard Burns, a chiropodist and president of an association of respectable black Carnival clubs, was quoted in 1964 by Trillin, "The Zulus," 60–61: "We met with the Zulus a number of times—if you can't beat them, join them, we figured. . . . But in subsequent meetings he

[the president of the Zulus] said there was one thing he was determined to keep and that was the black-face King, so negotiations broke down. We were willing to keep the name but *not* the blackface King. We thought we'd have a dignified parade, showing the progress the Negro has made in America. . . . To tell you the truth, we've just about given up on them. . . . I was talking with a doctor in town today about the possibility of some respectable Negroes joining the Zulus and changing the thing with their votes. Maybe that would work." Eureka!

60. See the story on the Zulu Coronation Ball in the *Times-Picayune*, February 28, 1987, sec. E, p. 5. Are pictures still taken of the king in "traditional costume," as he is shown in Laborde and Osborne, *Mardi Gras*, 131, or only in the new style, ibid., 133?

61. *Official Program 1980*, 3.

62. The King still wore a nose ring in 1964 (Trillin, "The Zulus," 41), and the Big Shot and dukes did too in the old days (Huber, *Mardi Gras*, 64: photographs).

63. Note also the female Zulus at the young man's side. This also is a recent innovation.

64. This contrast between the two records is the judgment of Berry, Foose, Jones, *Up from the Cradle*, after an extended, sensitive analysis of both productions, 224–36.

65. Ibid., 241–42: The films were Maurice Martinez's *Black Indians of New Orleans* (1976) and Les Blank's *Always for Pleasure* (1979). Martinez's film is reviewed by Francis A. De Caro, *Journal of American Folklore*, 91 (1978): 625–27, Blank's by Robert Gordon, ibid., 92 (1979): 261.

66. In 1987 the Louisiana State Museum in New Orleans exhibited Mardi Gras Indian "patches"—that is, the plaques which are placed at the center of the headdress and skirts and often elsewhere in the costume—made by fourth and fifth graders in the public schools in workshops conducted to observe a Black Heritage Festival (*Times-Picayune*, February 18, 1987, Mardi Gras Supplement, p. 16).

67. Reinecke, professor of English at the University of New Orleans and former editor of the *Louisiana Folklore Miscellany*, made this comment in the course of a joint lecture with Sister Mary Desales Oliver on November 14, 1979, at the New Orleans Public Library: "Growing up in New Orleans in the 1930s" (tape cassette available at Library).

68. Interview with Barbara Wallace, Mardi Gras Indian Queen, March 1, 1987. See also the undated photograph of the St. Louis Cemetery Marching Club, led by a skeleton masker, in Tassin and Stall, *Mardi Gras*, 42.

69. On the marching clubs in Mardi Gras, see pp. 293–94. Day, *Five Years*, in Abrahams and Szwed, *After Africa*, 269.

70. See n. 34 to this chapter. In Trinidad in the 1950s a masking group called the "Unburied Dead" paraded, "covered in yellowish mud and strung with eight still living krapo (*bufo marinis*) . . ." (Crowley, "Traditional Masques," 214).

71. See the extraordinary materials collected in Abrahams and Szwed, *After Africa*, chap. 4, "Religion and Magic: Beliefs and Practices."

72. Carnival's date, like Ash Wednesday's, is a movable one, depending on the date of Easter. So Carnival's relation to the Old Year-New Year division is a vague association, not a precise feeling. Christian leaders wanted to combat the nature-worshipping superstitions con-

nected with reverence for either the January or March kalends (January 1, March 1) as the beginning of the year.

73. A comprehensive record of the ceremonies, recorded by nineteenth-century ethnographers, is to be found in the thirteen volumes of James Frazer's *Golden Bough* (London, 1910–37, 3d ed.), especially in vols. 2, 4, and 8. The idea that the rituals were age-old and at the origin of Carnival seems to be an inversion of what happened: their attachment to Carnival was a gradual process from the Middle Ages to the nineteenth century, as was suggested in chap. 1.

74. On the death-of-Carnival ritual, see James Frazer, *The Golden Bough* 4 (1912): 222–40.

75. See pp. 107–8.

76. Joan Martin, "Life among Black Creoles in the Early 1900s," Public Lecture, October 9, 1980, New Orleans Public Library (conserved on tape cassette at Library).

77. See the reference to this stop in 1947 on p. 232 above. According to Young, *Mistick Krewe*, 209–10, Mr. Moss was a committed member of the Zulus, riding the floats with blackened skin and paying all costs not covered by other means. Young expresses the half amused, half horrified view of whites at such a setting in his concluding sentence about the Zulus: "The climax of their day is when the royal car halts at the mortuary parlor of Geddes and Moss on Jackson Avenue, where a toast is drunk to His Majesty, and where the entire cast [sic] dismount to enter the large room where wakes are held, there to participate in the royal dinner as guests of the proprietors."

78. The mixture of seriousness and joyousness expressed in New Orleans' "jazz funerals"—also on the way to disappearance, like the Zulus' traditions—is as mysterious and incongruous to white people as this funeral-parlor site of Carnival.

79. Hearn was struck by similar masks in Martinique where, according to him, they were commonplace. See *Two Years*, 210–11: "The masks worn by the multitude . . . as a rule . . . are simply white wire masks, having the form of an oval and regular human face. . . . It struck me at once that this peculiar type of wire mask gave an indescribable tone of ghostliness to the whole exhibition [here, as in the quotation in n. 29, he is speaking of Carnival in 1888 in a provincial town]. It is not in the least comical . . . it is colorless as mist,—expressionless, void, dead;— it lies on the face like a vapor, like a cloud,—creating the idea of a spectral vacuity behind it. . . ."

80. Even the macabre Death whom Day saw in 1848 produced guffaws: "Death . . . a skeleton . . . stalked about . . . a horse's thighbone in his hand; but his most telling movements only elicited shouts of laughter" (Abrahams and Szwed, *After Africa*, 269).

81. See the quotation from Young in n. 77 above: the "entire cast" of the Zulus "dismounts to go and banquet at the Geddes and Moss Funeral Home."

82. Berry, Foose, Jones, *Up from the Candle*, 244, come to sadly similar conclusions with respect to the "musical economy" of New Orleans. The end to school segregation in New Orleans between 1960 and 1962 incited much, although relatively short-lived bitterness. That story is briefly told by Benjamin Muse, *Ten Years of Prelude, the Story of Integration since the Supreme Court's 1954 Decision* (New York, 1964), 214–33 and 228–33.

83. The reference is to Saxon's account of Carnival in 1900, discussed at the end of chap. 5.

Chapter 9

1. Some of the water-color designs used to make Comus's floats for this parade are reproduced in Young, *Mistick Krewe*. I paraphrase here the extended description of the 1910 parades in George Douglas, *The American Book of Days* (New York, 1937), 97–107.

2. Laborde and Osborne, *Mardi Gras*, 103–4, describe Bacchus's invention by Blaine Kern and Owen Brennan. See ibid., 102, for an earlier version of Bacchusaurus, even more Disney-like with lower jaw flapping in a grin.

3. Nice developed a tradition of parading outsized, cartoon-like characters in the later nineteenth century. See Annie Sidro, *Le Carnaval de Nice et ses Fous* (Nice, 1979). Similar constructions were developed in New Orleans in the 1870s, "great papier-maché giants . . . monsters with huge and grotesque heads wobbling about on their necks" (Tallant, *Mardi Gras*, 163; see plate 7 above). After 1900 the big heads began to vanish in New Orleans, whereas they have remained popular in Nice. The dragon float of Nice was still largely made of wood and papier-mâché. Bacchusaurus' plastics, steel, and sophisticated cements were not available or adaptable. Incidentally, Bacchus also parades a "Bacchagator" rather closer to the Nice dragon in belligerence and on the same gigantic scale. Nice in 1979 produced "Carnavalosaure," a modern rival to Bacchusaurus (Sidro, *Carnaval de Nice*, 139).

4. Quoted from The New Orleans *Times-Picayune* Advertising Supplement for February 11, 1982, p. 13, advertising Bacchus's parade on February 21, 1982.

5. This scene is also illustrated in Laborde and Osborne, *Mardi Gras*, 106.

6. John Smith Kendall, *History of New Orleans* (Chicago and New York, 1922) 2:721. Kendall, 723, writes that Rex issues "nearly 15,000" invitations to outsiders each year; "it is not difficult for any reputable person, newly arrived in the city, to secure a card to its ball." Residents, on the other hand, were as severely restricted in attendance as at the other old-line balls.

7. See Laborde and Osborne, *Mardi Gras*, 74, and the *Times-Picayune*, Mardi Gras Supplement, February 18, 1987, p. 34.

8. Arthur Hardy, *Mardi Gras Guide (1987)*, 5.

9. The famous painting was created in 1876 as part of the centenary celebration of American independence. It has frequently been parodied. See Tassin and Stall, *Mardi Gras*, 82 and 84. This parade and others since the early 1970s also included two wildman figures adapted to comic-book dimensions: King Kong and—of course—Queen Kong.

10. Reported in *Gambit* (New Orleans weekly newspaper), February 28, 1987, p. 10.

11. Tassin and Stall, *Mardi Gras*, 93. The Wild Tchoupitoulas are a Mardi Gras Indian group who have joined with the Neville Brothers to produce a record album, as discussed in chap. 8.

12. The more dreamlike the projection of "reality," the more technology and organizational sophistication is required. Blaine Kern Enterprises (see n. 2 above) is by all odds the biggest business connected with

Carnival. His marketing strategies are as sophisticated and wide-flung as his float constructions.

13. See Jack Ludwig, *The Great American Spectaculars* (New York, 1976), 42.

14. Rayford, *Chasin'*, 98.

15. These themes were listed in the advertisement in the *Times-Picayune* (see n. 4 above). Diemert's Santa Claus was no doubt as Americanized as his other impersonations, with no shadow of the old belsnickle (St. Nicholas-in-fur: see p. 80). But let it be noted that I am speaking of only one side of Carnival's twentieth-century development here, the expansion of its middle-class component. Other sides of the present era are not consonant with this one.

16. Today Rex's members include some people from New York City. Some of Endymion's members fly in from London and Saudi Arabia. See the *Times-Picayune*, February 28, 1987, p. B-1.

17. Comic-strip characters began to appear after 1900 in New Orleans: "Happy Hooligan, the Katzenjammer Kids, Mutt and Jeff. A little later it was Maggie and Jiggs and Buster Brown. Still later it was Dick Tracy and Lil Abner." Political figures have always been caricatured in the streets as well as on the floats. "Teddy Roosevelt and his Rough Riders enjoyed years of popularity." Tallant, *Mardi Gras*, 163. In the 1960s the Mobile *Register* offered prizes for the best comic-strip costumes (Rayford, *Chasin'*, 133).

18. Victor Turner's interesting speculations on the relation of festivities like Carnival to the "liminal domain" created by tribal societies' rituals treat the modern industrial world's festivals as a "liminoid" variant of the "tribal-liminal." See Turner, "Variations on a Theme of Liminality," in Sally Moore and Barbara Myerhoff, eds. *Secular Ritual* (Assen, Netherlands, 1977), 43–47, and also his "Carnival, Ritual, and Play in Rio de Janeiro," in Alessandro Falassi, ed., *Time out of Time: Essays on the Festival* (Albuquerque, New Mexico, 1987), 76–90. But relating festival's modern condition to the old economy of ritual structures as its faded variant rather than its radical reorganization is misleading, however helpful it is as a historical reminder.

19. Ludwig, *Great American Spectaculars*, 3, 42, 189, 200ff.

20. See pp. 106–7.

21. A winning truck in the early 1980s is pictured in Tassin and Stall, *Mardi Gras*, 50. A trucker's cab is normally hitched to a flat trailer which has been decorated in a manner imitating the floats of the major krewes, while reserving relatively much more space to the merrymakers, as many as forty or fifty per float. A minimally ornamented truck in 1954, a species still common today, is shown in Laborde and Osborne, *Mardi Gras*, 77.

22. Laborde and Osborne, *Mardi Gras*, 74.

23. Ibid., 73. Neighborhood Carnival clubs engaged in assorted Carnival activities—balls, picnics, music-making, parading—are mentioned from the late nineteenth century in many parts of the city. See, e.g., Tallant, *Mardi Gras*, 163–64.

24. The Krewe of Little Rascals, for example, in nearby Metairie, is restricted to boys and girls aged five to sixteen. See Hardy, *Mardi Gras Guide 1987*, 35. Mobile gives greater public space to children's participation in Mardi Gras. The Floral Parade, the main parade on Saturday

afternoon before mardi gras, is mainly a children's affair. See Laborde and Osborne, *Mardi Gras*, 93, for a photograph of a king, queen, and court at a children's ball in the 1930s.

25. The flight had much to do with the obligation of the city to tax its citizens in order to preserve and supplement federal funds used to integrate schools and transportation after 1960. See Siegel, *New Orleans*, 130–34, and B. Muse, *Ten Years of Prelude*, 216–33, for the failure of white moderates to maintain direction of affairs in New Orleans when the school desegregation crisis developed in 1960.

26. Only a few of the many suburban parading krewes are listed, with maps of their parades, in Arthur Hardy's annual *Mardi Gras Guide*. Tassin and Stall, *Mardi Gras*, 41, estimated that there were over forty thousand members of Carnival societies in metropolitan New Orleans in 1984.

27. Laborde and Osborne, *Mardi Gras*, includes not only information on the gay krewes but many photographs of the gay balls' finery and views of the costume contest at the corner of St. Ann and Bourbon Street in the Quarter, generally dominated by gay men's inventions (frontispiece photographs, back cover of paperback edition, 115–25, 185, 187).

28. In early Philadelphia transvestism even on holidays was prosecuted as a civil offense. See Historical Society of Pennsylvania, *Collections* (Philadelphia, 1853), 258:

> *Philadelphia, the 4th of the 12th month*, 1702.—We, the Grand Jury for the City of Philadelphia, present John Smith of this citty, Living in Strabery Alley, for being Maskt or disguised in womens' aparell; walking openly through the streets of this citty and from house to house, on or about the 26th of the 10th month Last past, it being against the Law of God, the Law of this Province, and the Law of nature, to the staining of holy profession, and Incoridging of wickedness in this place. Signed in behalf of the rest. Abra. Hoopper, foreman.

The date, "the 26th of the 10th month last past," almost certainly refers to December 26 (*decem*-ber: "tenth" month), the day after Christmas, a time of holiday license. In the present-day Philadelphia Mummers Parade on New Year's Day "female impersonators," having begun in the early twentieth century to "mingle with the marchers," are now an "integral part" of the "Fancy Clubs" who spend "hundreds of dollars on their costumes," according to Charles Welch, "Oh, Dem Golden Slippers," *Journal of American Folklore* 79 (1966): 530.

29. Masking as a "bird of prey" was already noted in Havana in 1851 at the Epiphany parade of Afro-Caribbeans. See p. 55 above. See also the cloth mask covering the face of the provocatively dressed female masker at the center of the 1873 engraving (plate 13).

30. Tassin and Stall, *Mardi Gras*, 52. Photographs in Laborde and Osborne, *Mardi Gras*, 170–71, and passim, amply document the theme.

31. See p. 12 above on gadget costuming in New Orleans. Elsie Martinez was already struck by this in the 1930s as a young girl: "The maskers who impressed me most were those who completely covered themselves with odd things like playing cards, Coca-Cola bottle tops, buttons, or brass bells." Elsie Martinez and Margaret LeCorgne, *Uptown/Downtown: Growing Up in New Orleans* (Lafayette, Louisiana, 1986), 150.

32. Delaney, *Remember Mobile*, 225–27.

33. Dean, *Mardi Gras*, 197.

34. Ibid., 42.

35. *Mobile Press-Register*, February 14, 1988, sec. G, p. 1. Some of the Order of the Moonpies' earlier behavior is described in chap. 11 below. New Orleans' parallel to Mobile's Joe Cain parade is the Krewe of Clones, founded in 1979 by persons associated with the New Orleans Contemporary Arts Center. "Since its inception Clones has become New Orleans' audience participation parade, where nearly anyone with his own krewe and concept can register with the Contemporary Arts Center to march in the parade and parody the topic of his choice" (*Times-Picayune*, February 7, 1982, sec. 1, p. 36). The Clones have resisted the pressures of official orderliness and popular spectacle more successfully. "Artists this year transformed fullsized automobiles into art, one covered in intricate designs by Mardi Gras beads, another upholstered bumper to bumper in plaid fabric. Artist Dale Milford converted a pickup truck into his satirical creation. 'The New Right Mighty White Hawkettes, an all-white vehicle with a hawk-nosed front end, a cannon and one right wing" (ibid.). Although their parade was cancelled in 1986 because the police declared that "they could not patrol the parade and handle Super Bowl Eve crowds on the same night" (Hardy, *Mardi Gras Guide* [1987], 69), they reorganized and paraded in 1987. The Clones have also resisted the pressures which come with national funding (they receive money from the National Endowment for the Humanities), probably because they have not sought, and have not received, top tourist billing. As the group's charter states: "The Clones will pay homage to traditional Carnival format, but will simultaneously . . . giv[e] the tradition a good swift kick in the pants . . ." (69).

36. The following item caught my eye in the list of Mardi Gras events for Sunday, February 14, in the *Mobile Press-Register,* sec. G, p. 11: "Buccaneer Yacht Club Mardi Gras Barbecue and Billy Goat Race. Serving begins at 1:30 p.m."

37. Rayford, *Chasin'*, 147–48.

38. Ibid., 151.

39. Delaney, *Remember Mobile*, 216.

40. The reader will recall that in most cases Mobile's Carnival societies reserve the title of queen, as well as king, for the all-city selection of the clubs. However, an all-city black king and queen were not selected until 1939. See Dean, *Mardi Gras*, 86, 104, and 194–96.

41. Laborde and Osborne, *Mardi Gras*, 127. The same cultivation of white dancing and white costuming took place in Jamaica at Christmastime festivities by black slave women (with the avid assistance of their white mistresses). They developed the custom of "Set Girls" costuming and dancing. Annually on New Year's Day, Cynric Williams relates in his *Tour through the Island of Jamaica* (London, 1826), a contest between two parties of black women is prepared. "Each party wears an appropriate colour, one red, the other blue, of the most expensive materials they can afford. They select two queens, the prettiest and the best-shaped girls they can find, who are obliged to personate the royal characters, and support them to the best of their power and ideas. These are decorated with the ornaments, necklaces, earrings, bracelets, &c. of their mistresses, so that they often carry much wealth on their persons for the time. Each party has a procession (but not so as to encounter each other) with silk flags and streamers, in which the queen is drawn

in a phaeton, if such a carriage can be procured . . . they parade the towns, priding themselves on the number of their followers, until the evening, when each party gives a splendid entertainment. . . . Mirth and good humour prevail throughout, and the evening is concluded with a ball. . . . The music consisted of three fiddles, a pipe and tabor, and a triangle. The dancers, male and female, acquitted themselves famously well, and performed country-dances and quadrilles quite as well, if not better, than I had ever seen at the country ball in England." Reprinted in Abrahams and Szwed, *After Africa*, 251–52. See pp. 39–40 above for an earlier account of Jamaica's black Christmas dancing in imitation of the whites, a much less sympathetic view.

42. Dean, *Mardi Gras*, 103, 244–45. No descriptions of the floats have been preserved, according to Dean.

43. Ibid., 244, and Trillin, "The Zulus," 76.

44. Dean, *Mardi Gras*, 195–96.

45. Ibid., 195. There is also a federation of black Carnival clubs in New Orleans. Its President Burns is quoted with reference to the attack on the Zulus during the early 1960s in chap. 8, n. 59.

46. See pp. 13–15.

47. Trillin, "The Zulus," 56.

48. See John Stewart, "Patronage and Control in the Trinidad Carnival," in Edward Bruner and Victor Turner, eds., *The Anthropology of Experience* (Urbana, 1986), 289–315, esp. 308–14; and Julia M. Taylor, "The Politics of Aesthetic Debate: the Case of Brazilian Carnival," *Ethnology*, 21 (1982), 301–11.

Chapter 10

1. See pp. 12–13.

2. Cf. the discussion of inversionary theories of Carnival in chap. 1.

3. Folk culture has been a controversial concept almost from its first popularization by Herder and the Grimm brothers. While recognizing the limitations of the term "neighborly," I have nevertheless preferred its prosaic inadequacy, for my purposes here, to the amorphous overtones of "folk."

4. The themes of Comus are emblematic, as the following list shows (exceptions noted)

| | |
|---|---|
| 1857 | Demon actors in Milton |
| 1858 | Mythology |
| 1859 | English Holidays |
| 1860 | History of America (exception) |
| 1861 | Four Ages of Life |
| 1866 | Past, Present, Future |
| 1867 | Feast of Epicurus |
| 1868 | Lalla Rookh |
| 1869 | Five Senses |
| 1870 | History of Louisiana (exception) |
| 1871 | Spenser's Faerie Queen |
| 1872 | Dreams of Homer |
| 1873 | Missing Links (exception) |

The exceptions confirm the rule: they occurred just before and after the Civil War in the highly politicized circumstances related in an earlier chapter. In the twentieth century Comus's themes have gradually become less learnedly mythic, but they have remained studiously aloof from the here-and-now. A listing of themes down to 1956 is provided in *One Hundred Years of Comus*.

5. See p. 158.

6. La Cour, *New Orleans Masquerade*, 86.

7. Speaking of Jackie Gleason, Bacchus's "King" in 1975, Tassin and Stall, *Mardi Gras*, 61, write: "Like Hope and Harris, Kaye and Campbell, Nabors and Burr, Gleason had been a part of America's living rooms and dens for years. . . . The Honeymooners has become a television classic. Millions watch the reruns. . . ." See p. 292 below on the importance of the familiar and already-known as part of the popular-culture code.

8. Cf. Alex Rapheal's protest, quoted p. 210.

9. *Mobile Press-Register*, February 21, 1982, sec. G, p. 22.

10. He is called Felix III because the institution of an overall Carnival king for Mobile, selected by the association of mystic societies, has lapsed two times since the 1880s, when the willingness of the societies to support a common association collapsed. Thus when the first Mobile Carnival Association ended, so did the "reign" of Felix I, and when the second such association disappeared, so too did Felix II "die."

11. For example, the god Comus, the goddess Venus.

12. See La Cour, *New Orleans Masquerade*, 86, on the Atlanteans (founded 1891) and 115–16 on the Mystic Club. In later years recognition of debutantes found its way into the Mystic Club's balls. The Atlanteans were from the beginning concerned with recognizing highly regarded debutantes. Conversely, a few "mystic societies" in Mobile consist purely of married couples and do not occupy themselves with the debutante system.

13. Comus began announcing publicly in 1951 the names of the "pages to Comus" as well as those of its maids and queen.

14. Ludwig, *Great American Spectacular*, 209.

15. Who is masked, where, and how, is like nearly everything else at New Orleans a frequently changing variable, with a few exceptions like this custom of Comus. The identity of the captain in the krewes is supposed to be a closely guarded secret; he is the anonymous power behind the pseudo-king's throne. Yet the two superkrewe captains, those of Bacchus and Endymion, court publicity, offering interviews and unmasked photographs to newspapers. Even Comus's adherence to this custom is not absolute. Since nineteenth-century captains have "escaped from anonymity," their names and the dates of the parades which they managed were published in 1956 in *One Hundred Years of Comus*, 28. Iris's parade is led since 1986 not only by the captain but by her predecessor the captain emeritus, both of them masked.

16. One might consider a symbol of this anchorage of public in private power the following custom: Former holders of the title of Rex have the right to hang a large 6' by 9' purple-, gold-, and green-striped flag with the date of their rule embroidered on it before their *homes* for the last ten days of the Carnival season. More than half of the nearly forty flags honoring still-living Rexes fly in the city's most prestigious area, the so-called Garden District. Hardy, *Mardi Gras Guide* (1987), 64.

17. Both titles appeared in the New Orleans *Times-Picayune* for March 3, 1987, in sec. E, pp. 1, 3.

18. The best generalized description of the mores of twentieth-century elite Carnival societies remains that of Perry Young, *Mistick Krewe*,

207-18, whose chronicle of New Orleans Carnival as a whole is by far the most detailed record so far undertaken. The book is at the same time a sustained apology for Comus's preeminence in Carnival, which suggests that Young may have been an—of course never divulged—member. Here is his estimate of the soul of the festival, itself a suitable summary of the elite-culture code: "Carnival forbids injustice. Carnival is generous, but in its social aspects protects its own. If people are of established respectability they are accepted without regard for other qualities [Young's previous paragraph is devoted to the "guest list" for Carnival society balls]. Wealth is no consideration, nor is ancestry unless supported by becoming character. No qualities whatsoever are of any force unless an invitation is requested and issued through regular channels, and there are no other channels. Instead of fostering snobbery, carnival effectively prevents it. . . . The most prominent gentlemen of the city, abandoning frequently their urgent business obligations . . . spend their hours considering who shall be invited. . . . Rare and delicate judgment must ever be exercised in the selection of the courts, as the ladies are never masked and must be the most beautiful and in all other ways the most pleasing element of the scene." After all, as Young explains, even though power here is in the hands of "gentlemen," "the substantial social fabric must be founded, as everywhere, in the other sex" (ibid., 213–14).

19. Tallant, *Mardi Gras*, 197.

20. See on this theme the essay by Giuseppe Cocchiara in his *Il Paese di Cuccagna* (Turin, 1956). The myth of Cockayne was known, at least among some elite circles, at New Orleans. In 1814 the playhouse called the Spectacle de la Rue St. Pierre presented at noon on mardi gras "une representation du Roi de Cocagne . . . suivie du Tonnelier, opera buffon en un acte. . . ." Quoted from an advertisement of the Spectacle given in Young, *Mistick Krewe*, 28.

21. *Times-Picayune*, February 22, 1982, sec. 1, p. 1. Canizzaro's opening reference to general clamor is diagnostic. It is the generalized noise that intoxicates, and not any distinguishable words, as, for example, the customary cry of some decades ago: "Throw me something, mister." This cry is little used today, at least along the main parade routes.

22. See Moser, "Städtische Fasnacht," 181–82, and esp. n. 166, for a description of some fifteenth-century German quetes and throws.

23. This is my translation of K. Schwering's citation from the Kieler Schembartbuch of 1515 in Gunther Albrecht and Maria Schmidt, eds., *Masken und Narrentraditionen der Fastnacht* (Cologne, 1973), 29.

24. See Huber, *Mardi Gras*, 8 and 41 for the 1840s and 1881, and Laborde and Osborne, *Mardi Gras*, 81, for the 1871 instance.

25. Paper confetti, like the earlier flour pellets, had a short and troubled history in New Orleans and Mobile. In Mobile flour-throwing was still a problem in 1869, when the mayor banned it (Dean, *Mardi Gras*, 53); paper confetti was outlawed after only several years' use there in 1900. Nevertheless confetti and serpentines were being thrown again in Mobile in 1950 (ibid., 91, 118). In New Orleans paper confetti sporadically was thrown between 1897 and 1906 before being severely repressed from 1907 onward (Young, *Mistick Krewe*, 201).

26. The smearing is sometimes done at the time of the quetes and sometimes the next day. The wildman kukers, who make ritual visits to each village household and also chase people in the streets, are dis-

cussed in chapter 8. As suggested there (p. 222), it is tempting to see the "Mardi Gras run" (*le courir du Mardi gras*) performed by some Cajun communities in rural southern Louisiana as another variant of these customs.

27. "Dukes" discussing their experience on "Mardi Gras Highlights 1987," broadcast on Television Channel 6, New Orleans, February 27, 1987, 10:30 P.M.

28. See Trillin, "The Zulus," 100, for the quotation from Rex's captain. It is, however, true that the parameters of recognition, and the ambivalence which develops in relation to it, has for elites more to do with recognition from, and merging with, "their" crowd. Essential to this alternation of identity is the gossip which follows and enlarges upon the "private parties," by making them semipublic. Consider this exemplary account from William Davis, *Aiming for the Jugular in New Orleans*, 83:

> Doris and I stayed after the other guests left and sat with Germaine and her daughter Arnaud, on their patio, reminiscing about the balls and parties we'd attended during the previous Mardi Gras season. We laughed recalling the faux pas of some of the ball tableau announcers when they introduced the wrong personages to the auditorium audiences of thousands, the furor created when some of the balls' regal court came out into the spotlight on the ballroom floor so inebriated they had to be helped in walking, the shocked astonishment of all present when one of the ladies resplendent in her antebellum, hoop-skirted gown, relieved herself in the center of the ballroom at the St. Charles Hotel, and nonchalantly walked away from the very obvious puddle and the hilarity when she later announced it was impossible for her to go to the ladies' room and sit down in that "damn skirt!"

29. Inspiration for this passage comes in part from Michael Ventura, *Shadow Dancing*, 173, who writes in still broader terms than I have used here about the "audience" tendencies of twentieth-century Western culture.

30. Thomas di Palma, *New Orleans Carnival and Its Climax Mardi Gras* (New Orleans, 1953), unnumbered p. (8), entitled "Dedication," and 12 ("Foreword"). Capitalization, punctuation, italics as in the original.

31. Ibid., 16–17 and 20–21.

32. Hardy, *Mardi Gras Guide* (1987), 52.

33. Such was the boast of Ed Muniz, Endymion's captain, in an interview in 1982: *Times-Picayune*, Mardi Gras Supplement, February 11, 1982, p. 43.

34. Hardy, *Mardi Gras Guide* (1987), 23–24.

35. *Gambit* (New Orleans weekly newspaper), February 28, 1987, 16, concerning the Krewe of Pandora's theme, "Fantastic Flickers."

36. Hardy, *Mardi Gras Guide* (1987), 64. Hardy does not cite the number of parades falling into his ten most popular categories, he merely lists them in order; he makes no distinction between nineteenth- and twentieth-century popularity.

37. See n. 57 to this chapter.

38. Danny Barker and Jack Buerkle, *Bourbon Street Black* (Oxford and New York, 1973), 14, claim that marching brass bands became prominent in New Orleans in the generation after the Civil War simply because many brass instruments became available in second-hand stores

where they were left behind by the departed military bands of the occupying Union army. Jelly Roll Morton (Lomax, *Mr. Jelly Roll*, 78) says they were left by the confederate army bands. The richness of this tradition, which irrigated Carnival with fine music for generations, is captured in the books by Lomax, Barker and Buerkle, and also in the photographs and text in Rose and Souchon, *New Orleans Jazz*. In recent years high school bands from all over the South have increasingly displaced local musicians in the parades. They are, of course, cheaper.

39. Tassin and Stall, *Mardi Gras*, 42.

40. Student revelers from the University of Paris during Carnival of 1229 provoked a riot which eventually required calling in the city police after the students entered a tavern and "there found sweet, fine wine." See Henry Rashdall, *The Universities of Europe in the Middle Ages* (Oxford, England, 1936), 1: 334–35. The motif of drinking to excess in Carnival recurs from century to century throughout Europe, as may well be imagined.

41. James McLain, "The Economic Impact of Mardi Gras," Lecture, April 26, 1977, New Orleans Public Library, conserved on tape cassette at the Library. "Tourist business alone": the spending of local people, and above all of Carnival-society members, was not calculated.

42. The obvious exception was Comus's behavior in the 1870s when political conditions were so extreme that they provoked reaction in the "Missing Link" parade and some others. A second exception is the off-and-on political vocation of Momus, an old-line society which in 1987, for instance, produced an amusing set of floats with sharp satiric references to local and national issues by means of metaphorical use of the seemingly innocuous theme, "Children's Games." Perhaps the latter was itself a satire of the commonplaces in other parades.

43. Calvin Trillin, "The Zulus," 100, cites these examples and the general opinion that it is "bad manners" to speak of the city's part in Mardi Gras. Hard as it is to gauge such matters, it seems to me that this opinion has faded in the twenty-five years since Trillin wrote.

44. Young, *Mistick Krewe*, 99.

45. Waldo, *History of the Carnival*, 50.

46. Rayford, *Chasin'*, 138–39.

47. An anonymous *Gambit* (New Orleans weekly) writer, assessing the "Best and Worst of Carnival," concluded, February 28, 1987, p. 13, that this team with its "all pure precision" was the best drill team in Mardi Gras.

48. Hans Moser, "Archivalisches zu Jahreslaufbrauchen der Oberpfalz," *Bayerisches Jabrbuch für Volkskunde*, no volume number (1955), 169–70, cites archival documents concerning the parodic takeover of city hall in the Bavarian town of Hirschau in the 1520s, and also gives bibliographical references to parallel fifteenth- and sixteenth-century examples in Switzerland and Austria. The parodic takeover of the City Council by artisans in Romans, France, in 1579 had tragically bloody consequences for the artisans (see Le Roy Ladurie, *Le Carnaval de Romans*). The modern ritual in southwest Germany is discussed in Hans-Gunther Bäurer's superbly rich inventory of modern Carnival practices in that area, "Fasnet in Hegau, am Bodensee und im Linzgau," *Fasnet im Hegau und Linzgau*, ed. Herbert Berner (Konstanz, 1982), 154–56.

49. Rayford, *Chasin'*, 139–40.

50. Trillin, "The Zulus," 58. See also p. 274 above on Morial and the Zulus.

51. Dean, *Mardi Gras*, 91.

52. Huber, *Mardi Gras*, 38–39.

53. Ludwig, *Great American Spectaculars*, 242. See the quotation on p. 128 above.

54. "Meet de boys on de Battlefront," *The Wild Tchoupitoulas* (Island Records).

55. The reference is to the jargon of street gangs, black and white, in modern cities. "Our turf" versus "your turf": don't show up over here or you'll be mauled.

56. One of di Palma's stories provides at least an inkling of how the two Carnivals, black and white, looked to a black person in 1920, a far less lurid look than that which Lyle Saxon attributes to the black servant Robert. Di Palma (*New Orleans Carnival*, 24–26) is asked to conduct two masked women to Mardi Gras in his taxi and in effect to chaperone them for the day; they provide him with a costume and tell him to follow on foot, never too far behind. Di Palma recognizes one of the two, in spite of her disguise, as a married woman of high social status who has frequently made use of his services. But he can't place the second woman, masked as a black mammy, but not quite perfectly because she has left one blond curl showing. The day's street-masking adventures over, he conducts the woman whom he has recognized to a party, as she requests, and then is shocked when the blonde-curl mammy tells him to go to the Geddes Funeral Home, "where the queen of the negroes (the Zulu Queen) and her court and guests sit and toast their king." This place, di Palma adds, is "to the negroes what the Boston Club is to the white people." Di Palma is worried, "because the blonde curl told me clearly that the lady in all probability did not know what she was getting into." Even so, the mammy steps out of the car near the Geddes Funeral Home, hands di Palma a five-dollar bill and says, "I will really enjoy my Mardi Gras now." And di Palma in a flash realizes that the blonde curl was a decoy; the mammy is the high-society lady's black maid.

To a black woman in 1920 the street dancing and bizarre costuming on Canal Street, the Rex parade, and the rest of it were all right, but to really enjoy Mardi Gras, she wanted to be with her own people. It was not a question of high and low but of otherness.

57. The disputed origins of the Jefferson City Buzzards' name are discussed in Tassin and Stall, *Mardi Gras*, 41.

58. Rayford, *Chasin'*, 164, quotes a black dentist, Dr. Russell, the president of the Colored Carnival Association (presumably in about 1960), about the parades along Davis Avenue by the black Carnival societies: "People sort of looked for Mr. Colored Man to be a clown. But we have changed that attitude among our people. We seek dignity. . . . We go in more for the classical side. . . . We follow Mardi Gras as it has been set by the fathers of Mardi Gras. Mr. Sidney Simon and Mr. Alfred Staples [leaders in the white association of Carnival clubs] helped us to get started, and it was agreed that we should have, as much as possible, a classical parade. We did not care to have a burlesque." The reference to a "burlesque" was probably to the Zulus of New Orleans or to the Zulus of Mobile who, as we noted, were criticized as early as 1947 by Mobile

blacks. Obviously the dentist and his association do not represent the sentiments of all black people who participate in Mardi Gras. All I want to emphasize here is that the stiffness already noticed in white Mobile's Carnival has its strong counterpart on the black side.

59. In 1973 new regulations of the Fire Department banned all Carnival parades in the Quarter (Laborde and Osborne, *Mardi Gras*, 138).

60. Pierce Lewis, *New Orleans, the Making of an Urban Landscape* (Cambridge, Mass., 1976), 88–90, tells in brief the story of the saving of the Quarter from urban blight, superhighway construction, and commercial invasion. A Vieux Carré Commission was created in 1936; the WPA had an important hand in stimulating Orleanians to recognize the value of the Quarter. See also the excerpts from the 1968 "Plan and Program for the Preservation of the Vieux Carré," reprinted in Siegel, *New Orleans*, 135–37, and the richly developed chapter on the same subject in Robert Tallant, *The Romantic New Orleanians*, 307–28.

61. Oliver Houck, "Take Me to the Mardi Gras," *New Orleans Magazine* (March 1987), 45.

62. Ibid., 44.

63. See p. 193 above.

64. Pete Fountain, for example, did homage to this emanating power in 1982, as he described the activities of the Half-Fast Walking Club. "We start walking at seven in the morning and end up between one and five that afternoon. . . . Our biggest thing is just keeping ahead of Rex or Zulu—that's the only schedule we have to keep." Fountain goes on to explain that, in the time-honored tradition of the walking clubs, he and his friends had begun in 1959 by "walking in and out of the parades and floats" without a permit until they were caught. But today there's only one way left to keep in touch with the old spirit: "We're the craziest group that will go into the quarter and we make it *all over* the quarter that day so that's when it *really* loosens up." Carl Lineberry, "Peter Fountain: Struts His Stuff," *Arcade* (New Orleans), February 16, 1982, p. 8.

Chapter 11

1. There has been, however, according to Professor John Hafner of Spring Hill College, Mobile, in an interview published in the *Azalea City News and Review*, April 23, 1987, p. 4, "a real concerted official effort to stamp out Joe Cain Day . . . ," of which this float was part, by regulating participation in the parade to the point where the performance is scarcely worth the trouble (see chap. 9 above on this point).

2. Interview by the author with Maud Lyon, Curator of Costumes, Louisiana State Museum, New Orleans, February 27, 1987.

3. See chap. 9, n. 25.

4. Hardy, *Mardi Gras Guide* (1987), 33.

5. Did they turn inward even with respect to the immediate hinterland? One direction of research which requires further explanation for both black and white Carnivals is the connection of these cities' celebrations with plantation, Cajun, and black-Creole modes of Carnival. It is unreasonable to suppose that the influences on city festivals of rural Louisiana in particular entirely ceased in the civic period.

6. This precedence to the Rex parade might be interpreted as one more piece of white cunning. The Zulus had always looked suspi-

ciously like a black parody of Rex. But if the Zulus come before that which they satirize, who will make the connection?

7. On the very dust-jacket of Tassin and Stall's book celebrating the krewe of Bacchus, *Mardi Gras and Bacchus, Something Old, Something New,* black and white are shown together; the same is true of the photograph prominently placed opposite the table of contents; again on page 75 King Henry "the Fonz" Winkler trips it lightly with a scantily clad "Southern University coed."

8. See chap. 10, n. 58.

9. By "connection to elite society" I mean more than simply the relation of the Carnival-society balls to the social education and circulation of eligible young ladies and gentlemen. I refer to all the points made in this book about the way Carnival in these cities has become a part of school programs, the tourist industry, business connections, and government connections, not least of all through the functioning of the Carnival societies' influential, highly screened memberships. These connections constitute the chief advantage that New Orleans' celebration retains over the chronologically comparable but no longer today quite so complex festive tradition of Philadelphia. Recent studies by Susan Davis and Charles Welch (see Bibliography) have done much to recover the great richness of Philadelphia's festive past.

10. Like the Strikers, the Order of Dragons is a nonparading old-line mystic society in Mobile, founded in 1889. See Dean, *Mardi Gras,* 76–82.

11. Samuel Clemens [Mark Twain], *Life on the Mississippi* (New York: Bantam edition, 1945; first published 1883), 314–15.

12. In 1987 two krewes in New Orleans took New Orleans history as their theme (Sparta, Thor) and four others constructed their parades around scenes from Louisiana and U.S. history (Carrollton, Alla, Hercules, Thoth) See Hardy, *Mardi Gras Guide* (1987), passim.

13. Reproduced in Laborde and Osborne, *Mardi Gras,* 141.

14. See the extraordinary frontispiece chosen by Laborde and Osborne for their *Mardi Gras,* facing the title-page.

15. See the sumptuously illustrated *Carnavals et Mascarades,* ed. Pier Giovanni d'Ayala and Martine Boiteux (Paris, 1988), 72, 85, 121, 126, etc., for some of the many European ritualizations of the death of Carnival.

## Afterword

1. This position puts me at odds with nearly the first published scholarly article focusing on New Orleans' Mardi Gras (see also M. Edmonson's "Carnival in New Orleans"), which came to my attention just as this book goes to press: Francis A. De Caro and Tom Ireland, "Every Man a King: Worldview, Social Tension and Carnival in New Orleans," *International Folklore Review* 6 (1988): 58–66. "Carnival," they write, "symbolically mediates between two opposing social ideals: that of kingship, aristocracy and class hierarchy on the one hand; that of equality on the other. . . . The fusing of the expressions of these two opposing 'worldviews' into a single great celebration dispels a social contradiction in local social attitudes" (65). De Caro and Ireland qualify their social functionalism with references to the other two main bodies of source material on which I have drawn, "tradition" and "private fanta-

sies" (58–59). But they see the three as congruent: "In essence it is a matter of the celebration's simply being fluid enough to allow anyone to appropriate the central symbols and/or to allow outgroups to establish within the general festival their own range of symbolic behaviour" (62). So they conclude: "From its inception Carnival has been this force for social unity and harmony. . . . Surely it is the genius of a great ritual to work on the human mind subliminally and to provide an inner order in the midst of outward pandemonium and frolic" (66).

# Bibliography

Abrahams, Roger D. 1971. "British West Indian Folk Drama and the 'Life Cycle" Problem." *Folklore* 82: 241–65.

———, 1968, "'Pull Out Your Purse and Pay:' A St. George Mumming from the British West Indies," *Folklore* 79 (1968), 176–201.

———, 1964. "The Cowboy in the British West Indies," in M. C. Boatwright, W. M. Hudson, and A. Maxwell, eds., *A Good Tale and a Bonnie Tune*, 168–75. Dallas.

———. 1983. *The Man-of-Words in the West Indies: Performance and the Emergence of Creole Culture*. Baltimore.

———, and John F. Szwed, eds. 1983. *After Africa: Extracts from British Travel Accounts and Journals*. New Haven.

Achard, Paul. 1869. "Les chefs des Plaisirs." *Annuaire de Vaucluse* 20: 32–77.

Aebischer, Paul. 1952. "Les dénominations du Carnaval d'après les chartes italiennes du Moyen Age." In *Mélanges de philologie romane offerts à M. Karl Michaelsson*. Gothenburg.

Aimes, Hubert. 1905. "African Institutions in America." *Journal of American Folklore* 18: 15–32.

Albrecht, Gunther, and Maria Schmidt, eds. 1973. *Masken und Narrentraditionen der Fastnacht*. Cologne.

Alexander, James. 1833. *Transatlantic Sketches*. London.

Allain, Hélène. 1883. *Souvenirs d'Amérique et de France*. Paris.

Ancelet, Barry. 1980. "Courir du Mardi Gras." *Attakapas Gazette*. 15, no. 2; reprinted in *Louisiane* 54 (February 1982).

Aries, Philippe, and J.-C. Margolin, eds. 1982. *Les jeux à la Renaissance*. Paris.

Arnaudov, Mikhail. 1917. *Die bulgarische Festbräuche*. Leipzig.

———. 1920. "Kukeri i Rusalii" (in Bulgarian). *Sbornik za Narodni Umotrozenija i Narodpis* 34: 1–244.

Asbury, Herbert. 1936. *The French Quarter: An Informal History of the New Orleans Underworld*. New York.

d'Ayala, Pier Giovanni, and Martine Boiteux, eds. 1988. *Carnavals et Mascarades*. Paris.

*Azalea City News and Review*. 1981, 1982, 1987, 1988. Weekly newspaper, Mobile, Alabama.

Bakhtin, Mikhail. 1968. *Rabelais and His World*. Moscow, 1965; trans. 1968, Cambridge, Mass.

Barker, Danny. 1986. *A Life in Jazz*. London.

———, and Jack Buerkle. 1973. *Bourbon Street Black*. Oxford and New York.

Barron, Bill. 1975. *The Vaudreuil Papers: A Calendar and Index of the Personal and Private Records of Pierre de Rigaud de Vaudreuil*. New Orleans.

Bartram, William. 1791. *Travels in North and South Carolina*. New Haven.

Bascom, William, and Paul Gebauer. 1953. *Handbook of West African Art.* Milwaukee.

Baskerville, Charles. 1920. "Dramatic Aspects of Medieval Folk Festivals in England." *Studies in Philology* 17: 19–87.

Basso, Etolia, ed. 1948. *The World from Jackson Square.* New York.

Bastide, Roger. 1971. *African Civilizations in the New World.* London.

Baumann, Richard. 1972. "Belsnickling in a Nova Scotia Island Community." *Western Folklore* 31: 229–43.

Bäurer, Hans-Gunther. 1982. "Fasnet in Hegau, am Bodensee und im Linzgau." In Herbert Berner, ed., *Fasnet im Hegau und Linzgau,* Konstanz.

Bayley, Frederick. 1830. *Four Years' Residence in the West Indies.* London.

Beauvallet, Leon. 1856. *Rachel and the New World: A Trip to the United States and Cuba.* New York.

Beckwith, Martha. 1923. *Christmas Mummings in Jamaica.* Poughkeepsie, New York.

Beduschi, Lidia, 1981. "La vecchia di Mezza-Quaresima." *La ricerca folclorica,* no. 7, 37–46.

Beidelman, T. O. 1966. "Swazi Royal Ritual." *Africa* 36: 373–405.

Belisario, I. M. 1837. *Sketches of Character in Illustration of the Habits, Occupations, and Costume of the Negro Population in the Island of Jamaica.* Kingston, Jamaica.

Berkhofer, Robert, Jr. 1978. *The White Man's Indian.* New York.

Berlin, Ira. 1974. *Slaves without Masters.* New York.

———. 1980. "Time, Space, and the Evolution of Afro-American Society." *American Historical Review* 85: 44–78.

Bernardy, A. A. 1928. "Il 'rey de la Faba.'" *Studi medievali,* n.s., no. 3: 522.

Bernheimer, Richard. 1952. *The Wildman in the Middle Ages.* Cambridge, Mass.

Berquin-Duvallon. 1803. *Vue de la Colonie espagnole du Mississippi.* . . . Paris.

Berry, Jason. 1981. "Goodby Chief Pete." *Gambit,* November 11, 1981, 21–22. New Orleans.

———, Jonathan Foose, and Tad Jones. 1986. *Up from the Cradle of Jazz: New Orleans Music Since World War II.* Athens, Georgia.

Bettelheim, Judith. 1976. "The Jonkonnu Festival, Its Relation to Caribbean and African Mascarades." *Jamaica Journal* 10: 21–27.

———. 1979. "Jamaican Jonkonnu and Related Caribbean Festivals." In Franklin Knight and Margaret Crahan, eds., *Africa and the Caribbean* (Baltimore): 80–100.

———. 1985. "The Jonkonnu Festival in Jamaica." *Journal of Ethnic Studies* 13: 85–105.

Blassingame, John. 1973. *Black New Orleans 1860–1880.* Chicago.

Boiteux, Martine. 1976. "Les Juifs dans le Carnaval de la Rome Moderne (XVe–XVIIIe Siècles)." *Mélanges de l'Ecole Française de Rome* 88.

———. 1981. "Chasse aux Taureaux et Jeux Romains de la Renaissance." In P. Aries and J.-C. Margolin, eds., *Les Jeux à la Renaissance.* Paris.

Brand, John, 1853. *Observations on Popular Antiquities.* London.

Brasseaux, Carl. 1980. "The Administration of Slave Regulations in French Louisiana, 1724–1766." *Louisiana History* 21 (1980): 140–58.

Bremer, Fredrika. 1853. *Homes of the New World: Impressions of America*. 2 volumes. New York.

Bruner, Edward, and V. Turner, eds. 1986. *The Anthropology of Experience*. Urbana.

Burke, John. 1972. "The Wild Man's Pedigree. Scientific Method and Racial Anthropology." In Edward Dudley and Maximilian Novak, eds., *The Wild Man Within*, 259–80. Pittsburgh.

Burke, Peter. 1978. *Popular Culture in Early Modern Europe*. New York.

———. 1982. "Le carnaval de Venise, Esquisse pour une histoire de longue durée." In P. Aries and J.-C. Margolin, eds., *Les Jeux à la Renaissance*, 55–63. Paris.

Cable, George W. 1886. "The Dance in Place Congo." *Century Magazine* 31: 517–32.

Camberoque, Charles, and Daniel Fabre. 1979. *La Fête en Languedoc*. Toulouse.

Capers, Gerald. 1965. *Occupied City: New Orleans under the Federals 1862–65*. Lexington, Ky.

Carmichael, A. C. 1833. *Domestic Manners and Social Conditions of the West Indies*. London.

*Carnivaliana*. N.d. Paris.

Cassidy, Frederick. 1961. *Jamaica Talk: Three Hundred Years of the English Language in Jamaica*. London.

Castellanos, Henry. 1978. *New Orleans as It Was*. New Orleans, 1895; reprint New Orleans, 1978.

Chaudron, Louis de Vendel. 1912. *Mobile Mystics and the Story of the Mardi Gras Societies*. Mobile.

Chevalier, Louis. 1958. *Classes laborieuses et classes dangereuses à Paris pendant la première moitié du XIXe siècle*. Paris.

Citron, Alan. 1982. "Carnival All Year. . . ." *Times-Picayune*, February 22, 1982. New Orleans.

Clemens, Samuel [Mark Twain]. 1945. *Life on the Mississippi*. New York: Bantam edition; first published 1883.

Cocchiara, Giuseppe. 1956. *Il Paese di Cuccagna*. Turin.

Coleman, James, ed. 1885. *Historical Sketchbook and Guide to New Orleans*. New York.

Columbian Magazine. See Higman 1976.

Comus. See *One Hundred Years of Comus*.

Creecy, James. 1860. *Scenes in the South and Other Miscellaneous Pieces*. Philadelphia.

Crété, Liliane. 1981. *Daily Life in Louisiana 1815–1830*. Baton Rouge.

Crowley, Daniel. 1956. "The Traditional Masques of Carnival." *Caribbean Quarterly* 4: 194–223.

———. 1982. "Spettacolo e participazione nel Carnevale, uno studio comparato." *La ricerca folclorica*, no. 6: 81–86.

———. 1953. "American Credit Institutions of Yoruba Type." *Man* 53:80.

Curtis, Edward S. 1907–30. *The North American Indians*. 20 volumes. Seattle, Washington.

Da Matta, Roberto. 1984. "Carnival, Informality, and Magic." In Edward Bruner, ed., *Text, Play, and Story*. Washington, D.C.

Davis, Natalie. 1971. "The Reasons of Misrule: Youth-groups and Charivaris in Sixteenth-Century France." *Past and Present* 50: 41–75.

Davis, Susan. 1983. "Making Night Hideous." *American Quarterly* 35: 185–99.

———. 1986. *Parades and Power: Street Theater in Nineteenth-Century Philadelphia.* Philadelphia.

Davis, William H. 1976. *Aiming for the Jugular in New Orleans.* Port Washington, New York.

Dawkins, Richard. 1906. "Modern Carnival in Thrace." *Journal of Hellenic Studies* 26: 191–206.

Dean, Bennett Wayne. 1971. *Mardi Gras, Mobile's Illogical Whoopdedo.* Mobile.

De Caro, Francis A. 1978. "Folk Festival Films." *Journal of American Folklore,* 91: 625–27.

———, and Tom Ireland, 1988. "Every Man a King: Worldview, Social Tension, and Carnival in New Orleans." *International Folklore Review* 6 (1988): 58–66.

De Coy, Robert. 1967. *The Nigger Bible.* Los Angeles.

Dekker, Thomas. 1605. *The Honest Whore.* Part 2. London.

De la Beche, H. T. 1983. *Notes on the Present Conditions of the Negroes in Jamaica.* Reprinted in Abrahams and Szwed, *After Africa.*

Delaney, Caldwell. 1948. *Remember Mobile.* Mobile.

DeLeon, Thomas C. 1890. *Our Creole Carnivals: Origin, History, Progress and Results.* Mobile.

De Metz, Kaye. 1980. "Theatrical Dancing in Nineteenth-Century New Orleans." *Louisiana History* 21: 23–42.

Demeulenaere-Douyere, Christiane. 1982. "La promenade du boeuf gras à Paris," *Gavroche,* no. 7: 25–27.

di Palma, Thomas. 1953. *New Orleans Carnival and Its Climax Mardi Gras.* New Orleans.

Dirks, Robert. 1975. "Slaves' Holiday." *Natural History* 84 (December issue): 83–90.

———. 1979. "The Evolution of a Playful Ritual: The Garifuna's John Canoe in Comparative Perspective." In E. Norbeck and C. Farrer, eds., *Forms of Play of Native North Americans.* St. Paul, Minnesota.

Dominguez, Virginia. 1986. *White by Definition: Social Classification in Creole Louisiana.* New Brunswick, New Jersey.

Douglas, George W. 1937. *The American Book of Days.* New York.

Duchesne, Louis, ed. 1889. *Liber pontificalis.* 2 volumes. Paris.

Dunham, Katharine. 1937. *The Dances of Haiti.* New York.

Earle, Alice. 1912. *Colonial Days in Old New York.* New York.

Edmonson, Munro. 1956. "Carnival in New Orleans." *Caribbean Quarterly* 4: 233–45.

———, and John Rohrer. 1964. *The Eighth Generation Grows Up.* New York.

Eichold, Samuel. N.d. [1984?]. *Without Malice, The 100th Anniversary of the Comic Cowboys 1884–1984.* Mobile.

Eights, James. 1867. "Pinkster Festivities in Albany Sixty Years Ago." In *Collections on the History of Albany.* Albany. Reprinted in Abrahams and Szwed, *After Africa.*

Ellis, Alfred. 1887. *The Tshi-Speaking Peoples of the Gold Coast of West Africa.* London.

Ellison, Ralph. 1964. *Shadow and Act.* New York.

Epstein, Dena. 1977. *Sinful Tunes and Spirituals*. Urbana.

Fabre, Daniel. 1976. "Le monde du Carnaval." *Annales, E.S.C.* 31: 389–406.

*Fasnacht*, 1964. Ed. Tübingen University Group for the Study of Carnival. Tübingen.

Faure, Alain. 1978. *Paris Carême-prenant*. Paris.

Fiehrer, Thomas. 1979. "The African Presence in Colonial Louisiana: An Essay on the Continuity of Caribbean Culture." In *Louisiana's Black Heritage*, ed. Robert Macdonald, John Kemp, Edward Haas, 7–28. New Orleans.

First National Bank of Mobile, ed., 1940. *Highlights of 75 Years in Mobile*. Mobile.

Fitzstephen, William. 1877. "Vita Sancti Thomae." In *Materials Pertaining to Thomas a Becket*, ed. James Robertson, *Rerum Britannicorum Medii Aevi Scriptores* (Rolls Series), vol. 67, pt. 3. London.

Flint, Timothy. 1826. *Recollections of the Last Ten Years . . . in the Valley of the Mississippi*. Boston.

Flugel, F. 1924. "A Voyage Down the Mississippi in 1817," *Louisiana Historical Quarterly* 7: 428–42.

Fossier, Albert. 1957. *New Orleans of the Glamour Period 1800–1840*. New Orleans.

Frazer, James. 1910–15. *The Golden Bough*. 12 volumes. London.

Frégault, Guy. 1952. *Le Grand Marquis, Pierre de Rigaud de Vaudreuil et la Louisiane*. Montreal and Paris.

Froning, Richard. 1888. "Die Familie Rorbach." *Archiv für Frankfurter Geschichte und Kunst*. 3d series, vol. 2: 148–70.

*Gambit*, 1982, 1987, 1988. Weekly newspaper. New Orleans, Louisiana.

Gayarré, Charles. 1854–66. *History of Louisiana*. 4 volumes. New York.

Giroux, Françoise, ed. 1984. *Carnavals et Fêtes d'Hiver*. Paris.

Glassie, Henry. 1975. *All Silver and No Brass: An Irish Christmas Mumming*. Bloomington, Indiana.

Glotz, Samuel, ed. 1975. *Le Masque dans la tradition européenne*. Binche, Belgium.

Gluckman, Max. 1963. *Order and Rebellion in Tribal Africa*. New York.

Goethe, Johann Wolfgang von. 1789. *Das Römischer Karneval*. Reprinted in critical edition: Frankfurt, 1984.

Gordon, Robert. 1979. Review of Les Blank, *Always for Pleasure* (film), *Journal of American Folklore* 92:261.

Goreau, Laurraine. 1968. "Mardi Gras." In Hodding Carter, ed., *The Past as Prelude: New Orleans 1718–1968*, 341–73. New Orleans.

Gresemund, Dietrich. 1495. *Podalirii Germani cum Catone Certomio de furore germanico diebus genialibus Carnisprivii dialogus*. Mainz, 1495; republished in Joel Lefebvre. *Les fols et la folie*. Paris, 1967.

Grinberg, Martine, and Samuel Kinser. 1983. "Les Combats de Carnaval et de Carême, Trajets d'une Métaphore." *Annales: Economies, Sociétés, Civilisations* 38: 65–98.

Hall, Abraham O. 1851. *The Manhattan in New Orleans*. New York.

Halpert, Herbert, 1969. "A Typology of Mumming." In Halpert and M. Story, *Christmas Mumming in Newfoundland*, 34–61.

Halpert, Herbert, and G. M. Story, eds. 1969. *Christmas Mumming in Newfoundland*. Toronto.

Hardy, Arthur. 1987. *Mardi Gras Guide. 1987*. New Orleans.

Hearn, Lafcadio. 1883. "The Scenes of Cable's Romances." *The Century Magazine* 27: 43–50.

———. 1890. *Two Years in the French West Indies*. New York.

Helm, Alex. 1981. *English Mummers' Plays*. Cambridge.

Higginbotham, Jay. 1968. *Mobile, City by the Bay*. Mobile.

———. 1977. *Old Mobile*. Mobile.

*Highlights of 75 Years in Mobile*. See First National Bank of Mobile.

Higman, Barry, ed. 1976. "Characteristic Traits of the Creolian and African Negroes in this Island, etc., etc." From *The Columbian Magazine; or Monthly Miscellany* (Kingston, Jamaica, 1797). Mona, Jamaica (rare; partly reprinted in Abrahams and Szwed, *After Africa*, 233–35).

Hill, Errol. 1972. *Trinidad Carnival*. Austin, Texas.

Historical Society of Pennsylvania. 1853. *Collections*. Philadelphia.

Honorat, Michel. 1955. *Les danses folkloriques haitiennes*. Port au Prince, Haiti.

Houck, Oliver. 1987. "Take Me to the Mardi Gras." *New Orleans Magazine*, March 1987, 44–45.

Huber, Leonard. 1977. *Mardi Gras, A Pictorial History of Carnival in New Orleans*. Gretna, Louisiana.

Hübner, Joseph von. 1870. *La vie à Rome au temps de Sixte Quint*. 2 volumes. Paris.

Jackson, Joy. 1969. *New Orleans in the Gilded Age: Politics and Urban Progress 1880–1896*. Baton Rouge.

Jacobs, Claude. 1988. "Spirit Guides and Possession in the New Orleans Black Spiritual Churches." *Journal of American Folklore* 102: 45–67.

Jonson, Ben. 1969. *The Complete Masques*, ed. Stephen Orgel. New Haven.

Jordan, Winthrop, 1968. *White over Black: American Attitudes toward the Negro, 1550–1812*. Chapel Hill.

Joyaux, Georges. 1956. "Forest's Voyage aux Etats-Unis de l'Amérique en 1831." *Louisiana History Quarterly* 39: 457–72.

Kaslow, Alison Miner. 1977. See Miner, Alison.

Kaslow, Andrew, 1977. "From Waltz to Boogie: The Music of Mardi Gras." Taped lecture, May 24, 1977. Conserved on tape cassette at New Orleans Public Library.

Kemp, Jacob. 1906. "Zur Geschichte der Kölner Fastnacht." *Zeitschrift des Vereins für rheinische und westfalische Volkskunde*, 3: 241–72.

Kendall, John Smith. 1922. *History of New Orleans*, 2 volumes. Chicago and New York.

King, Edward. 1873. "Old and New Louisiana." *Scribner's Monthly* 7: 1–32.

Kinser, Samuel. 1983. See Grinberg and Kinser, 1983.

———. 1986. "Presentation and Representation: Carnival at Nuremberg 1450–1550." *Representations*, no. 13, 1–41.

———. 1990. *Rabelais' Carnival: Text, Context, Metatext*. Berkeley.

Klersch, Joseph. 1961. *Die Kölnische Fastnacht*. Cologne.

Kmen, Henry. 1966. *Music in New Orleans: The Formative Years, 1791–1841*. Baton Rouge.

———. 1972. "The Roots of Jazz and the Dance in Place Congo: A Reappraisal." *Yearbook for Inter-American Musical Research*, 5–16.

Knight, Franklin. 1978. *The Caribbean: Genesis of a Fragmented Nationalism*. New York.

———, and M. Crahan, eds. 1979. *Africa and the Caribbean*. Baltimore.

Kutter, Wilhelm. 1971. "Pelzmärtle und Christkindle in oberen Enztal und verwandte Gestalten." In *Ländliche Kulturformen in deutschen Sudwesten: Festschrift für Heiner Heimberger.* Stuttgart.

———. 1976. *Schwäbisch-Alemanische Fasnacht.* Salzburg.

Labat, Jean-Baptiste. 1724. *Nouveau Voyage aux Isles de l'Amérique.* The Hague.

Laborde, Errol, and Mitchell Osborne. 1981. *Mardi Gras, A Celebration.* New Orleans.

La Cour, Arthur. 1957. *New Orleans Masquerade.* New Orleans.

Latrobe, Benjamin. 1980. *Journals.* E. Carter, J. Van Horne, and Lee Formwalt, eds. 3 volumes. New Haven.

———. 1984. *The Diary and Miscellaneous Papers.* New Haven.

Laussat, Pierre. 1831. *Mémoires sur ma Vie, à Mon Fils.* Pau.

Lawes, Dianne N. 1984. *Fisher Annotated Travel Guides: Bahamas, 1984.* New York.

Leach, Edmund. 1961. *Rethinking Anthropology.* London.

Lecorgne, 1986. See Martinez, E., and Lecorgne, 1986.

Le Goff, Jacques, and Jean-Claude Schmitt, eds. 1981. *Le Charivari.* Paris.

Le Page du Pratz, Antoine. 1763. *History of Louisiana.* London.

Le Roy Ladurie, Emmanuel. 1979. *Le Carnaval de Romans.* Paris.

Lévi-Strauss, Claude. 1966. *The Savage Mind.* Chicago.

Lewis, Matthew G. 1834. *Journal of a West Indian Proprietor.* London.

Lewis, Pierce. 1976. *New Orleans, the Making of an Urban Landscape.* Cambridge, Mass.

Lineberry, Carl, 1982. "Pete Fountain: Struts His Stuff." *Arcade* (New Orleans), February 16: 8–9.

Liungman, Waldemar. 1938. *Traditionswanderungen von dem Euphrat bis zum Rhein.* Part 2. Helsinki.

Lomax, Alan. 1950. *Mr. Jelly Roll.* Berkeley.

———. 1970. "African-Afro-American Musical Style." In J. Szwed and N. Whitten, *Afro-American Anthropology, Contemporary Perspectives.* 181–201. New York.

Long, Edward. 1774. *History of Jamaica.* London.

Ludlow, Noah. 1880. *Dramatic Life as I Found It.* St. Louis; reprinted, 1966: Bronx, New York.

Ludwig, Jack. 1976. *The Great American Spectaculars.* New York.

MacMillan, Dougald. 1926. "John Kuners." *Journal of American Folklore* 39: 53–57.

Marcel-Dubois, Claudie. 1975. "Fêtes villageoises et vacarmes cérémonials, ou une musique et son contraire." In *Les Fêtes de la Renaissance,* ed. Jean Jacquot, volume 3. Paris.

———. 1981. "La musique de Charivari." In Jacques Le Goff and Jean-Claude Schmitt, *Le Charivari,* 45–53. Paris.

Marcus, Leah. 1986. *The Politics of Mirth.* Chicago.

Marmier, Xavier. 1851. *Lettres sur L'Amérique.* 2 volumes. Paris.

Marsden, Peter. 1788. *An Account of the Island of Jamaica.* Newcastle.

Martin, Joan. 1973. "Mardi Gras Indians, Past and Present." *Louisiana Folklore Miscellany* 3: 52–55.

———. 1980. "Life among Black Creoles in the Early 1900s." Taped lecture, October 9, 1980. Conserved on tape cassette at New Orleans Public Library.

———, 1980. "The Black Indians Don't Sing Your Mardi Gras." Taped lecture, October 2, 1980. Conserved on tape cassette at New Orleans Public Library.

Martinez, Elsie, and Margaret Lecorgne. 1986. *Uptown/Downtown: Growing Up in New Orleans*. Lafayette, La.

Martinez, Maurice, 1979. "Two Islands: The Black Indians of Haiti and New Orleans." *Arts Quarterly* (New Orleans), 1, no. 7: 18.

*Masken Zwischen Spiel und Ernst*. 1967. Ed. Tübingen University Group for the Study of Carnival. Tübingen.

McLain, James. "Behind the Mask: the Future of Mardi Gras." Taped lecture, May 31, 1977. Conserved on tape cassette at New Orleans Public Library.

McWilliams, Richebourg G. 1953. *Fleur de Lys and Calumet*. Baton Rouge.

Mercier, Louis-Sebastien. 1982. *Le Tableau de Paris*. J. Kaplow, ed. Paris.

Meyerowitz, Eva. 1951. *The Sacred State of the Akan*. London.

Milton, John. 1936. The *Poems of John Milton*, ed. James H. Hanford. New York.

Miner, Allison. 1973. "The Mardi Gras Indians." *Louisiana Folklore Miscellany* 3: 48–49.

———. [Allison Miner Kaslow.] "Coconuts, Indians, and Mambos: The Black Celebration of Carnival." Taped lecture, May 10, 1977. Conserved on tape cassette at New Orleans Public Library.

Moreau de Saint-Méry, Médéric. 1797. *Description topographique, physique . . . et historique de la partie française de l'isle Saint-Domingue*. Volume 1. Philadelphia and Paris.

Moser, Hans. 1955. "Archivalisches zu Jahreslaufbrauchen der Oberpfalz." *Bayerisches Jahrbuch für Volkskunde*, no volume number, 157–75.

———. 1967. "Städtische Fasnacht des Mittelalters." In *Masken Zwischen Spiel und Ernst*. Ed. Tübingen University Group for the Study of Carnival. Tübingen.

———. 1985. *Volksbräuche im geschichtlichen Wandel*. Munich.

Mumford, Lewis. 1961. *The City in History*. New York.

Muse, Benjamin. 1964. *Ten Years of Prelude, the Story of Integration since the Supreme Court's 1954 Decision*. New York.

*Narrenfreiheit. Beiträge zur Fasnachtforschung*. 1980. Ed. Tübingen University Group for the Study of Carnival. Tübingen.

Nketia, J. H. Kwabena. 1974. *The Music of Africa*. New York.

Olmstead, Frederick. 1856. *A Journey in the Seaboard Slave States*. New York.

*One Hundred Years of Comus*. 1956. New Orleans.

Orloff, Alexander. 1981. *Carnival, Myth and Cult*. Wörgl, Austria.

Ortiz, Fernando. 1921. "Los cabildos afro-cubanos." *Revista bimestre cubana* 16, no. 1, 5–39.

Oster, Harry. 1964. "Country Mardi Gras." In Richard Dorson, ed., *Buying the Wind*. Chicago.

———, and Revon Reed. 1960. "Country Mardi Gras in Louisiana," *Louisiana Folklore Miscellany* 1: 1–17.

*Oxford English Dictionary*. 1975. Oxford, England.

Ozouf, Mona. 1976. *La fête révolutionnaire 1789–99*. Paris.

Paul, Emmanuel, 1962. *Panorama du folklore haitien*. Port-au-Prince, Haiti.

Pearse, Andrew. 1956. "Carnival in Nineteenth-Century Trinidad." *Caribbean Quarterly*, 4: 175–93.

Phillippo, James, 1843. *Jamaica, Its Past and Present State*. London.

Pitré, Guiseppe. 1889. *Usi e costumi, credenze e pregiudizi del popolo siciliano*. 4 volumes. Palermo.

Platt, Orville. 1900. "Negro Governors." *Papers of the New Haven Colony Historical Society* 6: 315–35.

Post, Lauren. 1974. *Cajun Sketches*. Baton Rouge.

Rashdall, Henry. 1936. *The Universities of Europe in the Middle Ages*. Oxford, England.

Rayford, Julian. 1962. *Chasin' the Devil Round a Stump*. Mobile.

Rector, Monica. 1984. "The code and message of carnival: 'Escolas-de-Samba.'" In Thomas Sebeok, ed., *Carnival*. Berlin and New York.

Reid, Ira De A. 1942. "The John Canoe Festival." *Phylon* 3: 348–70.

Reidy, Joseph. 1978. "'Negro Election Day' and Black Community Life in New England, 1750–1860." *Marxist Perspectives* 1, no. 3 (Fall).

Reinders, Robert. 1964. *The End of an Era: New Orleans 1850–1860*. New Orleans.

———. 1965. "The Free Negro in the New Orleans Economy, 1850–60." *Louisiana History* 6:273–85.

Reinecke, George. 1970. "Mardi-Gras, Chooka Lapai: A Probable Meaning." *Louisiana Folklore Miscellany* 3, no. 1 (April): 77–79.

Renfrew, Colin. 1979. *Before Civilization*. New York.

Reynolds, Bernard. 1868. *Sketches of Mobile from 1814 to the Present Time*. Mobile.

Rice, Ann. 1979. *The Feast of All Saints*. New York.

Rightor, Henry, ed. 1900. *Standard History of New Orleans*. Chicago.

Röhrich, Lutz. 1976. *Sage und Märchen*. Freiburg.

Romaios, Constantin [Rhomaios, Konstantinos]. 1949. *Cultes populaires de la Thrace*. Athens.

Rose, Al. 1974. *Storyville*. Tuscaloosa, Alabama.

———, and Edmond Souchon, 1967. *New Orleans Jazz, A Family Album*. Baton Rouge.

Rozwenc, Edwin. 1973. *The Making of American Society*. Volume 2. Boston.

Rushton, William. 1979. *The Cajuns*. New York.

Sala, George. 1883. *America Revisited*. London.

Salaun, Zuma Young. 1983. *Mardi Gras Facts and Fancies*. New Orleans.

Saxon, Lyle. 1928. *Fabulous New Orleans*. New York.

———. 1929. *Old Louisiana*. New York.

———, Edward Dreyer, and Robert Tallant, eds. 1945. *Gumbo Ya-Ya, A Collection of Louisiana Folk Tales*. Boston.

Schultz, Christian, Jr. 1810. *Travels on an Inland Voyage Through the [United] States. . . .* New York.

Scott, Michael. 1881. *Tom Cringle's Log*. Edinburgh and London.

Shoemaker, Alfred. 1959. *Christmas in Pennsylvania*. Kutztown, Pa.

Sidro, Annie. 1979. *Le Carnaval de Nice et ses Fous*. Nice.

———, and Pierre Falicon, eds. 1984. *Carnavals à travers les Ages du Monde*. Nice.

Siegel, Martin. 1975. *New Orleans, a Chronological and Documentary History*. Dobbs Ferry, New York.

Singleton, Esther. 1927. *Dutch New York*. New York.

Smith, Michael. 1984. *Spirit World: Pattern in the Expressive Folk Culture of Afro-American New Orleans*. New Orleans.

Smollett, Tobias. 1979. *Travels Through France and Italy, 1763–65.* F. Felsenstein, ed. Oxford.

Stedman, J. G. 1796. *Narrative of a Five Years' Expedition Against the Revolted Negroes of Surinam.* Reprinted in Abrahams and Szwed, *After Africa.*

Sterkx, H. E. 1972. *The Free Negro in Ante-Bellum Louisiana.* Canbury, New Jersey.

Stewart, James. 1986. "Patronage and Control in the Trinidad Carnival." In Edward Bruner and Victor Turner, eds., *The Anthropology of Experience,* 289–315. Urbana.

Story, G. M., 1969. "Mummers in Newfoundland History," in Herbert Halpert and G. M. Story, eds., *Christmas Mumming in Newfoundland,* 163–75. Toronto.

Strong, Roy. 1973. *Splendor at Court: Renaissance Spectacle and Illusion.* London.

Summersell, Charles. 1949. *Mobile, History of a Seaport Town.* Tuscaloosa, Alabama.

Szwed, John. 1970. "Afro-American Musical Adaptation." In J. Szwed and Norman Whitten, *Afro-American Anthropology: Contemporary Perspectives,* 219–27. New York.

Tallant, Robert. 1948. *Mardi Gras.* Garden City, New York.

––––––. 1950. *The Romantic New Orleanians.* New York.

Tasistro, Louis. 1842. *Random Shots and Southern Breezes.* 2 volumes. New York.

Tassin, Myron and Gasper Stall. 1984. *Mardi Gras and Bacchus: Something Old, Something New.* Gretna, Louisiana.

Taylor, Julia M. 1982. "The Politics of Aesthetic Debate: The Case of Brazilian Carnival." *Ethnology* 21: 301–11.

Tcherkezova, Marina. 1975. "Les Jeux Carnavalesques bulgares." In Samuel Glotz, ed., *Le Masque dans la tradition européenne,* 112–26. Binche.

Thorndike, Lynn. 1944. *University Records and Life in the Middle Ages.* New York.

Tinker, Edward. 1953. *Creole City.* New York.

Tocqueville, Alexis de. 1946. *Democracy in America.* World Classics edition (abridged). Oxford.

Trautman, Frederick. 1984. "New Orleans, the Mississippi, and the Delta through a German's Eyes: the travels of Emil Deckert, 1885–1886." *Louisiana History* 25 (1984): 79–90.

Tregle, Joseph. 1952. "Early New Orleans Society: A Reappraisal." *Journal of Southern History* 18: 20–36.

Trexler, Richard. 1984. "Correre la Terra; Collective Insults in the Late Middle Ages." *Mélanges de l'Ecole française de Rome* 96: 845–902.

Trillin, Calvin. 1964. "The Zulus." *The New Yorker,* July 20. New York.

Turner, Victor. 1977. "Variations on a Theme of Liminality." In Sally Moore and Barbara Myerhoff, eds., *Secular Ritual,* 39–52. Assen, Netherlands.

––––––. 1986. "Dewey, Dilthey, and Drama." In Edward Bruner and Victor Turner, eds., *The Anthropology of Experience,* 33–44. Urbana.

––––––. 1987. "Carnival, Ritual, and Play in Rio de Janeiro." In Alessandro Falassi, ed., *Time out of Time: Essays on the Festival,* 76–90. Albuquerque, New Mexico.

U.S. Bureau of the Census. 1982. *State and Metropolitan Data Book.* Washington, D.C.

Vasari, Giorgio. 1963. *Lives of the Artists.* 4 volumes. London.

Ventura, Michael. 1985. *Shadow Dancing in the U.S.A.* Los Angeles.

Wade, Richard. 1964. *Slavery in the Cities: The South 1820–1860.* New York.

Waldo, J. Curtis. 1882. *History of the Carnival at New Orleans from 1857 to 1882.* New Orleans.

Walser, Richard. 1971. "His Worship the John Kuner." *North Carolina Folklore* 19: 160–72.

Weed, Thurlow. 1866. *Letters from Europe and the West Indies.* Albany.

Welch, Charles D., Jr. 1963. "'Common Nuisances:' The Evolution of the Philadelphia Drummers Parade," *Keystone Folklore Quarterly* 8: 95–106.

———. 1966. "'Oh, Dem Golden Slippers,' The Philadelphia Mummers Parade." *Journal of American Folklore* 79: 523–36.

———. 1970. *Oh Dem Golden Slippers.* New York.

Wetmore, Elizabeth Biskind. 1906. *The Life and Letters of Lafcadio Hearn.* 2 volumes. Boston.

White, Shane. 1988. "Pinkster: Afro-Dutch Syncretization in New York City and the Hudson Valley." *Journal of American Folklore* 102: 68–75.

Widman, Enoch. 1894. "Hofer Chronik." In Christian Meyer, ed., *Quellen zur Geschichte der Stadt Hof.* Hof, Germany.

Wilentz, Sean. 1983. "Artisan Republican Festivals." In Michael Frisch and Daniel Walkowitz, eds., *Working Class America,* 37–77. Urbana.

Wilhelmsen, Finn. 1973. "Creativity in the Songs of the Mardi Gras Indians of New Orleans, Louisiana." *Louisiana Folklore Miscellany* 3: 56–74.

Willett, Frank. 1971. *African Art, An Introduction.* New York.

Wiswall, Joseph T. 1864. *Mr. Christopher Katydid.* 2 volumes. London.

Wurdemann, Dr. J. G. 1844. *Notes on Cuba.* Boston.

Young, Perry. 1931. *The Mistick Krewe, Chronicles of Comus and His Kin.* New Orleans.

# Index

*Abeile,* L', New Orleans newspaper (French section), 72, 116, See also *Bee, The*

Abrahams, Roger, 327 n. 4, 336 n. 80, 338 n. 105, 365 n. 43, 368 nn. 68, 69, 372 n. 28, 383 n. 80

Alexander, James, 59–60, 127–28

American Circus Company, 88

Anderson, Tom, 128–29, 131

Animal maskers, 12, 49–56, 63–65, 69, 82, 87, 99, 153–56, 204–14, 242–48, 300–301, 304, 335 n. 75, 341 n. 38

Arnaudov, Mikhail, 376 nn. 8, 14

Asbury, Herbert, 364 n. 29

Ashanti, African tribe, 199, 211–14, 215, 223, 374 n .47, 377 n. 20

Ashe, Thomas, 330 n. 21, 332 n. 52

Atlanteans, Carnival society, 276, 279, 316, 389 n. 12

Baby Dolls, 132–36, 142, 356 nn. 40, 45, 357 n. 96

Bacchanalia, Roman and Greek, 3–5, 7

Bacchus, Carnival society, 107, 252–53, 255–58, 266, 277, 286, 313, 316, 384 nn. 2, 4, 389 nn. 7, 15, 395 n. 7

Bacchusaurus, 252–53, 256, 266, 384 n. 2

Bakhtin, Mikhail, xv, 171–72, 317, 327 n. 6

*Bal de bouquet,* 59–60

Balls: Carnival society, 11, 99–100, 103–4, 106, 107, 111, 119–25, 127, 270, 316, black Indian, 161; Colonial and other precedents for, 17–18, 22–31, 59–60, 63–65, 67–69, 71–72, 88–89, 93, 339 nn. 4, 7; "French," 128–29; Quadroon, 25–29, 63, 127–28, 329 n. 17, 330 n. 21; Storyville, 128–30; Zulu, 144–45

Bamboula, 36–40, 163, 332 n. 53, 333 n. 57, 364 n. 29

Barker, Danny, 175, 177, 235–36, 332 n. 50, 359 n. 71, 367 nn. 60, 61, 368 n. 63, 391 n. 38, 392 n. 38

Barriers, theory of Carnival, xiii–xxi, 14, 21, 34–35, 48, 73, 120, 148–49, 175–77, 275–92, 301–5, 308–10, 317–19; *See also* Carnival, first, second forms of

Bartram, William, 20

Bastide, Roger, 42–43

Batiste, Becate, 162–63

Bean cake, ceremony of the, 59, 119–20, 339 n. 3, 353 n. 2

Beauvallet, Leon, 47–48, 53–55, 338 n. 100

Bébé, dancing master, 17–18, 31, 140, 328 n. 1

Bedouins, Carnival society, 88, 90, 92, 103, 342 n. 41, 346 n. 33, 350 n. 77

*Bee, The,* New Orleans newspaper (English section), 27, 66, 72, 128, 343 n. 49, 355 n. 32

Beidelman, T. O., 206–7, 373 n. 35

Belisario, I. M., 218, 375 n. 2

Belsnickle, 80–81, 86–87, 159, 207, 344 n. 9, 376 n. 9

Berlin, Ira, 338 n. 98

Berquin-Duvallon, 22

Berry, Jason, 162–65, 167, 174, 363 n. 25, 369 n. 74, 382 n. 64, 383 n. 82

Bettelheim, Judith, 371 n. 21

Bienville, Carnival society. *See* Krewe de Bienville, Le

Bienville, Sieur de (Jean Baptiste Lemoyne), xiv, 17, 19, 358 n. 58

Blassingame, John, 348 n. 58, 354 n. 22, 358 n. 57

Boeuf gras, 8, 153–58, 242, 248, 297, 348 n. 63, 350 n. 81, 361 nn. 9, 10, 377 n. 22

Boston Club, xxi, 94, 121, 124, 247, 280, 281, 288, 347 n. 50, 353 n. 7, 393 n. 56

Bowdich, John, 211–14

Brand, John, 356 n. 34

Brasseaux, Carl, 333 n. 63

Bremer, Fredrika, 31, 45, 48, 85, 96, 171, 336 n. 77, 338 n. 101, 366 n. 49

British Guyana, African dance form in, 338 n. 102

Buechler, Johann, 36
Burke, Peter, 325 n. 1, 355 n. 32, 360
  n. 3, 361 n. 8

Cabildo: black organization in Latin
  America, 42–43, 45–48, 52–55, 74,
  171, 227, 263, 334 n. 72, 336 n. 77,
  338 n. 101; Spanish governmental
  body in New Orleans, 20, 25–27,
  32, 63, 329 n. 18, 330 n. 19
Cable, George, 37, 137, 140, 332 n. 56,
  333 n. 57, 357 n. 47, 359 n. 60
Cain, Joseph, 98–99, 107–10, 114, 348
  n. 54, 351 n. 95, 387 n. 35, 394 n. 1
Cajuns, 5–6, 22, 326 n. 4, 390 n. 26
Cake, See Bean cake, ceremony of the
Calenda or calinda, 37–39, 333–334 n.
  63
Callithumpians, 81
Camellia Ball, 278, 311
Canoe, John, 49–55, 57, 159, 201–2,
  205, 215–16, 336 n. 88, 337 nn. 95,
  96, 338 n. 96, 371 n. 12, 373 n. 39,
  374 n. 56, 375 n. 8; See John Canoe
Captains of Carnival societies, xv, 93,
  117, 152, 290, 316, 360 n. 2, 370 n.
  9, 389 n. 15
Capuchins, 20
Carmichael, A. C., 40, 334 n. 66
Carnival: European phases of, 3–9;
  European precedents in Gulf Coast,
  65–66, 68–71, 79–80, 96–97, 103,
  105, 112–13, 151, 207–9, 219, 221–
  23, 284, 295, 326 nn. 1, 2, 344 n. 9;
  first, second forms of, xix–xxi, 13–
  15, 301–5, 308–9, 317–19, 379 n. 36;
  Gulf Coast preparatory stage, 67–
  68, 71–74, 311–12; Gulf Coast civic
  phase, 75–77, 90, 97, 101–2, 104–5,
  312; Gulf Coast national phase,
  250–51, 255, 257–60, 272–74, 312–
  13; psychology of, 15, 171, 257–60,
  263–66, 273, 275, 277–78, 285–90,
  303–4, 314–18; sociology of, 61, 75–
  77, 90–92, 167, 170–75, 177, 215–16,
  226, 248–49, 277–82, 286–305, 310–
  17; theory of, xiv–xv, xvii, 112–13,
  204–5, 236, 275, 277, 280–82, 286–
  90, 299–305, 310, 312, 314, 317–18,
  325 n. 2; See also Barriers; Economy;
  Krewes; Satire in Carnival
Carnivalesque, 35, 47–48, 57–60, 78–
  81, 112–14, 282, 284, 313–14, 317–18
Cartoon and comic-strip masks and
  floats, 258, 313, 382 n. 17
Cassidy, Frederick, 336 n. 83
Castellanos, Henry, 332 n. 56
"Characteristic Traits" (1797), 49

Chaudron, Louis de Vendel, 344 n. 6
Chickasaws, 20, 98, 362 n. 20
Christmas celebrations, 2, 6, 11, 35,
  39–40, 48, 54, 59–60, 68, 75, 80–81,
  159, 207, 219, 311, 334 n. 68, 337 n.
  96, 338 n. 3, 339 n. 3, 344 n. 6, 346
  n. 31, 372 n. 28, 375 nn. 3, 7, 386 n.
  28, 388 n. 41
Churches: relation to Carnival of, 3–
  6, 8, 21, 70–71, 294, 297–98, 316,
  327 n. 8, 342 n. 49
Cirque Américain, 88
Civil War, 68, 70, 97–100, 112–14, 136,
  148, 339 n. 10, 343 n. 1, 350 n. 76,
  388 n. 4, 391 n. 38
Civism. See Carnival, Gulf Coast civic
  phase
Claiborne Avenue, New Orleans, 14–
  15, 273, 328 n. 14
Claiborne, William C., 28–29, 330 n.
  31, 334 n. 65
Clemens, Samuel L., 395 n. 11
Clubs and sticks, use of in Carnival,
  200–204, 341 n. 30, 371 nn. 19, 20
Clubs involved in Carnival. See Bos-
  ton Club; Elks Club; Pickwick Club.
  See also Marching clubs
Cockayne, Land of, 282, 284, 390 n.
  20
Codes, cultural, 274–305, 307
Coleman, James, 67, 340 n. 20, 341 n.
  30, 358 n. 56
Colonial period: Caribbean festivities
  in, 49–56, 337 nn. 95, 96; Gulf
  Coast festivities in, 17–58
Comic Cowboys, Carnival society,
  110–11, 146–48, 307, 352 n. 106, 354
  n. 21; queen of, 125
Commerce. See Economy
Commercialism, Carnival, 102–6,
  146–48, 255–57, 292–94, 384 n. 12
Communication theory, 275–76, 297–
  99, 311–12
Comus, Carnival society, 9, 28, 88–
  101, 103–7, 113–21, 128, 137–38,
  143–44, 155, 158–59, 249–55, 260,
  276–80, 288, 316, 346 nn. 33, 35,
  347 n. 56, 349 n. 71, 350 n. 76, 352
  n. 15, 353 n. 7, 355 nn. 25, 26, 357
  n. 52, 358 n. 54, 359 n. 64, 361 n. 9,
  362 n. 14, 384 n. 1, 388 n. 4, 389 nn.
  13, 15, 390 n. 18, 392 n. 42
Comus, Greek deity, 96, 115–16, 347
  n. 56
Cosimo, Piero di, 96
Courir du mardi gras, 6, 222, 326 n. 4,
  391 n. 26
Cowbellions, Carnival society, 80–92,

97, 107–9, 116, 158–59, 276, 315, 340 n. 21, 344 n. 6, 346 nn. 28, 35, 347 n. 47, 348 n. 63, 350 n. 76, 362 n. 15

Creecy, James G., 58, 63–64, 101, 338 n. 106, 340 n. 18, 341 n. 38

Creole: definition of, 339 n. 10; black, 133, 139–40, 162, 164–65, 177, 242, 326 n. 4, 365 n. 43, 368 n. 63, 378 n. 33; dialect, 161, 196, 374 n. 33; French, 8, 59–62, 64, 66, 70–72, 80–82, 88–93, 128, 131, 146–48, 250, 255, 276, 311, 330 n. 27, 342 nn. 48, 49, 346 n. 36, 347 n. 42, 364 n. 32; vs. Anglo culture, 146–48, 333 n. 56

Creole Wild West Tribe, 162, 364 n. 33, 369 n. 74

Crété Liliane, 329 n. 9, 338 n. 1

Crowley, Daniel, 196–97, 201, 204, 336 n. 80, 338 n. 102, 357 n. 45, 363 n. 23, 370 nn. 3, 5, 7, 373 n. 31, 382 n. 70

Cuba, festivities in, 23, 31, 34, 41–46, 48, 53, 59, 160, 335 n. 74, 336 n. 77

Curtis, Edward, 103, 138, 224, 349 n. 73, 377 n. 21

Da Matta, Roberto, xv

Dancing: Afro-American forms of, 32–42, 44–46, 56, 143–45, 160–63, 182–92, 213–14, 227–28, 230–31, 272, 333 n. 63, 334 n. 72, 336 n. 82, 364 n. 29, 372 n. 25, 378 n. 33; Voodoo rituals, 333 n. 57, See also Balls

Davis Avenue, Mobile, 15

Davis, Jefferson, 121

Davis, John, proprietor of Orleans Ballroom, 340 n. 20

Davis, Susan, 81, 334 n. 39, 346 n. 39, 395 n. 9

Davis, William, 353 n. 11, 391 n. 28

Day, Charles, 242, 370 n. 2, 380 n. 45, 383 n. 80

Dean, Bennett Wayne, 83, 86, 108, 125, 158, 327 n. 5, 345 n. 15, 348 n. 59, 351 n. 95, 353 n. 13, 360 n. 76, 362 n. 15, 388 n. 42

Deathlike maskers, 108, 242, 245–48, 383 nn. 79, 80, 395 n. 15

De Caro, Francis A., 382 n. 65, 395 n. 1

De Coy, Robert, 236

Dekker, Thomas, 356 n. 34

De la Beche, H. T., 331 n. 38

Delaney, Caldwell, 270–71, 328 n. 4, 343 n. 5, 345 n. 23, 347 n. 47

DeLeon, Thomas, 146–47

Devil maskers, 129, 245, 341 n. 38, 355 n. 26, 370 n. 4, 378 n. 33

Diamond, Jim-along-Josey, 62

di Palma, Thomas, 291–92, 296, 391 n. 30, 393 n. 56

Dirks, Robert, 373 n. 39

Distinctive Society, The. See Tea Drinkers Society

Dollis, Bo, 172

Dorson, Richard, 326 n. 4

Doubloons, 277, 282, 284, 292, 304

Dragons, Order of: Carnival society, 316, 395 n. 10

Dunham, Katherine, 227, 359 n. 69, 378 n. 28

Earle, Alice, 344 n. 7

Economy: Carnival benefits to, 9–10, 146–47, 170, 250, 327 n. 12; Gulf Coast character of, 75, 77, 145–46, 273, 330 n. 29, 343 n. 5, 345 n. 14

Edmonson, Munro, 327 n. 12, 367 n. 60, 368 n. 63, 395 n. 1

Eichold, Samuel, 352 n. 102, 354 n. 20, 360 n. 72

Eights, James, 44, 335 n. 75

Elexis, King of Mobile Carnival (black), 271, 308

Elks Clubs in Carnival, 15, 260, 270, 328 n. 13, 367 n. 61

Elves of Oberon, Carnival society, 280

Endymion, Carnival society, 84, 255–56, 277, 286, 292, 385 n. 16, 389 n. 15, 391 n. 33

Eva, Queen, 126

Fat Ox. See Boeuf gras

Faure, Alain, 327 n. 9, 341 n. 33, 342 nn. 41, 43

Felix, emperor of Mobile Carnival (white), 7, 107, 109, 121, 270–71, 279, 295–96, 351 n. 89, 389 n. 10

Fiehrer, Thomas, 333 n. 58

Fights in Carnival, 66–67, 165, 167, 170, 191–93, 200–204, 228–29, 359 n. 71, 365 n. 52, See also Clubs and sticks, use of in Carnival

Fitzstephen, William, 360 n. 1

Flambeaux, 138–39, 357 n. 52

Flint, Timothy, 35–36, 41, 48, 57, 228, 331 n. 28, 332 n. 49

Fluegel, J. G., 36, 332 n. 51

Forest, Pierre, 34, 38, 41

Forman, B. R., 327 n. 11

Fountain, Pete, 362 n. 22

French Quarter, 11, 14, 19, 22, 32, 61–62, 128, 131, 133, 140, 143, 162–63,

French Quarter (*continued*) 178, 249, 262–63, 303, 308, 312–13, 364 nn. 29, 32, 368 n. 64, 379 n. 36
Frontiers. *See* Barriers

Gadget costumes, 12, 266–68, 386 n. 31
Gays, males' and females' participation in Carnival, 262–63, 313, 386 n. 27
Gluckman, Max, xiv, xv, 325 n. 1, 373 n. 35
Golden Blades, Tribes, 168
Gresemund, Dietrich, 327 n. 7

H.S.S., Carnival society, 108, 351 n. 99
Haiti, festivities in, 37, 39, 160, 202–3, 215, 226–28, 359 nn. 69, 71, 372 n. 27, 378 n. 30; Gulf Coast contacts with, 37, 203–4
Half-Fast Walking Club, 293, 362 n. 22, 394 n. 64
Hearn, Lafcadio, 37, 135, 137, 163, 333 n. 57, 357 n. 47, 363 n. 29, 372 n. 26, 378 n. 33, 380 n. 45, 383 n. 79
Hermes, Carnival society, 255, 267
Higginbotham, Jay, 328 n. 3
High Priests of Mithras, Carnival society, 280
Hill, Beatrice, 133–34, 140, 162, 338 n. 102, 356 nn. 40, 45, 357 n. 45, 370 n. 3, 371 n. 17, 380 n. 45
Honorat, Michel, 228, 378 n. 30
Houck, Oliver, 394 n. 61

Iberville, Siêur d' (Pierre Lemoyne), xiv, 17, 19
Indescribables, Carnival society, 86
Indian maskers, 54–55, 143, 160–205, 248–49, 299–301
Infant Mystics, Carnival society, 108, 113, 277
Iris, Carnival society, 125, 224, 354 n. 15, 377 n. 22, 389 n. 15

Jazz, *See* Music
Jefferson City Buzzards, 11, 293, 302, 316, 359 n. 64, 393 n. 57
John Canoe (Jonkonnu), 49–55, 57, 159, 201–2, 205, 215–16, 336 n. 88, 337 nn. 95, 96, 338 n. 96, 371 n. 12, 373 n. 39, 374 n. 56, 375 n. 8
Jonson, Ben, 89, 115, 339 n. 3
Joyaux, Georges, 331 n. 47, 333 n. 59

Kennerly, Charles, 78–83, 344 nn. 6, 8
King, Edward, 104
King's Ball, 59

King's Cake. *See* Bean cake
Kings: black festive, 44–48, 53–54, 57, 227–28; of Carnival societies, xv, 7, 47, 102, 105, 107, 120–21, 123–24, 255–58, 270–72, 276–81, 294–96, 308; gorilla, 99–100; Zulu, 141, 144–45, 164, 210, 213, 232–34, 236, 238, 240, 247
Kirsch, Elise, 163, 372 n. 25, 377 n. 22
Knights of May Zulu Club, 272
Knights of Revelry, Carnival society, 13, 107–8
Koo-Koo or Actor Boy, 216, 218–19, 221–24, 227, 375 n. 2. *See also* John Canoe
Krafft, Michael, 78–81, 83–84, 86, 108, 315, 344 n. 6, 348 n. 63
Krewe de Bienville, Le, Carnival society, 269
Krewes: definition of, 114–18; Carnival society, 75, 152, 255, 278–81, 291, 293, 304, 328 n. 13, 341, 343 n. 51, 346 n. 33, 349 n. 74, 353 nn. 5, 11, 354 n. 16, *See also* names of particular Carnival societies
Kuker, 219, 221–23, 226, 285, 375 n. 8

Langlois, Nicholas, 19, 328 n. 5
Labat, Jean-Baptiste, 37, 333 n. 62
Latrobe, Benjamin, 27–28, 32–34, 36, 58, 330 n. 28, 331 nn. 42, 44
Laussat, Pierre, 36, 40, 70, 332 n. 53
Law, John, 19
Lecorgne, Margaret, 328 n. 17, 386 n. 31
Le Page du Pratz, Antoine, 333 n. 63
Le Roy Ladurie, Emmanuel, 325 n. 1, 339 n. 5, 392 n. 48
Levi, Dave, 110–11, 268, 352 n. 106
Lévi-Strauss, Claude, 170, 365 n. 42
Lewis, Matthew, 51, 337 n. 95, 366 n. 44, 371, 394 n. 60
Literate and learned culture. *See* Orally centered vs. letter-centered cultures
Lomax, Alan, 132, 358 n. 58, 367 nn. 57, 60, 372 n. 25, 373 n. 34, 392 n. 38
Long, Edward, 49, 51–52, 336 n. 82, 337 n. 95
Lord of Misrule, 35, 41, 100–101, 119, 339 n. 5
Lost Cause Minstrels, 99, 109, 351 n. 95
Louis XV, King of France, 19
*Louisiana Gazette*, 28, 72, 329 n. 16
Louisiana Purchase, 23
Ludlow, Noah, 115, 117, 329 n. 15, 344 n. 5, 345 n. 14

Ludwig, Jack, 257, 259
Lupercalia, Roman, 3, 4, 326 n. 1

Madison, James, president, 27–28,
  334 n. 65
Mammoth Parade, 15
Marching clubs, 293–94, 302
Marcus, Leah, 352 n. 113
Mardi Gras Indians, 14, 41, 134–55,
  159–63, 177, 193–94, 204–5, 207–9,
  211, 215–16, 218–19, 222–24, 226–
  32, 234, 236, 238, 290, 299–302, 356
  n. 43, 363 n. 25, 365 n. 35, 366 n.
  55, 367 n. 57, 369 n. 74, 370 n. 8,
  373 n. 31, 376 n. 12, 379 n. 36, 381
  n. 49
Mardi Gras Rangers, Carnival society,
  88, 92
Margins. *See* Barriers
Marigny, Henri, 62, 162
Marmier, Xavier, 55, 57
Marsden, Peter, 39, 334 n. 64
Martin, Joan, 328 n. 14, 363 n. 26, 365
  nn. 35, 40, 366 n. 55, 369 n. 74, 383
  n. 76
Martinez, Elsie, 328 n. 17, 386 n. 31
Martinez, Maurice, 363 n. 26, 368 n.
  64, 382 n. 65
Martinique festivities in, 23, 38–39,
  135, 245, 378 n. 33, 380 n. 45, 383 n.
  79
Masks. See under types of maskers:
  Animal, Deathlike, Devil, King,
  Queen, Transvestite, Gadget, Car-
  toon
McLain, James, 327 n. 12, 392 n. 41
Mercier, Louis-Sébastien, 70
Military participation in and influ-
  ence on Carnival, 152, 295
Milton, John, 89, 93, 115–17, 345 n.
  15, 352 n. 118, 355 n. 25
Moko Jumbie dancers, 338 n. 102
Momus, Carnival society, 97, 100–
  101, 107, 121, 138, 251–52, 255, 288,
  351 n. 92, 362 n. 14, 392 n. 42
Montana, Tuddy, 162–63, 228–29
Moon pies, 13, 284, 307
Moonpies: Order of Mystic, 270–71,
  307, 387 n. 35
Moreau de Saint-Méry, Médéric, 36–
  37, 39, 227, 333 n. 63
Morton, Jelly Roll, 132–33, 165, 358 n.
  58, 363 n. 25, 365 n. 35, 368 n. 62,
  372 n. 25, 392 n. 38
Moser, Hans, 326 n. 3, 390 n. 22, 392
  n. 48
Music: Afro-American forms of, 131–
  32, 163, 166–67, 172, 183–93, 230–
  31, 240–42, 368 n. 61, 379 n. 35

Mysterieuses, Les, Carnival society,
  125
Mystery, Carnival society, 280, 347 n.
  52
Mystic Club, Carnival society, 114,
  279, 347 n. 52, 389 n. 12
Mystics, Order of, Carnival society,
  10, 108, 113–14, 270, 277
Mythology, Carnival themes of. *See*
  Themes
Myths, Order of, Carnival society, 13,
  107–8, 277, 350 n. 83

Neighborhoods, 64, 141–45, 299–301.
  *See also* Codes
Neville Brothers, 183, 241–42, 256,
  384 n. 11
New Year's celebrations, 54, 59–60,
  75, 78–81, 84–88, 99–100, 206, 220–
  21, 326 n. 4, 337 n. 96, 338 n. 1, 344
  n. 9, 348 n. 63, 351 n. 92, 373 n. 35,
  387 n. 41
Nicholls, Thomas, 329 n. 17
Nketia, J. H. Kwabena, 373 n. 33, 379
  n. 34

Oberon, 280. *See* Elves of Oberon
Olmstead, Frederick, 354 n. 23
*One Hundred Years of Comus*, 346 n. 37,
  347 n. 46, 350 n. 76, 389 n. 15
Orally centered vs. letter-centered
  cultures, 167, 170–73, 193–94, 205–
  10, 216, 231–32, 365 n. 43, 374 n. 56
O'Reilly, Alexander, 20
Ortiz, Fernando, 334 n. 72, 336 n. 77
Overbury, Thomas, 356 n. 34

Parades: of Carnival societies, 11–12,
  78–89, 93, 98–99, 103–5, 108–12,
  133–36, 151–52, 232–40, 250–53,
  255–60; functions of, 67–69, 89–92,
  100–102, 137–38. *See also* Marching
  clubs; Truck parades
Parker, Charity, 38
Paul, Emmanuel, 333 n. 63
Paxton, John, 34
Pearse, Andrew, 201, 371 n. 19
Phillippo, James, 337 n. 95
Phunny Phorty Phellows, Carnival
  society, 112, 119, 311
Pickwick Club, 94, 96, 124, 353 n. 7
Police, 13, 29, 67, 163, 275, 294–97,
  299–301, 304, 308
Politics in Carnival, 100–101, 279–82,
  294, 296, 301, 385 n. 17, 392 n. 42
Prostitution, 92, 128–40, 262, 355 nn.
  28, 32, 356 n. 38, 358 n. 58
Proteus, Carnival society, 107, 121,
  251, 255, 280, 357 n. 52, 362 n. 14

Pseudo-king; -queen. *See* Kings; Queens

Quadroon, 25–28, 63, 126–29, 143, 175, 262, 330 n. 21, 332 n. 52, 333 n. 59, 354 n. 23. *See also* Balls
Queens: black festive, 42–43, 45–46, 54; black Indian, 167, 188, 190–91, 196; of Carnival societies, 29, 120–24, 270, 276–81, 291–92; of prostitute balls, 129–30; transvestite, 125–26, 233–34; Zulu, 232–33, 236, 240, 247
Quetes, 166–67, 221–22, 227–28, 283–90, 365 n. 37; definition of, 49, 336 n. 86

Race relations, xix–xx, 12, 14–15, 22–27, 39–41, 45, 53–54, 61–63, 90, 97–101, 111, 113, 126,129, 131, 134, 137, 141–45, 153, 174–177, 235–36, 240, 271, 296, 307–11, 329 n. 15, 330 n. 21, 348 n. 63, 349 nn. 68, 71, 73, 354 nn. 22, 23, 374 n. 44
Rayford, Julian, 269–70, 328 n. 5, 344 n. 8, 345 nn. 13, 18, 347 n. 47, 348 n. 63, 351 nn. 89, 98, 352 nn. 101, 106, 393 n. 58
Reid, Ira De A., 337 n. 96
Reidy, Joseph, 335 n. 74
Reinecke, George, 242, 374 n. 56, 382 n. 68
Rex, Carnival society, 7, 12, 47, 102–6, 120–21, 251, 258–60, 276–81, 294–97, 308–9, 349 n. 74, 354 n. 16, 359 n. 64, 384 n. 6
Reynolds, Bernard, 76, 84, 327 n. 11, 328 n. 4, 330 n. 29, 343 n. 1
Rice, Ann, 161, 329 n. 15
Rightor, Henry, 129, 138, 142, 146, 160–64, 181, 364 n. 32
Rituals, African festive, 205–8, 210, 214, 373 n. 39. *See also* Kings, black festive; Queens, black festive; Dancing; Music
Rising Generation, Carnival society, 34, 86
Romanov, Alexis, Grand Duke, 102
Rushton, William, 326 n. 4

Sala, George, 357 n. 47
Satire in Carnival, 108, 110–12, 233–36, 307–9, 380 n. 45, 381 nn. 50, 52, 387 n. 35
Saturnalia, Roman, 3–5, 7, 35
Saxe-Weimar Eisenach, Duke of, 26, 30, 70
Saxon, Lyle, 18, 140–44, 164, 171,

249, 328 n. 1, 329 n. 17, 343 n. 53, 393 n. 56
Scott, Michael, 50, 52–53, 207, 216
Semiotics, xviii, xix, 192, 195–214, 215, 218–19, 224, 226, 229–30, 250–53, 262–66, 268, 275, 321–22, 369 n. 1
Sets, women's, 51, 353 n. 14, 354 n. 17
Skeletons, black marching club, 242
Slackabamorinico, Chief, 99, 109, 119, 268, 315, 352 n. 101, 362 n. 19
Slavery, xiv, xix, 17, 20, 23–27, 30–32, 41, 56, 60, 72–73, 77, 205, 358 n. 57
Smith, Michael P., 173, 181, 186, 205, 366 n. 53, 370 n. 7, 373 n. 31, 376 n. 13, 377 n. 19
Societies, Carnival. *See* Carnival: Psychology of; and individual names
Spectacle de la rue St. Pierre, 24, 390 n. 20
Spitzer, Nicholas. 326 n. 4
Stedman, J. G., 331 n. 38
Stewart, James, 370 n. 6, 388 n. 48
Storyville, 129–33, 139, 142, 144, 164, 171, 355 n. 28, 356 n. 38, 358 n. 58, 367 n. 57, 379 n. 36
Strikers Independent Society, festive society, 84
Swazi, African tribe, 206–7, 209, 211, 215
Symbolic realism, 259, 293
Szwed, John, 336 n. 80, 383 n. 80

Tallant, Robert, 349 n. 74, 361 n.8
Tasistro, Louis, 66, 69, 342 n. 41
Taylor, Charles, 178–90
Taylor, James, 78–80, 83, 86, 388 n. 48
Tea Drinkers Society (T.D.S.), 84, 98–99, 107–8, 348 n. 63
Théatre d'Orleans, 24, 26, 72
Themes, kinds of, and relative popularity of parade, 12, 85, 96–99, 251–59, 271–72, 276, 292–93, 316, 388 n. 4
Throwing game, xvii, xix, 12, 134, 239, 282, 284, 285–88, 391 nn. 25, 26
Tillman, Robert "Brother," 369 n. 74
Tinker, Edward, 124
Tocqueville, Alexis de, 93, 347 n. 48
Tourism, and Carnival, 9, 101–3, 137–38, 198, 229, 239, 242, 249, 251, 255–57, 260, 267–68, 273–74, 294, 313, 337 n. 96
Transvestism, 12, 54–55, 64, 92, 125, 136, 233–34, 264
Tregle, Joseph, 346 n. 41

Trexler, Richard, 355 n. 33

Trinidad, festivities in, 40, 195–204, 219, 226, 241, 273, 336 n. 80, 338 n. 104, 356 n. 45, 365 n. 43, 370 n. 3, 371 n. 16, 372 n. 28, 382 n. 70; Fancy Indians of, 196–98, 200, 219, 370 n. 5; Indian Warrior Bands of, 196–97, 204; Red Indians, 196, 201, 370 n. 5, 371 n. 14; Wild Indians of, 196, 201–2, 226

Truck parades, 12, 261, 301–2, 328 n. 13, 385 n. 21

Turbinton, Wilson, 172, 241–42, 379 n. 35

Turner, Victor, xvii, 326 n. 3, 370 n. 6, 373 n. 35, 385 n. 18, 388 n. 48

Twelfth Night celebratoins, 6, 22, 59, 106, 311, 316, 338 n. 3, 339 n. 5

Twelfth Night Revelers, festive society, 100–101, 284, 311, 316, 349 n. 68, 350 n. 76

Two Well-Known Gentleman, Balls of, 128–30, 312, 355 n. 28

Vasari, Giorgio, 96, 340 n. 19

Vaudreuil, Marquis de, 17–18, 20, 22, 27, 328 n. 1

Ventura, Michael, 365 n. 44, 366 n. 44, 379 n. 36, 391 n. 29

Waldo, J. Curtis, 103–4, 138, 295, 349 n. 73, 350 n. 82, 358 n. 56, 361 n. 8

Wallace, Barbara, 382 n. 68

Weed, Thurlow, 334 n. 73

White Cloud Hunters Tribe, 169, 178–90, 223, 230

Wild Magnolias Tribe, 168, 172, 240–42, 365 n. 36, 366 n. 46, 373 n. 30;

European versions, 80–81, 219, 221–23

Wildmen: African precedents for, 204–14, 219, 223–24, 227–29, 242–43, 278, 300–301; in Carnival, xix, 151–94, 226, 236–37, 242; costuming, 222, 235, 321–22, 373 n. 31; European versions of, 80–81, 219, 221–23, 344 n. 9, 361 n. 7, 362 n. 18, 376 n. 9, 390 n. 26; in Western thought, 153

Wild Tchoupitoulas Tribe, 168, 172, 182–83, 191, 240, 255, 298, 363 n. 25, 365 n. 41, 384 n.11

Wilhelmsen, Finn, 366 n. 54

Williams, Cynric, 40–41

Wiswall, Joseph, 85–86, 347 n. 47

Women: participation in Carnival of, 24, 51, 55, 56, 70, 119–48, 186–88, 265, 278–80, 288, 313

Wurdemann, Dr. J. G., 41–43, 45–46, 334 n. 69, 335 n. 74

Yellow Pocahontas Tribe, 164, 365 n. 39

Young Men's Benevolent Association, 100

Young Men's Dress Society, 100

Young, Alfred, 362 n. 21

Young, Perry, 59, 349 n. 69, 383 n. 77, 389 n. 18, 390 nn. 20, 25

Zulu Social Aid and Pleasure Club, Carnival activities of, 46–47, 144–45, 164, 204, 206, 213, 232–40, 247, 272, 291, 296, 308, 380 n. 44, 381 nn. 46, 47, 59